Dictators and Democrats

Dictators and Democrats

MASSES, ELITES, AND REGIME CHANGE

Stephan Haggard and Robert R. Kaufman

PRINCETON UNIVERSITY PRESS

PRINCETON AND OXFORD

Copyright © 2016 by Princeton University Press

Published by Princeton University Press, 41 William Street,
Princeton, New Jersey 08540
In the United Kingdom: Princeton University Press, 6 Oxford Street,
Woodstock, Oxfordshire OX20 1TR

press.princeton.edu

Cover image courtesy of Anton Gvozdikov / Shutterstock

All Rights Reserved

ISBN 978-0-691-17214-9

ISBN (pbk.) 978-0-691-17215-6

Library of Congress Control Number: 2016941824

British Library Cataloging-in-Publication Data is available

This book has been composed in Sabon LT Std

Printed on acid-free paper ∞

Printed in the United States of America

1 3 5 7 9 10 8 6 4 2

Dedication

To Laura and Sharon

Factional conflict erupts everywhere on account of inequality, or at least it does if no proportion exists between those who are unequal. In general, people engage in factional conflict seeking equality.

—Aristotle, *The Politics*

When the rate of return on capital exceeds the rate of growth of output and income, as it did in the nineteenth century and seems quietly likely to do again in the twenty-first, capitalism automatically generates arbitrary and unsustainable inequalities that radically undermine the meritocratic values on which democratic societies are based.

—Thomas Piketty, *Capital in the Twenty-First Century*

Contents

Illustrations

Tables

Preface and Acknowledgments

THREE DEVELOPMENTS MOTIVATED THIS BOOK. The first was empirical: the global trend toward democratic rule captured by Samuel Huntington's metaphor of a Third Wave. Between 1980 and 1989, the number of democracies in the world showed a steady upward trend, jumped sharply around the collapse of the Soviet Union, and then continued to rise through the mid-2000s. These changes constituted the most sweeping expansion of political freedom in history, and they unquestionably transformed the global political landscape.

The Third Wave was not an unalloyed success, however. Some autocracies failed to budge, and the net increase in the number of new democracies masked substantial churning as some democracies slid back toward authoritarian rule. Notwithstanding the dramatic scope of the transitions toward democracy, therefore, we need also to account for reversals. Why did these transitions take place, and what drove some new democracies back toward dictatorship?

Our second motivation was theoretical. The longest-standing theory of democratization in political science is the modernization approach. Modernization theory linked competitive politics to long-run growth, the emergence of middle classes, and other economic and social-structural changes. In the 2000s, a powerful formal variant of this work—which we call distributive conflict models of regime change—suggested that both transitions and reversions were associated with inequality and ensuing social conflict over the distribution of the social pie. Authoritarian elites were less likely to cede power—even in the face of mass pressure—where income and assets were highly concentrated.

These theories had an optimistic face. The spread of economic growth to developing countries in the postwar period was encouraging not only for the material well-being of the majority of the world's population but for the prospects for self-governance as well. In at least some circumstances—when inequality was at low or moderate levels—mass mobilization over social grievances could displace dictators and establish new democratic regimes.

Yet these theories also had a darker side, playing into a wider anxiety about rising inequality across the world and its adverse effects on a range of outcomes from economic growth to public health. Did adverse trends in the distribution of income pose challenges to the future of democratic governance as well? The question was relevant not only to developing and postsocialist countries—our primary focus—but to advanced industrial states as well.

But were these theories true? We had doubts rooted in our prior collaborative work on democratization and the politics of social policy.[1] Inequality and distributive conflict seemed to be drivers of transitions in some cases, but others seemed elite-led affairs. If mass publics were involved, their grievances often extended far beyond inequality per se to poor performance, corruption, and the general fecklessness of government. Reversions from democratic rule often appeared rooted less in the defensive reactions of economic elites than the self-seeking behavior of militaries and political incumbents. The structural proclivities of both modernization and distributive conflict theories seemed distant from institutional and political factors that appeared more central to us. These included the specific institutional features of both authoritarian regimes and new democracies, the capacity for collective action on the part of social forces, and government performance.

Testing modernization and distributive conflict theories against the experience of the Third Wave was not altogether straightforward, as these theories combined structural and strategic components in a complex mix. Our third motivation was therefore methodological: to consider how complex theories of this sort could be tested deploying both quantitative and qualitative methods. Using select cases to illustrate or buttress arguments made principally in econometric form has become a tradition of book-length monographic work in political science. But transitions to and from democratic rule are rare events. It thus seemed possible to devise a method that obviated the ongoing problem of case selection altogether by selecting *all* transitions for structured causal process observation.

That is the big picture. More concretely, how did we actually get here? As with all work, the project followed a much more twisted path than such broad motivational statements suggest; it also relied on tremendous generosity on the part of family, friends, colleagues, and strangers willing to listen to us talk. In *Development, Democracy and Welfare States*, published in 2008, we considered the effects of democracy on social policy in new democracies but not how inequality and redistribution might influence the prospects for democracy. Although we were aware of emerging distributive conflict models while writing that book, they were somewhat orthogonal to our core interests.

Kaufman was the first to engage these theories directly. He did so in a skeptical piece for *Comparative Politics* published in 2009 titled "The Political Effects of Inequality in Latin America: Some Inconvenient Facts."[2] He then extended his observations on Latin America to a global sample in a "back-of-the envelope" way. Haggard urged that we check our doubts

---

[1] Haggard and Kaufman 1995, 2008.
[2] Kaufman 2009b. See also Kaufman 2009a.

more systematically, and together with Terence Teo, we jointly developed the first iteration of the qualitative dataset that undergirds this project.[3] We found that a large number of transitions and reversions during the 1980 to 2000 period did not even conform descriptively with distributive conflict models. Even when they did, inequality did not appear implicated in any systematic way. Kaufman presented that early study in 2011 at the Watson Institute of International and Public Affairs at Brown University, and we then published it in the *American Political Science Review* (*APSR*) in 2012.[4] Ron Rogowski and reviewers did outstanding editorial work to bring out the underlying message of the article. It benefited as well from very helpful comments by Carles Boix, Michael Bratton, T. J. Cheng, Ruth Collier, Ellen Commisso, Javier Corrales, Sharon Crasnow, Anna Grzmala-Busse, Allan Hicken, Jan Kubik, James Long, Irfan Nooruddin, Grigore Pop-Eleches, Celeste Raymond, Andrew Schrank, and Nic van de Walle. Their comments obviously carried over into this book-length elaboration.

Above all, our publication in the *APSR* gave us confidence to build the study out and present our critical engagement with distributive conflict models in a more extended way. We initially thought that one way to test these models was through a micro-level approach that dissected the relationship between inequality and individual preferences for redistribution, an axiomatic component of the theory. A 2007 symposium organized by John Echeverri-Gent offered Kaufman an opportunity to review the existing literature.[5] Together, Haggard and Kaufman presented early ideas on the topic at a lively workshop at Duke convened by Herbert Kitschelt, drawing on work that Kaufman had initiated with his graduate student Brian Cramer.[6] We both then worked with James Long to expand these findings to a global sample.[7] This work yielded interesting results, and cast doubt on the extent to which the poor necessarily favored redistribution. We ultimately concluded that this line of research was not as immediately central to the macro-level arguments as we had initially thought and in any case did not play to our comparative advantage. We moved back to our macro roots, but combining quantitative and qualitative approaches to the issue.

In developing the *APSR* article and in our subsequent research on the book, we had the good fortune to be able to work with Terence Teo, then a graduate student at Rutgers. Although Terence began as a research assistant, it quickly became apparent that he could play a more integral role

---

[3] Subsequently revised as Haggard, Kaufman, and Teo 2016.
[4] Haggard and Kaufman 2012.
[5] Kaufman 2009a.
[6] Cramer and Kaufman 2011.
[7] Haggard, Kaufman, and Long 2013.

in the implementation of the project. In addition to his collaboration on the construction of our qualitative dataset, he became an indispensable contributor to the design and analysis of the quantitative portions of our book. We credit him especially for his work on Chapters 2, 5, and 6.

Our work has also benefitted enormously from several opportunities to reside for a period of weeks with communities of scholars who shared our interest in democratization. In this regard, special thanks are due to Nancy Bermeo and the faculty of Nuffield College, who arranged for Kaufman to present our work in 2013 and for both of us to be scholars-in-residence during the fall of 2014. During that stay, Haggard gave talks at Nuffield College, Cambridge University, and the London School of Economics. Among the many people who offered feedback and advice during that stay in England were Ben Ansell, Nic Cheeseman, David Rueda, Maya Tudor, Robert Wade, Laurence Whitehead, and Joseph Wong.

Haggard also owes special thanks to Martin Dimitrov for convening a wonderful three-week workshop on authoritarian resilience at the American Academy in Berlin. He managed to get work done while learning from a group that included Paulina Bren, Linda Cook, Larry Diamond, Nara Dillon, Tom Gold, Nathalie Koch, Beatriz Magaloni, Elizabeth Perry, Joseph Sassoon, and Lisa Wedeen.

In addition to these relatively prolonged visits, we have each presented our work before numerous audiences over the past three years, and would like to thank the conveners of these meetings, as well as the many faculty and students who attended.

Haggard's seminars and presentations were organized by Carew Boulding at the University of Colorado; Jana Grittersova and Matthew C. Mahutga at the University of California, Riverside; Sarah Brooks at the Mershon Center; Tasha Fairfield at the London School of Economics; Nancy Bermeo, Ben Ansell, and David Rueda at Oxford; Mette Eilstrup-Sangiovanni at Cambridge; Dan Treisman, Dan Posner, and Barbara Geddes at the University of California, Los Angeles; and Aurel Croissant at the University of Heidelberg. These hosts were not simply conveners but took the time to offer focused comments as well.

Jong-sung You organized an unusually productive set of events for Haggard at the Australian National University in 2014. These included a workshop on the book with detailed comments from Ed Aspinall, Paul Kenny, Chungshik Moon, and Allen Hicken and some econometric schooling from Paul Burke. A master's class at ANU yielded extensive comments from Eve Warburton, Danielle Cave, Bayu Dardias, Danang Widjojoko, Burhanuddin Muhtadi, Kerry Eng, and Stephan Norman.

Kaufman made presentations at seminars and conferences organized by Kostis Kornetis at New York University; Kevin Narizny at Lehigh; Maria Victoria Murillo at Columbia University; Ozge Kemahlioglu at Sabanci

University, Istanbul; and Deborah Yashar at the Annual Meeting of the American Political Science Association. In the course of those presentations, in addition to the organizers mentioned above, he received highly useful comments from Valerie Bunce, Alicia Cooperman, and Lucan Way, who kindly provided an advanced look at relevant chapters of his new manuscript on "pluralism by default."

As the project moved toward completion, our thinking was sharpened further by the opportunity to work on a number of related contributions. Staffan Lindberg, Ben Smith, and Michael Bernhard—editors of the *Comparative Democratization Newsletter*—provided us the opportunity to guest-edit a symposium in which most of the protagonists in these debates presented their work and updated their views: Ben Ansell and David Samuels; Carles Boix; Christian Houle; and Daron Acemoglu, Suresh Naidu, Pascual Restrepo, and James A. Robinson.

Lydia Tiede's work with Haggard on the rule of law played into our joint work in subtle but important ways.[8] As the project was coming to a conclusion, Haggard collaborated with his wife Sharon Crasnow—a philosopher of social science—on a piece outlining the logic of a multi-method approach to the study of rare events.[9] Jack Snyder's invitation to write a review essay for the *Annual Review of Political Science* provided us an opportunity to carefully review a broad literature that had evolved under our feet as the book was being written.[10]

Among the many colleagues who have read and commented on the manuscript or offered us advice, including on the dataset, are Andy Bennett, Carles Boix, Valerie Bunce, Nic Cheeseman, T. J. Cheng, Ruth Collier, the late Ellen Commisso, Alicia Cooperman, Javier Corrales, Larry Diamond, Karen Ferree, Barbara Geddes, Clark Gibson, Anna Grzymala-Busse, Allan Hicken, Ethan Kapstein, James Long, Beatriz Magaloni, Jim Mahoney, Isabella Mares, Irfan Nooruddin, David Pion-Berlin, Grigore Pop-Eleches, Celeste Raymond, James Robinson, Nita Rudra, David Samuels, Andrew Schrank, Dan Slater, Maya Tudor, Nic Van De Walle, Lucan Way, Eric Wibbels, Joe Wong, and Jong-sung You. Very late in our efforts, Gary Goertz read the entire manuscript and weighed in with a very incisive and generous set of comments on the methodological and substantive issues. Eva Bellin also read the entire manuscript as it was in final revision, making important comparative points about the Arab Spring. Particular thanks also to Christian Houle for making his dataset available, and to Vincent Greco and Steve Weymouth for research assistance.

[8] Haggard and Tiede 2011.
[9] Crasnow and Haggard 2015.
[10] Haggard and Kaufman 2016.

In addition to the material in these pages, we have posted the qualitative and quantitative datasets online with supporting materials and robustness checks on the book's page on the Princeton University Press site at http://press.princeton.edu/titles/10879.html.

Families support these efforts by tolerating our distraction. Haggard began this project just as his daughter Kit was leaving for college, but Max had to put up with it; thanks to the boy. His wife, Sharon Crasnow, provided intellectual stimulus as well as moral support to the project, and even coauthored a paper that helped him to sharpen his thinking on the approach to causality deployed in the project. Laura Schoen, Kaufman's wife, did not become a coauthor. But she remained a very loving supporter and companion throughout this project, and as always, a highly valued critic of his many faults.

Introduction

REGIME CHANGE DURING THE THIRD WAVE:
FROM DICTATORSHIP TO DEMOCRACY AND BACK

DURING THE PAST TWENTY-FIVE YEARS, Huntington's metaphor of a "Third Wave" of democratization captured what appeared to be a steady worldwide movement toward more liberal political rule.[1] Beginning in Southern Europe in the mid-1970s, the wave spread to major Latin American and Asian countries in the 1980s: Brazil, Argentina, Mexico, Turkey, the Philippines, Taiwan, Korea, and Thailand. The trend accelerated dramatically in the aftermath of the fall of the Berlin Wall, and not only in Eastern Europe but in the poorer nations of the African continent as well. Even more recently, the "color revolutions" in Georgia, Ukraine, Kyrgyzstan, and Lebanon and the Arab Spring evoked hope that the former Soviet Union and the Middle East would more fully participate in the worldwide trend.

By the late-2000s, however, the net increase in the number of democracies slowed and the tide of democratization appeared to crest. This slowdown should not be altogether surprising; as the number of democracies increased, the remaining authoritarian regimes by definition constituted tougher cases. Mass mobilization against these remaining dictatorships often failed to produce successful democratic transitions, as the Arab Spring showed most clearly.[2] But other developments were somewhat more surprising. First the number of intermediate regimes—variously labeled illiberal democracies, semiauthoritarian, electoral authoritarian, or competitive authoritarian regimes[3]—held surprisingly constant. Some of these regimes arose in the wake of transitions from "harder" authoritarian rule, most notably in the former Soviet Union and parts of Africa. Yet others reflected the failure of new democracies to consolidate. Military coups have become less common over time, but we have seen an increase in what we call "backsliding" from democracy: actions on the part of nominally democratic incumbents that exploit the benefits of office—including economically—to

---

[1] Huntington 1991.

[2] Bellin 2012.

[3] On illiberal democracies, see Zakaria 1997, 2003; Diamond 2009. On semiauthoritarian regimes, see Ottaway 2003. On electoral authoritarian regimes, see Schedler 2002, 2009. On competitive authoritarian regimes, see Levitsky and Way 2002, 2010.

restrict political contestation and civil and political liberties. Prominent examples of such backsliding include Russia, Ecuador, Venezuela, Nigeria, Kenya, and, more recently, Turkey, Hungary, and Pakistan.

With this new pessimism has come a revival of structural theories of democratic transition and consolidation. During the Third Wave, modernization theory was cast into doubt by the spread of democracy to low-income countries, giving rise to an emphasis on elite negotiations and even outright contingency.[4] But the failure of many of these new democracies to consolidate has revived the focus on factors such as economic development and social structure. Attention initially focused on whether Lipset's observation of a cross-sectional correlation between level of development and democracy could be extended to the analysis of transitions to democratic rule.[5] Przeworski et al. argued that it didn't, reflecting in part his focus on the postwar period when transitions spread across the developing world.[6] But they were subsequently challenged by Boix and Stokes, who argued that a longer-term perspective—incorporating the early European transitions—in fact confirmed the relationship between level of development and the collapse of authoritarian rule.[7]

There was a much stronger consensus, however, that development is associated with the consolidation of democratic rule. Przeworski et al. famously showed that no democracy has ever reverted above a per capita GDP of $6,055, Argentina's level of development in 1975.[8] Przeworski followed with an important formal contribution, arguing that level of development influences the stability of democratic rule through class dynamics as well.[9] At higher levels of income, both richer and poorer classes develop vested interests in the democratic status quo and a generalized aversion to the uncertainties of authoritarian rule. Boix showed that this result was even stronger in the post–Cold War period when the international system was dominated—at least for a time—by a liberal hegemon, reducing the "drag" on these long-run structural factors from geostrategic and ideological rivalries.[10] It followed directly from such analysis that democracies are much more likely to fail in the poorer countries that transitioned during the second half of the Third Wave.

Growing concern about the adverse political effect of high inequality has played an important role in these structural arguments. The link

---

[4] O'Donnell and Schmitter 1986; Di Palma 1990.
[5] Lipset 1959, 1960.
[6] Przeworski, Alvarez, Cheibub and Limongi 2000.
[7] Boix and Stokes 2003. See also Epstein et al. 2006; Kennedy 2010.
[8] Przeworski, Alvarez, Cheibub and Limongi 2000.
[9] Przeworski 2005.
[10] Boix 2011.

between class conflicts over the distribution of wealth and regime change has had a long pedigree in the modernization literature. Arguments of these sorts were influential in analyses of transitions to democracy in Europe,[11] and have been revived to consider the potentially adverse effects of the concentration of wealth an income on political accountability, participation, and polarization in the United States and Europe.[12]

Class conflict models of regime change have also been deployed in comparative historical work on democratization and its reversal in developing countries.[13] Recently, these insights have been formalized in influential models of regime change rooted in the divergent preferences of elites and masses, not only over the distribution of income but over the political institutions that sustain or redress social inequalities.[14] A key finding of this literature is that high inequality constitutes a barrier to democratic rule, blocking transitions and increasing the risks of reversion.[15]

The central purpose of this book is to critically assess this new structural turn both theoretically and empirically. Theoretically, we seek to steer the discussion about transitions to and from democratic rule away from structural explanations emphasizing level of economic development and social inequality back toward more political accounts, rooted in factors such as the nature of authoritarian and democratic institutions, regime performance, and capacities for collective action on the part of civil society.

Empirically, our analysis seeks to exploit not only cross-national regression designs but a systematic attention to the entire population of cases as well. The book is based on 78 discrete democratic transitions and 25 reversions that occurred between 1980 and 2008 as coded in two widely used datasets. We show that structural factors have mixed effects on transitions to and reversions from democratic rule. This is particularly the case with inequality. Distributive conflict is evident in about half of the transitions in our sample, and in a smaller share of reversions. But even where democratic transitions do appear to emerge from distributive conflict, those cases do not seem to be driven by the level of inequality one way or the other. Rather, democratization driven by mass mobilization appears to hinge on political factors: how exclusionary or co-optive authoritarian regimes are and the extent to which publics are capable of

---

[11] Marshall 1950; Lipset 1960; Moore 1966.

[12] Mahler 2002; Phillips 2003; Jacobs et al. 2004; McCarty, Poole, and Rosenthal 2006; Solt 2008; Bartels 2008; Piketty 2013.

[13] O'Donnell 1973; Rueschemeyer, Stephens, and Stephens 1992; Bermeo 2003.

[14] Acemoglu and Robinson 2000, 2001, 2006; Acemoglu et al. 2013; Boix 2003, 2008, 2013; Przeworski 2005, 2009.

[15] See however Ansell and Samuels 2010, 2013a, 2013b, 2014.

mobilizing grievances into the political arena. Where class conflict does not appear as even a proximate cause of regime change, we need to look elsewhere for explanations, including to the role international forces have played and to elite calculations and intra-elite conflicts.

In our cross-national quantitative models, we find that a low level of development does play a role in reversions to authoritarian rule. But a closer examination of cases reveals a myriad of anomalies: low-income countries that survive and a handful of middle-income countries that revert. Moreover, as with transitions, we find that inequality does not have a significant effect on reversions and that there is a noticeable disjuncture between the postulated mechanisms in distributive conflict models and how reversions actually transpired. Third Wave democracies were only rarely destabilized by right-wing elites defending their income and assets. Failure was much more commonly attributable to what we have termed a "weak democracy syndrome": a complex of political and economic factors including histories of praetorianism, weak institutionalization, and poor economic performance, itself partly a function of poor governance.

In the remainder of this Introduction, we begin by defining core terms and justifying our focus on the Third Wave. We then preview the empirical findings of the book, which are grouped into two major sections: the discussion of democratic transitions (Chapters 1–4) and a chapter on the effects of these transitions paths (Chapter 5); and a section on reversions (Chapters 6–8). We close the Introduction with a note on method. Throughout, our purposes are not only substantive; our work also includes an effort to bridge two methodological cultures: that of quantitative analysis rooted in a focus on average treatment effects and qualitative, causal process observation, with its emphasis on uncovering causal mechanisms.

DEMOCRACY, DEMOCRATIZATION, AND REVERSION: STUDYING THE THIRD WAVE

As is common in the political science literature, we define "democracy" in procedural terms. Democracies are political regimes in which all adult citizens are entitled to choose chief executives and legislatures through competitive elections, with expectations that the results of those elections will be honestly counted and honored through turnover in government. To meet these conditions, however, it is also necessary for citizens to be protected by a range of civil and political liberties, including the ability to organize and assemble, freedom of speech, and access to competing sources of information. The guarantee of rights and liberties opens the door to wider, more substantive definitions of democracy, based on the idea of citizens as agents.[16] For our purposes, however, we view rights and liberties through their crucial—if more limited—role in sustaining open political contestation.

Of course, no regime satisfies all of these criteria perfectly,[17] and this poses critical problems in the analysis and measurement of transitions to and from democratic rule. In principle, the benchmark for regime change would be decisive movement toward or away from the "rules of the game" outlined above. O'Donnell and Schmitter, for example, suggest that "the first free election" marks the point at which transitions end and a new regime is installed.[18] And in some instances, particularly via the coup d'état, the reversion to dictatorship is unambiguous as well.

But two problems arise in identifying and coding regime change. First, moves to and from democracy need not be decisive, given that the major components of our definition could all pertain to different degrees. Where elections occur, they may be more or less competitive. Rights and liberties, similarly, may be more or less guaranteed. Both the competitiveness of the political system and the protection of political rights are ultimately continuous variables. This raises a second problem of temporality: that changes of regimes may not be sharply marked, but constitute more incremental processes occurring over time.[19] As we will see, more temporally elongated causal processes pose daunting problems for standard econometric methods, opening the space for complementary qualitative analysis.

These problems immediately raise issues of measurement. How much political freedom do we need to see before we say a democratic transition has occurred? How egregious do incumbents' arrogation of powers or abuses of political rights need to be before they constitute a reversion? These are crucial questions given the competitive authoritarian regimes that have emerged within the gray zone between full-blown democratic and autocratic rule.

Our approach to these problems is pragmatic. For some comparative purposes, particularly in our quantitative analysis, we treat transitions dichotomously while recognizing that this is an analytic artifice. At the same time, however, we emphasize throughout the importance of qualitative causal process observation that permits a more nuanced assessment of transition processes and the extent to which regimes satisfy democratic criteria.

To engage existing quantitative literature and to probe the comparability and replicability of its findings, we rely primarily on two panel datasets: the

[16] O'Donnell 2004.
[17] Dahl 1973.
[18] O'Donnell and Schmitter 1986: 59–64.
[19] Pierson 2004.

coding scheme developed by Przeworski et al. and extended by Cheibub, Gandhi, and Vreeland (subsequently the CGV dataset) and Polity IV; to ensure consistency with existing work, we only recode or discard cases in extraordinary circumstances where we can find little support for the coding in question.[20] We supplement these codings with reference to three other datasets when pursuing several related questions: the Freedom House dataset, which measures political rights and civil liberties more explicitly, and particularly nuanced coding schemes on the variety of authoritarian rule by Hadenius, Teorell, and Wahman and Svolik.[21]

The choice of the CGV and Polity datasets is appropriate not only because they are widely used. They are also grounded in different conceptualization and measurement strategies, providing the opportunity to check the robustness of findings to competing conceptions of democratic rule. CGV provides a dichotomous measure of regime change that hinges on the staging of free elections and evidence of subsequent turnover that vindicates the competitiveness of the transitional electoral process.[22] The CGV codings thus reflect a more minimalist conception of democratization but as a result are well-suited to capture sharp reversions to authoritarian rule in which elected executives are deposed and legislatures shuttered.

The Polity score is a continuous metric (–10 to +10) that takes into account the broader political framework, including the regulation, competitiveness, and openness of chief executive recruitment, checks on executive discretion—including through the judiciary or legislature—and the competitiveness of participation; this last component implies some indirect consideration of the protection of political liberties.[23] Although we exploit the continuous nature of the Polity data, we also follow the

[20] Przeworski, Alvarez, Cheibub and Limongi 2000; Cheibub, Gandhi, and Vreeland 2010.
[21] Hadenius, Teorell, and Wahman 2012; Svolik 2012.
[22] More precisely, the definition of democracy hinges on four coding rules: the chief executive is elected in popular elections; the lower house in the legislature is popularly elected; there is more than one party; and there is turnover. With respect to the last desideratum, countries are coded authoritarian if "the incumbents will have or already have held office continuously by virtue of elections for more than two terms or have held office without being elected for any duration of their current tenure in office, and until today or until the time when they were overthrown they had not lost an election" (Przeworski, Alvarez, Cheibub and Limongi 2000: 23; see also 19–20 and 28).
[23] Again more precisely the Polity "dem-auth" scale is based on the following component variables: the regulation of chief executive recruitment (XRREG), competitiveness of executive recruitment (XRCOMP), openness of executive recruitment and the independence of executive authority (XROPEN), executive constraints, political competition, and opposition (XCONST), and the regulation (PARREG) and competitiveness (PARCOMP) of participation. The last variable captures the protection of political and civil liberties and thus constitutes one of the more important differences from the CGV dataset, which relies on the existence of an opposition party alone.

convention in the discipline and in the Polity dataset itself of using a cutoff of 6 to indicate the dividing line between authoritarian and democratic systems.

The differences between the two datasets are evident in the fact that only 55.4 percent of the CGV transitions are also Polity cases. Conversely, 34 of the 78 cases coded as CGV transitions—43.6 percent—had Polity scores of less than 6. In some instances, CGV transitions might appropriately be seen as transitions to what Levitsky and Way call competitive authoritarianism rather than full democracy.[24] As a result of these differences, we do not pool the data but rather run all statistical tests on each dataset separately. Nonetheless, both datasets are clearly capturing important political changes and provide the opportunity to consider the robustness of our findings to the definition of regime change.

Why limit our study to the Third Wave? Our focus on the period between 1980 and 2008 arguably biases results from what might emerge from a study of transitions over a longer time frame. Indeed, precisely in the interests of avoiding such biases, a number of studies have argued that a consideration of democracy as a long-run socioeconomic equilibrium requires considering the entire life span of the political form, beginning with late 19th-century franchise extensions that marked the breakthrough.[25]

However, there are theoretical, empirical, and substantive reasons to consider more contemporary processes on their own terms. We are interested in the determinants not only of democracy in general but of democratization in our time. Both modernization and distributive or class conflict theories were inspired by the 19th- and early 20th-century experience of Europe.[26] Early work by Acemoglu and Robinson is explicit in considering how working-class pressures served to widen the franchise.[27] The sociological work of Rueschemeyer, Stephens, and Stephens also views working-class challenges as the key driver of democratization in Western Europe and seeks to extend those findings to Latin America.[28] Taking a somewhat different tack, Ansell and Samuels have relied heavily on illustrations from 19th-century Britain to advance their argument that it is the conflict between landed interests and rising commercial classes that drove democratization.[29]

[24] Levitsky and Way 2010.
[25] Boix 2003, 2008, 2013; Boix and Stokes 2003; Przeworski 2009; Ansell and Samuels 2010, 2013a, 2013b, 2014.
[26] It should be noted that these class conflict models have been challenged. Collier (1999) shows that in many early European cases, the impetus for democracy came from "insiders" already operating within narrowly based oligarchic systems.
[27] Acemoglu and Robinson 2001. See also Przeworski 2009.
[28] Rueschemeyer, Stephens, and Stephens 1992.
[29] Ansell and Samuels 2010, 2014.

However, it is not clear that these theories are appropriate to the very different political, economic, and social structures that characterize the contemporary developing and postsocialist worlds. In the earlier period, almost all transitions occurred from regimes that allowed some competition, but that limited franchises to propertied classes. The fight for democracy was thus equivalent to franchise extension. In the late 20th century, the overwhelming share of postwar autocracies have been military, one-party, and competitive authoritarian regimes, which exhibit quite different political dynamics because of the identity of political incumbents. Moreover, although economic development still implies a fundamental transition from rural agrarian to more urban and industrial economies, the economic and social structures of developing countries are vastly different from the early European democratizers, with a much larger role of foreign economic actors, a more ambiguous impact of manufacturing on growth, and the emergence of large informal and service sectors. Such differences impact class identifications, opportunities for collective action, and the political relations among competing economic sectors.

Long-run historical approaches also pose their own problems of sample heterogeneity. Standards for what constitutes democracy have shifted considerably over time. In the 19th century, for example, a country that excluded women and minorities from suffrage might still have been classified as democratic; by the mid-20th century, it definitely would not. Such a long-run approach also requires the causal factors at work to be defined in exceedingly general terms. To undertake analysis over a long period, inequality and class conflict have to be defined to encompass highly diverse social structures, a challenge even within the Third Wave period. Gains in generality and parsimony by "going long" are matched by equal if not greater losses in comparability of setting and context.

The international context of democratization is also quite different from earlier historical periods, in terms of both geopolitical configurations and international norms and ideas. An example of a quite significant change in context in the period of interest to us is the decline of East-West conflict and great-power patronage for client dictators and the rapid international diffusion of democratic norms and expectations. The importance of this changed international environment is captured by Geddes, Wright, and Frantz, who show that transitions to new authoritarian regimes were between two and three times more likely than transitions to democracy in the 1960s and 1970s.[30] During the 1980s—the beginning of the end of the Cold War—the odds that regime change would result in a democratic, rather than autocratic transition, were only slightly less than even. By the

[30] Geddes, Wright, and Frantz 2014.

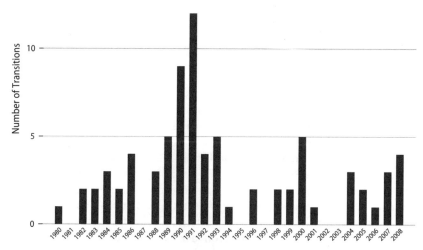

Figure 0.1 CGV Transitions during the Third Wave (1980–2008)

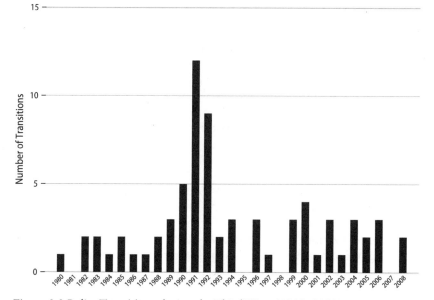

Figure 0.2 Polity Transitions during the Third Wave (1980–2008)

1990s and 2000s, democratic transitions outnumbered autocratic transitions by a ratio of more than two to one.

The temporal distribution of CGV and Polity transitions shown in Figures 0.1 and 0.2 provides an even more direct indication of the importance of changes in the structure of the international system. In both datasets, a large share of transitions—and what we classify as both distributive and elite-led cases—peaked with the collapse of the Soviet Union between 1989 and 1991. Some of these changes occurred in secessionist Soviet republics, such as the Baltic states and Ukraine, while others occurred in formally independent communist states of Eastern Europe. But the breakup of the Soviet Union also had repercussions among many client states in Africa and created a more benign environment for transitions outside of the Soviet sphere in Central America and Asia as well.

A second feature of the Third Wave that makes it distinctive is the spread of democratic practices to low-income countries with little experience with democracy and few expectations that they could become democratic at all. In an important article, Carles Boix shows that the impact of economic development on democracy grows stronger when a democratic hegemon dominates the international system, as was true in the 1990s and 2000s.[31] The end of the Cold War freed workers and the middle classes to mobilize in favor of democracy, a pattern consistent with regime changes in middle-income Eastern European and Latin American countries. However, it is striking that transitions also occurred in some of the poorest countries and most inhospitable environments, both regional and domestic.

Seeking to nest political change in this highly diverse set of countries in the still-more heterogeneous history of contemporary democracy since its late 19th-century origins has value; there may well be more generalized statements we can make by "going long." But it does not diminish more temporally localized findings of how developing countries democratized or returned to authoritarian rule during the Third Wave, particularly if we find that those processes don't correspond with theories motivated by earlier democratic experiences.

How and Why Does Democracy Emerge? Inequality, Distributive Conflict, and Elite-Led Transitions

Both modernization and distributive conflict theories see democracy emerging out of fundamental shifts in class structure and conflicting preferences over institutions across classes. How do struggles over the distri-

---

[31] Boix 2011.

bution of income and wealth affect transitions to democracy? And to what extent are these struggles related to differences in the degree of inequality? As we show in Chapter 1, formal theories developed by Boix, Acemoglu, Robinson, and others provide a useful theoretical point of departure.[32] These theories build on an important set of models of redistribution under democratic rule to give this analysis of regime change micro-foundations.[33] Their rationality assumptions are not typically shared by those with a more sociological perspective. But both sociological and rational choice models engage modernization theory with explicit predictions about how levels of inequality affect the prospects for both transitions to democratic rule and the stability of democracy once it is established.

As already noted, however, demand-driven theories of democracy are hardly new. Aristotle (*Politics*, Book 5, 1301a) states that "a system of government can be changed into a democracy when the size of the multitude of the poor increases." But he warns as well that "it is best for citizens in a city-state to possess a moderate amount of wealth because where some have a lot and some have none the result is the ultimate democracy or unmixed oligarchy. Tyranny can result from both these extremes. It is much less likely to spring from moderate systems of government."[34] Almost two millennia later, we find similar views expressed in the writings of Jefferson, who espoused the importance of family farms to democratic rule, and of de Tocqueville, whose warnings echoed those of Aristotle: "Almost all of the revolutions which have changed the aspect of nations have been made to consolidate or destroy social inequality. Remove the secondary causes which have produced the great convulsions of the world, and you will almost always find the principle of inequality at the bottom."[35]

More contemporary variants of these insights, similarly, converge around the core observation that the expansion of democratic rights provides groups excluded from political power with opportunities to reduce the inequalities of "conditions," including not only social and political conditions, but economic ones as well.[36] Both modernization and neo-Marxist theorists focused on the emerging middle classes as the crucial agent of political change, and these theories have been revisited in important work by Ansell and Samuels.[37] By the 19th century, however, mass democracy became a battle cry of the expanding European working classes, which challenged "bourgeois liberals" as well as the landed remnants of the old

[32] Acemoglu and Robinson 2000, 2001, 2006; Acemoglu et al. 2013; Boix 2003, 2008, 2013; Przeworski 2005, 2009; Ansell and Samuels 2010, 2014.
[33] Romer 1975; Roberts 1977; and particularly Meltzer and Richard 1981.
[34] Aristotle, *Politics*, book 5, 1301a; book 4, 1295a.
[35] De Tocqueville 1835: 302.
[36] Marshall 1950.
[37] Ansell and Samuels 2010, 2013a, 2013b, 2014.

social order. The idea that democratization in Europe was a function of the changing balance of class power has been seriously contested,[38] but it has remained an important component of the academic research agenda. Studies of franchise extension show that it was typically won through political protest rather than bestowed from above.[39] Rueschemeyer, Stephens, and Stephens claim—more broadly still—that working-class mobilization was the driving force behind the "democratic breakthroughs" of late 19th- and early 20th-century Europe.[40]

Narrowing differences in income and wealth were not universally viewed as the only objective of these challenges, nor were they clearly linked to objective measures of inequality. Nevertheless, it is by no means coincidental that liberal bourgeoisies as well as conservatives often viewed movements for democracy as threats to property and economic privilege. This assumption underlies Bismarck's attempt to co-opt the threat by extending social insurance to the most "dangerous" segments of the union movement. And the centrality of working-class economic demands in the transition to democracy is given greater credibility by the expansion of social programs and the reduction of inequality that followed democratic transitions.[41]

The corollary of such explanations for democratization is that extreme concentrations of income and assets, including landed wealth,[42] are major barriers to both regime transitions and the stability of democratic rule. Whether focused on the conflict between landed and middle classes—Moore's dictum of "no bourgeoisie, no democracy"[43]—or rising working classes, inequality is the enemy of democracy and democratization. In unequal authoritarian settings, elites have strong incentives to repress political challenges that would also have redistributive effects. In unequal democracies, economic elites pose an ongoing political risk, as they have the power to undermine democratic rule or overthrow it altogether.

The models we outline in Chapter 1 articulate these views more sharply and link them to explicit predictions about the likelihood of democratization at different levels of inequality. Even though democratization is ultimately driven by pressures from below, such challenges are likely to emerge and succeed only at low or moderate levels of inequality, when masses have the means and incentives to mobilize in favor of redistribution and elites prefer moderate concessions to incurring the cost of repression. At high levels of inequality, conversely, such challenges are unlikely to succeed.

[38] Collier 1999.
[39] Lizzeri and Persico 2004; Przeworski 2009.
[40] Rueschemeyer, Stephens, and Stephens 1992.
[41] For example, Lindert 2004.
[42] Ansell and Samuels 2014.
[43] Moore 1966: 418.

Distributive Conflict Transitions

It is important to emphasize that modernization and particularly class conflict theories are not—and cannot—be simply structural. They must operate through strategic interactions between existing and rising classes, elites and masses, and ultimately political incumbents and oppositions. All of these interactions hinge on capacities for collective action on the part of oppositions and the willingness and ability to repress or offer concessions on the part of elites. As a result, we focus throughout on two related but ultimately separable tests of modernization and distributive conflict theories. The first is the relationship between structural factors—level of development and inequality—and regime change. For example, although the role of inequality varies somewhat across different theoretical models, they converge on the expectation noted above that high inequality is a barrier to democratization.

The second question is whether observed transition processes conform to the stipulated causal mechanisms in the theory. These mechanisms are more worked out in the game theoretic models of distributive conflict, and we thus focus on them here. Even if inequality were found to be a significant deterrent to democratic transitions, it may not be as a result of class conflict over economic grievances. Inequality might operate through different channels, for example, marginalizing rather than mobilizing mass publics. Rather than arising out of class conflict, democracy may also prove an outcome of largely intra-elite processes or emanate from international pressures.

In Chapters 1 and 2—using somewhat different methods and measures—we find that inequality is not a significant determinant of democratic transitions one way or the other. It could nonetheless be the case that class conflict drives transition processes even if those conflicts are not rooted in the objective level of social stratification. To pursue this question about short-run causal dynamics requires that we code transitions. To do so, we create a qualitative dataset of within-case causal process observations that distinguishes between distributive conflict transitions of the type specified in the theory and what we call "elite-led" cases in which the stipulated mechanisms are absent.[44]

Distributive conflict transitions are defined as those in which (1) mass mobilization constitutes a significant and immediate threat to the ruling elite, (2) grievances associated with socioeconomic inequalities constitute at least one of the motives for mobilization, and (3) elites acquiesce to democracy in part in response to these threats. Elite-led transitions are not characterized by this sequence of threats and response; they work instead

[44]Haggard, Kaufman, and Teo 2016.

through initiatives undertaken by incumbents or rival elite groups that we describe in more detail below. Simply put, distributive conflict transitions can be characterized as "bottom-up" transitions that correspond at least in part to distributive conflict models while the elite-led transitions—from the "top down"—do not conform even descriptively or in their proximate causes to the theory.

We show in Chapter 1 that about half of the transitions we examine are the result of the mobilized de facto power envisioned by both the sociological and rational choice distributive conflict theories cited above. There are no clear standards by which a theory can be rejected by the presentation of anomalous cases; few theories take a rigidly deterministic or "necessary and sufficient" form under which any single case or even group of cases would be disconfirming. However, we also show in Chapter 2 that inequality does not have any statistically significant effect on transitions in general or on those transitions we identify as driven by distributive conflict. In line with the null statistical findings, the distribution of cases shows numerous anomalies, including not only high-inequality cases that transition through distributive conflict but low- and medium-inequality cases that transition in the absence of the postulated class dynamics. When the econometric results on inequality are taken together with the distributions based on our coding of the cases, these findings cast significant doubt on the generality of class conflict models.

However, the findings also raise the interesting question of the conditions under which excluded groups *do* demonstrate, strike, protest, or even threaten revolution in order to win democratic reforms. If such processes are not driven by inequality, then what does account for them? We explore this issue in Chapter 2 using statistical analysis, and in Chapter 3 through a consideration of the distributive conflict cases. We point to the significance of three more standard political factors: the repressiveness of the authoritarian regime, capacities for collective action, and regime performance as measured by short-run economic conditions.

Our first claim concerns the nature of authoritarian institutions. By their own admission, both the new and older class conflict theories are often institutionally spare; the same can be said for modernization theories. In class conflict theories, authoritarian regimes are defined in relatively undifferentiated ways, largely in terms of their role in sustaining socioeconomic inequalities through repression. But just as the new class conflict theories were generating debate, an extensive literature on authoritarian regimes was exploring their heterogeneity, including with respect to their reliance on repression and co-optation for managing opposition.[45]

[45] Geddes 1999; Smith 2005; Lust-Okar 2006; Magaloni 2006; Magaloni and Kricheli 2010; Brownlee 2007; Hadenius and Teorell 2007; Gandhi 2008; Gandhi and Przeworski

Paradoxically, we show in Chapters 2 and 3 that distributive conflict transitions are *less* likely in regimes that permit some space for political organization and representation than in more closed military and one-party regimes. From the perspective of the opposition, the principal challenge is to coordinate challenges to the regime. Regimes that allow limited pluralism and political opposition, however, not only repress but deploy resources to divide the opposition, co-opting some sectors and marginalizing others. Incumbents can manipulate cleavages, deflecting conflict away from class axes—along which oppositions have numerical advantages—and co-opting support through targeted patronage and clientelism.

By contrast, closed regimes that limit or eliminate channels of representation provide—virtually by definition—fewer opportunities for "de jure" influence or participation. Organized groups, such as unions and civil society associations, operate under tightly constrained circumstances or are driven underground entirely. Counterintuitively, such systems are more vulnerable to distributive conflict transitions.[46]

We do not test the relationship between repression, co-optation, and transitions through a consideration of institutions alone. We also find a strong relationship between a variety of indicators of repressiveness and the collapse of authoritarian rule via the distributive conflict route. In particular, we show that authoritarian regimes built around labor- or ethnically-repressive economic projects have an increased likelihood of leaving power in the face of distributive conflict. These findings are an important reminder that grievances in authoritarian regimes are by no means limited to inequality, but include wider injustices associated with the loss of freedoms.

A second major political lacuna in the modernization and new class conflict models centers on the role of collective action. Older, more sociological theories focused on the role that unions and working-class movements played in the extension of the franchise. Both modernization and newer class conflict approaches, however, largely sidestep the question of how excluded classes overcome—or fail to overcome—the disabilities associated with often-purposeful atomization imposed by autocratic rule.

Following the contentious politics literature,[47] we argue that the capacity for collective action depends not only on the opportunity structure

---

2006, 2007; Gandhi and Lust-Okar 2009; Blaydes 2010; Levitsky and Way 2010; Teorell 2010; Malesky and Schuler 2010; Hadenius, Teorell, and Wahman 2012; Svolik 2012; Wright and Escribà Folch 2012; Wahman, Teorell, and Hadenius 2012; Boix and Svolik 2013; Reuter and Robertson 2015.

[46] See also Svolik 2012: 111.

[47] Tilly 1986; Tarrow 1998; McAdam 1999; McAdam, Tarrow, and Tilly 2001.

available to excluded groups—which can be highly repressive as we have seen—but also on their organizational resources and strategies, including those that are nonviolent.[48] Resources depend in part on the availability of "protest repertoires"—knowledge of symbols, relevant public spaces, tactical information—that can be marshaled and coordinated by decentralized networks of leaders. Relatively decentralized and spontaneous forms of mobilization have long been a component of protest activity, and its potential may be increasing with the spread of social media.

Nevertheless, we show in Chapters 2 and 3 that longer-standing organizations are pivotal actors in turning people out in the streets and mounting sustained threats to authoritarian rule. These organizations can even play a triggering role if in abeyance under dictatorial rule.[49] A surprising finding given the spread of the Third Wave to lower income countries is the robust role played by unions not only in transitions in middle-income countries, but in lower-income countries as well. Organizational resources can also be provided by civil society groups and NGOs, as well as ethnic and religious groups. Indeed, in the absence of organizations, such challenges from below will not have the credibility to force political change; incumbents will wait them out.

Finally, building on earlier work,[50] we argue that regime change is associated not only with long-run economic growth—as in modernization theories—but shorter-run economic grievances that can be interpreted as measures of performance. The likelihood of a transition to democratic rule is inversely related to the economic performance of the incumbent authoritarian regime. A large number of transitions, and of all types, occurred in the context of severe economic difficulties, circumstances evident in the recurrent financial crises that coincided with the Third Wave: in Latin America and Africa in the 1980s, in the transitional economies in the first half of the 1990s, and again across a number of middle-income emerging markets from the mid-1990s into the early 2000s. Although economic crises sometimes exacerbated tensions between rich and poor, they were just as likely to have impaired the provision of rents to elites, military officers, and favored sectors of the public. As such they encouraged a defection of both elite supporters and appeared to have played a role in spurring mass mobilization as well.

---

[48] Sharp 1973; Helvey 2004; Zunes 1994; Ackerman and Kruegler 1994; Zunes, Kurtz, and Asher 1999; Ackerman and DuVall 2000; Schock 2005; Roberts and Garton Ash 2009; Chenoweth and Stephan 2011.

[49] Taylor 1989; Taylor and Crossley 2013.

[50] Haggard and Kaufman 1995.

Elite-Led Transitions

What about the large number of transitions that did not appear to be driven by demands from below? Adam Przeworski poses the puzzle of such transitions in the clearest terms: "Why would people who monopolize political power ever decide to put their interests or values at risk by sharing it with others? Specifically, why would those who hold political rights in the form of suffrage decide to extend these rights to anyone else?"[51]

In Chapter 4, we start with a substantial body of theory and empirical work showing how international factors may influence transitions, from direct military pressures and even intervention to the effects of international institutions and diffusion.[52] We organize our discussion around Levitsky and Way's distinction between leverage and linkage as sources of international influence. In four cases—Cyprus (1983), Grenada (1984), Panama (1989), and Haiti (1994)—outside intervention took a military form and directly displaced incumbents and/or established new democratic governments. Yet in all other cases, the political dynamics between outside actors and incumbents reflected more subtle tacit bargaining and what Putnam called two-level games.[53] Particularly in the wake of the end of the Cold War, the major powers became less tolerant of undemocratic regimes that appeared guilty of economic mismanagement and outright corruption. Threats or withdrawal of political and military support and economic aid—including from multilateral institutions—played an important role in motivating transitions in a group of low-income African countries in particular.

Except for cases of direct foreign displacement, however, these outside pressures always operate in conjunction with domestic political factors. Even in the absence of popular mobilization, intra-elite rivalries can constitute an important mechanism for spurring transitions. These rivalries may stem from competition among the political, military, and economic elites that constitute the authoritarian coalition—for example, when factions within the regime seek to displace incumbents—or from elite challenges from outside the regime altogether.[54] Some of these elite conflicts result in the replacement of one authoritarian leadership with another, a phenomenon we do not address. However, intra-elite conflicts can also generate transitions to democratic rule, particularly in the context of strong external inducements and constraints. Intra-elite conflicts often rotate

[51] Przeworski 2009: 291.
[52] Whitehead 1996; Pevehouse 2002; Levitsky and Way 2005, 2010; Brinks and Coppedge 2006; Gleditsch and Ward 2006; Wejner 2005; Boix 2011.
[53] Putnam 1988.
[54] Slater, Smith, and Nair 2014.

around differences over the costs and benefits of persisting with authoritarian rule. For example, while some military factions may favor a continued political role, others frequently see engagement in politics as carrying a variety of organizational costs, including to the core military mission. In about a third of all elite-led transitions, we found these conflicts central to transition processes.

Even when elites remain relatively unified, however, they may still acquiesce to—or even lead—democratizing reforms. This will occur if they believe they can retain leverage over the political process while reducing the costs of repression. Incumbent elites can do this in several ways, including through the design of political institutions that give them effective vetoes or through the organization of political parties that exploit other cleavages to dampen distributive conflicts. Dominant party systems—as opposed to true one-party systems—provide incumbent political elites with particular organizational advantages that can be redeployed in a more competitive context.

Note that each of the alternative domestic causal mechanisms we have sketched—intra-elite conflict or transitions led by incumbent elites seeking to retain office—may in fact be related precisely to the *weakness* of immediate threats from below. We find at least some indirect support for this claim in our statistical analysis in Chapter 2. While measures of the capacity for collective action are significant determinants of distributive conflict transitions, they play no role in elite-led cases. Where such threats are off the table or limited, elites are more likely to control the transition. Societies in which the poor are not mobilized through programmatic parties, unions, or other organizations may be especially prone to vote buying, patronage, and other forms of clientelistic control that would guarantee elite control of politics, even in nominally democratic settings.[55]

Transition Paths and the Stability of Democratic Rule

Drawing the distinction between distributive conflict and elite-led transitions is necessary to test class conflict models, but it raises a big "so what?" question. Do these transition paths ultimately reflect equifinality, the existence of multiple routes to the same outcome? Or does democratization through one path rather than another have a more enduring effect? We take up this question in Chapter 5, also setting the stage for a discussion of cases that revert to authoritarian rule.

Theoretical priors on this question by no means reflect a well-developed consensus. Mass mobilization may subsequently overwhelm fragile democratic institutions through polarization and the precedent that violence

---

[55]Kitschelt and Wilkinson 2006.

"works."[56] We argue, however, that mass mobilization may also constitute a check on government. It does so by raising the costs to both autocratic incumbents and their democratic successors of abusing executive power, derogating from the guarantee of human rights and civil liberties, and engaging in electoral fraud. Quantitative analysis provides some evidence that countries transitioning through the distributive conflict route appear more robust, and not only in the short run but as long as ten years after the transition. We also undertake paired comparisons between similarly situated distributive-conflict and elite-led transitions, showing the mechanisms through which this might occur. These cases provide additional evidence on how mass mobilization can increase the quality of transitional elections, reduce the capacity of hard-liners to resort to repression, and impede the scope of institutional "lock-ins" that give exiting elites veto power. More generally, mass mobilization that forces concessions from authoritarian rulers opens the political system to broader participation, a more competitive electoral and political system and more robust horizontal checks on executive power.

WHY DO DEMOCRACIES COLLAPSE?

Inequality and distributive conflict play a somewhat different theoretical role in authoritarian reversions than they do in democratization. High inequality is a barrier to democratization in distributive conflict theories. However among those countries that do transition to democracy, the logic is precisely reversed: highly unequal distributions of income are likely to trigger redistributive challenges to elites and tempt them to undermine or overthrow democratic rule. Mass mobilization also plays a somewhat different role in the logic of reversion. The exercise of "de facto" power is a central feature of distributive conflict transitions, but need not play a central role in what we call elite-reaction reversions, which can be triggered by the redistributive policies of governments even in the absence of mass protest.

The elite reaction model of reversion from democratic rule is highly plausible, and has a substantial pedigree. In the bureaucratic-authoritarian regimes of the Southern Cone of Latin America, for example, militaries did appear to intervene in the face of populist democratic challenges; Pinochet's overthrow of the Allende government in Chile is paradigmatic.

As with our discussion of transitions, our consideration of reversions in Chapters 6 through 8 begins with econometric tests of modernization

[56] Huntington 1968.

and class conflict models, with particular attention to the role of inequality. We then resort to causal process observation in Chapters 7 and 8 to see the extent to which reversions conform descriptively to the model. In addition to elite-reaction reversions and those in which class conflict is absent, we also code for a third reversion path: cases in which authoritarian rule emanates not from the right, but from populist disaffection with the performance of incumbent democratic regimes.

We find very little evidence that the Third Wave reversions conform to the elite reaction model and again in two senses. First, we find no evidence in cross-national panel models that inequality matters either for reversions in general or for elite-reaction reversions in particular. Moreover, there is even less evidence that reversions during the Third Wave conformed to the proximate causal processes identified in distributive conflict models. The share of elite-reaction reversions constitutes less than a third of reversions in both datasets, and that number includes a number of reversions that proved extremely short-lived. In only a very small handful of cases did such reversions result in the sort of enduring authoritarian rule visible in earlier authoritarian waves such as in the Southern Cone or the developmental states of East Asia.

Rather than a strong causal role for inequality and distributive conflict, we highlight a complex of three political and institutional factors, a "weak democracy syndrome" that makes democracies vulnerable to authoritarian installations: a history of praetorianism and weak civilian control over the military; weak institutionalization more generally; and poor economic performance, manifest not only in low average growth but in recurrent economic crises as well. Particularly significant in this regard is the concept of weak institutionalization, which refers not to any particular constitutional arrangements but to the absence of *any* significant and durable political institutions capable of constraining the political ambitions of incumbents and oppositions. In weakly institutionalized systems, not only are militaries more likely to intervene in politics but incumbents are more likely to treat politics as a "winner-take-all" game and abuse office with the purpose of permanently marginalizing oppositions.

We do find statistical support for modernization theory in Chapter 6. Reversions to authoritarian rule are indeed more likely to take place in poorer countries. In Chapter 7 we consider an array of low-income "reverters" drawn from Africa, Asia, Latin America, and the postsocialist world. However, even controlling for level of development, we find that the political factors we highlight—particularly praetorianism and weak institutionalization—continue to have explanatory weight. The cases reviewed in Chapter 7 provide strong evidence of these political factors in explaining the incentives of political elites to limit the scope of democratic rule.

The cases also show a more significant role for short-run economic factors than is visible in the regression analysis.

A closer consideration of cases also reveals a substantial number of anomalies with respect to modernization theory. We focus on two. First, even among low-income democracies that we expect to be particularly fragile, we find an ample number of cases that beat the odds. In Chapter 8, we explore these cases in more detail, showing how taming the military, incremental institutional innovations, and robust economic performance explain how these "survivors" built democracy in low-income settings. A second set of anomalies is composed of middle-income countries that would appear to have structural advantages with respect to democratization, but nonetheless revert. Typical of these cases is a process we call backsliding: the arrogation of powers on the part of incumbents and the abuse of that power to marginalize oppositions. There are multiple causes of such backsliding, with oil producers providing prominent examples. However we show how the weak democracy syndrome is implicated in these cases as well. Praetorianism, deinstitutionalization, and economic crises set the sage for the entry of outsiders into political office. Exploiting majoritarianism and the absence of robust party and civil society oppositions, elites are able to arrogate powers, weaken horizontal checks, subvert elections, and undermine the protection of civil and political liberties.

A NOTE ON METHOD, HEDGEHOGS, AND FOXES

In addition to our theoretical and empirical interests, this book also has a methodological purpose. Since the publication of King, Keohane, and Verba's important methodological manifesto *Designing Social Inquiry*, there has been a growing debate over the relationship between quantitative and qualitative methods in contributing to the goal of causal inference.[57] The authors made a strong case that if qualitative methods were to succeed, they essentially needed to mirror the rulebook of quantitative analysis.

Yet there has been a sustained countercurrent of disaffection with this reductionist claim, culminating with Gary Goertz and James Mahoney's important *A Tale of Two Cultures*.[58] Goertz and Mahoney come to the conclusion that the underlying approaches of quantitative and qualitative methods are fundamentally different. The former is grounded in a

[57] King, Keohane, and Verba 1994.
[58] Goertz and Mahoney 2012.

conception of cause as the revelation of average treatment effects, and the latter ultimately rooted in set theory, the analysis of necessary and sufficient conditions, and a mechanisms approach to causation.[59]

How these two approaches to the object of study (populations vs. cases) and even of underlying conceptions of cause can be bridged is by no means obvious.[60] As with other nested analysis,[61] we frame our analysis with cross-national panel designs. Technically, we treat most of our regression analysis as largely correlational, although we deploy a variety of widely used specifications in the literature on democratization and reversions from democratic rule including both multilevel models and the country fixed effects approach favored by economists.

But we are particularly intent on showing how causal inference can be improved by complementing statistical analysis with causal process observation. The concept of causal process observation that we employ grew out of an earlier stream of methodological work on process tracing initiated by Alexander George and subsequently joined by work on the empirical testing of formal models, including through "analytic narratives."[62] Although Collier, Brady, and Seawright distinguish between causal process observation and process tracing, we see them as essentially the same. We prefer the term "causal process observation" because it underscores the link to theory testing. The causal process that we seek to observe does not reflect naïve epistemological realism and is not a search for "causes in the world," so to speak. Rather, it reflects the effort to test whether there is empirical evidence for the causal processes stipulated in the chosen theory under test. It is through such observation that causal process tracing can complement statistical analysis, generate new data, and advance the objective of causal inference.

A central problem in all qualitative analysis, however, centers on case selection.[63] Beach and Pedersen go so far as to identify the approach with the consideration of individual cases.[64] Yet selection of individual cases always runs the risk of not only selection bias but also charges of cherry-picking conforming examples. This problem is not necessarily alleviated by simply expanding the number of cases through medium-N designs; the selection of those cases may be motivated as well.

---

[59] Falleti and Lynch 2010; Gerring 2007b, 2010; Hedstrom and Ylikoski 2010.

[60] Mahoney 2008; Crasnow and Haggard 2015.

[61] Lieberman 2005, 2015.

[62] On causal process observation, see Collier, Brady, and Seawright 2010; Beach and Pedersen 2013; Bennett and Checkel 2015. On process tracing, see George and Bennett 2005; George and McKeown 1985. On "analytic narratives," see Bates et al. 1998; Kuehn 2012.

[63] Gerring 2007a, 2012; Seawright and Gerring 2008; Goertz and Mahoney 2012.

[64] Beach and Pedersen 2013.

We therefore propose a somewhat novel approach to causal process observation of relatively rare events such as democratic transitions and reversions: to select *all* of the cases in the corresponding cross-national panel models for closer qualitative scrutiny. In addition to regime change, the subject of this book, such an approach is also relevant to many other types of rare events of interest to political scientists: wars, civil wars, state failure, genocides, financial crises, and pandemics.[65] Its advantages begin with the nature of the theories that are likely to be on offer. A scan of the list above immediately reveals that any explanation of a rare event is likely to be complex. Even relatively stylized models are likely to invoke both structural and institutional factors as well as strategic interactions among contending players, typically modeled formally or informally in game-theoretic terms.

This complexity has important implications for the testing of theory. These models may appear spare, but in fact rest on highly complex causal chains. In our case, these include inequality, distributive conflict, and strategic interactions between incumbents and oppositions over the nature of political institutions. Moreover, these processes unfold in variable temporal time frames and in different sequences that do not necessarily lend themselves to efficient econometric tests. In a quantitative model, the effects of either structural variables, such as inequality, or behavioral ones, such as protest, are estimated across a heterogeneous set of cases, some of which transition as a result of the stipulated causal mechanism and some of which do not. The focus on average treatment effects masks the heterogeneity of actual transition paths; the variable in question may be significant or not significant across a population, but this does not necessarily provide useful information on the outcomes in particular cases. By contrast, causal process observations do not ask whether the variable in question is significant across a population, but whether the cases conform with the causal process stipulated in the theoretical model, a causes of effects versus an effects of causes approach.[66]

In addition to their advantages in more closely testing the actual mechanisms specified in causal models, causal process observations also address a second important problem in standard quantitative panel designs: the mismatch between the temporal framework of a stipulated causal process and the constraints of country-year coding of cases. In cross-national panels, each country-year is coded as a transition or nontransition year; these codings constitute the dependent variable. The causal covariates are similarly either contemporaneous or antecedent with some lag structure. Yet the causal sequence of actor choices associated with transitions and

[65]The following draws on Crasnow and Haggard 2015.
[66]Mahoney 2008; Goertz and Mahoney 2012.

reversions is blurred when data are aggregated up to the country-year level. In fact, the panel year design may hide mismatches between antecedent conditions and subsequent events; they could, for example, be altogether reversed and nonetheless receive the same coding. Processes may also be more compressed or extended, not constant across cases, and thus similarly not well captured by the artifact of the country-year coding constraint. As we see later, many cases that are coded as transitions prove to be dubious when a more extended but variable temporal context is taken into account, a point emphasized more generally in the work of Pierson.[67]

In principle, multistage models can be constructed that work from structural causes through intervening behaviors to institutional effects.[68] Some critics of the mechanisms approach have argued that mechanisms may be nothing more than such chains of intervening variables.[69] Moreover, the temporal problems we note might be handled by higher-frequency data that would reduce sequencing problems. Although possible in principle, the continued reliance on reduced-form specification suggests that these strategies are both practically difficult to implement, in part because of the labor intensity of recoding existing datasets to conform more precisely with the theory being tested, and potentially not solvable in principle.

The approach proposed here raises its own challenges, including the well-known trade-off between breadth and depth that comes from a consideration of a large number of cases. However this is offset by the advantages gained by a sharp focus on the presence or absence of the complex—and often configurative—set of causes outlined in the underlying theoretical model under consideration. We illustrate the approach in more detail in Chapter 1, but it begins with a clear coding rule with respect to the causal mechanisms in the theory and a focused discussion of the extent to which each case conforms with the theory; these discussions constitute the qualitative dataset that undergirds the analysis throughout the book.[70]

In principle it is possible that all cases might conform with the theory, and a consideration of the distribution of all cases has occasionally been used in this way.[71] But it is more likely that we would find cases that do and do not conform with the model, or put differently, alternative causal pathways. In this case, we can probe these two different populations in more detail through both quantitative and second-round causal process observation that considers alternative hypothesis. We engage the modernization and distributive conflict theories in this fashion throughout the

[67] Pierson 2004.
[68] King, Keohane, and Verba 1994: 85–87.
[69] Beck 2006, 2010; Gerring 2007b, 2010; Hafner-Burton and Ron 2009.
[70] Haggard, Kaufman, and Teo 2016.
[71] Fortin 2010.

book, probing their implications through both quantitative analysis and causal process observation and proposing alternatives.

Despite our methodological ambitions, we should note that this book is indebted to Huntington and early theorists of the Third Wave for more than simply the metaphor. Our identification of multiple routes to and from democracy also reflects his skepticism that "the search for a common, universally present independent variable that might play a significant role in explaining (democracy) in such different countries is almost certain to be unsuccessful. . . . The causes of democratization differ substantially from one place to another and from one time to another."[72] It follows, he argues, that democratization is likely to result from highly endogenous combinations of causes, an approach we take in outlining the "weak democracy" syndrome.

To draw on Isaiah Berlin's well-known parable, the urge to be a "hedgehog" who knows "one big thing" is strong in social science. Theories of regime change rooted in inequality and class conflict are reflective of that urge. But given the complexity of the changes being analyzed, it is more appropriate to cast a wide empirical net but to move like a "fox" who knows many things. Being a fox does not imply a retreat into ideographic accounts where "everything matters."[73] Rather, we aim at a disciplined causal account that avoids, as Fukuyama puts it, both "the pitfalls of excessive abstraction (the vice of economists) and excessive particularism (the problem of many historians and anthropologists)."[74]

[72] Huntington 1991: 38.
[73] Berlin 1953.
[74] Fukuyama 2011: 25.

PART I

Inequality and Transitions to Democracy

CHAPTER 1

Inequality and Transitions to Democracy

IN THIS CHAPTER, WE TAKE A FIRST CUT at the relationship between inequality, distributive conflict, and regime change during the Third Wave of democratic transitions from 1980 to 2008. As discussed in the Introduction, the new distributive conflict models that have recently been formalized by Boix and Acemoglu and Robinson give a sharper edge to structural, class-conflict approaches to political change that have long been a part of the social science canon.[1] They have done so in part by outlining the causal mechanisms that link inequality, struggles between elites and masses, and regime change, and we begin by outlining the underlying theory in more detail.

At first glance, these theories appear amenable to relatively straightforward quantitative tests, and we take up this task in Chapter 2. Are demands for democracy driven by discontent over the distribution of income and wealth? Are they blocked by elites at high levels of inequality? If so, we should find that transitions to democracy are more likely to occur in societies that are either relatively equal (Boix) or in ones that are at least not highly unequal (Acemoglu and Robinson). Transitions should be far less likely where income and assets are highly concentrated.

As we noted in the Introduction, however, reduced-form statistical models have difficulty capturing the complex strategic interactions that constitute the intervening causal processes in these theories. They therefore tend to focus on the structural components of the theory, such as level of development or inequality, and regime change. But the empirical question is not only whether antecedent conditions are linked to the outcome via an average treatment effect. We also want to know whether this causal relationship operates through the mechanisms stipulated in the theoretical model and, if so, in what share of the cases.

In this chapter, we outline and demonstrate a different empirical approach that we use throughout the volume. The approach rests on a three-step process of causal process observation: coding all cases for the presence or absence of the stipulated causal mechanism, which can be used in both econometric and qualitative tests; showing distributions of actual

---

[1] Acemoglu and Robinson 2000, 2001, 2006; Acemoglu et al. 2013; Boix 2003, 2008, 2013; see also Przeworski 2009; Ansell and Samuels 2010, 2013a, 2013b, 2014.

outcomes as opposed to average treatment effects or predicted values; and considering smaller samples of cases to buttress causal inference.[2]

Two features of case selection in our approach are somewhat unorthodox. First, we select on the dependent variable, choosing cases on the basis of whether or not they underwent a transition to democratic—or in later chapters—authoritarian rule. This approach is justified because we are trying to assess the extent to which the causal mechanisms postulated in class conflict theories—i.e., political challenges to existing distribution of wealth and income—are actually present in the transitions in the sample. Second, in contrast to the more common practice of purposeful or random selection of cases for more intensive analysis, our approach is to select *all* transitions in the relevant sample period (1980–2008) identified in the Polity and CGV datasets.[3] Because transitions and reversions are rare, this appears to resemble other "medium-*N*" designs. In fact, however, it differs in not sampling at all and thus assessing conformity with the theory across the entire universe of cases.

In the following sections, we begin with a review of the theory and existing quantitative findings on the relationship between inequality and democratic transitions. We then turn to the findings we derive from the causal process observations and codings in our dataset. We show that the support for the distributive conflict model of regime change is weak, even under highly generous coding rules. And when these rules are tightened, the evidence is weaker still. In Chapter 2, we provide similar findings with multivariate analysis and outline some alternative theoretical ideas about the origins of distributive and elite-led transitions. Rather than socioeconomic inequality, our approach to distributive conflict transitions emphasizes the role of prior authoritarian institutions and social capacity for collective action, as well as regime performance. The elite-led transitions also have institutional and political roots, with elite conflicts and calculations and international factors playing a prominent role. These ideas are in turn explored in Chapters 3 and 4 through a consideration of select cases.

THEORY: DISTRIBUTIVE CONFLICT MODELS OF REGIME TRANSITION

The new distributive conflict approaches pioneered by Boix and Acemoglu and Robinson both trace their theoretical underpinnings to a class of economic models on redistribution under democratic politics, including

---

[2] Crasnow and Haggard 2015.
[3] Gerring 2006, 2007a, 2007b; Fearon and Laitin 2011; Crasnow and Haggard 2015.

Romer, Roberts, and particularly Meltzer and Richard.[4] The Meltzer-Richard model begins with a simple economy in which individuals differ in their productivity and, as a result, in their income. In the first period—or state of nature—all income is from wages; there are no government transfers. The distribution of productivity and income is skewed to the right, with most citizens falling at the lower and middle range of the distribution, and a small tail constituting the rich. As a result, the mean income is higher than the median income, a distribution that is consonant with the actual allocation of income in most countries. In a subsequent period, the government levies a proportional income tax and redistributes the resulting revenue in the form of a lump sum payment to each individual, supplementing wage income. This new distribution reshuffles the prior distribution of income, and also determines the size of the government.

Two features of the model determine the extent of redistribution. First, the tax rate is set by the preferences of the median voter, an assumption consonant with simple voting models derived from Duverger's Law.[5] Since median income is always below the average income, democratic government can always be expected to engage in some degree of redistribution. The second feature of the model, however, concerns the effects of inequality. The wider the divergence between the median and mean income—the more the median voters' income falls below average income—the more is to be gained from taxes-cum-transfers. As a result, the median voter will favor a higher tax rate and the government will be larger.

The model is typically interpreted as telling us about the effects of different income distributions in democratic systems; more unequal democracies should have more redistribution. But the model unexpectedly can also shed light on the franchise, political participation, and the incorporation of new groups into politics. Expansions of the franchise or increases in participation that bring poor voters into the electoral process will lower the median income relative to the mean and thus generate more redistribution.

Boix, and Acemoglu and Robinson build on the Meltzer-Richard framework to develop a theory of not only democratic responses to preferences over the distribution of income but how such preferences might lead to changes in political institutions. The Meltzer-Richard model assumes that, in democracies, mass preferences about redistribution are registered through elections, and in the model on a referendum on the tax rate and associated transfers. In autocracies, however, preferences can be registered only through mobilized demands both for redistribution and for the

[4]Romer 1975; Roberts 1977; Meltzer and Richard 1981.
[5]Duverger 1972.

extension of the franchise, what Acemoglu and Robinson term the exercise of de facto political power. Regime change occurs when elites calculate that it is less costly to yield political power than to undertake the risks and costs of repressing protest. The core question is therefore the conditions under which mass publics will succeed in exercising their de facto power in the interests of regime change and in which authoritarian incumbents will be displaced directly or accede to institutional change. Although Boix and Acemoglu and Robinson offer somewhat different answers, they each suggest how the level of inequality matters.

The demand side of both arguments begins with the micro-foundations provided in the Meltzer-Richard model. If democracies are more inclined than dictatorships to respond to the distributive demands of the median voter, then mass *preferences* for democracy can be taken as a given. But in autocracies, we also need to know whether popular majorities will actually assume the risk of mobilizing around such preferences. On this issue, the two models diverge.

Boix offers an informational model in which regime changes are triggered by exogenous shocks that weaken the elite or reveal its weakness, thereby providing openings for low-income sectors to mobilize for democracy.[6] But the prospects for regime change depend on the "political and organizational resources of the parties in contention." "[As] the poor become mobilized in the form of left-wing mass parties, the cost of repression increase for the rich."[7] Importantly, Boix does not predict when this type of mobilization might occur; it is exogenous to his model and can occur at any level of inequality. But "once the poor accumulate political resources and overcome their collective action problems," dominant elites are most likely to choose concession over repression at low levels of inequality, where the costs of redistribution are also relatively low. Although regime change may still be possible at "middle levels" of inequality, the prospects diminish in a linear fashion as income becomes more concentrated.

In contrast to Boix, Acemoglu and Robinson build predictions about the mobilization of demands for democracy directly into their model. They argue that such pressures are unlikely to occur in authoritarian governments with low levels of inequality because the incentives to actively demand institutional change are weak. Although subject populations might in principle gain more if political rights were expanded, the costs of mobilization are likely to exceed the gains that they currently receive from their share in the existing distribution of income. As inequality grows, however, the gains from mobilization for democracy rise. Thus, whereas

[6]Boix 2003: 28–30.
[7]Boix 2003: 20.

Boix argues that the chances for democracy diminish directly as inequality increases, Acemoglu and Robinson conclude that the relationship between inequality and democratic transitions should exhibit an inverted-U pattern: transitions to democratic rule are most likely to occur at intermediate levels of inequality where grievances are sufficient to motivate the disenfranchised to mobilize, but not threatening enough to invite repression.[8]

It should be emphasized, however, that although the two models differ in their predictions about the level of inequality at which the masses will mobilize around demands for democracy, they concur strongly that high inequality deters elites from making concessions. Building on Meltzer-Richard, Boix argues that as inequality increases, the potential level of transfers becomes larger.[9] But as a result the authoritarian inclinations of the wealthy also increase and the probability of democratization declines. Boix qualifies this argument by emphasizing the role played by capital mobility in mitigating the relationship between inequality and regime change.[10] High levels of capital mobility enhance the bargaining power of elites. Fixed assets, by contrast, limit the options of the wealthy and make them vulnerable to democratic redistribution and thus more resistant to it. But given the decision of the poor to mobilize, the incentives of upper-class incumbents to repress are ultimately a function of the level of inequality as well as the mobility of assets. Transitions are most likely when inequality is low, asset mobility is high, and elites have less to lose from competitive politics. Elites have stronger incentives to repress when assets are fixed.

Acemoglu and Robinson also argue that high inequality increases the incentives for authoritarian elites to repress demands for regime change. To this observation, they add an important point about how institutional change affects the credibility of commitments and compounds the risk of redistribution. When elites are confronted by mobilization from below, they can make short-run economic concessions to diffuse the threat even in situations of high inequality. But these concessions are unlikely to be credible to the mobilized citizens in the absence of institutional reforms that limit the power of the elites to renege. Yielding to demands for democracy provides an assurance that elites will commit to a more equal distribution of resources in the future as well as in the present. Commitment to the future, however, also compounds the cost of concessions and strengthens the incentives for elites to resist change at high levels of inequality.

[8] See also Burkhart 1997; Epstein et al. 2006.
[9] Boix 2003: 37.
[10] See also Freeman and Quinn 2012.

Quantitative Evidence: A Review

Despite the widespread interest in distributive conflict theories, the empirical support for a relationship between inequality and regime change is mixed at best. Acemoglu and Robinson do not present systematic empirical evidence in support of their claims.[11] Much of the book is taken up with a discussion of the underlying intuition of the theory,[12] and the presentation of a family of formal models of democratic and nondemocratic regimes and regime change.[13] They do present scatterplots showing a positive relationship between equality and the *level* of democracy in a cross-section of countries, including developed and developing ones.[14] But this relationship is clearly complicated by the fact that inequality declines as countries develop. They also provide short case studies of Great Britain, Argentina, South Africa, and Singapore.[15] But these correlations and cases are illustrative at best as the principle governing their selection is not clear. Revisiting the issue, moreover, Acemoglu et al. deploy a specification favored by economists—a panel design with country fixed effects and common trends with time effects—and come to the conclusion that inequality has no effect on transitions one way or the other.[16]

In his analysis of democratic transitions over the very long run (1850–1980), Boix finds that the distribution of land, proxied by the share of family farms, affects the likelihood of a transition to democratic rule.[17] More unequal societies are both less likely to transit and less stable when they do.[18] Boix also explores a highly uneven panel of countries for the 1950 to 1990 period (only 587 observations), including developed countries.[19] Using a Gini index as his measure of inequality, Boix finds some evidence that increases in the level of inequality reduce the likelihood of a democratic transition, but the findings are not altogether robust.[20] Boix returns to the issue using measures of both land and skill inequality and

---

[11]Their earlier work (2000, 2001) was motivated by experiences in 19th-century Europe and early 20th-century Latin America. But in those articles, as well as in the later book, the formal theory is cast in general terms, without specifying scope conditions that might apply to "Third Wave" transitions. In the book, moreover, the illustrations from South Africa and Singapore rely on much more recent developments.

[12]Acemoglu and Robinson 2006: 1–47, 80–87.
[13]Acemoglu and Robinson 2006: 89–172, 173–320.
[14]Acemoglu and Robinson 2006: 58–61.
[15]Acemoglu and Robinson 2006: 1–14.
[16]Acemoglu et al. 2013.
[17]Boix 2003.
[18]Boix 2003: 90–97.
[19]Boix 2003: 71–88.
[20]See, for example, Model 2A, Boix 2003: 79.

improved data on regime type and regime change. He finds confirming evidence for his favored inequality hypothesis with respect to both the likelihood of transitions and the stability of democratic rule.[21] Societies with a more equitable distribution of human capital have a higher probability of transiting to democracy (except for the very most equitable) and a lower likelihood of democratic breakdowns. Land equality does not influence the probability of transitions but has a democratic stabilization effect.

More recently, a number of other quantitative studies have taken up the challenge raised by Boix and Acemoglu and Robinson, but with similarly mixed results. Like Boix, Ansell and Samuels consider both long-historical and postwar samples (1850–1993; 1955–2004) but from a different theoretical perspective. They find that land concentration—a measure of rural inequality—makes democratization less likely. But they find that increases in overall income inequality as measured by a Gini coefficient make democratization *more* likely.[22] Their result is counterintuitive to class conflict models in which high—although not rising—inequality is a barrier to democratization but is consistent with alternative theoretical traditions. Ansell and Samuels argue that increasing income inequality reflects the emergence of a new capitalist class that challenges landed elites, a dynamic consistent with Boix's and Acemoglu and Robinson's extension of their models into three-class variants.[23]

Other tests in the literature generally fail to find a relationship between inequality and democratic transitions. A cross-section design by Dutt and Mitra finds a relationship between inequality measured by the Gini coefficient and "political instability," but fails to find a relationship between inequality and transitions to democratic rule.[24] Christian Houle creates a dataset using an alternative measure of inequality: capital's share of income in the manufacturing sector that we also use in our analysis below and in Chapters 2 and 6.[25] Using the dichotomous coding scheme developed by Przeworski et al. and Cheibub and Gandhi that we also deploy,[26] Houle shows that inequality bears no systematic relationship to democratic transitions over the 1960 to 2000 period, although it is a significant predictor of reversions to authoritarian rule. In a wide-ranging study of the determinants of democratization, Teorell also fails to find a relationship between a Gini coefficient and democratic transitions.[27]

[21] Boix 2013.
[22] Ansell and Samuels 2010, 2013b, 2014.
[23] Boix 2003: 47–59; Acemoglu and Robinson 2006: 266–86.
[24] Dutt and Mitra 2008.
[25] Houle 2009, 2013.
[26] Przeworski, Alvarez, Cheibub, and Limongi 2000; Cheibub and Gandhi 2004.
[27] Teorell 2010: 60.

CAUSAL PROCESS OBSERVATION OF TRANSITIONS TO DEMOCRATIC RULE

These theories, as we have already indicated, rest on an extraordinarily complex causal chain: discontent over inequality; mass mobilization around distributive grievances by the poor or—more commonly—by coalitions of low- and middle-income groups; elite calculations about the costs of repressing these challenges or offering political concessions; the strategic response of the masses to those elite decisions; and the ultimate outcome of regime maintenance or change.[28] Moreover, despite the compression of time in standard game-theoretic models, these interactions are typically iterated. Detailed case studies reveal that the mobilization-repression dynamic may occur dozens of times, in the majority of cases having no systemic effect. In some cases, however, it will produce a breakthrough.

Rather than beginning with our quantitative analysis—to which we return in Chapter 2—we turn first to a consideration of some simple distributions based on our qualitative dataset, which is set up to gauge the extent to which the cases conform or diverge from the causal mechanisms stipulated in the theory. These distributions also provide the opportunity to introduce the dataset, and particularly our coding of distributive and elite-led conflict transitions. This distinction structures our discussion in Chapters 2 through 5.[29]

The cases included in our dataset come from the dichotomous coding of transitions and reversions in Cheibub, Gandhi, and Vreeland (CGV) and from Polity IV.[30] For the continuous Polity IV metric, we use a cutoff of 6 to indicate a transition, a benchmark used in the dataset itself to denote that a regime has reached a democratic threshold. However, in contrast to country-year panel designs, causal process observation can isolate much more precisely the strategic interactions we associate with democratization. By "regime change," we mean quite precisely the decisions made by authoritarian leaders to make political concessions or withdraw altogether in favor of institutional arrangements that ultimately prove democratic under the coding rules of the datasets.[31] It is important to underscore

---

[28] For explication of the basic models, see particularly Boix 2003: 27–36; Acemoglu and Robinson 2006: 181–220.

[29] We personally researched all cases cited in the dataset and consulted closely with each other on each coding decision to ensure consistency across cases. Country and regional experts also reviewed coding decisions, particularly in ambiguous cases (see Haggard, Kaufman, and Teo 2016).

[30] Cheibub, Gandhi, and Vreeland 2010.

[31] For reversions, discussed in Chapters 6–8, we identify actions taken by challengers within or outside the government that result in the overthrow of democratic rule.

that this coding does not necessarily reflect a transition as the onset of a new set of political institutions, for example, a founding election. But as will be seen, it is appropriate for testing this particular theory, which rests as much on the displacement of incumbents as the forging of a new order.

Selecting all cases of transitions has the advantage of permitting what we call "stage 2" and "stage 3" analysis: the aggregation of the individual causal process observations to show distributions of conforming and nonconforming cases, including with respect to other variables of theoretical interest such as inequality; and the consideration of particular cases for more in-depth treatment. For example, we pay particular attention to high- and low-inequality cases because the theory has strong expectations about how such cases should behave.

For each transition, we provide a narrative that reconstructs the causal process leading to authoritarian withdrawal and assesses whether the key political decisions in question were a result of distributive conflicts; these are contained in the accompanying dataset.[32] Two mechanisms appear central for the theory to hold. First, elites must confront political-cum-distributive pressure from below in the form of mass mobilization, or at least a "clear and present danger" of it. In the absence of such pressures, it is not clear why elites would be motivated to cede power at all, as Przeworski's trenchant question cited in the Introduction suggests. Second, there must be some evidence, minimally in the temporal sequence of events, that mass mobilization either directly overthrows incumbents—a minority of cases—or forces incumbents to make institutional compromises.

We therefore code "distributive conflict" transitions as ones in which both of the following occurred:

- The mobilization of redistributive grievances on the part of economically disadvantaged groups or representatives of such groups (parties, unions, NGOs) posed a threat to the incumbency of ruling elites;
- *And* mass mobilization directly ousts incumbents, or the rising costs of repressing these demands force elites to make political compromises in favor of democratic challengers, typically indicated by a clear temporal sequence (mass mobilization followed by authoritarian withdrawal).

In coding the cases, we were deliberately permissive, writing coding rules that gave the benefit of the doubt to the theory.[33] First, our coding rule has the advantage of allowing us to consider a variety of distributive conflicts that may not be captured by any single inequality measure, from urban class conflicts to ethnic and regional ones. Yet such conflicts must

---

[32] Haggard, Kaufman, and Teo 2016.
[33] Haggard, Kaufman, and Teo 2016.

be fought around identifiable inequalities. Second, the economically disadvantaged or the organizations representing them need not be the only ones mobilized in opposition to the existing regime. We allow for the possibility of cross-class coalitions as long as disadvantaged sectors are significant actors in the mobilization of grievances. Finally, although mass mobilization must partly reflect demands for redistribution, it can be motivated by other grievances as well.

We coded all cases in which such threats from below did not occur at all or appeared to play only a marginal causal role as "elite-led transitions."

An important coding issue is the question of "potential" threats in the absence of actual mobilization. As Acemoglu and Robinson note in distinguishing between de jure and de facto power, the poor can be considered a potential threat in virtually any authoritarian setting.[34] However, we can plausibly assume that elites seeking to undermine long-term threats have time horizons that are substantially different from those responding to more immediate challenges. We do take potential threats into account where there has been a recent history of mass mobilization demanding democratic reforms that might weigh on incumbent decision making. Beyond that, however, we are wary of the coding challenges. Virtually any case can be coded as one in which there was a "potential" challenge from below, but this brings with it a corresponding decline in analytic leverage.

Table 1.1 provides evidence on the presence of distributive conflict in all of the transitions in the two datasets. The third and fourth columns divide the CGV transitions into distributive conflict and elite-led types; the fifth and sixth columns repeat the exercise for Polity transitions. We also identify the nonoverlapping cases. The last column shows the average Polity score from the time of the transition through either the end of the sample period or until an outright reversion to authoritarian rule, a measure of the extent to which democracy took hold in the case.

The information contained in Table 1.1 provides a powerful reminder of the significance of coding rules and the caution required with respect to the inferences drawn from quantitative analysis of these datasets. As we noted in the Introduction, only 55.4 percent of the CGV transitions are also Polity cases, and 34 of the 78 CGV transitions have Polity scores of less than 6. But even where the two datasets are in agreement, questions can be raised about the validity of the codings. Transitions in Guatemala (1986) and Honduras (1982) empowered nominally democratic governments that actually intensified repression of social movements that had redistributive objectives. Death squads continued to terrorize the opposition in El Salvador after the transition in 1984. Insiders and elites

---

[34] Acemoglu and Robinson 2006.

Table 1.1 Distributive Conflict and Elite-Led Transitions, 1980–2008.

Country	Year	CGV Distributive	CGV Elite-Led	Polity Distributive	Polity Elite-Led	Polity Score
Albania	1991	X				4.4
Albania	2002				X	8.1
Argentina	1983	X		X		7.6
Armenia	1991	X				7.0
Bangladesh	1986		X			3.4
Bangladesh	1991			X		6.0
Belarus	1991		X		X	7.0
Benin	1991	X		X		6.2
Bhutan	2007		X			3.0
Bolivia	1982	X		X		8.7
Brazil	1985	X		X		7.9
Bulgaria	1990	X		X		8.4
Burundi	1993	X				0.0
Burundi	2005	X		X		6.0
Cape Verde	1990–91		X (1990)		X (1991)	8.9
Central African Republic	1993		X			5.0

(*continued*)

Table 1.1 (*continued*)

Country	Year	CGV		Polity		Polity Score
		Distributive	Elite-Led	Distributive	Elite-Led	
Chile	1989–90		X (1990)		X (1989)	8.6
Comoros	1990		X			3.6
Comoros	2004		X			7.8
Congo	1992	X				5.0
Croatia	1991		X			-2.3
Croatia	2000				X	8.4
Cyprus	1983		X			10.0
Czechoslovakia	1989–90		X (1989)		X (1990)	9.6
Dominican Republic	1996			X		8.0
Ecuador	2002			X		5.9
El Salvador	1984	X		X		6.7
Estonia	1991	X		X		7.6
Fiji	1992	X				5.4
Fiji	1999				X	5.2
Georgia	2004	X		X		6.6

Country	Year					Value
Ghana	1993		X			−1.0
Grenada	1984		X			NA
Guatemala	1986	X				5.8
Guatemala	1996			X		8.0
Guinea-Bissau	2000		X			5.0
Guinea-Bissau	2004–5		X (2004)		X (2005)	6.0
Guyana	1992				X	6.0
Haiti	1990			X		7.0
Haiti	1994				X	6.2
Honduras	1982		X		X	6.2
Honduras	1989				X	6.5
Hungary	1990		X		X	10.0
Indonesia	1999	X		X		7.0
Kenya	1998	X				4.2
Kenya	2002			X		7.7
Kyrgyzstan	2005	X				3.3
Latvia	1991	X		X		8.0
Lesotho	1993			X		8.0

(continued)

Table 1.1 (continued)

Country	Year	CGV		Polity		Polity Score
		Distributive	Elite-Led	Distributive	Elite-Led	
Liberia	2006		X		X	6.0
Lithuania	1991	X		X		10.0
Macedonia	1991		X		X	7.2
Madagascar	1992–93	X (1993)		X (1992)		7.6
Malawi	1994	X		X		5.7
Malawi	2004				X	6.0
Malaysia	2008				X	6.0
Maldives	2008	X				NA
Mali	1992	X		X		6.7
Mauritania	2007		X			4.0
Mexico	1997				X	7.5
Mexico	2000		X			8.0
Moldova	1993				X	7.5
Mongolia	1990–92	X (1990)		X (1992)		9.8
Nepal	1990	X				5.3
Nepal	1999				X	6.0

Country	Year					
Nepal	2006–8	X (2008)		X (2006)		6.0
Nicaragua	1984		X			5.5
Nicaragua	1990				X	7.6
Niger	1992–93	X (1993)		X (1992)		8.0
Niger	2000	X				5.6
Niger	2004				X	6.0
Nigeria	1999	X				4.0
Pakistan	1988		X		X	7.8
Pakistan	2008	X				5.0
Panama	1989		X		X	8.8
Paraguay	1989		X			6.5
Paraguay	1992				X	7.3
Peru	1980	X		X		7.2
Peru	2001		X		X	9.0
Philippines	1986–87	X (1986)		X (1987)		8.0
Poland	1989–91	X (1989)		X (1991)		8.8
Romania	1990	X				7.3
Romania	1996				X	8.4

(*continued*)

Table 1.1 (*continued*)

Country	Year	CGV Distributive	CGV Elite-Led	Polity Distributive	Polity Elite-Led	Polity Score
Russia	2000				X	5.6
São Tomé and Principe	1991		X			NA
Senegal	2000		X			7.9
Serbia	2000		X		X	7.2
Sierra Leone	1996–98		X			4.0
Sierra Leone	2007		X			7.0
Solomon Islands	2003–4				X	8.0
South Africa	1992			X		8.8
South Korea	1988	X		X		7.0
Sri Lanka	1989	X				5.3
Sri Lanka	2006				X	6.0
Sudan	1986			X		7.0
Suriname	1988	X				0.0
Suriname	1991		X			5.0
Taiwan	1992				X	8.8

Taiwan	1996			X		9.3
Thailand	1992	X		X		9.0
Thailand	2008		X			4.0
Turkey	1983		X		X	7.5
Uganda	1980		X	X		2.5
Ukraine	1991	X		X		6.4
Ukraine	1994			X		6.6
Uruguay	1985	X		X		9.8
Zambia	1991			X		6.0
Zambia	2008				X	7.0
N		42	37	36	37	6.5
%		53.2	46.8	49.3	50.7	

Sources: CGV transitions from Cheibub, Gandhi, and Vreeland (2010); Polity transitions from Marshall, Gurr, and Jaggers (2013); transition types from Haggard, Kaufman, and Teo (2016).

Note: In the dataset, we treat any transitions that are coded within a two-year window as the same case (for example, the CGV coding of the Philippines transition occurring in 1986, the Polity coding as of 1987). Outside of this two-year window (for example, Paraguay) or where there is an intervening reversion (Sierra Leone), we treat the transitions as separate cases. There are no Polity scores for Grenada, the Maldives or São Tomé.

repressed opposition and/or exercised disproportionate control over them in the nominally democratic cases of Croatia, Niger, and Thailand. In at least four cases—Ghana under Rawlings; Kenya under Moi; Malawi, where an "insider" won the transitional election; and Romania—the military or incumbent elites continued to exercise disproportionate influence after the transition. In all of these cases, the transitions appear to conform more closely to what Levitsky and Way call "competitive authoritarianism" than to democracy.[35] Because we seek to engage the quantitative analysis that deploys such data, we do not discard or reclassify cases identified as transitions in the two datasets. But caution is clearly in order.

What does the coding show about the role of distributive conflict in democratic transitions? We found that distributive conflict played some proximate causal role in propelling transitions in about 53.8 percent of CGV and 53.8 percent of Polity transition cases, roughly half in both datasets. However, a full test of the theory requires that we also consider the relationship between inequality and distributive conflict, which we take up in a preliminary way below and explore in more detail in Chapter 2.

Before turning to that task, however, these preliminary findings about the distribution of cases need to be tempered by the generosity of our coding rules. Distributive pressure from below did play an unambiguously significant role in a number of middle-income countries, such as Argentina, South Korea, and South Africa. However our expansive coding rules also necessitated the classification of cases as distributive conflict where there was considerable ambiguity about its causal weight. The ambiguity stemmed from one or more of three factors. First, some distributive conflict transitions occurred in small, open economies that were highly vulnerable to pressure from donors or other international actors, which may have been substantial or even decisive. The class basis of protest constituted a second source of ambiguity; in many cases, protest included or was even dominated by middle- and in some cases upper-middle-class groups, calling into question the class dynamics of the model even if we allow for cross-class coalitions including the poor. A third source of ambiguity stemmed from judgments about the role played by redistributive grievances in opposition demands; in many instances, it was difficult to separate redistributive demands from grievances that focused on generalized dissatisfaction with authoritarian incumbents, issues such as poor economic performance and corruption or nationalist claims. Table 1.2 lists the ambiguous distributive conflict cases: the cases in the dataset where international pressures, the class composition of the protestors, or the extent of redistributive grievances made the coding of the case am-

[35] Levitsky and Way 2010.

Table 1.2 Ambiguous Distributive Conflict Transitions.

CGV Dataset		Polity Dataset	
Country	*Source of Ambiguity*	*Country*	*Source of Ambiguity*
Armenia (1991)	Grievance	Armenia (1991)	Grievance
Benin (1991)	Class	Benin (1991)	Class
Bulgaria (1990)	Grievance	Bulgaria (1990)	Grievance
Congo (1992)	Class	El Salvador (1984)	International
El Salvador (1984)	International	Estonia (1991)	Class/grievance
Estonia (1991)	Class/grievance	Latvia (1991)	Class/grievance
Fiji (1992)	International	Lesotho (1993)	Class/international
Kenya (1998)	International	Lithuania (1991)	Class/grievance
Latvia (1991)	Class/grievance	Malawi (1994)	Class/international
Lithuania (1991)	Class/grievance	Mali (1992)	Class
Malawi (1994)	Class/international	Mongolia (1992)	Class/grievance
Mali (1992)	Class	Niger (1992)	Class/grievance/international
Mongolia (1990)	Class/grievance	Ukraine (1991)	Class/grievance
Niger (1993)	Class/grievance/international		
Sri Lanka (1989)	Grievance		
Suriname (1988)	International		
Ukraine (1991)	Class/grievance		
Total	17		13
Percentage of total transitions	18.1		21.8

biguous. The table also shows the share of these ambiguous cases as a proportion of all distributive conflict transitions. A number of African transitions were ambiguous on the first two counts, and a cluster of post-socialist cases raise questions on the third; each category deserves somewhat more extended discussion.

A number of African cases, including Lesotho, Kenya, Malawi, and Niger, were ambiguous with respect to the role of international pressures, as were other small countries such as El Salvador, Fiji, and Suriname. Although domestic mobilization played a role in the exit of authoritarian incumbents in these cases, we cannot rule out the possibility that the transitions in question might not have occurred without international pressures. An example is provided by the shift from single-party to multiparty government in Malawi in 1993 and 1994. Student protests and strikes contributed to the decision by Hastings Banda, "President for Life," to tentatively agree to a referendum on whether to hold multiparty elections. But donors reacted strongly when Banda began to renege on his commitments by arresting a prominent regime opponent, Chakufwa Chihana, returning from exile. A decision by the donors to reject a major appeal for aid significantly increased the leverage of the internal opposition, which played a crucial role in guaranteeing the integrity of the referendum on multiparty rule and the subsequent election.

Notwithstanding our generous coding decision, it is also ambiguous at best to claim that the transition processes always mapped directly to the underlying Meltzer-Richard model, in which the poor are pitted against the rich. Ambiguity about the class composition of protest comes up in a number African cases in particular, including Benin, Congo, Lesotho, Malawi, Mali, and Niger. Even though all of these cases meet our coding rules because of the presence of mobilization "from below" that affected the transition, protest was primarily limited to civil servants, students, and other sectors of the urban middle class. Niger provides an example. The pivotal decision in this case was an agreement by the military strongman, General Ali Saibou, to convene a National Conference, which then assumed the role of a transitional government and organized competitive elections. Distributive protests played a role in Saibou's decision to yield authority. Yet the opposition came primarily from the Nigerien Workers Union, which represented Niger's 39,000 civil servants, and the Union of Nigerien Scholars, which represented about 6 percent of the country's school-aged population.[36] Both groups bitterly opposed tough adjustment programs demanded by the International Monetary Fund, but the conflicts did not appear to engage the poor, who were overwhelmingly rural. As Gervais writes, "the political stakes raised by . . . adjustment policies tended to compromise the benefits of the organized groups of the modern sector as much as the privileges of the traditional political class."[37]

The nature of grievances is a third source of ambiguity in the coding, and democracies that emerge from the secession from Yugoslavia and the former Soviet Union warrant special mention in this regard. In three such

[36] Gervais 1997: 93.
[37] Gervais 1997: 105.

cases—Croatia, Macedonia, and Belarus—the coding was unambiguously elite-led because mass mobilization on distributive lines was altogether absent or there was strong evidence that the political process of independence occurred as a result of intra-elite processes. Yet in the Baltic cases, as well as in Ukraine, Mongolia, and Armenia, there is theoretical ambiguity as to the nature of the claims made by groups engaged in mass mobilization. Several regional specialists whom we consulted objected that these cases did not fall easily into the distributive conflict category and should be seen as the outcome of cross-class secessionist or nationalist movements and the resulting collapse of multinational empires. In the Baltics in particular, we believed that the evidence of conflicts between indigenous populations and the Russians warranted a "distributive conflict" coding, but it is important to acknowledge the pivotal importance of strong nationalist aspirations that cut across class lines.[38]

The significance of these ambiguous cases is not trivial. If we were to shift all of them from the distributive to the elite-led category, the incidence of cases that conform even descriptively to the distributive conflict model would fall to fewer than a third in both datasets. At a minimum, we need to acknowledge that these are cases that only weakly conform with the theory.

Even with the expansive coding of distributive conflict transitions, we found a large share of cases—again, roughly half in both datasets—in which distributive conflict played only a marginal role in the transition process and which we coded as elite-led as a result. These cases followed several alternative causal pathways. Some were driven wholly or largely by international pressures. In a few, outside intervention was direct and unambiguously decisive. Transitions in Grenada (1984) and Panama (1989) were the result of US military operations that directly displaced incumbent rulers. In Haiti (1994), the military ruler negotiated his exit as an international force of 21,000 troops prepared to land on the island. Democratic rule in Cyprus followed competing interventions on the part of Greece and Turkey that resulted in de facto partition. However, in ten additional cases, outside military forces played a role even if they did not directly displace authoritarian incumbents:[39] Comoros 1990 and 2004, Guinea-Bissau 2000 and 2004, Liberia 2006, Nicaragua 1990, Serbia 2000, Sierra Leone 1996–98 and 2007, and Uganda 1980.

---

[38]These cases also posed a second coding problem: whether they should be treated as democratic transitions at all given that they are entirely new countries. We chose to include them in the dataset because they cross standard thresholds (Polity) or appear as new democracies (CGV); see Haggard, Kaufman, and Teo (2016).

[39]For the purpose of this count, we treat the two discrete transitions in Sierra Leone in 1996 and 1998 as a single case.

If we set aside the four cases of direct external military displacement of incumbents—Panama, Grenada, Haiti, and the somewhat different case of Cyprus—we see at least three other elite-led pathways that we explore in more detail in Chapter 4. First, we have cases of "displacement" in which competing elites displace incumbents, typically through a coup, and then accede to political liberalization and democratization. Second, are cases of "preemptive" transitions in which incumbents themselves lead the liberalization and democratization process. Finally, we identify a more incremental path in which incumbents—mostly in competitive authoritarian systems—undertake marginal institutional changes that have the effect of pushing the political system over democratic thresholds. As these types all suggest, elite-led conflict transitions hinge crucially on elite conflicts and calculations about the costs and benefits of maintaining power through authoritarian means.

What about the role of inequality in the distributive conflict cases? Table 1.3 shows how simple distributions can provide insight into causal claims, in this case with respect to both the underlying role that inequality plays as well as the causal mechanism that runs through distributive conflict. A consideration of the full sample of cases also allows us to identify cases that conform or are anomalous from the perspective of the theory.

The table shows distributive and elite-led transitions using the definition of transitions in the CGV dataset; we also report these distributions of cases based on Polity codings of regime change. The cases are arrayed according to three measures of inequality: Christian Houle's measure of capital's share of income in the manufacturing sector (capshare);[40] a Gini coefficient from the Standardized World Income Inequality Database;[41] and the Vanhanen measure of land inequality.[42] We divide the sample of all developing country-years for the full sample period (1980–2008) into terciles of high-, medium-, and low-inequality cases and identify the transitions that fall into each tercile.

The table shows that transitions occurred at all levels of inequality, regardless of which measure is used; this is to be expected in any distribution. But more anomalous is the fact that transitions at high levels of inequality were in fact quite common. If we exclude cases for which data are missing—a substantial number with respect to the family farms measure in particular—we find that 42.0 percent of transitions occurred in the most unequal tercile ranked by capshare, 37.1 percent ranked by the Gini, and 40.3 percent in terms of land distribution. Even more problematic for theoretical expectations in both Boix, and Acemoglu and Robinson,

[40] Houle 2009.
[41] Solt 2014.
[42] Vanhanen 2003.

Table 1.3 Distributive Conflict and Elite-Led Transitions by Level of Inequality, 1980–2008.

Level of Inequality	Inequality Measures					
	Capital Share of Income in Manufacturing Sector (Houle)		Gini Coefficient (Solt)		Share of Family Farms (Vanhanen)	
	Distributive	Elite-Led	Distributive	Elite-Led	Distributive	Elite-Led
High	Argentina 1983	Chile 1983	Bolivia 1990	Central African Republic 1982	Bolivia 1993	Belarus 1991
	Benin 1991	Ghana 1991	Brazil 1993	Chile 1985	Brazil 1990	Chile 1985
	Bolivia 1982	Mexico 1982	El Salvador 2000	Guinea-Bissau 1984	Bulgaria 2004	Czech Republic 1990
	Brazil 1985	Nicaragua 1985	Guatemala 1984	Honduras 1986	El Salvador 1982	Hungary 1984
	Burundi 1993	Pakistan 1993	Kenya 1988	Liberia 1998	Estonia 2006	Nicaragua 1991
	Burundi 2005	Paraguay 2005	Kyrgyzstan 1989	Mauritania 2005	Guatemala 2007	Panama 1986
	El Salvador 1984	Peru 1984	Madagascar 2001	Nicaragua 1993	Latvia 1984	Paraguay 1991
	Guatemala 1986	Sierra Leone 1986	Malawi 1996	Panama 1994	Lithuania 1989	São Tomé and Principe 1991
	Indonesia 1999	Sierra Leone 1999	Maldives 1998		Peru 1989	Suriname 1990
			Paraguay 2008			

(continued)

Table 1.3 (continued)

Level of Inequality	Inequality Measures					
	Capital Share of Income in Manufacturing Sector (Houle)		Gini Coefficient (Solt)		Share of Family Farms (Vanhanen)	
	Distributive	Elite-Led	Distributive	Elite-Led	Distributive	Elite-Led
	Nepal 1990	Turkey 1983	Mali 1992	Sierra Leone 1996	Romania 1990	
	Nigeria 1999		Nigeria 1999	Sierra Leone 1998	Suriname 1988	
	Peru 1990			Sierra Leone 2007	Ukraine 1991	
	Philippines 1986			Turkey 1983		
	Poland 1989					
	South Korea 1988					
	Sri Lanka 1989					
	Sudan 1986					
	Thailand 1992					
	Uruguay 1985					
N/%	19/65.5	10/34.5	11/45.8	13/54.2	14/60.9	9/39.1

Medium	Congo 1992	Bangladesh 1986	Argentina 1986	Mexico 1983	Argentina 2000	Cape Verde 1990
	Kyrgyzstan 2005	Cape Verde 2005	Burundi 1990	Uganda 2005	Armenia 1980	Central African Republic 1993
	Madagascar 1993	Comoros 1993	Fiji 1990		Benin 1991	Comoros 1990
	Malawi 1994	Czech Republic 1994	Nepal 1989		Kenya 1998	Honduras 1982
	Mali 1992	Guinea-Bissau 1992	Niger 2000		Malawi 1994	Pakistan 1988
		Hungary 1990	Peru 1990		Mongolia 1990	
		Panama 1989	Philippines 1986		Sudan 1986	
		Senegal 2000	South Korea 2000		Uruguay 1985	
		Serbia 2000	Sri Lanka 1989			
		Suriname 1991	Sudan 1986			
		Taiwan 1996	Thailand 1992			
			Uruguay 1985			
N/%	5/31.2	11/68.8	12/85.7	2/14.3	8/61.5	5/38.5

(continued)

Table 1.3 (*continued*)

Level of Inequality	Capital Share of Income in Manufacturing Sector (Houle)		Gini Coefficient (Solt)		Share of Family Farms (Vanhanen)	
	Distributive	*Elite-Led*	*Distributive*	*Elite-Led*	*Distributive*	*Elite-Led*
Low	Albania 1991	Belarus 1991	Armenia 1991	Bangladesh 1986	Burundi 1993	Bangladesh 1986
	Armenia 1991	Central African Republic 1991	Bulgaria 1993	Belarus 1990	Congo 1992	Croatia 1991
	Bulgaria 1990	Comoros 1990	Burundi 2004	Comoros 1993	Fiji 1992	Ghana 1993
	Estonia 1991	Grenada 1991	Estonia 1984	Croatia 1991	Indonesia 1999	Macedonia 1991
	Fiji 1992	Guinea-Bissau 1992	Indonesia 2004	Czech Republic 1999	Madagascar 1993	Sierra Leone 1996
	Georgia 2004	Honduras 2004	Latvia 1982	Ghana 1991	Mali 1992	Sierra Leone 1998
	Kenya 1998	Liberia 1998	Lithuania 2006	Hungary 1991	Nepal 1990	Taiwan 1996
	Latvia 1991	São Tomé and Principe 1991	Mongolia 1991	Macedonia 1990	Niger 1993	Turkey 1983
	Lithuania 1991	Uganda 1991	Poland 1980	Pakistan 1989	Nigeria 1999	Uganda 1980

	15/62.5	9/37.5	11/50	11/50	12/57.1	9/42.9
	Mongolia 1990		Suriname		Philippines 1986	Suriname 1988
	Niger 1993		Ukraine		Poland 1989	Taiwan 1991
	Niger 2000				South Korea 1988	Bhutan 2005
	Romania 1990				Sri Lanka 1989	Comoros 2004
	Suriname 1988				Thailand 1992	Grenada 2005
	Ukraine 1991					Guinea-Bissau 2008
						Guinea-Bissau 2008
						Liberia 2000
						Mauritania 2008
N/%	15/62.5	9/37.5	11/50	11/50	12/57.1	9/42.9
Missing Data	Maldives 2008	Bhutan 2008	Benin 2007	Bhutan 1991	Burundi 2007	Bhutan 2007
	Nepal 2008	Croatia 2008	Congo 1991	Cape Verde 1992	Georgia 1990	Comoros 2004
	Pakistan 2008	Macedonia 2008	Georgia 1991	Comoros 2004	Kyrgyzstan 1990	Grenada 1984
		Mauritania 2007	Nepal 2007	Grenada 2008	Maldives 1984	Guinea-Bissau 2000
		Sierra Leone 2007	Niger 2007	Guinea-Bissau 2000	Nepal 2000	Guinea-Bissau 2004
		Thailand 2008	Pakistan 2008	Peru 2008	Niger 2001	Liberia 2006
			Romania 1990	São Tomé and Príncipe 1990	Pakistan 1991	Mauritania 2007

(continued)

Table 1.3 (*continued*)

Level of Inequality	Inequality Measures					
	Capital Share of Income in Manufacturing Sector (Houle)		Gini Coefficient (Solt)		Share of Family Farms (Vanhanen)	
	Distributive	*Elite-Led*	*Distributive*	*Elite-Led*	*Distributive*	*Elite-Led*
				Senegal 2000		Mexico 2000
				Serbia 2000		Peru 2001
				Thailand 2008		Senegal 2000
						Serbia 2000
						Sierra Leone 2007
						Thailand 2008
N/%	3/33.3	6/66.7	7/41.2	10/58.8	7/35	13/65

Sources: Transitions from Cheibub, Gandhi, and Vreeland (2010); transition types from Haggard, Kaufman, and Teo (2016); capital share from Houle (2009); Gini from Solt (2014); share of family farms from Vanhanen (2003).

a substantial number of distributive conflict transitions transpired among the high-inequality cases.[43] When inequality is measured using the Gini, 45.8 percent of high-inequality transitions were distributive conflict transitions; the incidence of transitions driven by class conflict is higher still in the top tercile of land inequality (60.9 percent) and capital's share of income (65.5 percent). As this table suggests—and we show through multivariate regressions in Chapter 2—inequality effectively has no detectable causal role either in transitions in general or in distributive conflict transitions. Mass mobilization clearly generates democratic transitions, but only infrequently through the causal mechanism stipulated in the theory.

CONCLUSION AND THEORETICAL REPRISE

Viewed over the long run, the emergence of democracy in the advanced industrial states resulted in part from fundamental changes in class structures. Demands on the state from new social classes—first the emergent bourgeoisie and then the urban working class—played a role in the gradual extension of the franchise. These stylized facts played an important role in the formulation of both modernization approaches and new distributive conflict models of regime change. The existence of sizable middle classes has also been held out as an important factor sustaining democratic rule and even driving transition processes. Mass mobilization by urban middle classes was visible during the Third Wave in the Philippines, in Korea, in a number of the Eastern European countries, and, more recently, during the Arab Spring in Egypt and Tunisia.

Yet our analysis in this chapter indicates that as a general proposition, these models do not travel well to the very different international, political, and socioeconomic conditions that prevailed during the Third Wave of democratization. Standard panel designs have found mixed evidence for the inequality-democratization logic of the distributive conflict models, and we find no evidence in Chapter 2 of a link between inequality and distributive conflict transitions either. As we have seen, a simple analysis of the distribution of cases reveals that distributive conflict marks only one possible transition path. More troubling for the theory, however, is the ample number of anomalies: the many distributive conflict transitions that occurred in high-inequality countries rather than in those characterized by medium or low inequality as the theory would predict. Although more refined measures of inequality may ultimately shift cases or capture ethnic or regional cleavages that are underestimated, our causal process

---

[43] Boix 2003; Acemoglu and Robinson 2006.

observations are designed to capture at least the overt political manifes-
tations of such cleavages. It therefore seems likely that the problems'lie
with theory as well as measurement.

How should we respond to such findings? One avenue would be to
abandon the distributive conflict models entirely, at least as they pertain
to democratic transitions. But although distributive conflict cases cannot
be linked empirically to objective problems of inequality, they still constitute a substantial portion of these transitions. A more useful way forward
is to consider in more detail what drives alternative transition paths, including more conventional political variables. Our analysis of distributive conflict cases focuses on characteristics of authoritarian regimes and
the opportunities and capacity of excluded groups to mobilize protest
against them, factors that are underplayed or ignored in the formal models outlined above; we take up these theoretical issues in Chapter 2 and
provide more conventional tests of these competing models as well.

PART II

Pathways to Democracy

Modeling Democratic Transitions

DISTRIBUTIVE CONFLICT AND ELITE PROCESSES

(with Terence Teo)

WE FOUND IN CHAPTER 1 that cases of democratization driven by distributive conflict constituted only slightly more than half of the universe of transitions during the Third Wave, and that neither transitions in general nor those driven by distributive conflict were correlated with economic inequality. However, distributive conflict transitions did constitute one important path to democracy. In this chapter and the two following, we seek to understand why some transitions were propelled by the mobilization of the de facto power of citizens, while others appeared to be predominantly elite processes, with a greater role for international influences as well.

Ironically, a major contribution of the formal models discussed in the preceding chapter is to highlight the relationship between political institutions and distributive outcomes. These models conceptualize authoritarian rule as a means of maintaining unequal distributions of income and assets. They identify the risks to incumbent political and economic elites from redistribution under democracy and the grievances and potential gains of excluded social classes from institutional change. Despite their assumptions about the significance of political institutions, however, these spare models did not pay particular attention to how institutional differences among dictatorships might affect incentives for protest. As a rapidly growing literature has now documented, authoritarian regimes vary widely along a number of dimensions, including their reliance on repression and co-optation for managing opposition. We argue that differences in the reliance on repression and institutions of co-optation are consequential for transition paths. Counterintuitively, more repressive and exclusionary regimes are more likely to face distributive challenges from below than those that create controlled institutional mechanisms for representation.

A second lacuna of the distributive conflict models is that they do not address the capacity for collective action: how excluded groups manage to mobilize pressure from below. Contrary to "prairie fire" models of political mobilization, we show that enduring organizations play a crucial role in fomenting the mass protest that drives distributive conflict transitions, particularly unions and ethnonationalist organization. Moreover, we provide evidence that these factors do not give us purchase in explaining elite-led transitions. Rather, we show in Chapter 4 that elite-led transitions are driven to a greater extent by international constraints of various sorts and by intra-elite conflicts or calculations by incumbents that they can control redistributive challenges under democratic rule.

We begin with a discussion of our core theoretical arguments about the way authoritarian institutions and the capacity for collective action shape democratic transitions. We then undertake some statistical modeling of transitions during the Third Wave, turning to causal process observation of distributive and elite-led transitions in Chapters 3 and 4, respectively.

THEORY: AUTHORITARIAN INSTITUTIONS, ORGANIZATIONAL RESOURCES, AND COLLECTIVE ACTION

The arguments signaled above follow the contentious politics literature by noting that effective mobilization against the state is a function of two core factors: the opportunity structure provided by the authoritarian order, and the organizational resources available to challengers. What opportunities and constraints are associated with the strategies authoritarian rulers pursue and the institutions that they construct to govern? What resources—both organizational and symbolic—do challengers bring into the political arena?

Types of Authoritarianism and Opportunity Structures

Authoritarian regimes differ in the way they combine coercion and co-optation to maintain incumbents' positions, protect the interests of elite allies, and deflect opposition from below.[1] The most repressive and exclusionary regimes limit representation and rely on terror, widespread use of coercion, and direct penetration and control of social organizations. At the other end of the spectrum are what Levitsky and Way call competitive authoritarian regimes, which place much greater reliance on semicompetitive elections and co-optation and manipulation of political opposition.[2] Regimes also vary in the types of political resources they use to exercise

---

[1] Geddes 1999; Smith 2005; Lust-Okar 2006; Magaloni 2006; Magaloni and Kricheli 2010; Brownlee 2007; Hadenius and Teorell 2007; Gandhi 2008; Gandhi and Przeworski 2006, 2007; Gandhi and Lust-Okar 2009; Blaydes 2010; Malesky and Schuler 2010; Hadenius, Teorell, and Wahman 2012; Svolik 2012; Wright and Escribà Folch 2012; Wahman, Teorell, and Hadenius 2012; Boix and Svolik 2013; Reuter and Robertson 2015.

[2] Levitsky and Way 2010.

control—from extensive reliance on the military establishment, to greater emphasis on ruling parties and legislative assemblies.

Using data from the Authoritarian Regimes Dataset,[3] we can identify four types of authoritarian regimes in descending order of frequency: multiparty or competitive authoritarian regimes (37.3 percent of all authoritarian country-years), military regimes (22.9 percent), one-party systems (19.5 percent), and monarchies (12.5 percent).[4] Multiparty authoritarian regimes are those in which at least some opposition candidates are allowed to participate in elections. Military regimes are controlled directly or indirectly by the military, and are defined to exclude regimes in which military personnel compete in semicompetitive elections; such regimes are captured by the multiparty category. One-party regimes ban all other parties from participating in elections, and monarchies are based on hereditary succession. Average Polity scores for each of these types indicate that these regimes not only have distinctive institutional features, but also vary substantially in how closed they are to political contestation. Whereas the average Polity score for multiparty regimes is 0.5, military and one-party regimes—the other two main types on which we focus[5]—exhibit Polity scores of –5.4 and –7.3, respectively.

Geddes has shown that military regimes tend to be less stable than one-party regimes; military elites have the option of retreating to the barracks whereas rulers in one-party systems have a stronger stake in the political status quo.[6] However, as indicated in the work of Hadenius and Teorell and others cited above, it is important to distinguish between one-party systems that bar all competition, and dominant party and multiparty

[3] Hadenius and Teorell 2007; Hadenius, Teorell, and Wahman 2012; Wahman, Teorell, and Hadenius 2012.

[4] In addition to these main types, the subtypes ("regimeny") include the permutations and combinations of these types (military, military no-party, military one-party, military multiparty, monarchy, no-party monarchy, one-party monarchy, multiparty monarchy) as well as a variety of subtypes of the "other" category, including civil war cases, occupations, theocracies, transitional regimes, and yet another residual "other" category. "Regimeny" also includes a "rebel regime" coding as a type of military regime.

[5] Our dataset includes a number of monarchies, most of which do not transit at all during the period. The fact that these highly repressive regimes have a much lower likelihood of transitioning to democratic rule would appear anomalous from the perspective of the theory that follows. But an inspection of the cases reveals that a substantial majority of them are oil producers, with their well-known affinity with authoritarian rule (for example, Ross 2013). For the most part, these regimes were also lacking the organized civil society forces we discuss in more detail in Chapter 3. The monarchies in the sample are Bahrain, Bhutan, Brunei, Jordan, Kuwait, Morocco, Nepal, Oman, Qatar, Saudi Arabia, Swaziland, Tonga, and the United Arab Emirates. Of these cases, only Bhutan and Nepal underwent transitions during the 1980–2008 period.

[6] Geddes 1999.

systems that do not.[7] Notwithstanding their differences in longevity, we hypothesize that both military and one-party regimes are likely to be especially vulnerable to distributive conflict transitions.

How might differences in type of authoritarian regime affect opportunities for mobilization? This depends in part on the targets of authoritarian control and the kinds of grievances that are mobilized. In the next chapter, we discuss more explicitly how particular forms of economic and ethnic exclusion might contribute to or exacerbate distributive conflict transitions. Here, however, we focus on the way variations in institutions and the extent of political contestation can structure subsequent transition paths.

First, regimes that rely primarily on repression to close off avenues of political contestation leave few alternatives between quiescence and taking opposition to the streets. The debate about the effectiveness of repression in controlling dissent is a long-standing one, with inconclusive results.[8] Even when coercion works, a regime that has relied extensively on repression is vulnerable to mass mobilization in the face of external shocks or changes of leadership. Boix makes just such an argument in *Democracy and Redistribution*.

Furthermore, severe repression itself can trigger popular backlash. In one of the more systematic studies of this phenomenon in authoritarian regimes, Goodwin found that increased political contention was rarely a response to *declining* repression.[9] Rather, systematic repression backfired by generating more protest.[10] Coercion tended to delegitimize incumbents, clarify the ultimately political origins of material grievances, and mobilize dissent. This is particularly the case where social organizations are able to both organize dissent and provide effective frames for social resistance. Even targeted repression and exclusion of labor and ethnic groups can play a similar mobilizing role where unions and ethnonationalist groups are capable of overcoming barriers to collective action.

Complementary arguments have recently emerged in the literature on authoritarian institutions, particularly in the attention given to ruling parties, semicompetitive elections, and legislatures as instruments of authoritarian control and co-optation. A key empirical finding is that authoritarian regimes with legislatures are more durable than those without them.[11] A number of explanations for this durability have been put forward. One focuses primarily on the role of institutions in managing potential rivalries

[7] Hadenius and Teorell 2007.

[8] Tilly 1978; Lichbach 1987; Opp and Roehl 1990; Gupta, Singh, and Sprague 1993; Moore 1998; Rasler 1996; Goldstone and Tilly 2001; Schock 2005.

[9] Goodwin 2001.

[10] Lichbach 1987; Moore 1998; Chenoweth and Stephan 2011.

[11] Gandhi and Przeworski 2007; Boix and Svolik 2013.

within the ruling elite. Elections and legislatures provide mechanisms for power sharing and coup proofing,[12] generate information about sources of opposition,[13] and provide opportunities to demonstrate the intimidating reach of state power to potential defectors within the ruling coalition.[14]

For our purposes, it is also important to emphasize that semicompetitive elections, strong dominant parties, and legislatures have a broader function of both co-opting and dividing social opposition.[15] Even when military or one-party states rule with a relatively light touch, they limit institutional outlets for the expression of discontent. Such regimes are inherently exclusionary; oppositions must either stay underground or take to the streets. Ruling parties and legislatures, by contrast, provide opportunities for limited political participation and rents to those who conditionally cooperate. These institutions also minimize the impact of regime opponents that choose to remain outside the controlled institutional space. In a study of Russia, Reuter and Robertson make a direct link between such institutional arrangements and the incidence of protest.[16] Where regional legislatures allocated committee positions and associated rents to opposition leaders, they were able to deter mass mobilization.

Incumbents in competitive authoritarian regimes are by no means immune from the risks of ouster, most often by rival insiders or co-opted oppositions. Nonetheless, destabilizing protests from below are more likely to occur in military and single-party regimes that lack co-optive mechanisms of social control. Among regimes that have established such mechanisms, the early observation of Huntington still appears to hold: institutional links to the broader population—elections, parties, and legislatures—channel participation in ways that reduce the likelihood that regimes will exit through the distributive conflict route.[17]

Social Organization and the Capacity for Collective Action

If the strategies and institutions of authoritarian rule shape the opportunity structure facing oppositions, we still must consider the resources that opposition groups can bring to bear in challenging incumbents. One possibility is that mass mobilization results from short-run triggers and subsequent informational cascades. In some cases in our sample, protests did

---

[12] Gandhi and Przeworski 2006, 2007; Gandhi 2008; Wright 2008; Svolik 2012.

[13] Wintrobe 1998; Gandhi 2008.

[14] Magaloni 2006.

[15] Smith 2005; Lust-Okar 2006; Magaloni 2006; Magaloni and Kricheli 2010; Brownlee 2007; Blaydes 2010; Malesky and Schuler 2010; Wright and Escribà Folch 2012.

[16] Reuter and Robertson 2015.

[17] Huntington 1968.

appear to emerge almost spontaneously in uncoordinated "prairie fires."[18] Contingent factors such as the death of a leader or a particularly egregious abuse of power—the killing of a protestor or a corruption case—can spawn a surge of outrage and protest. Others make the decision to join this protest on the basis of signals they receive from state actions, or when they believe collective action itself suggests regime weakness. Once triggered, information about citizen preferences cascades as those opposed to the regime realize that they are not alone. The Tunisian uprising of 2011—triggered by outrage over a confrontation between a low-level security official and a street vendor—provides an example. Moreover, these prairie fires may be stoked by new organizational resources, such as social media, which permit relatively decentralized organizations to coordinate mass actions.

We argue, however, that the contingent nature of protest is most likely exaggerated. Even if protests appear spontaneous, they are unlikely to be sustained in the absence of organizations that can play a leadership and coordinating role. The Solidarity movement in Poland provides an example of a labor union playing that role; the mass uprisings in the Baltics in the last year of the Soviet Union are examples of emergent ethnonationalist movements.

Acemoglu and Robinson make an important theoretical argument about why organization is likely to matter, even if they do not focus on the implications.[19] If mass mobilization is transient, then incumbent authoritarian rulers are unlikely to yield; it makes more sense to coerce, make reversible concessions, and wait out the storm. The mass protests that topple regimes, by contrast, typically involve sustained, strategic interactions, in which elites first attempt to contain the protest through a combination of repression and partial concessions. These strategic interactions can go on for months or even years. Incumbents are ultimately forced to yield when protest persists and grows, backed by resources, organizations, and networks of communication that can be sustained over time. It is these organizational resources that ultimately back the claims of political counterelites.

Where do these organizations come from in the first place? In their abbreviated discussion of the issue, Acemoglu and Robinson build on Mancur Olson to argue that antiauthoritarian movements solve collective action problems with selective incentives, such as land for peasants in rebel territory or expectations of booty.[20] But these models rely upon the literature

---

[18]Kuran 1989; Lohmann 1994; Ellis and Fender 2011.
[19]Acemoglu and Robinson 2006.
[20]Acemoglu and Robinson 2006; Olson 1965.

on organized insurgencies—which only rarely lead directly to democratic transitions, as we will show in Chapter 3—and ignore other types of collective action in which such selective incentives seem less plausible.

The classic sociological approaches to democratization focused on long-run social and economic processes that lead to the emergence of new classes with the resources to challenge incumbents and engage in collective action. Barrington Moore and new work in this tradition by Ansell and Samuels focus on conflicts between emergent commercial, industrial, and middle classes, and predatory states, whether monarchic or more contemporary.[21] Other work gives greater attention to industrialization and the corresponding rise of working-class organizations in Europe in the late 19th and early 20th centuries.[22] Geographic and workplace concentration made it easier to organize, communicate and coordinate, and socialize followers into collective norms and repertoires of collective action. Proximity also allowed organizations to monitor individual behavior and check shirking.

The "social space" of the late 20th-century developing world is much more dense than that of 19th-century Europe, with a variegated texture including not only unions, but ethnonationalist and religious organizations, professional and producer associations, women's coalitions, human rights groups, and a plethora of other NGOs. In addition, this complexity is compounded by the growth of transnational social movements and organizations that can play a coordinating role as well.[23]

As suggested above, however, it is important to underscore that these organizations do not typically arise de novo in the transition process; history matters. Whether or not the strength of unions or civil society groups can be directly traced to processes of economic development, they typically originate in circumstances that predate the incumbent authoritarian regime. Indeed, authoritarian rule may itself be a response to threats that mass-based organizations posed in earlier periods; this was the case in the "bureaucratic authoritarian" regimes in Latin America and the labor-repressive dictatorships in East and Southeast Asia.[24] In these instances, authorities may jail, exile, or even murder the leaders of such groups and disrupt the organizations they led, for example by seizing bank accounts, shutting down headquarters and offices, and disrupting cells. During the 1970s, all of these tactics were deployed by military dictatorships in Argentina, Uruguay, and Chile against industrial unions, NGOs, and small

[21] Moore 1966; Ansell and Samuels 2010, 2013a, 2013b, 2014.
[22] Rueschemeyer, Stephens, and Stephens 1992; Przeworski 1985, 2008, 2009.
[23] Gourevitch, Lake, and Stein 2012.
[24] O'Donnell 1973; Kaufman 1979; Deyo 1993; Haggard 1990.

revolutionary organizations. The activity of such groups might be repressed and driven underground. However, a social movement in abeyance can provide the foundation for new rounds of mobilization through the persistence of activist networks, repertoires of goals and tactics, and the maintenance of collective identities that constitute a symbolic resource for subsequent mobilization.[25]

What role do organizations play in transition processes, and distributive conflict processes in particular? First and most obviously, they can turn out their members. To borrow a felicitous phrase from Acemoglu and Robinson, the political challenge to authoritarian regimes ultimately comes from the exercise of de facto power on the part of publics that are very much larger in number than the elites they seek to displace.[26] For Acemoglu and Robinson, the image of mass mobilization is revolutionary, with the implication of armed insurrection or less coordinated violence. There is, however, a wide-ranging literature on nonviolent campaigns,[27] which has documented the array of strategies available to oppositions and the fact that nonviolent collective action can be as effective as if not more effective than violent action.[28] Organizations help individuals overcome their natural reluctance to take risks and direct them to actions that impose costs on the regime and its allied economic elites.[29] These include everything from general strikes—paralyzing mass actions that effect economic activity—to more limited strikes and blockades of select industries, the capital city, or key roads, land occupations, sit-ins, and other forms of disruptive and noncooperative behavior.

Second, organizations facilitate looser horizontal coordination across groups. As we have argued, the dense organizational space that characterizes civil society in the late 20th-century developing world is populated by a plethora of organized social actors and nongovernmental organizations. As Tarrow argues, mobilization is most effective when linked by "connective structures" that coordinate and aggregate across organizations.[30] Horizontal coordination allows social movements to avail themselves of organizational capabilities residing in allied organizations. These organizations may have only partially overlapping interests but nonetheless can bring important resources to bear; examples include churches, cultural

[25]Taylor and Crossley 2013.
[26]Acemoglu and Robinson 2006.
[27]Sharp 1973; Helvey 2004.
[28]Zunes 1994; Ackerman and Kruegler 1994; Zunes, Kurtz, and Asher 1999; Ackerman and DuVall 2000; Schock 2005; Roberts and Garton Ash 2009; Chenoweth and Stephan 2011.
[29]Chenoweth and Stephan 2011.
[30]Tarrow 1994.

organizations, professional associations, and universities. Coalitions of organized civil society actors can serve as "force multipliers" that increase the de facto power brought to bear on authoritarian incumbents.

Yet there is a third role that organizations play, and it is explored most thoroughly in the sociological literature on contentious politics. A central theme of that work is that mobilization is a function not simply of the exercise of de facto power, but of framing that redefines individual interests, links them to collective identities, and thus helps overcome individual barriers to engaging in collective action.[31] Put differently, mobilization is about not only material forces but the redefinition of existing circumstances as unequal, unjust, and unfair. Such framing delegitimizes the status quo, both by characterizing it in a compelling way and by posing plausible socioeconomic and political alternatives. Particularly important for our purposes is the way in which political and social movement entrepreneurs connect underlying social and economic grievances to the political order and thus to political demands. These demands include liberalization and the relaxation of controls, political and electoral reform, and ultimately the withdrawal of authoritarian elites, the negotiation of democratic institutions, and the staging of free and fair elections.

In sum, transition paths will be affected by both the opportunity structure and capacities for collective action. Distributive conflict transitions are more likely to take place where the authoritarian order relies on coercion and exclusion at the expense of limited contestation and co-optation, and where enduring social organizations are more dense. Elite-led transitions are more likely to occur where regimes are less repressive and better at co-optation. Such circumstances might provide opportunities for civil society to organize, but by definition we do not expect social organization to matter one way or the other in explaining elite-led conflict transitions, as they are driven by quite different political processes, centering to a greater extent on external actors and elites.

MODELING DISTRIBUTIVE CONFLICT AND ELITE-LED TRANSITIONS

In the remainder of this chapter, we explore the foregoing ideas through some simple statistical tests. As empirical work on democratization has been forced to acknowledge, there are ample endogeneity problems to contend with. On the one hand, differences in the organizational characteristics of authoritarian regimes can shape both the opportunities and incentives for mobilizing protests against incumbent rulers. Yet, as we

---

[31] Goffman 1974; Swidler 1986; Gamson 1992; Tarrow 1994.

will see in Chapter 3, the institutional structure and strategies of these regimes may themselves be a response to challenges from below. Instruments might be developed to proxy for each of these key independent variables, as well as relevant controls. But these strategies put undue faith in the availability and quality of the instruments and of the cross-national data, including with respect to regime change itself. Our more modest strategy is to provide a correlational mapping of statistical relationships that is broadly in line with the other work in this genre,[32] but to rely as well on causal process observation of distributive and elite-led transitions (Chapters 3 and 4, respectively).

Given our distinction between distributive and elite-led transitions, our empirical strategy differs from those that seek to present a unified model of democratic transitions; such an approach errs in combining disparate paths that may not have similar determinants.[33] Although we consider a pooled model, its results are scattered. Rather, we present a mixed effects multinomial logit model. This model allows us to consider the determinants of the distributive conflict and elite-led paths and also the more demanding question of whether these determinants indicate distinct causal processes. We run all tests separately on the CGV and Polity transitions, both as a robustness check and also because the two datasets are capturing somewhat different conceptions of democratization. Such an approach does not rule out the possibility of common causal factors; that is an empirical question. We hypothesize, however, that the two transition paths are characterized by different determinants.

In building such a model, we seek to maintain simplicity while controlling for some of the more important factors that have received attention in the literature. We begin by testing for the effects of inequality—the central focus of distributive conflict models. We use linear and quadratic specifications, per expectations derived from Boix and Acemoglu and Robinson; as the measure of inequality we use Houle's capital share measure as discussed in the previous chapter.[34] We next examine the effects of two alternative clusters of institutional and organizational factors discussed in the previous section and of several of the international factors discussed in the Introduction and Chapter 1.

First, we consider the nature of the authoritarian status quo ante: whether the institutional form of authoritarian rule and the level of contestation matter for the transition path. To proxy for this expectation, we create a dummy for all country-years with either military or one-party regimes—the

---

[32] Including Boix 2013 and Acemoglu et al. 2013; for a review, see Teorell 2010.
[33] See also Svolik 2012.
[34] Houle 2009. We also check the robustness of those results using a Gini (Solt 2014) as well.

primary authoritarian types lacking representative institutions—with multi-party regimes as the residual category.[35] The coefficient on this dummy thus provides a direct comparison of these more exclusive regimes with their multiparty authoritarian counterparts.[36] As an alternative to this specification—and as an indicator of restrictions on competition—we also consider the Polity score at t–3.

Two variables are taken as indicators of the capacity for collective action. The first is union density: the per capita membership in unions affiliated with the International Trade Union Confederation (ITUC), which was formed through a merger of the International Confederation of Free Trade Unions (ICFTU) and the World Confederation of Labor (WCL).[37] Not all unions have established this international tie, so many countries are given scores of zero; moreover, scores for other countries may also underrepresent the extent of unionization. Nevertheless, the history of the ITUC as the successor to the ICFTU and WCL has certain advantages. The WCL was a Christian Democratic labor confederation formed in 1920; the ICFTU broke off from the World Federation of Trade Unions in 1949 to establish itself as an explicitly anticommunist organization. As a result, with just a few exceptions[38]—and ones that weight findings against the hypothesis—almost all of the countries with scores of zero are ones in which unions are in effect appendages of the state and/or where unionization rates are in fact low. We log this variable to reduce the skew.

As an alternative proxy, we also consider a socioeconomic measure in line with more structural approaches—the manufacturing sector's share of GDP.[39] We assume that a relatively large manufacturing sector will imply a larger and more concentrated workforce, with attendant opportunities for communication, coordination, and organization that could result in the mass mobilization we associated with distributive conflict transitions. To avoid issues of endogeneity, we estimate the effects of the manufacturing sector separately from the regressions that include unions.

We also examined the effects of strikes, riots, and demonstrations at t–1.[40] By definition, we would expect these variables to be significant in distributive conflict transitions, and they were. We do not show those results here, but they are significant and provide a useful check on the validity of the distributive conflict concept.

---

[35] We also estimate the effects of each of these variables separately; Hadenius and Teorell 2007; Hadenius, Teorell, and Wahman 2012; Wahman, Teorell, and Hadenius 2012.

[36] Monarchies (12.5 percent of the sample) are excluded from the analysis.

[37] Teitelbaum n.d.

[38] Notably, Uruguay and Bolivia.

[39] World Bank 2013.

[40] Banks 2013.

In the Introduction and Chapter 1, finally, we suggested that constraints emanating from the international system might play an important role in explaining why some transitions occur in the absence of distributive pressures from below. These would include vulnerability to direct pressures from external actors and/or exposure to diffusion processes operating through geographic proximity, regional institutions, or emulation. Our measure of vulnerability (aid dependence) is official aid and development assistance as a percentage of GDP.[41] Our proxy for diffusion effects is the percentage of democracies within a 500-kilometer radius of the country in question.[42]

Our approach to controls is to focus on clusters of variables that capture other prominent bodies of theory about the determinants of regime change. These include

- Levels of economic development, central to the modernization approach to regime change and measured as GDP per capita[43]
- Regime performance: GDP growth/capita in t–1[44]
- Ethnolinguistic fractionalization, a measure of vulnerability to ethnic challenges[45]
- Resource rents[46]

The existence and extent of these rents are measured as the difference between the world price and the domestic production costs of oil, natural gas, coal, and minerals, expressed as a percentage of GDP; the larger this wedge, the larger the rents. Authoritarian regimes with access to such rents should be less vulnerable to transitions than those reliant on broader forms of taxation and/or more mobile forms of commercial capital.[47]

The descriptive statistics for each of these variables are presented in Table 2.1.

Our most significant *negative* finding is that neither transitions in general nor distributive transitions in particular are affected by linear or qua-

[41] World Bank 2013.
[42] Svolik 2008.
[43] World Bank 2013.
[44] We eliminated the following outliers—*high growth*: Liberia 1997 (106), Bosnia 1996 (89), Equatorial Guinea 1997 (71), Lebanon 1991 (38), Equatorial Guinea 2004 (38), Rwanda 1995 (35), Azerbaijan 2006 (35), Bosnia 1997 (34), Kuwait 1993 (34), Chad 2004 (34), Liberia 1998 (30), Equatorial Guinea 1996 (29), Sierra Leone 2002 (27), Lebanon 1990 (27), Azerbaijan 2005 (26), Kuwait 1989 (26), Liberia 2000 (26), Azerbaijan 2007 (25); *low Growth*: Liberia 1992 (–35), Liberia 1993 (–33), Liberia 2003 (–31), Tajikistan 1992 (–29), Guinea-Bissau 1998 (–28), Liberia 1989 (–27), Azerbaijan 1993 (–23). Results do not change, however, when they are included; World Bank 2013.
[45] Alesina et al. 2003.
[46] World Bank 2013.
[47] Boix 2003: 76.

Table 2.1 Modeling Democratic Transitions: Descriptive Statistics.

Variable	Mean	SD	Range
Military/one-party dummy	0.28	0.45	
Union (logged)	0.88	1.09	−2.43/3.30
Manufacturing	14.61	8.01	0.36/45.97
Strikes	0.29	1.09	0/23
Riots	0.54	1.60	0/26
Demonstrations	0.23	1.04	0/28
Aid dependence	0.04	0.06	0.01/0.89
Neighboring democracies	0.26	0.29	0/1
Capital share	0.68	1.12	0.29/0.93
GDP per capita (logged)	8.04	1.12	5.02/11.47
GDP growth t-1	3.61	5.70	−22.9/14.2
Ethnolinguistic fractionalization	0.40	0.31	0/1
Resource rents (logged)	1.11	2.10	−4.61/5.37

dratic measures of inequality. These regression results are consistent with our analysis of the distribution of transition types in Chapter 2. With respect to the effects of authoritarian institutions, we find that military and one-party authoritarian regimes are more likely than multiparty regimes to undergo distributive conflict transitions. And similarly, we find evidence that the likelihood of a distributive conflict transition is significantly related to the potential for collective action—as proxied by both the size of unions and the manufacturing sector. Elite-led transitions are most consistently predicted by one of our proxies for international influences—the percentage of neighboring democracies.

Some—although not all—of these variables also systematically predict *differences* between distributive and elite-led transitions. The effects of the size of the manufacturing sector, the regime dummy in the Polity dataset, and the percentage of neighboring democracies all provide evidence that there are distinctive causal processes at work.

Model Specification

As a baseline, we first run a mixed effects logistic regression model on a time-series cross-sectional (TSCS) dataset of all developing countries from 1980 to 2008. The model estimates the probability of any democratic transition in a given country-year, pooling both distributive conflict and elite-led transitions. To assess factors that might separately affect distributive conflict and elite-led transitions, we use a mixed effects multinomial logit regression model that codes distributive conflict transitions as 1, elite-led transitions as 2, and no transitions as 0. These estimate the likelihood of a change in each type of transition from a baseline of no transition. Finally, we regress distributive conflict transitions against a baseline of elite-led transitions to estimate whether any of the causal factors predict significant differences between the two transition routes.

TSCS data present two main challenges to inference. First, with respect to the time-series aspect of the data, we must account for temporal dependence that can lead to biased standard errors and false inference. Following Carter and Signorino, we use a cubic polynomial of time to model temporal dynamics in all models.[48] Second, the cross-sectional aspect means that we must account for country-specific factors not included in the models that may influence the probability of a distributive conflict or elite-led transition, the issue of unit heterogeneity. If left unaddressed, unit heterogeneity leads to omitted variable bias and biased parameter estimates. The typical solution to this problem is the fixed effects (or "no pooling") model. This approach uses country-varying intercepts that essentially absorb all cross-sectional variation, and allows the analyst to focus on how temporal variation in a predictor affects an outcome.

However, fixed effects models are unable to deal with time-invariant or slow-moving variables and generally exclude these from the analysis.[49] This presents a problem for our analysis, as our key predictors, such as union membership and the proportion of democracies, do not change much over time. More importantly, as students of comparative politics, we are interested in cross-national differences, which fixed effects models cannot capture.

Consequently, we deploy a mixed effects or multilevel model that allows us to address the unobserved heterogeneity at the country-level by treating cross-country variation as random without resorting to a fixed effects model. This "partial pooling" approach not only accounts for unit heterogeneity, but allows the inclusion of slow-moving variables (a significant drawback of the fixed effects model). Aside from its desirable statistical properties, a considerable advantage of the mixed effects model is that it allows us to make substantive interpretations of how a particular predictor impacts an outcome both across time (within country) and space (across country). However in the appendix to this chapter, we also report

[48] Carter and Signorino 2010.
[49] Beck 2001; Beck and Katz 2001.

the logic of and results from other specifications, including random and fixed effects models, a rare event logit, and hazard model.

We treat our TSCS dataset as multilevel or hierarchical data in which level 1 units are annual observations of each variable and level 2 units are countries. The time period ranges from 1980 through 2008, with a maximum number of time points, T, of 29, and the maximum number of countries (or cross-sectional units), N, of 143. Assuming no missing data, the dataset contains 4,147 possible level 1 units nested within 143 possible level 2 units.

Results

Table 2.2 reports the results for the pooled (all transitions) model for each dataset, and Tables 2.3a and 2.3b show how each variable affects the likelihood of a distributive or an elite-led transition in a given country-year, with "no-transition" set as the baseline category. Each table begins with a model that looks only at the effect of inequality. Economic and political variables are then added in subsequent models. In Table 2.3c, finally, we show the results of a logit model in which distributive conflict transitions are regressed against elite-led transitions as a baseline category. These models show whether a given variable can predict whether a transition will occur through a distributive or elite route.

We begin with a look at the pooled model (Table 2.2). As noted, results are scattered; for a number of variables, signs are even reversed between the two datasets. Transitions are not affected by either low or moderate levels of inequality, a null finding that is also evident in the tests of distributive and elite-led transitions below. Low growth increases the likelihood of a transition in the CGV dataset, but is not significant in the full Polity models. The availability of resource rents deters transitions in the CGV and Polity models that enter unions as the collective action proxy, but lose significance when manufacturing is substituted. Among the political variables, the military/one-party dummy is significant in all specifications of the CGV and in one of the full Polity models (with manufacturing). The proportion of neighboring democracies is significant in one of the CGV models, but is not significant and reverses sign in the Polity regressions. And neither unions nor manufacturing have significant effects. In sum, with the partial exceptions of resource rents and authoritarian regime type, there are no clear indications of a single set of underlying causal factors that affect transitions in general.

We turn next to a separate examination of distributive conflict and elite-led transitions in Tables 2.3a (CGV) and 2.3b (Polity). We look first at the determinants of distributive conflict transitions. As in the pooled model, we find no support for hypotheses that link distributive transitions to

Table 2.2 Likelihood of Transition, 1980–2008: Pooled Model. (Mixed Effects Logit Regression Estimates)

	CGV			Polity				
Capital share	−11.55 (10.68)	−11.01 (11.85)	−14.43 (14.91)	−1.89 (15.14)	8.76 (15.59)	10.75 (17.05)	20.42 (22.49)	28.72 (21.51)
Capital share squared	11.15 (7.70)	10.46 (8.54)	13.24 (10.64)	3.11 (10.92)	−4.48 (11.11)	−6.10 (12.18)	−13.28 (16.03)	−20.18 (15.53)
GDP per capita		−0.24* (0.13)	−0.25 (0.27)	−0.28 (0.26)		−0.12 (0.13)	−0.36 (0.24)	−0.42 (0.26)
Growth		−0.04** (0.02)	−0.06*** (0.02)	−0.07*** (0.02)		−0.03** (0.02)	−0.03 (0.02)	−0.04 (0.03)
Resource rents		−0.03* (0.02)	−0.04* (0.02)	−0.02 (0.02)		−0.05** (0.02)	−0.05* (0.03)	−0.05 (0.03)
Manufacturing				0.02 (0.03)				0.06** (0.03)
Union membership			0.06 (0.05)				0.06 (0.04)	

Military and single party dummy$_{t-3}$			1.24*** (0.41)	1.27* (0.67)			0.59 (0.39)	0.71* (0.41)
Proportion of democracies			1.32* (0.69)	-2.27 (3.52)			-1.05 (3.47)	1.14 (0.69)
Aid (% of GDP)			-1.02 (3.29)	0.41 (0.62)			-0.07 (0.62)	-0.95 (3.60)
Ethnolinguistic fractionalization			0.62 (0.64)					
N	3,676	3,213	1,990	1,944	3,676	3,213	1,990	1,944
Groups	142	135	90	94	142	135	90	94
Log-likelihood	-314.15	-279.45	-182.54	-183.75	-312.68	-278.50	-191.82	-175.53
AIC	642.29	578.90	395.08	397.50	639.36	576.99	413.64	381.06
BIC	685.76	639.65	479.02	481.09	682.82	637.74	497.58	464.65

Note: Standard errors are in parentheses. All variables are at t-1 unless otherwise specified. Cubic polynomials are not shown.

*p < .1. **p < .05. ***p < .01.

Table 2.3a Likelihood of CGV Distributive Conflict and Elite-Led Transitions, 1980–2008. (Mixed Effects Multinomial Logit Regression Estimates)

	Distributive Conflict vs. No Transition				Elite-Led vs. No Transition			
Capital share	-16.71	-14.16	-7.51	13.33	-11.62	-14.22	-26.65	-17.29
	(11.11)	(12.79)	(18.16)	(23.08)	(17.51)	(19.06)	(17.03)	(14.03)
Capital share squared	15.03*	12.65	7.80	-8.77	10.89	12.72	22.63*	15.51
	(7.74)	(9.19)	(12.54)	(15.98)	(13.73)	(14.71)	(12.74)	(10.63)
GDP per capita		-0.16	-0.26	-0.41		-0.34*	-0.13	0.11
		(0.15)	(0.30)	(0.28)		(0.19)	(0.43)	(0.37)
Growth		-0.06***	-0.07***	-0.10***		-0.02	-0.04	-0.03
		(0.01)	(0.02)	(0.03)		(0.03)	(0.03)	(0.04)
Resource rents		-0.02	-0.03	-0.02		-0.03	-0.09**	-0.01
		(0.01)	(0.03)	(0.04)		(0.02)	(0.04)	(0.03)
Manufacturing				0.06**				-0.05
				(0.03)				(0.04)
Union membership			0.06**				0.01	
			(0.03)				(0.0)	

Military and single party dummy$_{t-3}$			1.37*** (0.51)	1.29*** (0.49)			1.27 (0.79)	0.98 (0.58)
Proportion of democracies			0.21 (0.76)	0.28 (0.78)			2.66*** (0.71)	1.71** (0.70)
Aid (% of GDP)			−5.66 (4.50)	−5.70 (4.92)			5.17* (2.70)	2.63 (2.97)
Ethnolinguistic fractionalization			−0.08 (0.81)	0.07 (0.85)			1.75 (1.17)	0.77 (0.88)
N	3,633	3,170	1,990	1,944	3,633	3,170	1,990	1,944
Groups	142	135	90	94	142	135	90	94
Log-likelihood	−365.44	−324.71	−207.03	−210.16	−365.44	−324.71	−207.03	−210.16
AIC	742.88	673.42	458.06	464.32	742.88	673.42	458.06	464.32
BIC	780.06	746.16	581.17	586.91	780.06	746.16	581.17	586.91

Note: Standard errors are in parentheses. All variables are at t-1 unless otherwise specified. Cubic polynomials are not shown.
*$p < .1$. **$p < .05$. ***$p < .01$.

Table 2.3b Likelihood of Polity Distributive Conflict and Elite-Led Transitions, 1980–2008. (Mixed Effects Multinomial Logit Regression Estimates)

	Distributive Conflict vs. No Transition				Elite-Led vs. No Transition			
Capital share	2.98 (26.62)	4.19 (29.19)	61.36 (73.86)	60.14 (40.79)	15.28 (17.35)	17.45 (18.81)	11.23 (20.44)	4.67 (20.19)
Capital share squared	1.21 (18.25)	−0.06 (20.28)	−39.12 (49.71)	−40.78 (27.90)	−10.60 (12.42)	−12.25 (13.53)	−9.54 (14.97)	−4.52 (14.74)
GDP per capita		−0.13 (0.15)	−0.16 (0.20)	−0.67** (0.26)		−0.10 (0.15)	−0.43* (0.25)	−0.18 (0.24)
Growth		−0.04** (0.02)	−0.05 (0.03)	−0.08* (0.04)		−0.04* (0.02)	−0.01 (0.03)	0.10 (0.03)
Resource rents		−0.05** (0.02)	−0.05 (0.04)	−0.06 (0.05)		−0.05** (0.02)	−0.05* (0.03)	−0.05* (0.03)
Manufacturing				0.12*** (0.03)				−0.00 (0.03)
Union membership			0.07** (0.03)				0.03 (0.05)	

Military and single party dummy$_{t-3}$			1.29** (0.55)	1.51** (0.59)			-0.54 (0.66)	-0.24 (0.67)
Proportion of democracies			-0.70 (0.82)	-1.19 (0.81)			2.12** (0.83)	2.00** (0.79)
Aid (% of GDP)			-3.25 (3.67)	-5.45 (5.30)			-0.34 (3.51)	0.72 (4.90)
Ethnolinguistic fractionalization			-0.63 (0.66)	-0.89 (0.74)			0.44 (0.67)	0.34 (0.70)
N	3,633	3,170	1,990	1,944	3,633	3,170	1,990	1,944
Groups	142	135	90	94	142	135	90	94
Log-likelihood	-358.39	-318.66	-215.06	-190.10	-358.39	-318.66	-215.06	-190.10
AIC	728.78	661.33	474.12	424.20	728.78	661.33	474.12	424.20
BIC	765.97	734.07	597.23	546.79	765.97	734.07	597.23	546.79

Note: Standard errors are in parentheses. All variables are at t-1 unless otherwise specified. Cubic polynomials are not shown.

*p < .1. **p < .05. ***p < .01.

variations in the level of inequality. On the other hand, we do find evidence consistent with our hypothesis about regime type and collective action. Single-party and military dictatorships are more vulnerable than multiparty regimes to distributive transitions, and the likelihood of such transitions is also increased where union density and the size of the manufacturing sector are high. We obtain essentially the same results when we substitute the Polity score at t–3—another proxy for restrictions on competition—for the regime dummy.[50]

Figure 2.1 estimates how military or one-party regimes affect the likelihood of a transition via a distributive-conflict route in any given country-year. Since transitions are rare events, we can assume that the probabilities will be quite low; what is substantively important, however, is the extent to which differences in authoritarian regime type affects these probabilities. With all other variables held at their means, the probability of a distributive transition is almost four times higher in military/one-party regimes (2.7 percent versus 0.7 percent for CGV transitions and 2 percent versus 0.5 percent for Polity transitions). Figures 2.2 and 2.3 provide the same estimate for union strength and the size of the manufacturing sector. Each shows that the probability of a distributive transition approximately doubles with a 10 percent increase in union membership and manufacturing.

Finally, although authoritarian institutions and collective action are the most consistent predictors of distributive conflict transitions, we also see that they are significantly (inversely) affected by growth in the preceding year in all of the CGV models and in one of the three Polity models; the weaker economic performance, the more likelihood of a transition. This result is also robust to all of the specifications shown in the appendix to this chapter. This is an important finding: it suggests that while inequality may not be the source of increased grievance and mass mobilization, poor economic performance could well be. Figure 2.4 shows that as growth rates increase from 0 to 5 percent, the probability of a transition declines by about 50 percent in the CGV cases and about 35 percent in the Polity transitions.

If anything, moreover, the significance of economic performance may be larger than these results suggest, because our measure of growth is re-

[50]We also consider a number of alternative specification strategies that have been used in the democratization literature as robustness checks, including random and fixed effects approaches, rare event logits, and hazard models (Appendix 2.1). The results for the theoretical variables of interest generally hold in the random effects and survival models. In both the CGV and Polity datasets, the regime dummy and manufacturing have a significant effect on distributive conflict transitions in both the random effects and survival models; union strength is also significant in the random effects model, although it falls below the threshold in the survival regressions.

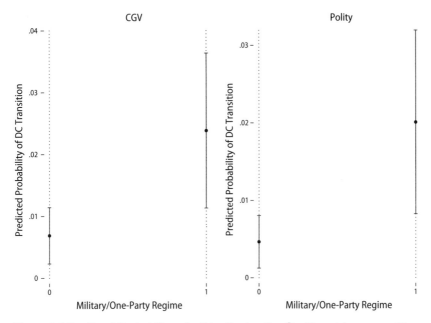

Figure 2.1 Predicted Probability of a Distributive Conflict Transition versus No Transition (Military and Single-Party Regime)

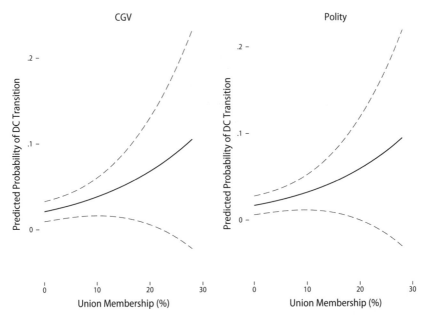

Figure 2.2 Predicted Probability of a Distributive Conflict Transition versus No Transition (Union Density)

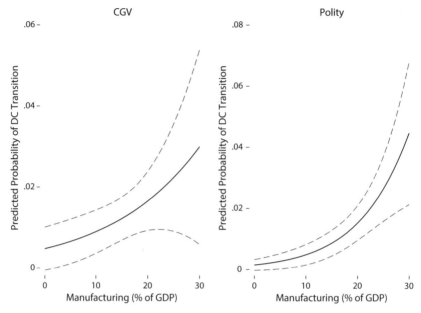

Figure 2.3 Predicted Probability of a Distributive Conflict Transition versus No Transition (Manufacturing)

stricted to the year immediately preceding the transition (t–1). For many of the countries in question, the debt crisis of the 1980s and the deep transitional recessions that followed the decline and breakup of the Soviet Union clearly had consequences for incumbent authoritarian regimes that persisted well after the worst shocks had passed. In Peru, Brazil, and the Philippines, there were actually growth rebounds of over 4 percent in the year prior to their transitions, but these were preceded by severe recessions. Peru's first economic crisis came in the mid-1970s as a consequence of populist policies pursued under the military government. When the government undertook a delayed stabilization, it faced fierce opposition from corporatist labor unions that it had counted on to support the regime. After a massive general strike in 1977, protesting austerity policies, the military rulers yielded to demands for a Constituent Assembly, leading to the Polity transition coded in 1980. The Brazil and Philippine cases are quite similar. In each country, the transitions occurred as the economy was turning up. But the mass mobilization of protest in these instances built on the back of severe recessions in preceding years, which generated sustained critiques of the economic failures of the incumbent regimes. If anything, moreover, short-term rebounds in African countries

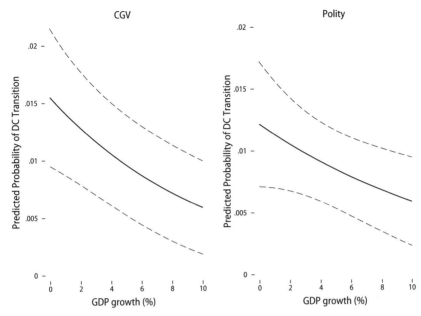

Figure 2.4 Predicted Probability of a Distributive Conflict Transition versus No Transition (Growth)

had been preceded by even more severe shocks. Burundi, Lesotho, and Malawi all experienced growth that exceeded 4 percent in the year prior to their transitions; but each had gone through sustained economic crises under authoritarian rule, prolonged and ultimately failed structural adjustment efforts, and mass protest and political destabilization.

We turn next to an examination of elite-led transitions in Tables 2.3a and 2.3b. Here we find results consistent with expectations about the effects of international factors. The proportion of neighboring democracies—"neighborhood effects"—was a consistently significant predictor in our mixed effects model and is robust to the random effects and survival models presented in the appendix to this chapter. These neighborhood effects can work through a multiplicity of channels, ranging from direct encouragement by neighboring governments, to more subtle forms of economic and cultural influence; we explore these in more detail in Chapter 4.

Figure 2.5 shows the substantive effects of an increase in neighboring democracies on the likelihood of an elite-led transition.[51] As the

[51] These are estimated when unions are entered into the regression. But results are essentially the same when manufacturing is entered.

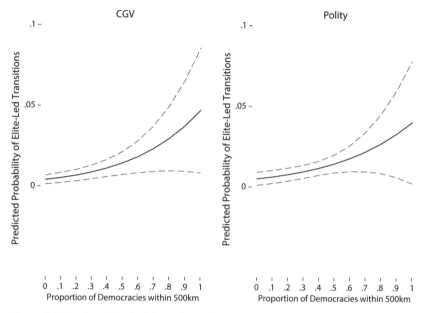

Figure 2.5 Predicted Probability of an Elite-Led Transition versus No Transition (Neighborhood Effects)

proportion of neighboring democracies increases from 20 to 80 percent, the probability of a CGV transition increases over four times (from about 1 to 4.5 percent) and the probability of a Polity transition doubles (from about 2 to 4 percent). As noted above, these are substantial changes in probabilities, given the low overall likelihood of transitions to begin with. In the absence of pressures from below, international factors appear to play a much more significant role in the elite-led transitions than in their distributive conflict counterparts.[52]

Finally, we turn to assessments of whether the variables we have examined above can predict differences between the two transition paths. This test is much more difficult because the comparison is restricted to only

[52] Aid dependence—the other international variable included in the regressions—had no effect in the Polity models and was significant in only one of the CGV models. In the model in which it was significant, however, the substantive effect was considerable: the predicted probability of an elite-led transition is almost five times higher at aid levels of 40 percent of GDP compared to 10 percent of GDP (5.4 percent vs. 1.3 percent). The cases we consider in Chapter 4 repeatedly confirm that aid dependence and donor conditionality appear to be significant factors in a number of the low-income cases.

Table 2.3c Likelihood of a Distributive Conflict vs. Elite-Led Transition.

	CGV		Polity	
Capital share	19.13	30.62	50.12	55.47*
	(27.90)	(29.11)	(65.46)	(33.04)
Capital share squared	−14.83	−24.28	−29.58	−36.25
	(19.87)	(20.58)	(44.26)	(23.23)
GDP per capita	−0.12	−0.52	0.27	−0.49
	(0.57)	(0.50)	(0.32)	(0.34)
Growth	−0.03	−0.07	−0.04	−0.08*
	(0.04)	(0.05)	(0.04)	(0.05)
Resource rents	0.06	−0.01	−0.01	−0.01
	(0.06)	(0.05)	(0.05)	(0.06)
Manufacturing		0.12**		0.12***
		(0.05)		(0.04)
Union membership	0.04		0.04	
	(0.09)		(0.06)	
Military and single party dummy$_{t-3}$	0.10	0.31	1.83**	1.75*
	(0.96)	(0.79)	(0.89)	(0.91)
Proportion of democracies	−2.45**	−1.42	−2.82**	−3.19***
	(1.16)	(1.12)	(1.22)	(1.18)
Aid (% of GDP)	−10.83**	−8.33	−2.91	−6.17
	(5.09)	(5.35)	(4.91)	(7.01)
Ethnolinguistic fractionalization	−1.82	−0.71	−1.07	−1.23
	(1.52)	(1.32)	(1.04)	(1.06)
N	1,990	1,944	1,990	1,944
Groups	90	94	90	94
Log-likelihood	−207.03	−210.16	−215.06	−190.10
AIC	458.06	464.32	474.12	424.20
BIC	581.17	586.91	597.23	546.79

Note: Distributive conflict transitions = 1; elite-led transitions = 0. Standard errors are in parentheses. All variables are at t-1 unless otherwise specified. Cubic polynomials are not shown.
*$p < .1$. **$p < .05$. ***$p < .01$.

the small number of transitions themselves. Not surprisingly the findings are mixed; both the confirming and disconfirming evidence from the regressions needs to be examined through causal process observation and a closer examination of the distribution of cases. Nonetheless, there are a number of findings that suggest distinct causal pathways. We show results in Table 2.3c.

With regard to the domestic political variables, the most consistent effect is for the size of the manufacturing sector—one of our proxies for collective action capability. The regressions in both the CGV and Polity models show that the larger the manufacturing sector, the more likely it is that a transition will be distributive rather than elite-driven. Regime type also distinguishes between the two transition paths in the Polity model, although it fails to do so in the CGV dataset; among the Polity cases, distributive conflict transitions are more likely than elite-led ones to emerge in military and single-party authoritarian regimes. Results for economic performance are much less consistent, but we do see a significant difference between distributive conflict and elite-led transitions in one of the full Polity models (when manufacturing is substituted for unions); in the cases we explore how poor performance may be implicated in transitions involving mass mobilization from below.

International factors also differentiate the two paths to an important extent. Coefficients for the proportion of democracies are negative and significant in both Polity models and in one of the full CGV models (with unions). In other words, transitions in "good neighborhoods" are less likely to be distributive and more likely to be elite-driven. One CGV model, similarly, shows that dependence on creditors is also more likely to lead to an elite-driven transition than a distributive one.

To reiterate, the bar for showing distinctive causal processes is high given the small number of cases; precisely for that reason we rely heavily on complementary causal process observation. But the findings here are suggestive. Not only do we see the institutional and collective action factors we have highlighted showing up in the distributive conflict samples, but there is at least some evidence that the mix of domestic and international causal factors differs between the two types of transition.

Conclusion

Our objectives in this chapter were twofold. First, we outlined some theoretical expectations about the factors that might drive distributive conflict and elite-led paths. We focused particular attention on the opportunity structures associated with authoritarian regimes of different sorts and the capacity to exploit those opportunities via collective action. Second, we sought to validate the distinctive characteristics of these two transition paths by showing empirically that they were driven by different clusters of factors that comported broadly with our theoretical expectations. Although the regressions do not allow us to fully identify and isolate the precise causal pathways leading to these different transition paths, they do suggest that efforts to generalize across all transition paths are likely to obscure the causes of democratic transitions. More specifically, we find support for the following observations.

In regressions that separately examined the likelihood of distributive conflict and elite-led transitions:

- The chances for a distributive conflict transition in a given country-year were higher under military and one-party regimes than under multiparty regimes that tolerated some channels of political contestation and representation.
- The chances of a distributive conflict transition also increased where high union density and large manufacturing sectors enhanced the capacity for collective action.
- Poor economic performance (low growth) increased the likelihood of distributive conflict transitions.
- The likelihood of an elite-led transition in any country-year was increased by a high proportion of neighboring democracies.
- Less conclusively, a high dependence on external economic aid increased the chances of an elite-led transition.

Some—although not all—of these variables also predicted whether a country would transition via a distributive conflict or elite-led route:

- Distributive conflict transitions were more likely than elite-led transitions in countries with large manufacturing sectors.
- In the Polity models, closed authoritarian regimes also increased the likelihood that a country would transit through the distributive conflict, rather than the elite route.
- In one Polity regression, countries with low growth were also more likely to transit via distributive conflict than through an elite route.
- Elite-led transitions, conversely, were more likely than distributive conflict transitions to occur in countries with a high proportion of democratic neighbors.
- In a single CGV model, a high dependence on external aid increased the probability of an elite-led transition.

We have argued that reduced-form panel designs of this sort, even if fully specified, still face hurdles in drawing strong causal inference because of the difficulty of tracing postulated causal mechanisms. In the following two chapters, we take up this challenge by looking in more detail at the distribution of cases undergoing the two transition paths and by selecting a variety of different cases for closer scrutiny.

APPENDIX

Modeling Transitions To and From Democratic Rule

The literature on democratization and reversion to authoritarian rule has deployed a variety of specification strategies for testing various causal theories. In addition to the mixed effects model that we favor, these include random effects models, hazard or survival models (and of different sorts), and a fixed effects approach favored by economists. In this appendix we outline the logic of each of these models and also report on the findings we get when following alternative specifications; we undertake a similar exercise in Chapter 6 with respect to reversions.

For the pooled models (Tables A2.1 and A2.2), we show random effects estimates, a survival model, and a rare events model. The hierarchical models that examine separate results for distributive and elite-led transitions do not allow for rare events corrections, but we show results for random effects and survival models in Tables A2.3 and A2.4. We have argued in the chapter that fixed effects models are not suitable for examining the cross-national variations we seek to capture in our theory. Nevertheless, to display the full range of options and to see if the causal variables we highlight are significant within countries, we include the results of these as well.

Random Effects Models

The random effects (or "complete pooling") model assumes that there is no covariance between the variables specified in the model and unobserved country-level effects. That is, the model is correctly specified—all relevant variables are included in the model—and there is no unit heterogeneity.[53] While this approach can accommodate time-invariant variables, the assumption that there are no omitted variables is a rather heroic one; if this assumption does not hold, parameter estimates will be biased. It is possible, however, to adjust the standard error estimates of these models to account for the within-country dependence of observations by country using clustered standard errors. Using country-clustered standard errors allows

---

[53] More precisely, the complete pooling model assumes that the residuals are independent and identically distributed. However, since observations within a country share some common characteristics, this assumption is often violated in TSCS data.

observations to be correlated within a country but assumes the independence of cross-country observations. While this may be sufficient for our purposes, this approach does not explicitly model the variables that vary across countries.

Rare Events Logit Models

Since transitions to democratic rule occur rarely—i.e., the number of nontransitions is far greater than the number of transitions—standard logistic regression models may lead to biased estimates and a loss of efficiency.[54] In practice, not accounting for the "rare" nature of a transition may lead to an underestimation of the probability of a transition. In addition, the likelihood of biased estimates increases as the ratio of nonevents to events becomes more skewed. In our sample, there are only 78 CGV and 73 Polity transitions out of a possible 1,990 country-year observations. As such, we use King and Zeng's rare events logistic regression with country-clustered standard errors that applies a bias correction for the rarity of a transition.[55]

Hazard, Survival, or Event History Models

The key concept in event history (or survival) analysis is the hazard rate (or function). The hazard rate is the probability that an event will occur at a particular point in time given that the event has yet to occur. In our analysis, this event is a transition to democracy or reversion to authoritarian rule, coded 1 if a transition/reversion occurred, and 0 otherwise. Two components make up the hazard rate: (1) a baseline hazard function that indicates the rate of event occurrence with time only, that is, the "natural" rate of a reversion with the passage of time, and (2) a set of covariates hypothesized to affect the timing of the event (transition/reversion).

Since we do not have a priori assumptions about the effect of time on the baseline hazard, we use a baseline Cox proportional hazards model with time-varying covariates. Such a model does not require us to specify a parametric form for the baseline hazard, and allows us to model the impact of explanatory variables that change over time on the probability of a reversion.

In order to compare differences in the complex of factors affecting distributive conflict and elite-led transitions, we have two possible options: a stratified Cox model and a competing-risks model. The stratified Cox

[54]King and Zeng 2001.
[55]King and Zeng 2001.

model considers each observation to be at risk of experiencing a distributive conflict transition, an elite-led transition, or no transition. It assumes that the effects of covariates are the same across each type of reversion, and models heterogeneity in terms of the risk of different events through different baseline hazards. However, since we expect the impact of our predictors to differ across elite reaction and nonelite reversions, we use a competing-risks model instead. To do this, we model the risk of each type of reversion separately, which allows us to capture heterogeneity by allowing covariate effects to vary across the two reversion types.

Significant results for the pooled and multilevel models are shown in Tables A2.1 and A2.2, and in Tables A2.3 and A2.4. Full results are shown in the online appendix at http://press.princeton.edu/titles/10879.html.

Table A2.1 Pooled Models (CGV Transitions): Summary of Robustness Checks.

Variable	Mixed Effects		Random Effects		Survival		Rare Events Logit		Fixed Effects	
Union membership					+		+			
Manufacturing										
Military and single party dummy$_{t-3}$	+	+	+	+	+	+	+	+	+	+
Neighboring democracies	+		+	+	+	+	+	+		
Capital share										
Capital share squared							+			
GDP per capita									–	–
Growth	–	–	–				–		–	
Aid (% of GDP)										
Resource rents	–		–		–				–	
Ethnolinguistic fractionalization										

Note: In this and following tables, marked cells indicate significant coefficients. Pluses and minuses indicate the direction of the effect. Under each model specification, the first column shows the results with union membership, the second the results with manufacturing.

Table A2.2 Pooled Models (Polity Transitions): Summary of Robustness Checks.

Variable	Mixed Effects		Random Effects		Survival		Rare Events Logit		Fixed Effects	
Union membership					+		+			
Manufacturing		+		+		+		+		+
Military and single party dummy$_{t-3}$		+	+	+		+		+	+	+
Neighboring democracies					+	+				
Capital share										
Capital share squared										
GDP per capita							–			
Growth										
Aid (% of GDP)										
Resource rents	–		–		–		–			
Ethnolinguistic fractionalization										

Note: Marked cells indicate significant coefficients. Pluses and minuses indicate the direction of the effect. Under each model specification, the first column shows the results with union membership, the second the results with manufacturing.

Table A2.3 Determinants of Distributive Conflict and Elite-Led Transitions (CGV): Summary of Robustness Checks.

Variable	Mixed Effects		Random Effects		Survival		Fixed Effects	
Distributive Conflict vs. No Transition								
Union membership	+		+		+			
Manufacturing		+		+		+		+
Military and single party dummy$_{t-3}$	+	+	+	+	+		+	+
Neighboring democracies								

(*continued*)

Table A2.3 (*continued*)

Variable	Mixed Effects		Random Effects		Survival	Fixed Effects	
Capital share						+	
Capital share squared							
GDP per capita					–	–	
Growth	–	–	–	–	–	–	–
Aid (% of GDP)					–		
Resource rents							
Ethnolinguistic fractionalization							

Elite-Led versus No Transition

Variable	Mixed Effects		Random Effects		Survival	Fixed Effects	
Union membership							
Manufacturing					+		
Military and single party dummy$_{t-3}$			+		+	+	
Neighboring democracies	+	+	+	+	+		
Capital share							
Capital share squared	+		+				
GDP per capita						–	
Growth							
Aid (% of GDP)	+	+					
Resource rents	–	–	–		–	–	
Ethnolinguistic fractionalization							

Note: Marked cells indicate significant coefficients. Pluses and minuses indicate the direction of the effect. Under each model specification, the first column shows the results with union membership, the second the results with manufacturing.

Table A2.4 Determinants of Distributive Conflict and Elite-Led Transitions (Polity): Summary of Robustness Checks.

Variable	Mixed Effects		Random Effects		Survival		Fixed Effects	
Distributive Conflict vs. No Transition								
Union membership	+		+					
Manufacturing		+		+		+		+
Military and single party dummy$_{t-3}$	+	+	+	+	+	+	+	+
Neighboring democracies								
Capital share				+		+		
Capital share squared						−		
GDP per capita	−		−		−			
Growth	−	−	−	−	−			
Aid (% of GDP)								
Resource rents					−	−		
Ethnolinguistic fractionalization								
Elite-Led vs. No Transition								
Union membership								
Manufacturing								
Military and single party dummy$_{t-3}$								
Neighboring democracies	+	+	+	+	+	+		
Capital share							+	
Capital share squared							−	
GDP per capita	−		−					
Growth								
Aid (% of GDP)								
Resource rents	−	−	−		−			
Ethnolinguistic fractionalization								

Note: Marked cells indicate significant coefficients. Pluses and minuses indicate the direction of the effect. Under each model specification, the first column shows the results with union membership, the second the results with manufacturing.

CHAPTER 3

Distributive Conflict Transitions

INSTITUTIONS AND COLLECTIVE ACTION

In Chapter 2, we found some support for our proposition that distributive conflict transitions were more likely to occur in more repressive regimes. These findings suggest that grievances and incentives for collective protest may be driven not by economic inequalities but by the nature of authoritarian rule: the absence of channels for representation and the extent of exclusion and repression. We also found that the likelihood of a distributive conflict transition was increased by union strength and the share of manufacturing in the economy, two proxies indicating a capacity for collective action.

To explore these propositions further, we turn to causal process observation of the distributive conflict and elite-led transition processes. Selecting on the dependent variable, we consider all of the cases in the two datasets with respect to variables of core theoretical interest: the authoritarian status quo, the organizational foundations of mass mobilization, and features of the exit of authoritarian rulers. We also consider briefly the role played by elections and political parties in these transitions, although we argue these factors typically enter the process of regime change at a fairly late stage.

Our method is to trace this arc first through a consideration of distributions of causal factors across the two transition paths and then through more focused causal process observation of how these factors operate in selected cases. We begin in the first section with a consideration of how the nature of authoritarian rule can affect modes of transition, drawing comparisons with the elite-led cases. Causally relevant features of these systems analyzed in the previous chapter include limits on contestation and representation. In addition, we consider here in more detail both the repressiveness of the system and the social and economic targets of repression. All authoritarian elites deploy instruments of control and coercion to extract rents from some subset of the underlying population and transfer them to supporters. A number of the distributive conflict transitions, however, occur in regimes that rely heavily on the support of landed or private-sector interests or ethnic minorities and that systematically target rural workers, the urban working class, or ethnic majorities and the organizations that seek to represent them. We expect this type of authoritarian project to be especially vulnerable to the mobilization of redistributive grievances.

The remaining sections focus on features of the distributive conflict subsample. The first examines the organizational foundations of mass mobilization and the denouement of such processes in authoritarian exit. Consistent with our regression results and an earlier class-based literature on Europe and Latin America,[1] we find union involvement in an overwhelming share of distributive conflict transitions. This is evident, moreover, even at low levels of per capita income where public sector unions frequently play a crucial role. By definition such political forces do not actively challenge regimes in the elite-led cases. We also find that despite the null statistical finding on ethnolinguistic fractionalization, there is a sizable minority of distributive conflict transitions—about a third—in which ethnonationalist political organizations play a leading or decisive role. Although fragmentation per se doesn't appear to have causal affect, ethnic organization does.

In this section, we also consider the strategies of regime opponents and how authoritarian exit actually occurs in the distributive conflict cases. In line with other recent literature on social resistance,[2] we find that the role of violence in distributive conflict transitions is less than might be thought, with the majority of transitions driven by peaceful mass mobilization. In fewer than a third (30.7 percent) did mass mobilization directly force incumbents to unconditionally yield power to opposition leaders. Regardless of the mode of exit, however, distributive pressures from below opened the way to the emergence of new configurations of political leadership that ultimately shaped—and benefitted from—the regime transition.

Finally, we examine the role of these emerging political entrepreneurs. We argue that because of the exclusionary and repressive nature of the status quo ante, neither elections nor political parties take on the central role they sometimes do in elite-led transitions. Opposition parties typically emerge relatively late in the transitional process, and are enabled to do so precisely because of the de facto power that organized social forces have brought to bear. We also suggest that the interests of political and civil society actors are not fully aligned and it is therefore wrong to ignore the distinction between them, as distributive conflict approaches sometimes do.

Given that our causal process observation is conducted on all transitions, the foregoing sections consider distributions of cases along the dimensions described. To what extent do those distributions conform to causal processes stipulated in distributive conflict models and our proposed alternative approach emphasizing the role of institutions and collective action? In the second half of the chapter, we descend to the level

[1] Rueschemeyer, Stephens, and Stephens 1992; Collier 1999.
[2] Chenoweth and Stephan 2011.

of individual cases. Because we consider all transitions, we can sample much more broadly than standard qualitative analysis. We examine cases from different regions and levels of development as well as those driven by different social organizations, particularly labor unions as opposed to ethnonationalist groups and the handful of cases such as South Africa were the two coincide. We consider distributive conflict transitions from the right-wing military regimes of Latin America, the one-party systems of Eastern Europe, African military and one-party regimes, and states based on ethnic exclusion. The objective is to demonstrate some of the underlying similarities across these apparently heterogeneous examples, particularly in the nature of the authoritarian status quo ante and organizational capacities that facilitate mass mobilization.

Authoritarian Institutions, Repression, and Distributive Conflict Transitions

Table 3.1 provides summary information on a variety of features of the authoritarian status quo ante in both the CGV and Polity datasets. Institutional features of the old regime are drawn from the Hadenius, Teorell, and Wahman dataset used in the Chapter 2 regressions.[3] Polity and Freedom House civil liberties scores provide more direct metrics of repressiveness. As noted, we also identify labor- and ethnic-exclusionary regimes based on our own coding. The country codings on which the table is based are provided in Tables A3.1a to A3.2b.

To capture the long-term features of the incumbent regimes, codings are generally lagged five years prior to the transition, with adjustments to take into account relevant developments within that five-year period. In some cases, transitions are preceded by multiple changes in regime type or by the overthrow of democracy and the installation of authoritarian regimes within the five-year window. In others, transitions are preceded by short-term "openings": the deposition of a longtime ruler, a last-minute liberalization initiative, or promises of elections. These latter changes may offer excluded groups the opportunity to mobilize, but do not reflect the equilibrium nature of the authoritarian status quo that drove distributive conflict transitions. All changes that deviate from the scores at t–5 are identified and justified in the notes to the appendix tables.

[3] Hadenius, Teorell, and Wahman 2012.

Complementing the regressions in Chapter 2, we expect a comparison of the distributive conflict and elite-led cases to reveal:

- Among all countries undergoing a transition, military and one-party regimes are more likely than multiparty regimes to experience a distributive conflict transitions, and multiparty regimes are more likely than the closed regimes to experience elite-led transitions.
- Among countries undergoing transition, regimes with higher levels of repression, as given by Polity and Freedom House scores, are more likely to experience distributive conflict transitions.
- Among all transition countries, labor- and ethnically-exclusive regimes are more likely to experience distributive conflict transitions.

The distributions in Table 3.1 generally support these expectations. We start by considering the share of distributive conflict and elite-led transitions that emerge from different authoritarian regime types. In the CGV dataset, about 60 percent of all the one-party and military regimes that undergo transitions do so through the distributive conflict route, as compared to about 40 percent of the multiparty regimes. The differences are even sharper in the Polity sample: 69 and 74 percent of the one-party and military regimes that transition did so through the distributive conflict route. By contrast only about one-fifth (22 percent) of the multiparty regimes underwent distributive conflict transitions.

One noteworthy observation to emerge from this exercise is the fate of the communist one-party regimes of the former Soviet Union and Eastern Europe. Ten of those regimes that transitioned in the late Soviet period did so via the distributive conflict route; two others that transitioned at a later point of time (Georgia 2004 and Kyrgyzstan 2005—by then no-longer one-party regimes) also fell as a result of pressure from below. By contrast, only three one-party regimes—Belarus, Czechoslovakia, and Macedonia—transitioned via the elite-led route, and a fourth (Serbia) transited in 2000, after almost ten years of multiparty rule.[4]

Polity and Freedom House scores provide insight into the repressiveness of regimes ultimately undergoing different transition paths. In the CGV sample, Polity scores averaged –5.6 at t–5 in the cases that subsequently experienced distributive conflict transitions and –3.0 in those undergoing elite-led transitions. In the Polity sample, average Polity scores at t–5 diverged even more sharply: –4.5 for the sample ultimately undergoing distributive conflict transitions and –.7 for those going the elite-led route.

---

[4]For the Polity cases, the differences are somewhat less stark but nonetheless broadly similar: nine communist regimes transition in the wake of distributive conflict, nine through the elite-led route. As in the CGV dataset, however, four of the elite-led cases transitioned much later under multiparty regimes, after communist parties had forfeited their monopoly of power (Albania 2002, Croatia 2000, Romania 1996, Serbia 2000).

Table 3.1 Distribution of Transitions by Authoritarian Regime Type.

	CGV Transitions			Polity Transitions		
	Distributive Conflict	Elite-Led	Total	Distributive Conflict	Elite-Led	Total
I. Authoritarian regime type						
One-party	12/60%	8/40%	20	11/69%	5/31%	16
Military	20/59%	14/41%	34	17/74%	6/26%	23
Multiparty	7/39%	11/61%	18	7/22%	25/78%	32
Monarchy	2/67%	1/33%	3	—	—	—
No-party	1/100%	—	1	—	—	—
Other	—	2/100%	2	1/50%	1/50%	2
Total	42/54%	36/46%	78	36/49%	37/51%	73
II. Labor repressive	8/80%	2/20%	10	8/80%	2/20%	10
III. Ethnically exclusive regimes	10/100%	0/0%	10	4/50%	4/50%	8
III. Average Polity scores	-5.6	-3.0		-4.5	-0.7	
IV. Average Freedom House civil liberties index	5.4	5		5.2	4.7	

Freedom House scores show parallel, if somewhat smaller, differences. The civil liberties index, which ranges from a score of 1 (full protection) to 7 (most abusive), focuses on freedom of expression and belief, freedom of association, rule of law, and personal autonomy and individual rights. Because the index is calculated separately from the Political Rights index, it can capture cases in which some civil liberties are protected in politically closed regimes, or in which nominally more open systems violate these liberties. We again see differences in both samples (5.4 to 5 in the CGV sample, 5.2 to 4.7 in the Polity sample). In sum, the availability of channels for co-opting dissent and the extent of repressiveness appear to distinguish regimes that exit through distributive conflict and elite-led routes, but in a somewhat counterintuitive way: governments that exit via mass mobilization show signs of being more repressive.

Finally, we expect that authoritarian regimes that exit via distributive conflict are more likely to repress lower-class or ethnic groups in pursuit of exclusive economic models favoring advantaged classes. We therefore code two additional types of rule that in principle can cut across all of the foregoing institutional forms. The first are regimes we call "labor repressive." These are organized with the explicit intent to systematically control rural or urban working classes, including the unions and left or labor parties that seek to represent them. Indeed, these regimes frequently come to power in the context of class polarization and mass mobilization that dominant elites seek to suppress. Prominent among the practices of such regimes are restrictions on the ability of labor to organize. They typically include both direct repression of labor organizations and complementary policies that expand the discretion of landlords and managers at the expense of labor. Examples include the bureaucratic authoritarian regimes of Southern Cone Latin America and similar cases in East Asia, such as South Korea and the Philippines.

The second type of regime is what we call "ethnic-exclusionary." Ethnic variants of these exclusionary models seek to limit opportunities for large ethnic minorities—and in some cases, such as South Africa, majorities—through similar strategies. These include either official favoritism toward incumbent ethnic groups or restrictions on the economic activity and opportunity of excluded minorities with respect to government employment, particular economic activities, and even property ownership. In many ethnically exclusionary systems, ethnic and class stratification overlap; South Africa again provides an example. We include in this category some of the Soviet republics—in which ethnic majorities were disadvantaged by Russian nomenklatura and immigrants—as well as Burundi, Sri Lanka, and Malaysia—in which, to varying degrees, one ethnic group was favored over others.

A simple count of the incidence of labor repressive regimes among the two transition types shows an even stronger representation than the distributions based on institutional form. In both the CGV and Polity datasets, eight of the ten transitions from labor repressive regimes were via distributive conflict; Chile and Turkey were the two exceptions. The patterns are less strong with respect to transitions in ethnic-exclusionary regimes, which are evenly split between distributive conflict and elite-led transitions in the Polity dataset. In the CGV dataset, however, all of the ethnically exclusionary regimes ultimately fall in the face of mass mobilization from below.

MASS MOBILIZATION AND REGIME CHANGE: SOCIAL FOUNDATIONS, STRATEGIES, AND MODES OF AUTHORITARIAN WITHDRAWAL

Authoritarian regimes, especially those that rely heavily on repression, cannot be effectively challenged unless excluded publics overcome barriers to collective action. Yet the new generation of distributive conflict models has paid surprisingly little attention to this issue. In this section, we focus on the distributive conflict cases and follow up on our regression finding that union density—an indicator of this capacity—was a significant and robust predictor of distributive conflict transitions. We do so by examining whether these correlations are supported by causal process observations of the distributive conflict transition cases, and by a count of the cases in which such processes appear to work as expected. In how many distributive conflict transitions were unions and other organized social forces involved in mass mobilization against incumbents?

We follow with an examination of two issues that were not captured by the quantitative analysis at all. First, was this mobilization generally peaceful, or did it involve violence in the form of riots or organized insurgencies? Did mobilization directly displace authoritarian leaders, or did they negotiate their exit? The answers to these questions shed light on exactly how mass mobilization works to oust incumbents and install new democratic orders.

Organizational Foundations of Mass Mobilization

Table 3.2 and Table A3.3 show the distributive conflict cases in which unions appeared to play a significant role in mobilizing opposition against the incumbent authoritarian regime. We define "union transitions" as those in which unions were leaders or core members of antiregime coalitions and/or when strikes or walkouts by these organizations added significantly to the overall pressure on the regime.

As can be seen, a large share of distributive conflict transitions—over two-thirds regardless of dataset—fall into the "union" category. The role of organized labor in the wave of South American transitions of the early

Table 3.2 The Social Foundations of Distributive Conflict Transitions,
1980–2008.
(Number of Cases and Shares)

	Union Transitions	Ethnonationalist Transitions	Riots	Presence of Revolutionary Armies or Militias
CGV distributive conflict transitions (N = 42)	30/71.4%	11/26.2%	8/19.0%	13/30.1%
Polity distributive conflict transitions (N = 36)	25/69.4%	11/30.6%	6/16.7%	12/33.3%
CGV and polity transitions (N = 52)	36/69.2%	16/30.8%	10/19.2%	17/35.7%

Note: The CGV and Polity total reflects all discrete transitions in the data set, including those that overlap as well as those that appear only in one or the other.

1980s—in Argentina, Brazil, Bolivia, Peru, and Uruguay—has been documented in the work of Ruth Collier, and we return to it in our case studies below.[5] But we see unions playing surprisingly similar roles in middle- and even lower-income communist countries. Strikes by both official and outside unions were instrumental in pushing out communist regimes in Ukraine and Poland, respectively, and even Albania and Bulgaria saw general strikes during the transition.

Union support for general strikes or large-scale work stoppages and blockades—triggered by economic crises—also posed critical challenges to incumbent rulers in a number of low-income African cases including Benin, Congo, Lesotho, Malawi, Mali, Niger, Sudan, and Zambia. Industrial unions played a role in some cases, most notably Zambia's copper workers in the Copperbelt protests of 1986–87, but in most African cases, state-sector workers were key actors. These workers not only were unionized, but enjoyed strategic advantages through their positions in the civil service or state-owned enterprises. Acting in concert or parallel with other urban groups, such as students, these unions exercised disproportionate influence through their capacity to mobilize against relatively weak, and even fragile, states.

[5] Collier 1999.

A distinctive feature of unions is that they operate in both the political and economic spheres. They can bring pressure to bear against authoritarian regimes directly by serving as leaders or key allies in wider antiregime social movements and mass mobilizations. However, they can also play a pivotal role in challenging the economic foundations of labor-repressive political economies—or any political economy—through general strikes, work stoppages, sit-ins, occupations, and a variety of other noncooperative strategies that weigh against economic elites' interests.

We also identify a cluster of transitions that we call ethnonationalist cases, similar to the union cases. We identify such transitions as those in which ethnonationalist groups were leaders or core members of antiregime coalitions, or when protests by these organizations added significantly to the overall pressure on the regime. The ethnonationalist cases include five transitions in which the incumbent authoritarian regime was the Soviet Union and the demands for regime change were, in effect, demands for independence: Armenia, Ukraine, and the three Baltic countries, Estonia, Latvia, and Lithuania. However, these ethnonationalist cases also included civil conflicts in Latin America, in which indigenous peoples played a role (Guatemala [1986 and 1996]) and transitions in societies with polarized ethnic-cum-regional cleavages (Burundi, Kyrgyzstan, Sri Lanka, and the Sudan).

It is important to underscore that the codings are not mutually exclusive, nor are all cases coded as one or the other. Four cases—Ecuador, Fiji, South Africa, and Ukraine—were coded as both union and ethnonationalist, while the transitions in the Philippines, Thailand, Kenya, and Haiti were the result of mass mobilization in which neither unions nor ethnonationalist movements played a role. The fact that the Polity and Polity plus CGV lines appear to sum to 100 percent is thus coincidental. However, it does make a substantive point: that in the vast majority of all discrete transitions—94.2 percent—one or the other of these types of organizations played a key role in the mass mobilization that undermined authoritarian rule.

Strategies, Violence, and Authoritarian Withdrawal

Acemoglu and Robinson sometimes conceive of regime transitions as revolutionary processes, in which force is brought to bear against the regime and its socioeconomic inequities. Yet, an emergent empirical literature on nonviolent resistance suggests that violence may be less prevalent in such challenges—and even less efficacious—than peaceful protest.[6] How, precisely, does mass mobilization work to displace incumbents?

Table 3.2 also considers all distributive conflict transitions in the two datasets and codes for the presence of riots—spontaneous violence that

[6] Chenoweth and Stephan 2011.

went beyond mass protest—and the presence of armed insurgent groups and militias, typically operating in rural areas. Perhaps the most clear-cut illustration of a case in which spontaneous violence proved decisive in the ouster of an incumbent leader was in Haiti in 1990–91, where widespread rioting helped to drive Colonel Prosper Avril from office (at the urging of the US government), and then helped to derail a brief military uprising aimed at preventing the popularly elected Jean-Bertrand Aristide from taking office. In approximately ten other cases, rioting played at least some role, yet the Haitian case is the only one in which rioting in support of an opposition alternative appeared decisive in the transition. Even where present, rioting was typically accompanied by much more durable and centralized forms of class or ethnic organization that ultimately convinced elites that repression was not a sustainable strategy for staying in power.

The table also shows that in 17 of the 52 discrete distributive conflict cases in the two datasets (35.7 percent), incumbent authoritarian regimes faced armed insurgencies, with half of those ethnonationalist in nature. El Salvador and Guatemala constitute classic civil war cases. In the other cases, the scope of insurgent violence ranged from major ethnic conflicts—as in Sri Lanka—to the operation of terrorist networks—as in Pakistan—to more episodic and scattered insurgent efforts. It is highly plausible that these conflicts reflected both objective spatial inequalities and subjective assessments of regional and ethnic injustice. It is important to note, however, that in none of these cases did democratization occur as a result of the outright victory of insurgent forces over the government. Rather, insurgent violence mattered only in conjunction with other forms of mobilization, and frequently with mobilization that was not even directly connected with the underlying insurgency.

Mass mobilization ousted incumbents through one of two routes. In cases of direct displacement, the magnitude of mass mobilization relative to existing state capacity made coercive responses physically or politically impossible, or rendered them unsuccessful. Incumbent rulers were forced to resign—and even flee—in favor of interim governments, national constitutional conferences, or oppositions. About a third of the distributive conflict cases (16 of 51 or 30.7 percent) conform to this displacement path.

However, in the majority of cases—nearly 70 percent—incumbents faced pressures from below, but retained at least some leverage in negotiations over the terms of their withdrawal. Whether the differences between "pacted" and forced transitions are consequential for the subsequent stability of democratic regime has been a matter of considerable debate.[7] We take up this issue in Chapter 5, and argue that the distinctions between

[7]Rustow 1970; Linz 1978; O'Donnell, Schmitter, and Whitehead 1986a; Share 1987; Karl 1990; Huntington 1993; Collier 1999.

pacted and non-pacted transitions are analytically less significant than whether the transition involved mass mobilization or not.

From Mass Mobilization to the Emergence of Democratic Rule: The Role of Political Entrepreneurs and Parties

Who are the political elites that ultimately assume leadership of the transition process, and what is their relation to the civil society groups that we have described above? The distinction between political and civil society raises two important questions. First, do elections constitute focal points for the mass mobilization we observe in these cases?[8] Related to this, to what extent—and at what point—do electoral politicians and political parties contribute to the mobilization of resistance to authoritarian rule? If parties are consequential for mass mobilization, it could challenge our claims about the importance of civil society organizations.

Table 3.3 provides some initial purchase on these questions. In the first column, we identify the distributive conflict cases in which fraudulent or postponed elections constituted a focal point for mass mobilization. This was manifest in only 11 of the 52 cases in our sample, consistent with the null findings on this issue in both the broader statistical work of Hadenius, Teorell, and Wahman,[9] and in regional case studies collated by Lindberg.[10] The reasons derive from our discussion of the authoritarian status quo ante in the first section of this chapter. Incumbent regimes were, for the most part, one-party or military-dominated regimes in which elections were plebiscitary or prohibited altogether. As we will see in Chapter 4, this contrasts with an important group of elite-led cases in which elections were more consequential.

The table also distinguishes between distributive conflict cases in which parties played no or a secondary role in mass mobilization, and those in which either established or new parties did in fact mobilize mass opposition.[11] In over half of the transitions (56 percent), parties played a minimal or, at most, a secondary role in the mobilization of protest; the

---

[8] Lindberg 2006; Schedler 2002, 2006; Tucker et al. 2006.

[9] Hadenius and Teorell 2007; Hadenius, Teorell, and Wahman 2012; Wahman, Teorell, and Hadenius 2012.

[10] Lindberg 2009.

[11] We define established parties as those with recognizable names, organizational histories, and leadership networks formed prior to the onset of challenges against the incumbent regime. Some established parties—such as the Peronists in Argentina—predated the authoritarian order altogether but were driven into quiescence. Others—such as Uruguay's Colorado and Blanco Parties—survived and were allowed to operate under strict authoritarian limits. We define new parties as those forged within the five years prior to the transition.

central challenges to incumbent authoritarian regimes came from organized civil society groups.

Parties in the remaining cases were more actively engaged in these challenges, but many of them were highly dependent on their links to organized social forces to turn people out in the streets. Party leaders were at the forefront of challenges in about 20 percent (10 cases) of all distributive conflict transitions. In about half of these cases, however, parties relied on unions or other civil society organizations to mobilize protest rather than the other way around. Examples include Brazil's Workers Party, Fiji's Labour Party, the South African ANC, Solidarity in Poland, and Zambia's Movement for Multiparty Democracy, headed by former labor union leader Frederick Chiluba.

In 13 cases (25 percent of the total), new parties joined, and sometimes assumed leadership of, protests against incumbent authoritarian regimes. However, seven of these cases were former Soviet republics. As we outline below in our discussion of the Baltics, parties were able to play a mobilizing role in these cases because of their presence in existing republic institutions. If we remove the established parties that relied on union bases of support and new parties that relied on organizational platforms provided by Soviet-era dumas, we are left with only 11 cases out of 63—17.5 percent—in which parties independently organized mass mobilization.

As noted, the repressive and exclusionary nature of the status quo ante does much to explain why elections and political parties are not more central to the patterns of mass mobilization. A significant majority of transitions that took place via the distributive conflict route were from one-party or military regimes, the overwhelming majority of which banned competing parties altogether.[12] In these cases, political entrepreneurs and parties were not in a position to enter the scene until *after* mass mobilization had weakened the incumbents' grip on power. Parties that were in abeyance or allowed to operate in competitive authoritarian regimes had been subjected to the imprisonment or exile of their leaders, repression, and efforts to disband or disrupt their organizational structures and networks. Such parties were most likely to have influence where they could rely on allied social organizations even if subject to similar constraints. New parties were even weaker, emerging initially as loose coalitions of counterelites forged around electoral aims and initially lacking in the instruments for reaching the broader society, including the media.

---

[12] Among the CGV transitions, the Hadenius, Teorell, and Wahman dataset identifies only three military regimes as also having multiparty elements: Indonesia, South Korea, and Pakistan. The Polity sample, similarly, identifies only three such regimes: Bangladesh, Indonesia, and South Korea. See Tables A3.1a and A3.2a.

Table 3.3 The Role of Elections and Parties in Mass Mobilization. (Distributive Conflict Transitions, N = 52)

Elections as Focal Points for Mass Mobilization	Party Sources of Mobilization		Not Significant or Secondary
	Established Parties	New Parties	
Dominican Republic 1996, Georgia 2004, Kyrgyzstan 2005, Madagascar 1992, Maldives 2008, Nepal 2006/8, Niger 2000, Nigeria 2000, Pakistan 2008, Philippines 1986, Thailand 1992	Bangladesh 1991, Brazil 1985, Dominican Republic 1996, Fiji 1992, Indonesia 1999, Nepal 1990, Nepal 2006, South Africa 1992, Sri Lanka 1989, Sudan 1986	Armenia 1991, Estonia 1988, Georgia 2004, El Salvador 1990, Kyrgyzstan 2005, Latvia 1991, Lithuania 1991, Maldives 2008, Mali 1992, Niger 2000, Poland 1989–1991, Ukraine 1991, Zambia 1991	Albania 1991, Argentina 1983, Benin 1991, Bolivia 1982, Bulgaria 1990, Burundi 1993, Burundi 2005, Congo 1992, Ecuador 2002, El Salvador 1984, Guatemala 1986, Guatemala 1996, Haiti 1990, Kenya 1998, Lesotho 1993, Madagascar 1992, Malawi 1994, Mongolia 1990, Niger 2000, Nigeria 2000, Pakistan 2008, Peru 1980, Philippines 1986, Romania 1990, South Korea 1988, Suriname 1988, Thailand 1992, Ukraine 1994, Uruguay 1985
n = 11 (21.2%)	n = 10 (19.2%)	n = 13 (25%)	n = 29 (55.8%)

The distinction between civil society actors and those in the political sphere points to an underlying tension in distributive conflict transitions that has complex implications for democracies. From the perspective of civil society groups, the transition to democracy is expected to address the grievances that gave rise to mass mobilization in the first place. Yet political leaders are typically forced into compromises that necessarily open a space between political leaders and less moderate factions of their social base. As we have seen, in almost 70 percent of distributive transitions, incumbent elites maintained sufficient authority to negotiate their exit or even to retain power in founding elections.[13] In a majority of cases, anti-incumbent parties did win decisive initial victories. But winning coalitions often broke up quite quickly as the interests between new political elites and their supporters diverged.[14] Even when transitions do not involve explicit agreements, new governments are likely to tread lightly on the interests of economic, military, and political elites with the capacity to derail the transition altogether.

In short, although mobilization may alter the playing field in important ways during distributive conflict transitions, it is unlikely to mark a definitive end to the struggles that led to regime change in the first place. The dangers this poses to democratic stability are well known. The expectations of antiauthoritarian demonstrators are ones that new democratic governments are often poorly equipped to meet. This is especially true in transitions that are spurred by economic crises, during which new governments are under strong external and domestic pressure to undertake unpopular adjustment policies. In such circumstances, a highly active civil society can contribute to polarization and stalemate, with a significant increase in the risk of democratic reversals.

Against these obvious risks, however, we must also weigh the dangers posed to democracy where transitions are effected in the absence of pressure from below. Where transitions are strictly the result of elite politics and/or external pressures, there may be fewer constraints on abuse of power by elected governments. In democratic governments propelled by mass demands and distributive conflict, politicians may be less vulnerable to these temptations, even when they are unable to meet the distributive

---

[13]Examples include the communist regimes in Mongolia, Romania, and Ukraine (1991, 1994), as well as Fiji (1992), South Korea (1988), and Kenya (1998). In four Central American cases (Guatemala 1986 and 1996, and El Salvador 1984 and 1990), revolutionary groups that challenged the authoritarian order were excluded from negotiations and/or were consigned to opposition roles following the transition.

[14]For example, Solidarity in Poland, the Vital Force in Madagascar, the Baltic Popular Front governments, and new governments in Bulgaria and Nepal. In Latin America, labor-based political movements that had spurred much of the protest in Argentina, Brazil, Peru, and Bolivia moved almost immediately into opposition following the founding elections.

demands of the public. Disruptive and potentially destabilizing though it might be, the contentious politics generated by distributive demands can have a positive effect on the longer-term quality of pluralistic competition and political accountability. We explore these dynamics in more detail in Chapter 5.

AUTHORITARIAN INSTITUTIONS, COLLECTIVE ACTION, AND REGIME CHANGE: CASES

The preceding sections sought to advance our argument by comparing the distributive conflict and elite-led samples with respect to the authoritarian status quo ante and considering the social foundations and mechanics of transition in the distributive conflict cases. In this section, we provide causal process observation of individual cases to probe more deeply into how these characteristics of incumbent regimes and the organization of excluded social and ethnic groups combined to destabilize authoritarian rule. In each case, we begin with the exclusionary features of the authoritarian regime, then focus on the opposition and how it was organized. In most of these cases, labor played a central role even when other opposition forces and even external actors were also involved. We end each case with the response of authoritarian incumbents and their ultimate exit.

The cases also permit us to consider some of the other causal factors that appear in the regression analyses in Chapter 2. We pay particular attention to the role that economic crises or regime performance plays; economic sources of both mobilization and grievance come out strongly in the cases considered here as well.

Because we consider all distributive conflict cases, we can sample widely. We consider five different clusters of cases, selecting them to maximize variance on several dimensions: region and, in relation, level of development as well as international alignments. We also choose cases to show some of the underlying similarities between those that involve labor as a key actor and those that are ethnonationalist in nature.

- Argentina and Bolivia provide examples—at different levels of development and engaging different types of working classes—of the fall of right-wing military regimes in a region with close proximity to the United States. These military regimes were characterized by labor repression, an exclusive governing structure, and mass mobilization by resurgent unions.
- Poland provides an example of the distributive conflict transitions in a number of the Eastern European one-party states that had developed as Soviet clients. These cases combined absence of controlled party competition with spatially concentrated and highly organized working classes.

- Niger and Congo provide examples of transitions in poor, African military and one-party regimes, respectively, with unions of state workers playing a role parallel to industrial working classes elsewhere. They also represent examples of Western and Soviet client states, respectively, and the changing international environment that arose at the end of the Cold War.
- South Africa and the Baltic states, finally, exemplify transitions in ethnically exclusive authoritarian regimes in which excluded groups organized mass mobilization. Again, these differ in international context as well, with South African vulnerable to an international sanctions movement among the democracies and the Baltics liberating themselves from Soviet dominance.

Transitions from Right-Wing Military Rule in Latin America: Argentina and Bolivia

South America provides strong examples of union-led protest against right-wing military regimes broadly in the American orbit.[15] In most union cases—including Brazil, Peru, and Uruguay—labor contributed to mass mobilization in the context of broader coalitions that included civil society groups, middle-class forces, and sometimes even business organizations. However, Argentina and Bolivia, two countries at very different levels of development, constitute near ideal types of the causal mechanisms we associate with distributive conflict transitions. Both had highly repressive, right-wing military regimes with limited channels for representation. In both cases militant unions organized and spearheaded the opposition that ultimately forced the withdrawal of authoritarian incumbents. In both cases, we also see the complementary role that economic crises played in spurring mass mobilization and regime breakdown.

ARGENTINA (1983 CGV AND POLITY)

As with many of the regimes we code as labor repressive, the military regime in Argentina seized power in 1976 in a period of economic collapse and escalating violence.[16] Institutionally, the junta ruled directly, closing Congress and subordinating state and municipal government to the military. The regime was particularly repressive, designating their program euphemistically the National Reorganization Process. In addition to banning parties and strikes and imposing censorship, the Videla regime initiated a massive campaign against the opposition centered around a clandestine

---

[15] Valenzuela et al. 1989; Drake 1996; Collier 1999; Levitsky and Mainwaring 2006.
[16] Kaufman 1979; Cavarozzi 1986a, 1986b.

system of military and police detention and disappearance that came to be known as the "dirty war." In addition to direct purges of labor-based Peronist adversaries, an important component of its strategy was the introduction of neoliberal economic reforms, including reforms of the labor market designed to curtail union power. However, these plans had wider effect than targeted repression and created a focal point for the mobilization of Peronist and labor opposition; even factions of the military itself had doubts about the neoliberal project. Opposition was spurred by poor economic performance as well as structural dislocations. The economy entered a period of volatility during the late 1970s; and in 1981 and 1982, the years just prior to the 1983 transition, the economy shrank by 5.7 and 5.0, respectively.

The union movement, among the most powerful and militant in the developing world,[17] was initially divided over whether to attempt to negotiate with the regime or oppose it outright. However, the military campaign of repression hardened the resolve of the confrontationist wing of the movement, and the arrests of many of the more conservative older leaders cleared the way for the emergence of a younger, more combative cadre of militants.[18] Despite repression, these more combative factions organized a wave of strikes and general strikes, beginning in 1977.

In the midst of the deep recession in 1981, the military high command replaced General Jorge Videla, the initial leader of the 1976 coup, with Roberto Viola, a more moderate figure expected to offer some concessions to labor, in part by moderating market reforms. The union movement, however, responded by increasing pressure on the regime.[19] In July 1981, the CGT (Confederación General del Trabajo) launched another massive general strike, which deepened divisions between hard-line officers and the more moderate president. After a second mobilization, the military command forced Viola to resign and replaced him with another hard-line officer, Leopoldo Galtieri, but militant opposition to the regime only increased. On March 30, 1982, the CGT led the largest demonstration since the 1976 coup, now joined for the first time by human rights organizations and political parties.

Just two days later, on April 2, the government launched an invasion of British-held Falkland Islands to divert this popular pressure and rally both the military and society around nationalist loyalties. This, however, was a desperate and eventually unsuccessful maneuver, which ended in humiliating defeat at the hands of Great Britain. The fate of the regime might, to be sure, have been different if the invasion had succeeded. But the decision to

[17] James 1994; McGuire 1997.
[18] Collier 1999: 123.
[19] Collier 1999: 119–26; McGuire 1995b; Munck 1998.

invade was itself a major gamble that was directly precipitated by growing pressure from below and the increasing internal rifts within the regime itself that resulted from the surge in mass mobilization.

In the event, protest surged as information about Argentine losses spread and the economy continued to deteriorate. Faced with these political and economic challenges, the navy and air force withdrew their representatives from the ruling junta, and the army command appointed a caretaker government under retired General Reynaldo Bignone to organize elections in negotiation with an opposition coalition of Peronist politicians, Radical Party leaders, and Peronist labor unions.

The question of amnesty for military crimes constituted a major sticking point in these negotiations. Although the opposition coalition repeatedly refused to accept an amnesty, rumors did begin to circulate that conservative factions of the Peronist labor movement had agreed to refrain from bringing charges against the military, in exchange being allowed to control key unions.[20] "Had the Peronists won in 1983 and delivered their end of the reported bargain," McGuire argues, "Argentina's transition might well have been interpreted as . . . carefully staged [and] incumbent controlled."[21] But the momentum of the popular opposition would have made it extremely difficult to sustain such a deal. Months before the rumor surfaced, a more formal proposal for legal amnesty had been withdrawn in the face of a massive opposition rally.[22] Moreover, the rumors themselves generated a heated backlash. Denunciations were loudest among Radical Party leaders, the Peronists' principal competitors; indeed, the backlash contributed to their victory over the Peronists in the transitional elections. But more liberal factions of the Peronist unions also denounced the idea of a union-military pact, and both military and conservative union leaders themselves denied that they had made such a deal. Whatever the truth of the allegations, moreover, the pact was not consummated. By early 1983, incumbent the military government essentially abandoned attempts to negotiate immunity, and the transition to a competitively elected government went forward in October of that year without preconditions.

BOLIVIA (1982 CGV AND POLITY)

Although at a much lower level of development, Bolivia exhibits similar patterns, including a labor-repressive military regime with few channels of representation, a strong history of union involvement in politics, and highly erratic economic performance and recurrent crises. From 1971 to

---

[20] McGuire 1995a: 189.
[21] McGuire 1995a: 181.
[22] McGuire 1995a: 188.

1978, the country was ruled by a right-wing military regime controlled by Hugo Banzer. The 1971 coup that brought Banzer to power left several hundred dead,[23] and the government immediately banned left-leaning parties and the main labor federation, the Central Obrera Boliviana, installing "coordinators" in place of independent labor leaders. Initially ruling with support from two right-wing parties (the Movimiento Nacionalista Revolucionario and the Falange Socialista Boliviana), Banzer ultimately banned all political activity, exiled remaining party leaders, and ruled directly through the military. A brief opening in 1978–79 was followed by a return to hard-line rule after a coup engineered by General Luis García Meza (1980–82). From the mid-1970s onward, however, both Banzer and his successors faced strong, mobilized opposition from the Bolivian union movement, exacerbated by a rapidly deteriorating economy and by IMF pressure to undertake painful economic adjustments.[24] Over the next decade, unions played a dual role, protesting deteriorating economic conditions, neoliberal reforms, and the political order that sought to impose them.

Confrontations first erupted in 1976, with a prolonged strike organized by the officially banned federation of mine workers. Banzer initially responded with severe repression, occupying the mines and arresting union leaders, but then followed with plans to hold a stage-managed election in 1978 designed to install a chosen successor. But the unions played a key role in disrupting this initiative. A hunger strike staged by wives of the detained miners provided the initial trigger for the protest. When government "coordinators" attempted to organize union opposition to the hunger strikers, the union rank-and-file revolted, forcing the government to allow the unions to resurface as independent organizations and to operate openly. Resistance then quickly escalated and broadened, with support from the Church and human rights movements. Within weeks, "over a thousand protesters were on strike in churches and public places all over the republic."[25] Within months, the protests forced both Banzer and his handpicked successor from office.

The defeat of Banzer's attempt to retain power in 1978 was followed by a succession of elections and military coups in which neither the military nor a deeply divided civilian opposition was able to gain control. The unions, however, played a key role in deterring the reassertion of military dominance. After a new round of strikes and demonstrations, moderate military factions agreed to hold new elections in July 1979. And when the military attempted to overthrow the weak interim government that

---

[23] Collier 1999: 143–49; Dunkerly 1994: 251–67; Whitehead 1986: 71.
[24] Klein 1992: 246–87; Whitehead 1986: 65.
[25] Whitehead 1986: 59.

followed, union protests again forced the new military government from power after only 16 days. Popular mobilization against coups continued during the run-up to a new election scheduled for 1980, and although the prodemocracy coalition included leaders from across the political spectrum, the Workers' Confederation maintained the most persistent pressure through roadblocks and strikes.[26]

In the 1980 election, no candidate won the necessary 50 percent of the vote. The new Congress awarded the presidency to the plurality winner, the union-backed candidate Hernán Siles Zuazo. Before Siles could take office, however, another coup installed General Luis García Meza in power and the new government unleashed the harshest repression since the demise of the Banzer regime. All avenues of representation were once again closed, the Congress was placed in recess, the parties were suspended, and all union activity was outlawed. Siles himself, along with most of the major political leaders, retreated into exile.

García Meza seized power evoking the image of Chile's Pinochet as a model. In fact, however, both he and his military faction were deeply implicated in corruption and drug trafficking, and he quickly encountered opposition not only from unions, but also from business and middle-class groups and crucial sources of international aid. In the face of this broad opposition, García Meza was ousted by rival military factions after only a year and might have fallen anyway even without pressure from the unions. It is hard to deny, however, that union pressure contributed to this outcome, and it is even clearer that it placed García Meza's military successors on the defensive.

Initially, the new military authorities had planned to retain power at least until the elections scheduled for 1983, and neither they nor other more conservative sectors of Bolivian society were anxious to open the way to the left-wing political coalition headed by Siles. Nevertheless, in response to a wave of general strikes and marches, the military government lifted the formal ban on unions and agreed to allow Siles and other exiled political leaders to return to the country. Reluctantly, the government also abandoned plans to extend its time in power and simply reinstated the Congress that had been deposed in 1980. In turn, Congress reaffirmed its selection of Siles for the presidency. This decision by no means ended the destabilizing struggles that marked Bolivian politics during the 1980s, but it did mark the end of the transition.

Several features of this case are of interest to our theoretical and methodological interests. First it is interesting to note that the causal processes we describe here involving a repressive regime with few channels of representation and strategic interaction with unions are repeated over

[26]Collier 1999: 147.

several iterations before the transition finally occurs. Economic crises also play a crucial role, exacerbated by external policy demands. Yet the fundamental dynamics comport with the distributive conflict model in which pressures from below make it impossible for the military to sustain authoritarian rule.

The Collapse of Communism in Eastern Europe: Poland (CGV 1989, Polity 1991)

As we argued above, the one-party communist states in the Soviet Union and Eastern Europe constitute a second cluster of regimes that appeared to be vulnerable to distributive conflict transitions. Communist political systems, such as Poland's, did not tolerate electoral challenges from even nominally opposition parties.[27] We do not code the Eastern European and Soviet cases as labor repressive because of their quite distinctive socialist political economies, although such a coding might well be warranted. Communist parties did seize control of existing union movements in the early postwar period and despite de-Stalinization, brutally suppressed popular protest from below, including by workers, in East Germany (1953), Hungary (1956), and Czechoslovakia (1968). Poland is exemplary of this trajectory, witnessing leadership changes associated with cycles of protest in 1953 and again in 1970 and 1980–81. Each time, the regime initially responded with efforts to quell dissent by improving living standards, only to be followed by economic retrenchment and a return to reliance on repression.

By the 1980s, repression had eased marginally and these regimes had evolved into bureaucratized state socialist systems that relied heavily on the socialist social contract to keep the population in line.[28] As in the Latin American cases, however, opposition to the system began to crystallize around a slowdown in growth, increasing inflation, and the erosion of the social guarantees that had bolstered the old regime. Ironically, the emphasis on industrialization, the concentration of workers in large establishments and cities, and the party-controlled unions had the effect of providing the organizational foundation for mass mobilization. Union opposition was a central feature of the collapse of the old regime in all four of the East European distributive conflict cases, including Bulgaria, Romania, Albania, and Poland, our focus here.

[27] In Poland, to be discussed in more detail below, the Communists did incorporate two small satellite parties into a "Unity Front," which ran essentially unopposed. At the onset of the Solidarity uprising in 1980, the Front was declared winner with 95.5 percent of the valid votes in a 98.8 percent turnout of eligible voters (Ekiert 1996: 227).

[28] Haggard and Kaufman 2008, chap. 4.

In June 1979, a visit from the newly elected Polish Pope, John Paul II, drew massive crowds; this played a key role in stripping away Communist legitimacy and reframing the thinking about the possibility of regime change.[29] The most concerted organizational challenge, however, emerged with the formation of an independent trade union movement and a wave of strikes in the early 1980s. These began as sit-ins in the Gdansk shipyards, with demands for lower prices, better benefits, and independent trade unions. In hopes of defusing the movement, the regime initially recognized the Solidarity unions with the Gdansk Agreement, but this unleashed a flood. Within months, membership in Solidarity swelled to over ten million, and strikes and protests swept the country.

In October 1981, the Soviet Union responded to these developments with pressure on the regime to crack down; and the Polish military establishment—under General Wojciech Jaruzelski—complied. Jaruzelski assumed direct control of the government and the Communist Party, and imposed martial law. But although Solidarity leaders were imprisoned and the union movement driven underground,[30] the social networks forged during the protests remained intact. The risk, therefore, of a renewed social explosion remained a serious impediment to the government's efforts to undertake economic adjustments.[31]

In 1985, the Polish regime issued an amnesty for Solidarity leaders, after Gorbachev assumed leadership of the Soviet Union and Soviet pressure eased. But the movement itself remained illegal, and tensions remained high. As the government struggled to contain deteriorating economic conditions with a new round of market-oriented reforms, Solidarity resurfaced in 1988 as an active political force, leading the largest wave of street protests and strikes since 1981. Although the movement rallied around nationalist and religious symbols, the dramatic slowdown in growth and material grievances were important motivating factors.

By this point, reform factions had assumed the leadership of the Polish Communist Party, and they became increasingly convinced that neither economic nor political stabilization would be possible without the collaboration of the Solidarity movement. In the absence of formal institutional channels of participation (and with Solidarity still officially illegal), they invited Solidarity to participate in ad hoc negotiations in which the Vatican initially served as an intermediary. The government's hope was that by granting Solidarity a limited representation, the movement could be induced to share political responsibility for painful but necessary

[29] Staniszkis 1981; Kubik 1994; Ash 2002; Smolar 2009.
[30] Staniszkis 1981.
[31] Osa 2003.

economic reforms. In February 1989, these negotiations evolved into more formal Round Table Talks.

The political agreement concluded several months later permitted Solidarity to compete for only 35 percent of the legislative seats; the Communists were to retain control of the rest. To the surprise of the government, however, Solidarity swept all of the seats it was allowed to contest, an indication of its continuing capacity to mobilize widespread popular challenges to the regime. The conclusion drawn by the party leadership was that its belated effort at limited co-optation was unsustainable and that containment of the deteriorating economic situation required a more fundamental transfer of power. The Communist-dominated legislature thus ceded executive authority entirely to a new Solidarity-led government. Once in power, the social movement itself quickly splintered into multiple competing factions and was ultimately defeated.[32] This new government, however, was the first to preside over full parliamentary elections in 1991.

As is the case with many distributive conflict transitions, union demands were only one component of a much broader social and political movement for change. As indicated above, moreover, the Soviet commitment to perestroika was clearly a precondition of the transition. Nevertheless, it was certainly pressure from the Solidarity movement that pushed this process well beyond the preferences and expectations of reformists within the Polish Communist Party. The Polish case, moreover, reflects processes visible not only in the other communist distributive conflict cases, but in this class of cases more generally. Deteriorating economic performance and the descent into crises provided the backdrop for popular disaffection. A regime that provided few mechanisms for political participation sought to survive through ad hoc political and policy concessions. But it faced an organic organization of blue-collar workers that was capable of mobilizing mass protest and putting economic as well as political pressure on the incumbent regime.

African Transitions from One-Party and Military Rule: Niger and the People's Republic of the Congo

A third cluster of distributive conflict transitions occurred in African military or one-party regimes. These exclusionary African regimes include Benin, Lesotho, Malawi, Mali, Nigeria, Sudan, Zambia, and the two cases we consider here, Niger (1993), more closely tied to the West, and the Republic of the Congo (1992), a Soviet client. Unlike the Latin American cases, these regimes did not pursue economic models that dictated labor repression. Most espoused anticolonial and nationalist ideologies, and if

[32] Ost 2006.

ethnic exclusion occurred, it was opportunistic rather than reflective of a wider economic project directly exploiting underrepresented minorities. Nonetheless, the nine cases listed above had average Polity scores of –7.8 at t–5, and were substantially more closed to competition and repressive than the average for all distributive conflict transitions.

Unions took quite different forms in these African countries when compared to their middle-income counterparts, concentrated among civil servants, state-owned enterprises, students, and professionals.[33] In our dataset, we note that both of the cases considered here are "ambiguous" with respect to the class composition of the protest. Unlike Argentina, Bolivia, and the other middle-income Latin American cases, unions and student organizations in Niger and the Congo represented a relatively privileged, urban slice of the population. Both countries were overwhelmingly rural, and poverty was concentrated in the countryside. Nevertheless, authoritarian states were also weaker, with greater vulnerability to urban and union protest that emerged in response to economic deterioration and crises.[34] In the absence of effective channels for co-opting opposition forces, unions were able to exploit their strategic and organizational advantages to play an important role in the transition process.

NIGER (1993 CGV, 1992 POLITY)

For the first 14 years after its independence in 1960, Niger was ruled by a single-party civilian regime. The Nigerien military came to power via a military coup led by Seyni Kountché in 1974.[35] Kountché dissolved the National Assembly—although completely monopolized by the Nigerien Progressive Party–African Democratic Rally party—and governed directly through a Supreme Military Council. The regime did make some concessions. It freed political prisoners and allowed some exiled political activists back into the country; and in the early 1980s, it brought some civilians into the Supreme Military Council and engineered a referendum on a national charter. But this charter provided for only nonelective consultative assemblies appointed at the regime's discretion. Until the transition in 1992 and 1993, therefore, political contestation was strictly limited; Polity scores remained at –7 during the entire period.

Kountché died in 1987 after 13 years in power, and was succeeded by General Ali Saibou, who returned the country to one-party rule in 1989 through a referendum and presidential and parliamentary elections with a single slate of candidates. Economic grievances played a major role in

[33] Kraus 2007.
[34] Schillinger 2005.
[35] On the cycles of breakdown, see Villalón and Idrissa 2005.

mobilizing union opposition to the Saibou regime.[36] The main unions, which had been subjugated by the Kountché regime, became substantially more militant and independent, particularly around structural adjustment measures imposed by the IMF and the French. In 1990, students and civil servant unions backed strikes and protests against an austerity program—which the regime repressed—and supported the formation of left-oriented opposition parties. The unions also maintained clandestine alliances with Marxist associations appealing to the Hausa (about half the population) and to the underdeveloped northern region.

In response to these pressures, Saibou and the military announced that they would convene a National Conference. The National Conference mechanism had first appeared in Benin in 1990, where it was forced on the reluctant authoritarian incumbent by the threat of a general strike and quickly went on to declare itself sovereign and oust him from office. This experience had an important effect in Niger as well. Saibou initially signaled his willingness to permit the formation of a multiparty system, clearly with the intention of controlling the transitional process.[37] However, the National Conference quickly fell under control of two emergent political and social forces in Niger. The first was a civilian political elite that—while divided—had common interests in democratic norms. The second was the major civil society groups that had mobilized pressure against the regime, most notably students and unionized workers. We code the case as "ambiguous" with respect to its class composition; these groups hardly represented the rural poor. But they did have strong corporate interests in defending their prerogatives, including through opposition to structural adjustment programs imposed by the outside, as well as their freedom to organize and strike.[38] As a number of analyses have noted,[39] these conferences were not uniformly successful: some ushered in democratic regimes, and incumbents in other cases managed to resist them altogether. And the subsequent path of democracy in Niger was far from smooth.[40] But because of prior mobilization against the regime and the weight of the groups represented, the National Conference had the heft to dissolve the incumbent government and assume control of the transition process. The winner of the 1993 presidential election was Mahamane Ousmane, leader of one of the new parties formed during this period, the Democratic and Social Convention.

[36] Charlick 2007: 83–123; Gervais 1997.
[37] Gervais 1997; Davis and Kossomi 2001; Villalón and Idrissa 2005.
[38] Villalón and Idrissa 2005: 28–29.
[39] Robinson 1994; Clark 1994a; Fomunyoh 2001.
[40] Villalón and Idrissa 2005.

THE CONGO (1992 CGV)

The nominally Marxist-Leninist one-party government in the People's Republic of the Congo came to power in a coup in 1968 that abolished the national assembly and subsequently established the Congolese Labor Party (PCT), in fact dominated by the military. In the absence of broader political contestation, politics was dominated by intra-elite conflicts, plots, and recurrent instability. The first president, Marien Ngouabi, was assassinated in 1977, and his successor was deposed after two years. The succession to Denis Sassou N'guesso in 1979 ushered in a period of political continuity, buoyed until the mid-1980s by growing revenues from petroleum, but with contestation tightly limited, as reflected in a Polity score of –8 throughout the decade of the 1980s.

Like other poor African states, Congo was hit hard by the global economic shocks of the 1980s as well as the decline and then collapse of the Soviet Union. Oil-rich Congo was hit especially hard by the collapse of petroleum prices, with revenues declining from $800 million in 1985 to only $160 million in 1989, reducing rents available to the military, civil servants, and students.[41] In response to these developments, the PCT leadership sought to make political and economic concessions, announcing in mid-1990 that it would abandon Marxism-Leninism, allow multiparty competition, free some political prisoners, and relax control over the economy.[42]

However, this initiative was not accompanied by a strategy or institutions for co-opting the opposition. In the fall of 1990 the country experienced a wave of mass demonstrations and strikes culminating in a standoff between the government and leading trade unions, concentrated in the public sector. When Sassou N'guesso demanded an end to the strikes, the unions called a general strike that shut down the government and signaled a loss of control. The strike leaders demanded not only higher wages but also autonomy from the government and political reform. As the government ceded to the demands of the unions and allowed the formation of opposition parties, the opposition was fed by the defection of a number of prominent PCT politicians.

As in Niger, a confluence of opposition political aspirants and a plethora of civil society groups, including the unions and churches, converged on demands for a National Conference outside the control of the PCT, following the model of other Francophone predecessors.

Substantial conflict ensued over the structure and process of the national conference. Initially, Sassou N'guesso sought to control the political

[41] Clark 1997: 64.
[42] Clark 1994b.

process by convening an all-party national conference in February himself. However, the opposition immediately protested the composition of the body as unrepresentative, and when it reconvened in March the opposition gained an absolute majority of both total delegates and seats on the conference's governing body. As in Niger, the conference took the decision early to declare itself "sovereign." Sassou N'guesso was constrained by the breadth of the opposition to accept this decision. The conference proceeded to elect a slate of leaders that completely excluded the PCT and to effectively dismantle the authoritarian state by creating new institutions. At the end of the conference, it chose an interim government for one year and appointed a technocratic leadership. The interim government scheduled presidential and legislative elections for March and June 1992 and, despite several crises involving the military and charges of election fraud, weathered challenges to hold these elections.[43]

Despite their nominally different political orientations and divergent foreign ties, the two regimes in Niger and the Congo exhibit surprising similarities that conform to the distributive conflict model. Neither authoritarian regime built institutions for co-opting potential opposition forces, relying on patronage and repression to keep the opposition and unions under control. As patronage resources declined as a result of economic shocks, structural adjustment, stabilization efforts, and the threat of reduced assistance, both regimes faced growing opposition from civil society. In both countries, the social base of unions was limited and arguably ambiguous from a class conflict perspective; unions represented relatively privileged sectors. Nevertheless, unions and other civil society groups organized around economic grievances allied with political aspirants and provided a crucial base of support for both the constitutional convention and the opposition that pushed the regime from power.

Ethnic Conflict and Regime Change 1: South Africa (1992 Polity)

Although class and economic grievances propelled the majority of distributive conflict transitions in our sample, a significant number were also driven by grievances about ethnic exclusion. Fiji, Guyana, and Burundi provide examples of ethnically exclusionary authoritarian regimes that fell as a result of distributive conflicts. Ethnonationalist cleavages played a significant role in the independence and democratization movements in the former Soviet Union as well. However, South Africa is a paradigmatic case of an ethnonationalist transition, and one in which black unions played a critical role as well. We argue that the Baltics, at the epicenter of the breakup of the Soviet Union, were also characterized by such cleavages.

[43]Clark 1994b.

South Africa is classified as a semicompetitive political system in the dataset used for the regressions in Chapter 2 because of the electoral competition allowed among white voters. However it is in fact a strong example of an economically exclusive authoritarian regime with few channels of representation for the vast majority. The strategy of "grand apartheid" was rooted not only in segregation but in the physical separation of the races, enforced by the notorious pass laws. Apartheid rested on the effective disenfranchisement of black and colored voters through measures such as segregation of voting roles, indirect representation and ultimately the creation of Bantustans that sought to strip the majority of their citizenship altogether. Repression was grounded in a sweeping Suppression of Communism Act (1950) that defined communism broadly to include any effort to disrupt the racial status quo. Racial injustice was therefore the overarching issue in the fight for democracy in South Africa.[44] The transition—spearheaded by the African National Congress—involved a highly organized struggle against all aspects of the exclusionary apartheid regime that included the full range of contentious politics, from demonstrations and strikes to armed struggle.

Within that context, however, the ANC gained critical support from a highly militant labor movement.[45] During the 1960s, leaders of the ANC had been exiled or—as in the case of Mandela—imprisoned; in the 1970s, however, strong popular challenges reemerged. Initially, this took the form of uprisings of neighborhood associations in the segregated townships in response to police brutality. Unionization, however, became a second major front in the mounting challenge to the apartheid regime. In the late 1970s, a recommendation to increase productivity by relaxing labor controls led to the formation of increasingly militant unions, which culminated in 1985 in the formation of the Congress of South African Trade Unions.

Both international pressures and elite defections played a role in the transition, to be sure.[46] But the actions of international actors and domestic business elites were themselves a response to the conflicts within the townships and the workplace. Growing international condemnation of the repression posed a clear challenge to the large corporations and elites that dominated the South African economy. In turn, as conflicts heated up, foreign and domestic investment declined, and the main business organizations began to press the government for political reform, a free vote, and an end to racial exclusion. Their efforts included trips abroad to confer with the ANC leaders in exile, and as important, calls for the release of

---

[44] Wood 2000.
[45] Adler and Webster 1995, 2000.
[46] Wood 2000, 2001.

Mandela. The ruling National Party also came under increasing pressure from its own Afrikaner base, dissatisfied with the economic downturn.

In 1990, incumbent Prime Minister Botha was replaced by F. W. de Klerk, who immediately had to deal with a rapidly deteriorating economy; growth was negative in 1990, 1991, and 1992. He lifted the ban on the ANC and ordered the release of Mandela, and this in turn opened the way to the negotiations that ended in the transitional 1994 election.[47]

Despite external and elite pressures on the regime, there can be little doubt that the absence of institutionalized channels of representation and protest from the black majority—with the significant participation of the militant union movement—were pivotal factors in the collapse of authoritarian rule. The recurrence of widespread violence—although renounced by Mandela—was an ever-present danger. The decision to hold elections in 1994 reflected the view of de Klerk and much of the white elite that South Africa's political isolation and deteriorating economic circumstances could be eased only through an accommodation with the ANC and its allied union base. Such accommodation would permanently remove the sustained pressure they had mobilized on both the political and economic fronts.

Ethnic Conflict and Regime Change 2: The Baltics (1991 CGV and Polity)

A final cluster of cases would appear quite distinctive on many dimensions, but also share key antecedent conditions with the other distributive conflict cases discussed above. Within the Soviet Union, "ethnic republics" were constituted principally as a means of controlling and subjugating non-Russian populations.[48] The official ideology acknowledged national identities while simultaneously subsuming them within a broader Soviet citizenship. Although we do not see the kind of overt ethnic repression found in other ethnically exclusive autocracies, such as South Africa, the one-party and nomenklatura systems—controlled from Moscow—as well as migration and employment policies, clearly favored the Russian diaspora within the Soviet Union and effectively discriminated against indigenous peoples.

The potential for conflict over such issues was especially evident in Estonia, Latvia, and Lithuania because of the way they were absorbed into the Soviet Union. The three Baltic countries were ceded to the Soviet Union under the Stalin-Ribbentrop Pact in 1939, subsequently occupied by the Nazi regime, and then reabsorbed into the Soviet Union as Stalin's armies marched through the Baltics. Moscow, it should be noted, did not

---

[47]Price 1991; Giliomee 1995; Sparks 1996.
[48]Motyl 1992; Martin 2001; Shanin 1989.

immediately attack indigenous culture, language, and religion; but it did seek to fundamentally change the ethnopolitical balance by deporting partisans who resisted Soviet rule, appointing Russian officials, and encouraging immigration of Russian workers.[49] Compared to their percentage in the population, ethnic Balts were underrepresented in the party membership, while Russian access was disproportionately high.[50] Top leadership in the republic parties was also restricted to "Russified Balts" and to Russian "minders," and beginning in the 1970s, the regime began a concerted campaign to promote the use of Russian at the expense of the ethnic languages.[51]

Patterns of discrimination extended into the economic sphere. Local control over economic policy was limited not only by the highly centralized planning system in Moscow, but also by cross-republican industrial committees that diluted the participation of ethnic Balts. Worsening economic conditions during the 1980s—including even recurrent food shortages—were widely interpreted to result from exploitation by Moscow. "The Balts," noted Alexiev, "generally consider themselves highly skilled and industrious people, and the Communist system and Soviet domination are seen by many as the only barrier to economic prosperity for their nations."[52]

This history of Russian domination—rejected not only by the West, through its policy of nonrecognition, but also by indigenous populations themselves—laid the basis for the secessionist movements that emerged in all three countries as the Soviet Union began to disintegrate. Our coding of these cases as distributive conflict transitions is arguably problematic, since the protests were framed in terms of nationalist demands for independence and redefining the territorial boundaries of the Soviet polity as a result. As suggested, however, these movements were also driven by driven by anti-Russian, ethnic grievances aimed at redefining socioeconomic boundaries within the polity itself.[53]

Beissinger has called the Baltics "early risers within the secessionist tide" that swept through the Soviet Union.[54] Given single-party dominance, the space for independent civil society was initially quite limited. Dissident movements operated at the margins of those societies at best. But in the more liberal environment of the mid-1980s, small nationalist

[49]Vardas 1966; Alexiev 1983.
[50]Alexiev 1983: 8.
[51]Alexiev 1983: 18.
[52]Alexiev 1983: 14.
[53]These objectives were made abundantly clear in the postindependence period by the redefinitions of citizenship that severely discriminated against the local Russian population and privileged the ethnic Balts. Ulfelder 2004: 24.
[54]Beissinger 2002: 166.

groups began to organize demonstrations marking key dates, such as the anniversary of the Molotov-Ribbentrop Pact of 1939. Helsinki-86, a small organization named after the Helsinki accords and the year it was founded, was the first such anticommunist organization to form. Gorbachev's liberalization policies opened opportunities for these small independent organizations to test the limits of protest. Intellectuals within the republic-level institutions also began to criticize excessive centralization of authority within the party bureaucracy, gradually exploiting existing organizations within the party and state, particularly organizations involving intellectuals. Over time, these pockets of dissidence within the state apparatus quickly grew into much wider "popular front" organizations that split republican elites.

These organizations mobilized initially in support of perestroika, but increasingly in favor of independence.[55] In Estonia, a joint meeting of the cultural unions expressed a lack of trust in Karl Vaino, the Estonian First Secretary, and prompted calls for a Popular Front of both official and dissident groups, which was ultimately formed in April 1988. Escalating mass protests led to the removal of Vaino in June and his replacement by Vaino Valjas, who openly supported the newly formed Popular Front. In Lithuania, efforts by the Republican Communist Party leadership to impose delegates to the Nineteenth Soviet Party Congress produced a stormy backlash among reformers in the Lithuanian Academy of Science and the formation of a popular front known as Sajūdis (or Movement for Perestroika in Lithuania). Expressions of support by Alexander Yakolev, a key Gorbachev lieutenant, opened the way to even wider mass protests and, as in Estonia, the replacement of the Republican First Secretary by a strong supporter of the Sajūdis.

In Latvia, mass protests were triggered by the Writers' Union and other official cultural organizations, which spotlighted long histories of ethnic exclusion by calling for demonstrations to commemorate Stalinist deportations of 1949. There, as well as in Lithuania, mass demonstrations split the Communist Party. Popular front forces converged in the massive Baltic Way protests of August 23, 1989, when human chains were formed across all three states on the 50th anniversary of the Stalin-Ribbentrop Pact. Gorbachev's acknowledgment of the pact, which had sanctioned Soviet occupation of the Baltics, unleashed another wave of protest and more and more explicit rejection of Soviet authority.

Gorbachev tried unsuccessfully to use force to repress the nationalist movements—most notably in Lithuania in February 1991—and independence was not formally resolved until the aftermath of the August putsch and the effective dissolution of the Soviet Union. Nonetheless, in all three

[55] Beissinger 2002: 171–76.

Baltic cases, as well as Armenia,[56] the Soviets faced the same constraints: the exploitation of existing organizations by intellectuals within the state and party apparatus, the rapid expansion of nationalist organizations and protest, followed by the seizure of state or party organizations that were ultimately turned to nationalist ends.

Although the Soviet Union clearly matches our conception of a regime that closes off contestation, the secessionist movements in the Baltics and elsewhere in the Soviet Union would appear to challenge our emphasis on the importance of long-standing organizational resources. Although these movements drew on nationalist identifications maintained through language, literature, the church, and historical associations, they were led initially by relatively small nationalist organizations that did not have deep roots in civil society. Are these cases anomalies to our theoretical expectation that organization matters? Did "prairie fire" mobilizations matter in these cases?

In fact, the initial organizational deficiencies of nationalist oppositions were overcome first by liberalizing concessions that provided an opportunity for groups to form and grow and then by the capture of existing Soviet institutions themselves. The effective capture of state institutions was quickly turned to broader nationalist purposes and ultimately resulted in "popular fronts" with wider organizational foundations. Thus, although somewhat different from the civil society organizations in the union and other ethnonationalist cases, these examples nonetheless confirm the importance of institutional resources for mounting sustained challenges to authoritarian incumbents.

CONCLUSION

The new distributive conflict models have not generally considered either variation in the nature of authoritarian rule, political exclusion, and repression, or capacity for collective action as key variables linking social and political grievances to mass mobilization and regime change. Nor does overall economic performance play a central role in these models;

---

[56]The Armenian nationalist movement played out much more violently than those in the Baltics, with armed conflicts over the Armenian ethnic enclave in Azerbaijan, called Nagorno-Karabakh (N-K). Again, however, local Soviets played a crucial role in the mobilizations. The conflicts were triggered by a decision of the N-K parliament to secede from Azerbaijan and join with Armenia. This move was supported by the Armenian Communist Party, but it was decisively defeated in the Soviet elections by a newly formed Armenian Nationalist Movement (ANM). Now dominated by the ANM, the Armenian Supreme Soviet quickly declared sovereignty and the incorporation of N-K, and broke with the Soviet Union in August 1991.

grievances are assumed to arise primarily out of socioeconomic inequalities. In this chapter, we challenged these omissions by using our causal process observations in two ways. First, we painted a stylized arc of a distributive conflict transition—from authoritarian status quo ante to mass mobilization and the exit of incumbents—and considered some simple distributions of these characteristics as a way of identifying the share and identity of cases that conformed and did not conform with our theoretical priors. We began with the vulnerability of different types of authoritarian regimes to mass mobilization from below and considered the significance of organizational resources, particularly unions and ethnonationalist organizations, to the collapse of authoritarian rule. We also noted other features of the transition process that are germane to current debates about democratization. Violence and direct displacement of incumbents did occur in some of the distributive conflict cases, but the dominant pattern of exit was credible and sustained mobilization that raised the costs of continued authoritarian rule. Elections did play a focal point in some cases, as did political parties, but even where they did, it was typically in conjunction with the mobilization of both protest and grievance on the part of civil society organizations.

We then turned to more focused cases, but selected to reflect a wide diversity of countries: by region, level of development, and economic circumstances. We used these cases to trace causal mechanisms more closely, and also to take note of several other causal factors that operated. Most notable in this regard was confirmation of the significant role played by poor economic performance and economic crises in igniting opposition and weakening the capacity of the state to respond.

Our findings are somewhat counterintuitive, and even appear contradictory in one important respect. Regimes that are more repressive and lacking in channels of representation are more rather than less likely to experience distributive conflict transitions. These dynamics suggest the significant difficulties repressive regimes face in maintaining political rule over the long run, even when they appear relatively successful. The installation of labor- and ethnically-repressive regimes often followed earlier waves of distributive conflict in a pattern we take up in more detail in our discussion of reversions. However, the ability to fully repress organizations with long-standing histories, identities, and repertoires of collective action proved extraordinarily difficult, even in single-party systems such as Poland and Romania. In the face of mobilization from below, repression ultimately proved untenable.

APPENDIX

Table A3.1a CGV Distributive Conflict Transitions.
(N = 42)

	Hadenius-Teorell-Wahman Regime Type and Subtype (t-5)	Labor Repressive or Ethnically Exclusionary Regimes	Polity Score (t-5)	Freedom House Civil Liberties Index (t-5)
Albania 1991	One-party		−9	7
Argentina 1983	Military	Labor repressive	−9	5
Armenia 1991	One-party	Ethnic exclusionary	−7	7
Benin 1991	One-party		−7	7
Bolivia 1982	Military	Labor repressive	−7	4
Brazil 1985	Military	Labor repressive	−4	3
Bulgaria 1990	One-party		−7	7
Burundi 1993	Military	Ethnic exclusionary	−7	6
Burundi 2005	Military	Ethnic exclusionary	−1	6
Congo 1992	Military/military one-party		−8	6
El Salvador 1984	Military	Labor repressive	−4	4
Estonia 1991	One-party	Ethnic exclusionary	−7	7
Fiji 1992	Military	Ethnic exclusionary	−3	5
Georgia 2004	Multiparty		5	4
Guatemala 1986	Military	Labor repressive	−5	6
Indonesia 1999	Military/military multiparty		−7	6
Kenya 1998	Multiparty		−5	6
Kyrgyzstan 2005	Multiparty		−3	5

(*continued*)

Table A3.1a (*continued*)

	Hadenius-Teorell-Wahman Regime Type and Subtype (t-5)	Labor Repressive or Ethnically Exclusionary Regimes	Polity Score (t-5)	Freedom House Civil Liberties Index (t-5)
Latvia 1991	One-party	Ethnic exclusionary	−7	7
Lithuania 1991	One-party	Ethnic exclusionary	−7	7
Madagascar 1993	Multiparty		−6	5
Malawi 1994	One-party		−9	6
Maldives 2009	No-party		NA	4
Mali 1992	Military/military one-party		−7	6
Mongolia 1990	One-party		−7	7
Nepal 1990	Monarchy/no-party monarchy	Ethnic exclusionary	−2	4
Nepal 2008*	Monarchy	Ethnic exclusionary	−6	4
Niger 1993	Military		−7	6
Niger 2000*	Multiparty		−6	5
Nigeria 1999	Military		−7	6
Pakistan 2008	Military/military multiparty		−5	5
Peru 1980	Military		−7	4
Philippines 1986	Multiparty	Labor repressive	−8	4
Poland 1989	One-party		−7	5
Romania 1990	One-party		−8	7
South Korea 1988	Military/military multiparty	Labor repressive	−5	6
Sri Lanka 1989	Multiparty	Ethnic exclusionary	5	4
Sudan 1986	Military/military one-party		−7	5
Suriname 1988	Military		−6	6
Thailand 1992*	Military		2	3

Table A3.1a (*continued*)

	Hadenius-Teorell-Wahman Regime Type and Subtype (t-5)	Labor Repressive or Ethnically Exclusionary Regimes	Polity Score (t-5)	Freedom House Civil Liberties Index (t-5)
Ukraine 1991	One-party		–7	7
Uruguay 1985	Military	Labor repressive	–7	5

Sources: Hadenius, Teorell, and Wahman (2012); Freedom House (2014b); Marshall, Gurr, and Jaggers (2013). Freedom House scores are on a scale of 1–7, with 1 the greatest protection of civil liberties, 7 the least.

Note: Asterisks indicate cases in the Hadenius-Teorell-Wahman dataset that undergo changes in coding in the five years prior to the transition; we seek to identify the dominant authoritarian form in the following notes and in some cases also adjust Polity and Freedom House scores accordingly. The following notes explain these codings.

Notes on CGV distributive conflict cases: Nepal reverted from multiparty to monarchical rule in 2002 and is coded "other/transitional" in 2006–7 and multiparty authoritarian in 2008. We code the authoritarian status quo ante as monarchical. Niger (1992) is coded as military from 1987 until 1990, and then as "other/transitional" in 1991–92; we code it as military. For Niger (2000), the Polity coding is 8 for 1995, but it reverts in 1996–99 to –6; we code it as –6 for the preauthoritarian period. Thailand is coded as military/military multiparty in 1987, but transitions to multiparty authoritarian in 1988–90, before reverting to military in 1991. Throughout this period, the military remained the dominant political force in the country, and we code the authoritarian status-quo ante as military. Regime codings and Polity and Freedom House scores for Armenia, Estonia, Latvia, and Lithuania are the codings for the Soviet Union in the relevant years.

Table A3.1b CGV Elite-Led Transitions.
(*N* = 36)

	Hadenius-Teorell-Wahman Regime Type and Subtype (t-5)	Labor Repressive or Ethnically Exclusionary Regimes	Polity Score (t-5)	Freedom House Civil Liberties Index (t-5)
Bangladesh 1986*	Military		–4	5
Belarus 1991	One-party		–7	7
Bhutan 2007	Monarchy/ no-party monarchy		–10	5
Cape Verde 1990	One-party		–3	6
Central African Republic 1993	Military/military one-party		–7	6

(*continued*)

Table A3.1b (*continued*)

	Hadenius-Teorell-Wahman Regime Type and Subtype (t-5)	Labor Repressive or Ethnically Exclusionary Regimes	Polity Score (t-5)	Freedom House Civil Liberties Index (t-5)
Chile 1990	Military	Labor repressive	–6	5
Comoros 1990	One-party		–7	6
Comoros 2004	Military		NA	
Croatia 1991	Multiparty		NA	4
Czechoslovakia 1989	One-party		–6	6
Ghana 1993*	Military		–7	6
Grenada 1984	Military/rebel regime		NA	5
Guinea-Bissau 2000	Multiparty		3	3
Guinea-Bissau 2004*	Multiparty		5	3
Honduras 1982*	Military		–1	3
Hungary 1990	One-party		–7	5
Liberia 2006*	Multiparty		0	6
Macedonia 1991	One-party		–6	5
Mauritania 2007*	Military	Ethnic exclusionary	–6	5
Mexico 2000	Multiparty		4	4
Nepal 1999	Multiparty		5	4
Nicaragua 1984	Military/rebel regime		0	5
Pakistan 1988	Military/military no-party		–7	5
Panama 1989	Military/military multiparty		–6	3
Paraguay 1989	Multiparty		–8	5
Peru 2001	Multiparty		1	3
São Tomé and Principe 1991	One-party		NA	7
Senegal 2000	Multiparty		–1	5
Serbia 2000	Multiparty		–7	6

Table A3.1b (*continued*)

	Hadenius-Teorell-Wahman Regime Type and Subtype (t-5)	Labor Repressive or Ethnically Exclusionary Regimes	Polity Score (t-5)	Freedom House Civil Liberties Index (t-5)
Sierra Leone 1996*	Civil war		−7	6
Sierra Leone 1998*	Civil war		−6	7
Sierra Leone 2007	Multiparty		5	4
Suriname 1991	Military		−5	6
Taiwan 1996	Multiparty		−1	3
Thailand 2008*	Military/military multiparty		9	3
Turkey 1983*	Military	Labor repressive	−5	5
Uganda 1980	Military		−7	7

Notes on CGV elite-led transitions: Asterisks indicate cases in the Hadenius-Teorell-Wahman dataset that undergo changes in coding in the five years prior to the transition; we seek to identify the dominant authoritarian form in the following notes and in some cases also adjust Polity and Freedom House scores accordingly. Bangladesh is coded as a military multiparty regime in 1981, but reverts to a traditional military regime from 1982; we code it as military. Ghana is coded as a traditional military regime from 1988 until 1991, but as a multiparty regime in 1992; we code it as military. Guinea-Bissau is coded as military in 1999, but is coded multiparty in both 1994–98 and again in 2000–2001. It is then coded as "other" in 2002 and military in 2003 before the transition; we code the dominant authoritarian form as multiparty. Honduras is coded as military from 1977 to 1981, except for an "other/transitional" coding in 1979; we code it as military. Liberia is coded multiparty in 2001–2, "other/transitional" in 2003–4, and multiparty again in 2005. We code it as multiparty. Mauritania is coded as multiparty from 2002 to 2004, but reverts to military in 2005–6; we code it as military. Sierra Leone is coded as one-party in 1991, military from 1992 to 1995, multiparty in 1996, then as "other/civil war" from 1997 to 2000, transitional in 2001, and multiparty from 2003 to 2006. We have coded the case as "civil war" for 1996 and 1998, but multiparty for 2007. Suriname is coded as military in 1986–87, as a democracy in 1988, then military again in 1989–90; we code it as military. Taiwan is coded as multiparty in 1991, democracy in 1992, multiparty authoritarian in 1993, then democratic through 1996. We code the case as multiparty due to the gradual opening of the electoral system. Thailand was democratic from 2003 to 2005, but reverts to military/military multiparty rule in 2006. We code the case as military because the immediate context of the transition was the coup of 2006. Turkey was a democracy in 1978–79, but reverted to military rule from 1980 to 1982. The immediate political context of democratization was the military regime; Polity and Freedom House scores are for 1980–82.

Regime codings and Polity and Freedom House scores for Belarus are for the relevant Soviet years; regime codings and Polity and Freedom House scores for Macedonia are for the relevant years for Yugoslavia.

Table A3.2a Polity Distributive Conflict Transitions.
(N = 36)

	Hadenius-Teorell-Wahman Regime Type and Subtype (t-5)	Labor Repressive or Ethnically Exclusionary Regimes	Polity Score (t-5)	Freedom House Civil Liberties Index (t-5)
Argentina 1983	Military	Labor repressive	−9	5
Armenia 1991	One-party	Ethnic exclusionary	−7	7
Bangladesh 1991	Military/military multiparty		−5	5
Benin 1991	One-party		−7	7
Bolivia 1982	Military	Labor repressive	−7	4
Brazil 1985	Military	Labor repressive	−4	3
Bulgaria 1990	One-party		−1	6
Burundi 2005	Military	Ethnic exclusionary	−1	6
Dominican Republic 1996*	Multiparty		6	3
Ecuador 2002*	Democracy		8	3
El Salvador 1984	Military	Labor repressive	−4	4
Estonia 1991	One-party	Ethnic exclusionary	−7	7
Georgia 2004	Multiparty		5	4
Guatemala 1986	Military	Labor repressive	−5	6
Haiti 1990*	Military		−9	6
Indonesia 1999	Military/military multiparty		−7	6
Latvia 1991	One-party		−7	7
Lesotho 1993	Military		−7	5
Lithuania 1991	One-party	Ethnic exclusionary	−7	7
Madagascar 1993	Multiparty		−6	5
Malawi 1994	One-party		−9	6
Mali 1992	Military/military one-party		−7	6
Mongolia 1990	One-party		−7	7

Table A3.2a (*continued*)

	Hadenius-Teorell-Wahman Regime Type and Subtype (t-5)	Labor Repressive or Ethnically Exclusionary Regimes	Polity Score (t-5)	Freedom House Civil Liberties Index (t-5)
Nepal 2006	Multiparty		6	4
Niger 1992	Military		–7	6
Peru 1980	Military		–7	4
Philippines 1987	Multiparty	Labor repressive	–8	4
Poland 1991	One-party		–7	5
South Africa 1992	Multiparty		4	6
South Korea 1988	Military/military multiparty	Labor repressive	–5	6
Sudan 1986	Military/military One-party		–7	5
Thailand 1992*	Military		2	3
Ukraine 1991	One-party		–7	7
Ukraine 1994*	Multiparty		5	4
Uruguay 1985	Military	Labor repressive	–7	5
Zambia 1991	One-party		–9	5

Notes on Polity distributive conflict transitions: Asterisks indicate cases in the Hadenius-Teorell-Wahman dataset that undergo changes in coding in the five years prior to the transition; we seek to identify the dominant authoritarian form in the following notes and in some cases also adjust Polity and Freedom House scores accordingly. The Dominican Republic was democratic in 1991–93 before reverting to multiparty authoritarian rule in 1994–95. Ecuador is coded as continuously democratic in the HTW dataset; the transition reflects a very short military intervention that almost immediately returns to democratic rule; we have excluded it from the event counts in Table 3.1. Haiti is coded as one party in 1985, but shifts to military rule from 1986 to 1989. Regime codings and Polity and Freedom House scores for Armenia, Estonia, Latvia, Lithuania, and Ukraine (1991) are the scores for the Soviet Union in the relevant years. For the Ukraine (1994), the Polity and Freedom House scores are for the period of reversion to multiparty authoritarian rule in 1993.

Table A3.2b Polity Elite-Led Transitions.
(N = 37)

	Hadenius-Teorell-Wahman Regime Type and Subtype (t-5)	Labor Repressive or Ethnically Exclusionary Regimes	Polity Score (t-5)	Freedom House Civil Liberties Index (t-5)
Albania 2002	Multiparty		5	4
Belarus 1991	One-party		−7	7
Cape Verde 1990	One-party		−3	6
Chile 1989	Military	Labor repressive	−6	5
Comoros 2004	Multiparty		−2	6
Croatia 2000	Multiparty		−5	4
Czechoslovakia 1990	One-party		−6	6
Fiji 1999	Multiparty	Ethnic exclusionary	5	4
Guinea-Bissau 2005*	Multiparty		5	3
Guyana 1992	Multiparty		−7	5
Haiti 1994*	Military		−6	7
Honduras 1982*	Military		−1	3
Honduras 1989	Democracy		6	3
Hungary 1990	One-party		−7	5
Kenya 2002	Multiparty		−2	6
Liberia 2006*	Multiparty		0	6
Macedonia 1991	One-party		−6	5
Malawi 2004	Multiparty		6	3
Malaysia 2008	Multiparty	Ethnic exclusionary	3	5
Mexico 1997	Multiparty		0	3
Moldova 1993*	Multiparty		5	5
Nepal 1999	Multiparty	Ethnic exclusionary	5	4
Nicaragua 1990	Multiparty		−1	5
Niger 2004	Multiparty		5	5

Table A3.2b (*continued*)

	Hadenius-Teorell-Wahman Regime Type and Subtype (t-5)	Labor Repressive or Ethnically Exclusionary Regimes	Polity Score (t-5)	Freedom House Civil Liberties Index (t-5)
Pakistan 1988	Military/military no-party		−7	5
Panama 1989	Military/military multiparty		−6	3
Paraguay 1992	Multiparty		−8	6
Peru 2001	Multiparty		1	3
Romania 1996	Multiparty		5	5
Russia 2000	Multiparty		3	4
Senegal 2000	Multiparty		−1	5
Serbia 2000	Multiparty		−7	6
Solomon Islands 2003	Multiparty*		NA	4*
Sri Lanka 2006*	Multiparty	Ethnic exclusionary	5	3
Taiwan 1992	Multiparty		−1	4
Turkey 1983*	Military	Labor repressive	−5	5
Zambia 2008	Multiparty		5	4

Notes on Polity elite-led transitions: Asterisks indicate cases in the Hadenius-Teorell-Wahman dataset that undergo changes in coding in the five years prior to the transition; we seek to identify the dominant authoritarian form in the following notes and in some cases also adjust Polity and Freedom House scores accordingly. The Comoros is coded as military in 1999, then multiparty from 2000 to 2003. Guinea-Bissau is coded as military in 1999, but is coded multiparty in both 1994–98 and again in 2000–2001. It is then coded as "other" in 2002 and military in 2003 before the transition; we code the dominant authoritarian form as multiparty. Haiti is coded as multiparty in 1990, but military in 1989 and again in 1991–93; we code it as military. Malawi is coded as democratic in 1999–2000 before reverting to multiparty rule in 2001–3. The codings for Moldova reflect its transition to a multiparty authoritarian regime in 1991–92; Polity scores are for those two years, Freedom House scores are for 1992. The Solomon Islands is coded as democratic in 1998–99 but reverts to multiparty authoritarian rule in 2000–2002. Polity codings are for a transitional regime; Freedom House score is for 2000–2001. Sri Lanka is coded as multiparty authoritarian in 2001–2, but then as democratic in 2003–5; we code it as multiparty authoritarian. Polity and Freedom House scores are for 2003–5. Turkey was a democracy in 1978–9, but reverted to military rule in 1980–82. The immediate political context of democratization was the military regime; Polity and Freedom House scores are for 1980–82.

Table A3.3 The Social Foundations of Distributive Conflict Transitions, 1980–2008: Cases.

Country	Democracy Coding	Union Transitions	Ethnonationalist Transitions	Riots (Distinct from Protests)	Revolutionary Armies and Militias
Albania 1991	CGV only	X		X	
Argentina 1983	CGV/Polity	X			
Armenia 1991*	CGV/Polity		X	X	X
Bangladesh 1991	Polity only	X			
Benin 1991*	CGV/Polity	X		X	
Bolivia 1982	CGV/Polity	X			
Brazil 1985	CGV/Polity	X			
Bulgaria 1990*	CGV/Polity	X			
Burundi 1993	CGV only		X	X	X
Burundi 2005	Polity only		X	X	X
Republic of the Congo 1992*	CGV only	X			
Dominican Republic 1996	Polity only	X			
Ecuador 2002*	CGV only	X	X		

El Salvador 1984*	CGV/Polity	X			X
El Salvador 1990*	CGV/Polity	X			X
Estonia 1991*	CGV only	X	X		
Fiji 1992*	CGV/Polity	X	X		
Georgia 2004	CGV only	X			X
Guatemala 1986	Polity only		X		X
Guatemala 1996	Polity only		X		X
Haiti 1990	Polity only			X	
Indonesia 1999	CGV/Polity	X			
Kenya 1998*	CGV only				
Kyrgyzstan 2005	CGV only		X		
Latvia 1991*	CGV/Polity		X		
Lesotho 1993*	Polity only	X			
Lithuania 1991*	CGV/Polity	X	X	X	X
Madagascar 1992–1993	CGV/Polity	X			
Malawi 1994*	CGV/Polity	X			X
Maldives 2008	CGV only	X			
Mali 1992*	CGV/Polity	X			X

(continued)

Table A3.3 (*continued*)

Country	Democracy Coding	Union Transitions	Ethnonationalist Transitions	Riots (Distinct from Protests)	Revolutionary Armies and Militias
Mongolia 1992*	CGV/Polity	X			
Nepal 1990	CGV only	X			
Nepal 2006–8	CGV/Polity	X			
Niger 1992–93*	CGV/Polity	X			
Niger 2000	CGV only	X		X	
Nigeria 1999	CGV only	X		X	X
Pakistan 2008	CGV only				
Peru 1980	CGV/Polity	X			
Philippines 1986	CGV/Polity				
Poland 1989–1991	CGV/Polity	X			
Romania 1990	CGV only	X			X
South Africa 1992	Polity only	X	X		X
South Korea 1988	CGV/Polity	X			X

Sri Lanka 1989*	CGV only		X		X
Sudan 1986	CGV/Polity		X		X
Suriname 1988*	CGV only	X			
Thailand 1992	CGV/Polity				
Ukraine 1991*	CGV/Polity	X	X		
Ukraine 1994*	Polity only	X	X		
Uruguay 1985	CGV only	X		X	
Zambia 1991	Polity only	X			
CGV transitions (42)		29	11	8	13
Polity transitions (36)		25	11	6	12
CGV and Polity transitions (52)		36	16	10	17

Note: Asterisks denote cases in the dataset coded as "ambiguous" for the reasons reviewed in Chapter 2.

CHAPTER 4

Elite-Led Transitions

INTERNATIONAL FACTORS AND POLITICS AT THE TOP

IN THE ABSENCE OF THE PRESSURES FROM BELOW that characterize distributive conflict transitions, what would induce autocratic rulers to acquiesce to—or even initiate—democratic reforms? We focus here on both the international and domestic political factors that might lead incumbent elites or their rivals to conclude that there is more to be gained by accepting a transition than by defending the status quo. The international influences include what Levitsky and Way call both "leverage" and "linkage," but we think of both as operating through the incentives they create for authoritarian incumbents and contending elites.[1] Although these pressures may also operate in distributive conflict transitions, they are complementary or secondary to the mobilization of mass protest.

In elite-led transitions, by contrast, we would expect international inducements and constraints to play a larger role in the calculations of authoritarian incumbents. The collapse of the Soviet Union and its empire in Eastern Europe, as well as Yugoslavia, removed protections that client elites had enjoyed and as a result were directly responsible for a number of both distributive conflict and elite-led transitions in this period; as we saw in Figures 0.1 and 0.2, democratic transitions clustered around 1990. But even before that collapse, the waning of the Cold War had fundamentally altered the incentives of the major powers with respect to their authoritarian clients. In about a third of the elite-led cases, outside powers openly abandoned authoritarian states they had previously supported or even intervened directly to promote democracy. In an overlapping set of cases, donors used aid to induce authoritarian incumbents to undertake political as well as economic reforms.

International influences were not limited to loss of foreign protection or direct leverage. In our regressions in Chapter 2, we showed that "neighborhood effects"—the share of an authoritarian regime's neighbors that were democratic—also had consistently positive effects in the models of elite-led transitions. In this chapter, we show some of the channels through which

---

[1] Levitsky and Way 2006, 2010.

these neighborhood forces operated, including through both positive and negative incentives emanating from regional institutions.

However, the multiple channels of foreign influence ultimately operated in conjunction with the domestic political calculus of authoritarian rulers, elite allies, and their competitors. Setting aside the small number of cases in which external actors directly imposed democratic rule, we identify three different elite-led pathways to more democratic rule. In elite-displacement transitions, authoritarian incumbents were ousted by rival domestic elites, who in turn initiated liberalization and democratization processes. In preemptive transitions, incumbents themselves initiated transition processes. In contrast, institutional transitions involve more incremental changes—ones that are captured only by the continuous Polity measure. In these cases, incumbent elites decided to abide by constitutional constraints or allow elections that they themselves put into place.

Each of these pathways reflected different proximate causal processes. But all ultimately rested on calculations of at least some within the ruling coalition that they could benefit by making institutional compromises. Such transitions appear more likely where incumbents—or competing factions—have organizational resources such as party organizations, control over patronage, or broader advantages of incumbency that lead them to believe they can operate in a more competitive political environment.[2]

In the remainder of the chapter, we address these international and domestic political factors in turn. In each, we consider both distributions of cases exhibiting the proposed causal mechanisms—both international and domestic—and cases that exhibit the commonality of these causal processes despite other identifiable differences such as region and level of development.

International Factors in the Elite-Led Cases

A growing literature has found a wide array of international factors that might contribute to the protection of human rights, political liberalization, democratic regime change, and the protection of democratic rule from authoritarian reversion. These factors range from direct military intervention (although hotly contested), sanctions, and "naming and shaming" pressures, to more subtle forces, such as the effects of membership in international organizations, transnational linkages, diffusion,

---

[2] Slater and Wong 2013.

and socialization.[3] These factors, to be sure, played a role in a number of distributive conflict transitions as well; in Chapter 1 we identified six cases that we coded as "ambiguous" because of the role played by outside actors in the transition process (El Salvador, Fiji, Kenya, Lesotho, Malawi and Niger). Nor can we rule out the fact that diffusion was at work in some of the mass mobilizations that we treat as largely domestic; the demonstrations that brought down communist regimes in the Baltics, and the Arab Spring are plausible examples.

As noted, however, we would expect that external forces would be more consequential in elite-led transitions. Following Levitsky and Way, we group these international factors into two broad categories.[4] The first is the exercise of *leverage*: actions by outside parties that directly induce authoritarian incumbents to reform or step aside. The policy tools for doing so range from direct military intervention and threats to sanctions and other forms of political and economic isolation, but also include conditional inducements such as the extension of aid. The second cluster of factors, what Levitsky and Way call *linkage*, encompass a variety of political and economic ties and transnational relationships that operate on leader incentives more indirectly.[5] Although the scope of these factors is wide, we focus particular attention on neighborhood effects and the role of regional institutions, both as a proxy and as a direct influence on institutional choices.

As Levitsky and Way argue, leverage and linkage are not mutually exclusive. For example, if an authoritarian regime has dense linkages to Western powers or more democratic neighbors, those ties can increase the salience of political developments for outside actors and thus increase the likelihood that it will be subject to more direct leverage. But

[3] On military intervention, see Kegley and Hermann 1997; Gleditsch, Christiansen, and Hegre 2007; Goldsmith 2007. On sanctions, see Pape 1997; Marinov 2005; Escribà Folch and Wright 2010. On "naming and shaming" pressures, see Hafner-Burton 2013. On international organizations, see Pevehouse 2002; Mansfield and Pevehouse 2006; Hafner-Burton 2013. On transnational linkages, see Levitsky and Way 2006, 2010. On diffusion, see Gleditsch 2002; Gleditsch and Ward 2006; Leeson and Dean 2009; Elkink 2011. On socialization, see Kelley 2006; Simmons, Dobbin, and Garrett 2006.

[4] Levitsky and Way 2006, 2010.

[5] Although we focus primarily on inducements, as noted above others have highlighted learning, emulation, and socialization as well. Levitsky and Way distinguish five types of linkage, most of which could be seen as affecting elite incentives and capabilities vis-à-vis oppositions: *economic*, operating not through specific exercise of leverage but of the generalized benefits from maintaining particular ties; *geopolitical*, which includes ties to Western governments and Western-led alliances and organizations; *social*, which includes tourism, migration, diaspora communities, and elite education in the West; *communication*, which includes cross-border telecommunications, Internet connections, and Western-media penetration; and *transnational civil society* linkage, which includes ties to international NGOs, churches, party organizations, and other networks.

Levitsky and Way do not believe that leverage and linkage are perfect substitutes, or that leverage alone is likely to be effective in generating robust democratic transitions; to the contrary, they are suspicious of the political effects of leverage alone, as are others.[6] However, our purpose is not to adjudicate among the variety of external factors that operate, nor to make strong claims about their general causal effect. Our aim is simply to outline some of the more prominent mechanisms through which external factors affected the incentives facing authoritarian incumbents and thus contributed to the elite-led transition processes that we describe.

Leverage

Four transitions in our dataset were the result of foreign military interventions that directly removed an authoritarian incumbent and/or established a democratic regime. Regime changes in Grenada and Panama came in the wake of American military interventions that ousted the governments of Bernard Coard and Manuel Noriega, respectively. In Haiti, General Raoul Cedras yielded power to a transitional civilian authority and was escorted out of the country in the face of an explicit threat of intervention by a US-led multinational military force of 21,000 troops. In Cyprus, the transition to a democratic regime in the Turkish part of the island occurred following competing interventions on the part of Greece and Turkey that resulted in de facto partition.

Moreover, as Table 4.1 shows, there are an additional ten discrete cases in which outside military forces played a role, even if they did not directly displace authoritarian incumbents:[7] Comoros 1990 and 2004, Guinea-Bissau 2000 and 2004, Liberia 2006, Nicaragua 1990, Serbia 2000, Sierra Leone 1996–98 and 2007, and Uganda 1980. In total, fully 15 of 51 elite-led transitions—just under 30 percent—involved outside military intervention, and this does not include cases such as Suriname (1991), in which domestic negotiations among competing parties took place under the shadow of possible outside intervention.

The causal mechanisms at work in these ten cases exhibit strong commonalities. In eight of the ten,[8] the mode of transition was what we call "elite displacement": incumbents were initially displaced by rival domestic elites, which then cooperated with external actors and domestic stakeholders in a transitional process. Indeed, just over half of *all* elite displacement

[6]Enterline and Greig 2008; Goldstein 2008; Gleditsch, Christiansen, and Hegre 2007; Peksen 2011.

[7]For the purpose of this count, we treat the two discrete transitions in Sierra Leone in 1996 and 1998 as a single case.

[8]Comoros 1990 and 2004, Guinea-Bissau 2000 and 2004, Liberia 2006, Sierra Leone 1996–98 and 2007, and Uganda 1980.

cases (8 of 15) involved such outside intervention. In another case of out-side intervention—Nicaragua—the incumbent leadership undertook po-litical reforms preemptively to reduce the threat of the armed opposition backed by the United States.[9]

Not surprisingly, such interventions were particularly prevalent among smaller, less-developed countries that were also heavily dependent on ex-ternal assistance (Table 4.1). These included Serbia and Cyprus in Europe and the Central American and Caribbean cases in Latin America. Yet the role of such intervention is particularly marked in Africa, where it accounted for a third of all Polity elite-led transitions in that region, and over half of all such transitions in the CGV dataset.

Outside intervention took a variety of forms. In some cases, major pow-ers or more powerful neighbors intervened bilaterally. In Nicaragua, the Sandinista regime undertook preemptive moves toward liberalization fol-lowing the loss of Cuban and Soviet support, but also in the context of long-standing American backing for the *contra* rebels. In the Comoros, a French show of force was crucial in forcing coup conspirator Bob Denard out of the country in 1990. Nor were these interventions limited to the major powers. Tanzanian troops fought alongside Ugandan exiles in the intervention that overthrew Idi Amin in Uganda in 1979. Less effectively, Senegal and Guinea—at French urging—intervened in Guinea-Bissau in 1998, followed by the establishment of a West African peacekeeping force.

In other cases—again, most notably low-income cases—major and re-gional powers intervened in the context of complex multilateral efforts. These interventions sought to settle long-standing civil conflicts, mitigate dire humanitarian challenges, and provide longer-run economic and po-litical assistance, including through election assistance and monitoring. Although the transitions in these civil war cases did not involve the elite/mass cleavages postulated by distributive conflict cases, they did take place against the backdrop of extremely violent, multisided civil conflict among a multiplicity of competing elites, including regional militias, tribal lead-ers, and external actors. In such situations, outside intervention and me-diation was a necessary condition for bringing the conflict to an end.

The transitions in Sierra Leone (1996–98 and 2007, both CGV only) il-lustrate the complexity of such interventions and the long time periods

---

[9] Serbia is the only case where outside intervention was coupled with what we call an "institutional" transition. Following the outbreak of the Kosovo War in 1998, Serbia (Yu-goslavia) first faced Western trade sanctions and then NATO airstrikes on Serbian targets. Initially, this led to an upsurge in nationalist support for Milosevic, but this eroded quickly as external economic pressure and the destruction of infrastructure took a severe economic toll. Milosevic was forced to accept a multilateral settlement of the Kosovo issue, and the electorate subsequently punished him at the polls and forced him to step down.

Table 4.1 Leverage: Aid Dependence and Military Intervention in
Elite-Led Transitions.
(Cases and Shares of Regional Cases)

	Military Intervention		Aid Dependence t-1 (Aid/GDP)	
	CGV Cases/Share of All Regional Cases	Polity Cases/Share of All Regional Cases	CGV Cases	Polity Cases
Europe and Former Soviet Union	Cyprus 1983; Serbia 2000 2/7 = 28.6%	Serbia 2000 1/11 = 9.1%	0.07	0.38
Asia	—	—	—	—
Latin America and the Caribbean	Grenada 1984; Panama 1989 2/9 = 22.2%	Haiti 1994; Panama 1989; Nicaragua 1990 3/10 = 30%	2.05	3.23
Africa	Comoros 1994 and 2004; Guinea-Bissau 2000 and 2004; Liberia 2006; Sierra Leone 1996–8 and 2007; Uganda 1980 8/15 = 53.3%	Comoros 2004; Guinea-Bissau 2004; Liberia 2006 3/9 = 33.3%	11.48	11.37

Note: Cases in italics reflect direct external ouster of authoritarian incumbents (Panama, Grenada, and Haiti) or creation of a new democratic regime (Cyprus).

over which they have an effect.[10] In 1996–97, a failed peace agreement brokered by a UN special envoy was followed by closer involvement on the part of the Economic Community of West African States (ECOWAS), with strong Nigerian involvement through the use of ECOMOG (the ECOWAS Monitoring Group) troops. An ECOWAS group negotiated a new peace plan that included sustained presence on the part of ECOWAS, ECOMOG, the United Nations, and the UN High Commission on Refugees; this early phase of outside involvement helps account for two of the earlier transitions in the country coded in 1996 and 1998.

This international consortium subsequently had to respond to rebel attacks, which it did in part through UN Security Council sanctions and

[10]Zack-Williams 1999; Kandeh 2003; Fithen and Richards 2005; Chistensen and Utas 2008.

the creation of a United Nations Observer Mission in Sierra Leone, supported by military liaison officers and security advisory personnel. When overmatched UN forces were forced to withdraw, the Security Council authorized yet another multilateral force (UNAMSIL) with a wider military mandate as well as support for civil affairs, civilian police, and other administrative and technical support functions.

In this context, the British military played a key role. Its mission was initially limited to evacuating nationals and peacekeepers, but expanded to supporting the government in its fight with the RUF rebels. The RUF gradually began to disarm under pressure, and the Sierra Leonean government eventually signed a ceasefire that required RUF fighters to enter a Disarmament, Demobilization, and Reintegration program in which the British also played a significant role. Subsequently, British forces also assisted in advising and restructuring the armed forces and were redeployed in 2003 in support of the Special Court for Sierra Leone. Although the 2007 elections were still marred by violence among youth gangs and militias associated with the competing parties, it is doubtful that those elections would have occurred without the succession of UN, ECOWAS, and British interventions spanning over a decade.[11]

The other civil war cases in the sample—Guinea-Bissau 2000 and 2004–5 and Liberia 2006—mirrored Sierra Leone, with crucial mediating roles played by consortia of outside actors, including UN peacekeepers, regional military forces, and multilateral and bilateral donors.[12] International consortia were also critical in the resolution of political crises in the Central African Republic in 1993 (the so-called GIBAFOR coalition, consisting of the United States, France, Germany, Japan, the EU, the UN, and the World Bank) and in the Comoros 2004 (African Union).

Direct intervention was not the only means through which outside pressure was brought to bear on small, poorer countries. Sometimes—although not always—authoritarian leaders were vulnerable to the gradual rise of democracy promotion policies, political conditionality with respect to multilateral and bilateral assistance, corresponding reductions in aid, and even sanctions against authoritarian holdouts.[13] As the Cold War waned, the United States not only engineered cosmetic political changes in some aid-dependent clients (for example, Honduras 1989), but also turned its back more sharply on several dictators it had long tolerated (Paraguay 1989). Similarly, the timing of transitions in Nicaragua (1990) and São Tomé and Principe (1991) are suggestive of the influence

[11]National Democratic Institute 2007.
[12]On Guinea-Bissau, see Birikorang 2005 and Marshall, Gurr, and Jaggers 2013 (Polity IV Country Report). On Liberia, see Kieh 2011; Harris 2012.
[13]Carothers 1999, 2004; Carothers and Ottaway 2000; Marshall 2014; Bush 2015.

that declining Soviet support had on its clients. Both of these countries moved toward democracy as a result of preemptive moves on the part of incumbents to politically reposition themselves in the face of a rapidly changing geostrategic landscape.

Over time, the credibility of the efforts on the part of donors to use aid as leverage was buttressed by legislation that restricted aid to authoritarian regimes, albeit with ongoing strategic limitations.[14] Language in the annual foreign operations appropriations legislation of the United States from 1985 forbade aid to any country where a democratic leader was deposed by military coup d'état or decree. The United States took particular interest in several high-profile cases, such as Kenya, where pressure on arap Moi around the elections of 2002 was overt.

We discuss the complex influence of the EU on the European periphery in the next section, but note here that leverage vis-à-vis the African, Caribbean, and Pacific (ACP) partners through the Lomé and Cotonou Agreements was increasingly overt over time.[15] Under articles 366a of the Lomé Convention, and particularly Article 96 of the Cotonou Agreement, signed in 2000, the EU was authorized to call for consultations in the case of coups d'état, flawed electoral processes, or violations of democracy, rule of law, and respect for fundamental human rights and freedoms. From the signing of the Cotonou Agreement through the endpoint of our dataset in 2008, the EU held consultations with 14 countries under these provisions; among them were no fewer than 7 of our elite-led transition cases, including the Comoros (consultations in 1999), Guinea-Bissau (1999 and 2004), Liberia (2001), the Central African Republic (2003), Fiji (2000 and 2007) Niger (1996 and 1999), and Mauritania (2007). Among this group only Liberia was ultimately sanctioned (in 2002) during the time period under consideration here.[16] But "consultations" did take place under the shadow of the ability to withdraw aid, a recurrent complaint on the part of the ACP states.

Linkage: Neighborhood Effects and the Role of Regional Institutions

Although international influence sometimes took the form of the overt exercise of leverage, the geographic clustering of democratization suggests that more subtle external inducements and constraints were also at work

[14] Carothers 2004; Bush 2015.

[15] Bradley 2005; Hazelzet 2005; Mackie and Zinke 2005; Laporte 2007; Andersen 2010.

[16] Sudan, Togo, Haiti, Liberia, Zimbabwe, and Guinea were ultimately sanctioned during the 2009–13 period.

Table 4.2 Neighborhood Effects: Average Percent Share of Democratic Neighbors.
(Elite-Led Transitions by Region, t-1)

	CGV Transitions		Polity Transitions	
	Cases	*Average % Neighboring Democracies*	*Cases*	*Average % Neighboring Democracies*
Europe (including Turkey)	10	27.4	10	45.2
Former Soviet Union	8	0.0	10	49.2
Asia	16	29.4	13	21.1
Latin America	17	64.2	20	67.0
Africa	27	11.7	19	5.9

Note: Proportion of neighboring countries within 500 km of the transition country that were democratic at the time of the transition.

on authoritarian incumbents.[17] Dense economic, social, and communications ties between authoritarian regimes and democratic neighbors can increase the weight of domestic groups with a stake in the country's international standing, provide resources to opposition groups, and even protect them from repression by increasing the visibility of such actions.[18] Social communication and learning can trigger mass mobilization, as the Arab Spring suggests, but can also affect elite calculations about their own stance toward democracy.

We can map these linkage effects geographically by considering the regional distribution of our "neighborhood" variable: the share of countries within a 500-kilometer radius of the transitioning country at t–1 that are democratic (Table 4.2). It is important to emphasize that this variable captures negative as well as positive diffusion effects. As can be seen, the African countries that managed to democratize underwent transitions in much less auspicious neighborhoods than their Asian, European, and Latin American counterparts. The former Soviet cases in the CGV dataset had *no* democratic neighbors, in part because the dataset captures earlier electoral transitions. On the other hand, positive neighborhood effects are particularly apparent in Eastern Europe, the former Soviet Union's Polity

[17]Gleditsch 2002; Gleditsch and Ward 2006; Simmons, Dobbin, and Garrett 2006; Leeson and Dean 2009.
[18]Ooi 2009; Levitsky and Way 2006.

transitions, and Latin America. Although European neighborhood scores appear low, particularly in the CGV dataset, the pull of states to the west of the newly democratizing countries of Eastern Europe was clearly more powerful than those to the east. In both regions, the share of democratic countries and norms, policies, and instruments evolved over time, providing increasingly explicit support for democratic rule.

The mechanisms through which these neighborhood effects operate— as noted—are multiple and complex. But we focus here on one important channel: developments in regional institutions and the inducements and constraints that they bring to bear. Particularly in Europe and Latin America, we see the emergence of formal rules and norms under which democratic rule and the protection of human rights became a condition for participation in regional institutions. In both regions, a complex mix of diplomatic intervention, inducements, constraints, and socialization processes played at least some role in incentivizing changes to democracy.

EUROPE: THE LURE OF MEMBERSHIP AND THE EMERGENCE OF POLITICAL CONDITIONALITY

In Europe, the EU developed accession processes that permitted quite explicit political quid pro quos. In the early European elite-led transitions in our sample—Czechoslovakia and Hungary—a general public aspiration to join Europe and the West clearly operated, as did the opening of numerous channels of social linkage and communication. But there were no international institutional mechanisms in place to promote those objectives. The early elite-led transitions in the Balkans (Macedonia 1991, CGV/Polity, and Croatia 1991, CGV only) were driven by intra-elite conflicts and calculations around the rapid disintegration of Yugoslavia rather than direct European involvement.

In June 1993, however, the Copenhagen Conclusions outlined explicit political conditions for membership by requiring that aspirant countries had "achieved stability of institutions guaranteeing democracy, the rule of law, human rights and respect for and protection of minorities" along with the two other sets of conditions regarding the existence of a functioning market economy and the ability to take on the complex obligations of the Community's *acquis*.[19] The major instruments of conditionality involved intrusive benchmarking and monitoring of candidate countries at different stages along the accession process,[20] with the quid pro quo of

[19] Smith 2000; Grabbe 2001; Schimmelfennig and Sedelmeier 2004; Kelley 2006.

[20] The stages in this process included entry into Stabilization and Association Agreement negotiations, accession negotiations, negotiation ("opening" and "closing") of the thirty-one chapters of the *acquis*, signing of the Accession Treaty, ratifying the Accession Treaty, and ultimately entering the European Union.

privileged access to trade and aid. These negotiations began in earnest only in 1997, and with democracies that were already consolidated. We would therefore expect that these processes played a much more significant role in countries that transitioned later: Romania (1996, Polity), Serbia (2000, CGV/Polity), Croatia (2000, Polity), and Albania (2002, Polity). However, political conditionality also affected the quality of democracy in countries that had transitioned earlier, for example in wide-ranging political reforms undertaken by Turkey following its designation as a candidate country at the Helsinki Summit in 1999.[21] It is important to acknowledge that these complex policies, combining inducements, constraints, and socialization, were by no means consistently successful, even within Eastern Europe proper: Romania in the first half of the 1990s, Slovakia under the Mečiar government, Croatia under Tuđman, and Serbia under Milosevic are examples of holdouts. Furthermore, European influence necessarily waned with geographic distance and reduced likelihood of actually being able to join the EU; we take up the case of Turkey in Chapter 8.

CAUSAL PROCESS OBSERVATION: ROMANIA AND ALBANIA

Nonetheless, Romania and Albania show the mechanisms through which neighborhood effects in Europe operated. The transition from a Communist regime in Romania in 1991 was marked by widespread violence and the execution of longtime dictator Nicolae Ceausescu. Although the case is coded as a democratic transition in the CGV dataset, progress toward democratic rule was limited at best.[22] Much of the opposition to the old regime, led by Ion Iliescu, was initially orchestrated by members of the Communist security forces.[23] Iliescu's National Salvation Front (FSN), dominated by former Communists, came to power in a highly controlled election in 1990. Immediately following the election, the Security Force mobilized thousands of miners to attack opposition party headquarters and politicians. The regime subsequently deployed censorship, legal pressures, and physical force to harass and intimidate opponents.

[21] Although not relevant to the cases in our sample, the Commission outlined the so-called European Neighbourhood Policy in May 2004 (ENP; Kelley 2006). While distinct from a path to membership, the ENP offered to extend preferential ties to North African and Middle Eastern countries that had sea borders with the EU as well as the Ukraine, Belarus, Moldova, and the countries of the Caucasus, based on "mutual commitment to shared values," including democracy, human rights, and rule of law. Aydin-Düzgit and Keyman 2004 and 2013.

[22] In fact, Polity codes the country as a 5 from 1990 to 1995, just below the democratic threshold.

[23] Siani-Davies 2003.

These abuses, however, met with strong reactions from Europe and the United States, and the government was forced to acquiesce to democratic reforms. The EU froze desperately needed aid in response to the miners' attack of 1990,[24] and a coalition of European powers effectively postponed consideration of Romania's bid to join the Council of Europe.[25] Continued pressure from the EU and the United States induced the Iliescu government to accede to new elections in 1992, which, though characterized by fraud and manipulation, allowed the opposition to regroup and forced Iliescu into a second-round runoff. In 1993, an accession agreement with the European Union strengthened incentives to liberalize the political system: press censorship eased and the opposition received technical and financial support from Western foundations and NGOs. By 1996, "most of Romania's political actors were aware that the country could not afford to become the pariah of the international community."[26] The regularly scheduled 1996 elections were largely free and fair and won by the liberal opposition Democratic Convention headed by Emil Constantinescu. It was at this point that Romania crossed Polity's 6-point democratic threshold.

Albania shows a similar pattern;[27] CGV marks a transition in 1991, but Polity scores average only 4 from 1991 to 2001. The Communists continued to control parliament after the elections of 1991; and turnover to the Democratic Party government in the 1992 elections did not mark a fundamental change as the new ruling party similarly exploited the powers of office. In the elections of 1996, the Democratic Party's Sali Berisha, a former Communist, overwhelmingly defeated the Socialist Party, but with considerable restrictions on campaigning, the opposition, and press freedom. In 1997, the collapse of a massive Ponzi scheme led to armed revolts and a loss of government control over large parts of the country. Berisha declared a state of emergency, ordered security forces to repress revolt, restricted public gatherings, and imposed additional press censorship.

The Polity transition occurring in 2002, by contrast, came about as a result of strong European inducements and constraints on rival parties In March 1997, the Organization for Security Co-operation in Europe (OSCE), led in this case by Italy, mediated an agreement between Berisha and the opposition for early elections and a government of reconciliation. The opposition Socialist Party won an overwhelming victory under Fatos Nano, but resorted to similar tactics as the Democratic Party by taking

[24] Crowther 2003.
[25] Levitsky and Way 2010: 101.
[26] Tismaneanu 1997, cited in Levitsky and Way 2010: 102.
[27] Biberaj 1999.

actions to suppress the opposition. Although approved by the OSCE, the elections of 2001 generated a political crisis. The Socialist Party was internally split between warring factions; the opposition boycotted parliament and the legislative process and blocked the selection of a president.

In 2002, however, EU foreign ministers explicitly threatened that Albania's entry into the Stabilization and Association Process, a prelude to negotiations over EU entry, would be blocked in the absence of fundamental political compromises. The parties agreed on a consensus candidate for president. The PSS leader Fatos Nano became prime minister but appointed a government of reconciliation that included prominent members of the opposition. Following the political settlement, Romano Prodi, president of the European Commission, was blunt about the quid pro quo: that democracy was part of the European bargain.[28]

THE EVOLUTION OF THE DEMOCRACY NORM IN LATIN AMERICA AND AFRICA

Rapidly changing regional norms are equally apparent in Latin America and Africa, even though the instruments of influence remained considerably weaker than in Europe. The early democratic wave in Latin America—Uruguay, Brazil, Argentina, Peru, and Bolivia—was dominated by distributive conflict transitions, which sharply increased the share of democracies in the region. Early elite-led transitions such as Honduras (1982) and Nicaragua (1984) occurred in Central America, where fewer than half of their neighbors were democratic, but over which the United States exercised substantial influence. By the time of the transitions in Chile and Paraguay in 1989–90, however, 75 percent and 80 percent of the neighbors of these two countries, respectively, were democratic.

These neighborhood effects operated in part through institutional developments.[29] The Organization of American States' (OAS) condemnation of the human rights record of the Somoza regime in Nicaragua was an early precedent, followed by the Protocol of Cartagena de Indias (1985) that first articulated a modest, nonbinding regional democracy norm. The OAS condemned Manuel Noriega's annulment of the 1989 presidential election, and issued similar resolutions vis-à-vis Haiti (1991, including sanctions and endorsement of the UN military mission), Peru (1992), and Guatemala (1993). The OAS's failure to act with respect to Panama set the stage for the American intervention, but the intervention in turn stimulated renewed efforts to strengthen regional norms. The 1991 Santiago Commitment and Resolution 1080 expanded the OAS toolkit by

---

[28] Gjomema 2007.
[29] Cooper and Legler 2001, 2005; Levitt 2006; McCoy 2006.

forcing deliberation in the event of any interruption of democratic government. The Washington Protocol (1992) added the capacity to suspend nondemocratic members, and the Managua Declaration (1993) and the Inter-American Democratic Charter (2001) nominally made the OAS an organization of democracies only.[30]

As Poast and Urpelainen argue in an important study, the effectiveness of these rules in preventing reversions has been limited at best.[31] Rules evolved in ways that could not easily address creeping authoritarianism or what we call "backsliding" in countries such as Ecuador and Venezuela; indeed, the first invocation of the democratic charter was actually in support of Venezuelan president Hugo Chávez following a coup attempt against him in 2002.[32] These norms did, however, encourage value change among domestic political actors and reinforced political and social groups positively inclined toward democratic practices and constitutional government.[33]

Finally, it is worth noting that while Africa is rightly considered a "bad neighborhood," regional organizations in Africa have even gone further than those in Latin America in undertaking direct interventions to support democracy in a number of civil war cases. Moreover, we see a similar pattern of norm evolution.[34] In 1999, the Organisation of African Unity (OAU) banned heads of state installed by coups from attending its meetings; in 2000, this norm against unconstitutional changes of government was institutionalized, resulting in the temporary suspension of Mauritania's and Niger's membership in 2008 and 2010, respectively. This norm is arguably self-interested, since it protects both democratic governments and civilian regimes that have overreached; nonetheless, the change is significant.

International Influences: A Reprise

In sum, we see a diverse range of international influences operating in the elite-led transition cases, including both leverage and linkage. A handful of cases—mostly in smaller Latin American and African cases—were vulnerable to direct military intervention. Aid also proved a surprisingly powerful external lever. Virtually all of the "elite displacement" cases, in

[30] Following these developments, subnational organizations including MERCOSUR also developed democracy clauses.

[31] Poast and Urpelainen 2015.

[32] In an event occurring outside our dataset, the OAS also suspended Honduras's membership following a constitutionally dubious ouster of sitting president Manuel Zelaya in 2009 (Meachem 2014). But the move did not succeed in restoring Zelaya to office.

[33] Mainwaring and Pérez-Liñán 2014.

[34] Ndulo 2012.

which military factions overthrow incumbents in order to liberalize, came in the context of internal debates about the future course of foreign aid; Pakistan is the sole exception to this rule. As we will see, external forces operated in a number of preemptive and institutional transitions as well, as elites sought to reposition their foreign policies to exploit financial inducements.

Linkage effects involve a variety of social as well as political influences from outside, many of which are difficult to capture. We focused particular attention on the evolution of regional institutions, in part in their own right, in part as a proxy for how the broader neighborhood effects captured in our regressions might operate. Particularly in Europe, regional democratization norms were matched with powerful instruments of influence, both within the European space and through agreements with former colonies. However we find some incipient development of such norms in Latin America and Africa as well.

THE DOMESTIC POLITICS OF ELITE-LED TRANSITIONS

In Table 4.3, we pool all of the elite-led transitions in the two datasets, noting where codings overlap or diverge, and group them into the three broad transitional pathways noted above: elite displacement, preemptive, and institutional.[35] Because of differences in coding rules, the incidence of the three pathways differs substantially in each dataset. The CGV dataset defines democratization in terms of relatively abrupt changes that initiate competitive elections and lead to subsequent democratic turnover; as a result the dataset is better suited to capture elite displacement and preemptive transitions.[36] On the other hand, because the Polity coding captures not only elections but also competitiveness, participation, and the openness of political recruitment, it picks up more incremental changes, including the vast majority of what we call institutional transitions.[37]

The table also includes information on the nature of the institutional status quo ante. Although elite displacement and preemptive transitions emerge in a variety of institutional settings, 19 of the 20 institutional transitions emerged out of multiparty authoritarian regimes in which there

[35]We exclude the four cases in which external actors directly deposed authoritarian incumbents (Grenada, Panama, and Haiti) or established the new democratic order (Cyprus).

[36]Fourteen of the 15 elite displacement cases are coded in the CGV dataset, five of which overlap with Polity codings. Only one elite displacement transition is a Polity-only transition. Out of a total of 18 preemptive transitions listed in Table 4.3, eight are CGV-only and six more overlap with Polity. Only four preemptive cases are coded as transitions by Polity only.

[37]Nineteen of the 20 institutional transitions listed in the table are coded in the Polity dataset. Three of these cases overlap with CGV, but only one is coded exclusively by CGV.

Table 4.3 A Typology of Elite-Led Transitions.
($N = 53$)

Elite Displacement	Preemptive Democratization	Institutional Transitions
Central African Republic 1993 (CGV), Military	Bangladesh 1986 (CGV), Military	Albania 2002 (P), Multiparty
Comoros 1990 (CGV), One-party	Belarus 1991 (CGV/P), One-party	Croatia 2000 (P), Multiparty
Comoros 2004 (CGV/P), Military	Bhutan 2007 (CGV), Monarchy	Fiji 1999 (P), Multiparty
Czechoslovakia 1989–90 (CGV/P), One-party	Cape Verde 1990–91 (CGV/P), One-party	Honduras 1989 (P), Military
Guinea-Bissau 2000 (CGV), Multiparty	Croatia 1991 (CGV), One-party	Kenya 2002 (P), Multiparty
Guinea-Bissau 2004–5 (CGV/P), Multiparty	Ghana 1993 (CGV), Military	Malawi 2004 (P), Multiparty
Liberia 2006 (CGV/P), Multiparty	Guyana 1992 (P), Multiparty	Malaysia 2008 (P), Multiparty
Mauritania 2007 (CGV), Military	Honduras 1982 (CGV/P), Military	Mexico 1997 (P), Multiparty
Pakistan 1998 (CGV/P), Military	Hungary 1990 (CGV/P), One-party	Mexico 2000 (CGV), Multiparty
Paraguay 1989 (CGV), Multiparty	Macedonia 1991 (CGV/P), One-party	Moldova 1993 (P), Multiparty
Sierra Leone 1996 and 1998 (CGV), Civil war	Nicaragua 1984 (CGV), Military	Nepal 1999 (P), Multiparty
Sierra Leone 2007 (CGV), Multiparty	Nicaragua 1990 (P), Multiparty	Niger 2004 (P), Multiparty
Suriname 1991 (CGV), Military	Paraguay 1992 (P), Multiparty	Peru 2001 (CGV/P), Multiparty
Uganda 1980 (CGV), Military	São Tomé and Príncipe 1991 (CGV), One-party	Romania 1996 (P), Multiparty
	Taiwan 1992 (P), Multiparty	Russia 2000 (P), Multiparty
	Taiwan 1996 (CGV), Multiparty	Senegal 2000 (CGV/P) Multiparty

(*continued*)

Table 4.3 (*continued*)

Elite Displacement	Preemptive Democratization	Institutional Transitions
	Thailand 2008 (CGV), Military	Serbia 2000 (CGV/P), Multiparty
	Turkey 1983 (CGV/P), Military	Sri Lanka 2001 (P), Multiparty
		Sri Lanka 2006 (P), Multiparty
		Zambia 2008 (P), Multiparty
15 (CGV only, 9; Polity only, 1; CGV/Polity, 5)	18 (CGV only, 8; Polity only, 4; CGV/Polity, 6)	20 (CGV only, 1; Polity only, 16; Polity/CGV, 3)
Military, 6; One-party, 2; Multiparty, 5; Civil War, 2	Military, 6; One-party, 6; Multiparty, 5; Monarchy, 1	Military, 1; One-party, 0; Multiparty, 19

Memo items

CGV/P cases	15
Polity cases	37
Polity-only cases	22, of which 16 are institutional transitions
CGV cases	35
CGV-only cases	20, of which 9 are elite displacement

Note: The table excludes four cases—Panama, Grenada, Haiti, and Cyprus—that underwent transitions as a result of foreign military intervention and direct displacement of authoritarian incumbents. CGV: CGV only; P: Polity only; CGV/P: cases coded as transitions in both datasets. Chile 1990 is not included in the table because it combined elements of all three processes and none of the three clearly dominates. The case resembles an institutional transition because it occurred as a result of political opposition organized around constitutional provisions for a plebiscite. Negotiations subsequently secured extensive influence for sectors of the old regime, conditions that allowed the displacement of Pinochet from power.

was already a degree of political competition. This reflects the fact that these incremental political changes are occurring in authoritarian regimes that are already close to the democratic threshold (i.e., with Polity scores of 4 or 5). However we show that the high incidence of multiparty institutional transitions also reflects a distinctive political logic and the trade-offs that surround the staging of elections in particular.

The common feature uniting all of these cases is that incumbents and/ or their elite challengers conclude that it is too costly to rely on repression to remain in power. But what would induce such a calculation? Even in the absence of mass mobilization, the risk of continued repression clearly plays a role. In most—although not all—of the elite-displacement transitions, the combination of external pressures outlined above and the potential threats from domestic rivals posed strong incentives to participate in power-sharing efforts or to move out of the line of fire by withdrawing from political activity altogether.

Overall, however, a very large number of the elite-led transitions also reflected perceived opportunities as well as threats: reforming elites calculated that they would be able to compete successfully in a more open electoral environment. These expectations played an important role in virtually all of the preemptive and institutional transitions, and in a significant minority of elite-displacement transitions as well. The very weakness of mass oppositions may well be one of the factors that induce authoritarian rulers to risk a more competitive political environment. But institutional and organizational resources should also matter. As Slater and Wong argue in the cases of one- and dominant-party systems, these calculations may rest on the institutional and organizational assets associated with such parties.[38] However, the political assets of incumbents extend to a variety of other advantages, including tools such as clientelism, and the more generalized advantages of incumbency that we take up in our discussion of "weak democracies" in Chapter 6. As we show, these advantages did not always pan out, and we provide examples of miscalculation. But expectations of electoral success—even if based on a manipulation of the political system— appear a recurrent theme in most, if not all, of the elite-led cases.

Elite Displacement

Elite-displacement transitions bear one important resemblance to distributive conflict transitions: incumbent elites are directly displaced or forced to leave office. They are impelled to do so, however, by contending elites and their external allies rather than mass pressures. Their successors— typically military factions—then acquiesce to democratic reforms. In some

---

[38] Slater and Wong 2013.

cases (Comoros 1990, Comoros 2004, Paraguay 1989–93, and Uganda 1980), the political forces displacing incumbents simultaneously sought to maintain office for themselves. As noted above, elite behavior in these cases reflected an assumption—similar to those in preemptive and institutional transitions—that they could prevail in a competitive political environment.

In nine of the elite-displacement transitions, however, the leaders of the initial coup acquiesced to pressures from external forces and internal rivals to relinquish power to interim governments, which then staged competitive elections.[39] This was the case, for example, in Mauritania (2007), where military coup leaders came under strong external pressure to pledge that they would not run for office.

What accounts for this pattern? A strong clue is provided by the fact that the vast majority of elite-displacement transitions during the Third Wave took place in the context of violence: recurrent military conspiracies, interstate and civil wars, generalized social unrest, and complex combinations of all of these elements. Paraguay 1989 and possibly Pakistan 1988 are the sole exceptions. These background conditions also provided the motive for the external interventions we tracked in the last section. In elite-displacement transitions that transpired in the context of civil wars in particular, outside forces sought to contain the violence while simultaneously allying with domestic political and military elites engaged in intense struggles for power. In short, a combination of internal violence and strong external pressure generated divisions within the political elite that paved the way for displacement of incumbents and regime change in a democratic direction favored by outsiders.

Other military and one-party cases provide examples of this sort of intra-elite conflict that occurs outside the context of civil war, including the Central African Republic (1993, military), the Comoros (2004, one-party), Mauritania (2007, military), and Suriname (1991, military). In these cases, elite-displacement transitions occurred when incumbents were forced to yield power through challenges by opposing military factions or insurgent groups, often supported—sometimes even decisively—by external political and military actors.

Sierra Leone, discussed in the preceding section through an international lens, provides an illustration of the way domestic rivalries intersect with international forces. The complex transitional processes in 1996–98 took place against the backdrop of the civil war that began in 1991. A coup in 1992 brought the military into power under Captain Valentine Strasser

[39] Central African Republic 1993, Czechoslovakia 1989/1990, Guinea-Bissau 2000 and 2004, Liberia 2006, Mauritania 2007, Pakistan 1988, Sierra Leone 1996 and 1998, and Suriname 1991.

following a period of personalist rule under Joseph Saidu Momoh (1985–92). Strasser was unable to staunch the violence, however, in part because of growing divisions in—and defections from—the underpaid military. In 1996, he was overthrown by his minister of defense, Julius Maada Bio, who sought to resolve the country's difficulties—including with outside actors—by staging elections and negotiating with the rebels.

The elections were won by Ahmad Tejan Kabbah of the Sierra Leone People's Party, an economist who had spent much of his career working for the UN. The Kabbah government, however, also had difficulty maintaining military loyalty, particularly as he sought to build his own base of support among mobilized civil defense forces known as the Kamajors. Kabbah was ousted from power twice more: in 1997, led by factions of the military that were aided by the insurgents on their final assault on Freetown; and again in 1999, after he had managed to briefly regain office with the assistance of Nigerian and mercenary forces. Nonetheless, outsiders supported a negotiated peace process, backed ultimately by the British intervention described above.

Despite significant political concessions to the insurgents—remade as a political party—Kabbah was able to reassume office and declare the conflict ended by 2002. In 2007, outside forces subsequently ensured that the Kabbah government ceded power to a successor. Similar alliances between external forces and complex coalitions of domestic challengers to authoritarian incumbents in civil war settings were also visible in Guinea-Bissau (2000) and Liberia (2006).

Several features of the elite-displacement transitions are worth reiterating. By definition such cases rested on intra-elites splits, typically involving the military. These conflicts generally unfolded in contexts characterized by violence: war, civil war, large-scale social unrest, and a history of coups, although Paraguay provides an important exception. The military or insurgents played a central role in displacing incumbents, even in authoritarian regimes that were not military in form. It is therefore not surprising that these cases largely appear as examples of democratization only in the CGV dataset, with its much more minimalist conception of democracy as an electoral phenomenon. These transitions took place to what we call "weak democracies" that subsequently fell well short of robust democratic rule or were vulnerable to outright reversion; we return to this issue and a number of these very same cases in Chapters 6 and 7.

Preemptive Transitions: Incumbents as Reformers

A surprisingly large number of the elite-led transitions (18, 34 percent of all cases) were preemptive: initiated by authoritarian incumbents themselves, without significant pressure from below—and often not even from competing counterelites. These provide the most clear-cut cases of constitutional and electoral reforms motivated by the expectation that the risks of such steps would be mitigated by either winning elections or exercising effective vetoes over political challenges. We would thus expect these transitions to occur in settings in which incumbents enjoyed at least some support and the organizational resources to compete, and/or in which oppositions were weak, divided, and unable to mount a coherent challenge. Although these calculations sometimes proved correct, several preemptive transitions either led to the defeat of incumbents or weakened them to a much greater extent than had been anticipated. As we show in our discussion of reversions, several of these transitions, including Belarus, Honduras, and Thailand, were followed by returns to autocratic rule.

Preemptive transitions took place from a diverse array of authoritarian predecessors: military (6), one-party (6) and multiparty (5) regimes, and one monarchy. Although the cases appear to be evenly distributed across authoritarian regime types, however, single and dominant party systems were more likely to believe they enjoyed organizational advantages.[40] We provide examples from European and former Soviet communist one-party cases and two multiparty systems with dominant parties, Taiwan and Nicaragua.

All of the post-Soviet and Eastern European cases were, of course, powerfully affected by the geostrategic shifts associated with the end of the Cold War in Europe. As the Soviet Union began to crumble, reformers within communist parties in Eastern Europe, the Soviet Union, and Yugoslav republics all sought to control the scope and pace of political reform, and failing that, to define institutional parameters that would permit them to live to fight another day. In roundtable discussions in Eastern Europe, for example, communist parties advanced electoral proposals such as proportional representation with low thresholds that would at least allow them to survive if not prevail.[41]

The results of these efforts took several different forms. In some cases, incumbents or successors managed to maintain authoritarian rule, most starkly in the Central Asian republics of Kazakhstan, Turkmenistan, and Uzbekistan, and in several of the former Yugoslav republics, most notably Serbia; these changes from communist to postcommunist authoritarian rule do not show up in our dataset. By contrast, in the cases we described in the last chapter, communist incumbents or their reformist successors were overwhelmed by protest or its prospect: this occurred in the distributive conflict transitions in Albania, Armenia, Bulgaria, Poland, the Baltics (Estonia, Latvia, and Lithuania), and Ukraine, as well as

---

[40] Slater and Wong 2013.
[41] Geddes 1995.

in East Germany, which is not included in our dataset because of the unusual circumstances of its ultimate merger with the West.[42]

Four postcommunist transitions in our sample, however, can be categorized as preemptive transitions. In these cases, reform communists led the political reform process and managed to remain in office—at least initially—under at least nominally democratic rule. Perhaps the clearest case of such preemptive reform is Belarus (1991), where the Communist Party was pushed to independence as much by events in Russia as by an indigenous opposition. The party effectively retained power through the transition by decisively winning transitional elections. In Hungary (1990), the transition was initiated by reformers who ousted longtime dictator Janos Kadar in 1988 and began to liberalize the political system.[43] The breakup of Yugoslavia provides examples of continued authoritarian rule in Serbia but also cases—Croatia (1991, CGV only) and Macedonia (1991, CGV/Polity)—in which party insiders seized the initiative and launched democratizing reforms, in both cases exploiting nationalist themes that resonated with voters to maintain office.

The effect of the collapse of the Soviet Union was also felt in small single- or dominant-party regimes highly dependent on Soviet and Eastern bloc or other socialist largesse. Rulers in both Cape Verde and São Tomé and Principe undertook preemptive liberalizing steps when faced with the prospective loss of aid. Both countries moved toward multiparty rule in the late 1980s and early 1990s. In Cape Verde, the expectations of the dominant party were not realized: despite starting from scratch, the opposition Movement for Democracy won both the presidency and a parliamentary majority in the transitional elections. In São Tomé and Principe, the prime minister was an exiled dissident from within the dominant party, but the opposition won a majority of legislative seats. In Nicaragua as well, the substantial organizational resources available to the dominant Sandinista party were undoubtedly central to its decision to allow elections to go forward in 1984 and 1990. The Sandinistas clearly hoped to leverage international support and restrain pressures emanating from the United States.[44] Its unexpected loss of power in the 1990

[42] In Mongolia, the transition was initially driven by distributive conflict, but reform elements in the party managed to prevail in founding elections nonetheless.

[43] With the benefit of hindsight, it may appear that Hungary is an ambiguous case because party elites initiated compromises in anticipation of collective action, and even violent collective action, from below. But it was by no means clear at the time that the opposition would force the government from office, or that publics couldn't be swayed by promises of reform socialism and a "third way."

[44] The Nicaraguan transitions occur in 1984 in the CGV dataset—when it is coded as transition from military rule—and 1990 in the Polity dataset, when the transition occurred from a multiparty authoritarian setting.

election resulted from widespread public fatigue with the "contra" war, but even in these circumstances, the Sandinistas deep links to civil society and very favorable public opinion polls provided the incumbents with good reasons to think they could win.

TAIWAN

The transition in Taiwan provides a useful illustration of how the resources derived from a well-organized ruling party can affect elite calculations outside of the Soviet sphere.[45] From the nationalist flight from the Chinese mainland in 1949, Taiwan was governed by a powerful, highly centralized one-party regime. The ruling party, the Kuomintang (KMT), maintained the position that it was the sole legitimate government of China and that someday it would reoccupy the mainland. Its top leadership consisted almost exclusively of elites from the mainland and it exercised strict control over the ethnic Taiwanese population.

In 1978, Ching-kuo succeeded his father and longtime ruler, Chiang Kai-shek (Jiang Jieshi), and after consolidating his authority within the party, began a process of very gradual liberalization.[46] Taiwanese political leaders formed incipient political organizations around magazines and capitalized on the liberalization process to run so-called *dangwai* ("outside the party") candidates and to ultimately form an opposition party in 1986, the Democratic People's Party. But the transition was tightly controlled by the KMT as its gradual nature attests. In 1987, the KMT abolished martial law and subsequently enacted a set of new laws guaranteeing freedom of speech, association, and public assembly. In 1990, the government sponsored a National Affairs Conference that sought to forge a consensus on the main elements of political reform, including an eventual transition to the direct election of president. In 1991, the government ended the authoritarian measures and the state of emergency that had prevailed since the retreat to Taiwan, and held elections for the National Assembly; thus the Polity coding of the transition as occurring in 1992. By 1994, the framework of a constitutional democracy was essentially in place, with the direct election of the president in 1996 as the final step; that date is the one chosen as the transition by the CGV dataset.

Although the regime in Taiwan faced little direct pressure for political reform from the United States, a changing international and regional

---

[45] The transition is coded as taking place in 1996 in the CGV dataset and 1992 in Polity.

[46] Cheng and Haggard 1992; Tien and Cheng 1997; Rigger 1999; Slater and Wong 2013.

environment was at least one factor in the elite calculus. From the mid-1970s onward, Taiwan faced the prospect of isolation from the opening between the United States and mainland China and the growing diplomatic recognition of the Communist government by countries around the world. Neighborhood effects also appeared to influence the government's calculus; by the late 1980s and early 1990s, formerly authoritarian regimes in Korea, the Philippines, and Thailand had made transitions to more competitive systems. For the Taiwanese rulers—already faced with a drift of the United States toward China—clinging to authoritarian controls appeared an increasingly serious impediment to international legitimacy and support.

What about domestic incentives? Continued political exclusion, of course, did carry a potential for instability, and it is conceivable that the elite's initiative was based simply on a farsighted recognition of the challenges that mass mobilization might eventually pose for the regime. But the regime had successfully repressed mass mobilization in the past, most notably in the so-called Kaohsiung Incident of 1979, and at best, such an explanation seems incomplete. As suggested in the introduction to the chapter, elite initiatives are more likely when incumbents possess organizational and political capabilities that can allow them to prevail—or at least survive—in more competitive political settings. In Taiwan, high growth and the extraordinary political assets of the KMT increased the likelihood that it could control the political transition by co-opting Taiwanese into the KMT camp.[47] Ruling party victories in the 1991 National Assembly elections allowed Chiang's successor, President Lee Teng-hui—of Taiwanese descent—to push the political reforms along despite conservative resistance within the KMT. It is doubtful that these outcomes would have been possible in the absence of a well-endowed and well-organized ruling party.

Although the logic of preemptive democratization is most obvious under single- and dominant-party systems that can exploit their organizational advantages, a number of military rulers, and even a monarchy (Bhutan 2007), also initiated transitions from above. Not coincidentally, however, the military regimes in our sample (Bangladesh 1986, Ghana 1993, Honduras 1982, Thailand 2008, Turkey 1983) appeared to have somewhat greater difficulty in sustaining their authority in more democratic settings. In Ghana, longtime military ruler Jerry Rawlings did successfully engineer a transition under pressure from external donors, with the expectation—which proved correct—that he would be able to win multiparty elections through his combination of charisma and populist appeals. In other cases in which incumbents retained power, there were serious questions about

[47] Haggard and Kaufman 1995.

whether they should be considered transitions at all. For example, the 1986 elections in Bangladesh largely served to "civilianize" the Ershad regime that had come to power in a coup in 1982. Repression of opposition groups even increased following the transition in Honduras in 1982; not surprisingly, both of these transitions are coded as such in the CGV dataset only.

In Turkey and Thailand, by contrast, militaries had a much harder time maintaining control in the wake of preemptive transitions. In Turkey, the military had seized power with the expectation that it would extricate itself from government once it had stabilized the political turbulence that had roiled the country in the late 1970s. In 1983, it moved forward with a plan to exit office, but only after drafting a constitution that reserved substantial authority in military hands. By the end of the 1980s, however, military influence was subjected to constitutional challenge and its ability to exercise a direct policy veto was weakened. In Thailand, the outcome was even less favorable to the military in the short run, and it ultimately reversed its decision to withdraw from power. Military leaders, backed by the king, drove populist tycoon Thaksin Shinawatra from office in 2006, and promoted the ratification of a new constitution aimed at preventing his return. Elections went forward as promised in December 2007, but despite the military's efforts, the populist political forces loyal to Thaksin regained control of the parliament, prompting the military to intervene again in 2008 and in 2014.

In sum, the unifying feature of this group of cases is that authoritarian incumbents themselves initiated major political reforms in the absence of distributive pressures from below or serious challenges from rival elites. These preemptive transitions, to be sure, reflected an anticipation that pressures on authoritarian rule might grow in the future. But the possibility of such threats exists in all cases; to invoke such risks is to make the distributive conflict theory true virtually by definition. International factors played a role in all of these cases, but incumbent rulers clearly acted in the belief that they could maintain effective control, or even political office, under more democratic auspices. This confidence typically stemmed from a combination of incumbent advantages and significant organizational resources, including control over dominant party machines, and the corresponding weaknesses of the opposition.

INSTITUTIONAL TRANSITIONS

The final type of elite-led transition is a more incremental process of change that we call "institutional" transition. These processes reflect an inherent tension in the competitive authoritarian model, emphasized by

Beatriz Magaloni in particular.[48] On the one hand, as we argued in Chapters 2 and 3, institutions such as elections, legislatures, judiciaries, and partial protection of political and civil liberties serve to sustain authoritarian rule: through power sharing, building mass support, co-opting wider oppositions, distributing rents, and revealing information on the identity and strength of possible challengers. On the other hand, these institutions can achieve these objectives only if they entail some risks for incumbents; otherwise, they would lack any credibility and thus reduce the controlled participation they seek to encourage. The liberalizing reforms that define these transitions reflect decisions by incumbents that the cost of reverting to overt controls outweighs the benefits or—as with preemptive democratization—the belief that incremental changes in the political order can be managed.

The overwhelming share of these institutional transitions are Polity transitions (19 of 20; Table 4.3). Of the 20 transitions, moreover, 19 occurred in multiparty authoritarian regimes. In these multiparty systems, incumbent rulers headed dominant parties and maintained power, in part, through a formal electoral process, while also using state resources and selective intimidation to ensure electoral majorities and limit the scope of collective action on the part of opposition forces.

The combination of scheduled elections and successions to new leadership within the authoritarian coalition were particularly important moments when ruling coalitions had to assess the risks of staging elections. Succession played a role in institutional transitions in Croatia (2000), Kenya (2002), Malawi (2004), Peru (2001), and Zambia (2008). Croatia provides the clearest example of the difficulties of sustaining strongman rule. When Tuđman fell ill, the Supreme Court appointed an interim president to oversee elections. But Tuđman's ruling HDZ could not hold together in the absence of its leader and ended up losing the elections badly. In Kenya, Daniel arap Moi was bound by a constitutional two-term limit. He subsequently failed to manipulate the electoral process to ensure victory for his protégé, Uhuru Kenyatta, in the 2002 elections, in part because of international pressures, but in part because of defections from the ruling party and the forging of a broad opposition coalition.

Although these successions pushed Polity scores across the democratic threshold, they did not always lead to a significant turnover of government. In Malawi (2004), for example, incumbent president Bakili Muluzi was forced by international pressures and legislative opposition to abandon his effort to override term limits. In contrast to developments in Kenya, however, his chosen successor, Bingu wa Mutharika, prevailed in the 2004 elections. The elections were plagued by fraud, and Levitsky

---

[48] Magaloni 2006; Magaloni and Kricheli 2010.

and Way argue that the system remained competitive-authoritarian after 2004.[49] But the defeat of Muzuli's attempt to perpetuate his rule and Mutharika's incorporation of some opposition forces were modest steps forward and appear to account for the marginal improvement in the Polity score from 5 to 6.

In some cases, apparently small changes in scores did in fact mark important shifts in power. The Polity rankings of Honduras (1989), Moldova (1993), and Russia (2000) improved to the threshold of 6 because the elections in those years marked the first time power had been passed from one elected government to the opposition. In Nepal, after a period of stalemate among fragmented parliamentary parties, the Nepal Congress Party was allowed to form a single-party minority government in 1998 on the condition that it would hold elections the following year. After it lived up to that commitment in 1999, Nepal's Polity score increased from 5 to 6. In Romania, the defeat of Ion Iliescu in 1996 was more substantial, as the change in Polity score suggests (from 5 to 8). These political systems were marked by a number of other disabilities, but electoral or other constitutional commitments were honored by incumbent authoritarian parties.

Senegal and Mexico: Transitions in Dominant Party Systems

It is important to note that even fairly well-developed ruling parties were vulnerable to these dynamics, particularly where economic and political circumstances provided opportunities for oppositions to exploit scheduled elections. Senegal (2000 CGV/Polity) and Mexico (1997 Polity; 2000 CGV) provide two quite diverse examples that demonstrate both the strengths and ultimate vulnerabilities of competitive authoritarian regimes.

Until his resignation in 1980, Léopold Senghor and the Parti Socialist (PS) dominated postindependence Senegal. Senghor opened the system to limited electoral competition in 1976 at the time he appointed his successor, Abdou Diouf, prime minister. However, the opening of the electoral process in 1981 had the effect of splintering the opposition and allowing continued PS domination; the PS won the 1983 elections convincingly. In 1988, fraud-ridden elections further split the opposition; Diouf won with 73.2 percent of the vote. Following widespread protest, however, the government undertook electoral reforms that increased the leverage of the opposition and encouraged the incorporation of some its leaders into coalitions led by the dominant PS.

[49] Levitsky and Way 2010: 287.

This protest-accommodation cycle did not ultimately lead to a regime change, but instead led to yet another cycle of small institutional changes designed to co-opt and divide the opposition.[50] Following an opposition boycott of local elections in 1990, Diouf offered to create a Government of National Unity and undertook decentralizing reforms that granted local officials greater autonomy over their budgets. Nonetheless, Diouf again won the 1993 elections, albeit with a substantially reduced majority (58.4 percent). After the elections, however, economic reforms diluted the capacity of the PS to maintain its complex patronage networks, including religious leaders who delivered the rural vote. Several Socialist Party leaders defected from the party, and Diouf failed to achieve a first-round victory in the 2000 elections despite gaining a plurality (41 percent). The rural constituencies that voted for Diouf in 1988 and 1993 turned against him 2000, and the opposition candidate, Abdoulaye Wade, won in the second-round runoff, marking the first democratic turnover in the country's history.

Mexican politics was dominated from the late 1920s by the Partido Revolucionario Institucional (PRI). The regime rested on a variety of co-optive mechanisms, including direct payoffs to labor allies and party personnel, corporatist channels of representation for unions and peasant organizations, and the tolerance of opposition parties that had little influence but represented dissident middle-class oppositions. High growth facilitated the operation of this system during the 1950s and 1960s, and the party routinely ran up supermajorities in semicompetitive, but manipulated elections. Control by the party came under strain, however, following a series of economic shocks beginning in the 1970s, and particularly with the onset of the debt crisis in 1982 and the subsequent adoption of neoliberal reform strategies. Unlike their trade union counterparts in the distributive conflict transitions of South America, Mexico's corporatist unions remained allied closely with the party's conservative old guard and in fact resisted political change.[51] The principal opposition emerged instead within the electoral arena.

The initial challenge came in 1987, with the defection of prominent left-wing leaders of the ruling party. In 1988, they launched a serious electoral campaign against the PRI's presidential candidate and were beaten back only through highly visible vote-counting fraud. The protests that ensued in this and in subsequent elections were costly to the regime, in terms of both its domestic legitimacy and its increasingly close ties with the United States. The leaders of the PRI thus responded to these strains

[50] Creevey, Ngomo, and Vengroff 2005.
[51] Middlebrook 1995.

with a succession of limited concessions aimed at dividing and co-opting the opposition.

In the wake of the controversies surrounding the 1988 elections, the government founded the Federal Election Institute in 1989; as charges of fraud continued, it acquiesced to a series of reforms during the 1990s that increased its independence from the executive branch.[52] To deflect challenges from the left parties, the neoliberal leaders of the ruling party also drew closer to the center-right PAN, allowing it to capture a number of governorships and legislating in cooperation with its congressional delegation. As noted, the purpose of these steps was to maintain the dominant party regime, but their cumulative effect was to progressively weaken the party's hold over the electorate and the reins of government. In 1997, the PRI accepted the loss of its absolute congressional majority and began to depend entirely on the cooperation of the PAN to pass its legislative program. In the presidential elections of 2000, it accepted the loss of the presidency, relinquishing presidential power to the PAN candidate.

In closing our consideration of these institutional transitions, it is worth drawing a contrast to the distributive conflict transitions discussed in Chapter 3. We found that electoral fraud or delays in scheduled elections did, at times, trigger mass protest that produced regime change. However, the incidence of this sequence of events was quite limited, occurring in just over 20 percent of all distributive conflict transitions.[53] We showed that this result stemmed, in part, from the fact that the regimes most vulnerable to distributive conflict transitions were repressive military and one-party authoritarian systems that lacked the mechanisms—including electoral mechanisms—to blunt such protest.

Yet our analysis here suggests that elections can generate their own vulnerability, though of a different sort. Transitions in the institutional cases were typically brought about by the very constraints these regimes placed on themselves. Although we agree with the new literature on authoritarianism that elections may be little more than a tool of soft authoritarian rule, there do appear to be cases in which authoritarian leaders find themselves facing Hobson's choices with respect to them. On the one hand, they can maintain power by overturning electoral outcomes and continuing to tinker with the system in order to maintain control but with some risk of inducing a wider political backlash. On the other hand, they can accept temporary electoral setbacks or even defeat but with the hope that

[52] Eisenstadt 2004.

[53] DR (1996), Georgia (2004), Kyrgyzstan (2005), Madagascar (1992), Maldives (2008), Nepal (2006–8), Niger (2000), Nigeria (2000), Pakistan (2008), Philippines (1986), and Thailand (1992).

their defeat will not be permanent and they can survive to fight another day. We cannot assume that all semicompetitive regimes necessarily succeed in staying so; some do appear to transition to more democratic forms, as both the Mexico and Senegal cases demonstrate.

Conclusion: The Diversity of Transition Processes

The distributive conflict pathway by no means captures the full diversity of the democratization process. Our analysis in this chapter explores cases in which distributive conflicts are absent, again posing Adam Przeworski's challenge as to why in the absence of pressure from below authoritarian incumbents might cede power.

In this chapter, we offered two complementary answers. The first is that international influences can have profound effects on elite calculations. We found that such pressures were particularly strong following the waning of the Cold War and in small countries that were vulnerable to direct intervention—particularly civil war cases—and the exercise of leverage from multilateral, regional, and major power donors. We noted that in a number of these cases, external pressures help explain a pattern we call elite displacement, in which authoritarian incumbents are thrown out by competing elites within the regime, who then pave the way for more democratic politics.

It is important to underscore that our observation of international influences in our cases does not speak to the general success of such efforts; we seek to establish only that they did appear to have influence in a number of the elite-led transitions. The cases we explore, however, do raise questions about the efficacy of leverage. The reasons for this limited influence have to do with constraints on the ability of external actors to shape domestic political developments, but also reflect important selection effects. Countries vulnerable to outside pressures also tend to be smaller, weaker, and less developed, and thus face a variety of headwinds in moving toward democratic rule. As we show in Chapters 6 to 8, a number of cases that we describe here end up subsequently reverting to authoritarian rule.

However, it is important to note that the more direct leverage effects did not exhaust external influences, which also operated through complex neighborhood effects. We offered one explanation for this statistical finding: that regional organizations in the post–Cold War period exercised at least some influence on the democratization process. These inducements and constraints operated most powerfully in Europe, and not simply through the aspirations to join an apparently winning organization. The EU also leveraged access to the community to directly influence political developments in a number of cases in Eastern Europe, and in the cases of Romania and Albania, all the way up to the very nature of the regime. Although Latin American and African regional organizations did not have the same resources, they did gradually develop the power to encourage democratic practices and, at times, to censure more visible challenges to democratic incumbents.

The second and more important point we seek to explore is how elite calculations about domestic politics might generate more democratic outcomes. Our efforts in this regard are in the first instance typological: to simply trace the proximate causal processes associated with the transition paths involving elite displacement, preemptive democratic moves by incumbents, or more marginal institutional changes. A common feature of all of these elite-led cases, however, is that they center on elite assessments of the costs and benefits of sustaining authoritarian rule. In elite displacement cases, the cleavage between incumbents and their elite challengers is precisely on this point, typically within divided militaries. In preemptive and institutional transitions, elites took the risk of an uncertain democratic future because they believed that they could continue to prevail. This, in turn, was more likely where incumbents controlled organizational resources, particularly parties and patronage, and where oppositions were weak.

An important question is whether the two transition paths we have traced here have any effect on the subsequent development of democratic rule. It is this question that we turn to in Chapter 5.

Transition Paths and the Quality of Democracy

(with Terence Teo)

THE EFFECTS OF MASS MOBILIZATION ON DEMOCRATIZATION have been the subject of considerable debate. Early advocates of "pacted" transitions emphasized the risks of polarization for the transition process. Democratization was more likely when moderate leaders controlled "maximalists" within their own ranks—and in the streets—and reached compromises with incumbent rulers and their backers,[1] or "softliners" within the authoritarian coalition.[2] Critics countered that the transitions driven by such elite processes not only generated conservative biases but could even limit the scope of democracy altogether.[3] Some recent research has revisited these arguments, claiming that democracies emerging through revolution and even civil war may be more robust than those that develop more peacefully.[4]

We revisit this debate by asking whether the nature of the transition—distributive conflict or elite-led—has any effect on the robustness of subsequent democratic rule. Does distributive conflict contribute to a more (or less) competitive, well-institutionalized, and open democratic order? And if so, through what mechanisms? Or do transition paths exhibit equifinality, providing alternative routes to broadly similar end points?

From the outset, it is important to acknowledge a significant endogeneity problem in seeking to answer this question. We argued in Chapter 2 that distributive conflict transitions were partly the result of prior capacities for collective action, often with deep historical roots. Even if we control for an array of structural factors that affect the quality of democracy, we are left with a substantial challenge. Regardless of whether distributive conflict played a role in the transition, we would expect polities with strong civil societies to check the likelihood of authoritarian reversal. How do we distinguish between the effects on democracy of the underlying organizational capacity of social groups—unions, ethnic associations, NGOs—and the short-run dynamics of the transition itself?

---

[1] O'Donnell and Schmitter 1986; Di Palma 1990; Huntington 1991.
[2] Przeworski 1991.
[3] Karl 1990.
[4] Bermeo forthcoming; Albertus and Menaldo 2014.

Although we cannot fully resolve these issues econometrically, causal process observation can help us distinguish among three causal mechanisms that might influence subsequent democratic development: social organization dating to the authoritarian period, elite-mass conflict during the transition, and new social organizations that emerge only in the wake of the transition. While we believe existing or new social organizations are likely to have a direct impact on democratic outcomes, there are also good theoretical reasons to believe that mass mobilization *during* the transition might have enduring consequences as well. As we have argued throughout, *capacities* for collective action—captured in structural variables, such as industry or manufacturing share of output, or even organizational ones, such as union density—are just that: indicators of a *potential* for collective action. It is mass mobilization itself, however, that actually demonstrates what Acemoglu and Robinson call "de facto power" and makes it credible. Mass mobilization reveals information on the balance of power between state and civil society. In distributive conflict transitions, outgoing elites, democratic successors, and potential authoritarian entrants gain updated information on the ability of civil society to respond to repression and derogations from democratic norms.

Transitions propelled by mass protest can affect the bargaining power of contending political elites and the design of new democratic institutions in at least three ways. First, mass pressures increase the likelihood of more open and competitive founding elections. Authoritarian regimes restrict political participation; the threat of mass mobilization widens the space for contestation and limits the capacity of outgoing elites to restrict the emerging electoral space.

Second, pressure from below can affect broader institutional design as well. Providing some institutional assurances to potentially dangerous beneficiaries of the old order may well be necessary for successful transitions, as the analysts cited above argued in the early days of the Third Wave. But when such assurances are institutionalized, including through pacts, they not only bias outcomes toward conservative political and social interests,[5] but can limit the representation of interests, the competitiveness of the political system, and even basic rights and liberties. Mass mobilization reduces the power of outgoing elites to negotiate institutional "lock-ins" that permanently enhance their veto power. Conversely, mobilization provides a political and social foundation for more robust institutional checks on new democratic governments. Governments coming to office in the wake of distributive conflicts face greater constraints on their ability to manipulate politics through the variety of techniques

---

[5]Karl 1990.

identified in the growing literature on competitive authoritarianism.[6] Related to this, mass mobilization can also reduce the control of authoritarian incumbents over organizational, economic, or military resources that can be wielded as instruments of repression. As we will argue in Chapter 6, moreover, the challenges to authoritarian rule come not only from exiting elites, but from the temptation for new democratic incumbents to tilt the political playing field in their favor. Mass mobilization also constrains their control over such organizational resources and thus facilitates stronger and more enduring horizontal checks on executive power.

Finally, mass mobilization should lead to more robust defense of political and civil liberties. The very act of organized resistance to authoritarian rule reflects de facto exercise of the full range of political rights and civil liberties, including most significantly the freedoms of association, assembly, and speech. Once unleashed, the exercise of these rights becomes more difficult to reverse. As Bueno de Mesquita and his coauthors put it, "When the press, speech and assembly are free, government finds it much more difficult to use oppression to quash opposition."[7] Such pressures from below should also limit the capacity of new democratic incumbents to erode such liberties.

In short, we emphasize that checks on political incumbents come not only from institutional design but also from the revealed balance of power between the state, political elites, and social forces. Open manifestation of those social capabilities provides information on that balance of power. We hypothesize that distributive conflict leads to greater electoral contestation, more effective checks on state power, and more robust protection of political rights and civil liberties. And as we argue in Chapter 6, these very factors in turn are highly consequential for the very stability of democratic rule.

Exploring these hypotheses is not straightforward. First, we expect the effects of mass mobilization during the transition—as distinguished from the underlying organizational factors in which they are rooted—to fade over time. Indeed, it seems quite likely that the quality of democracy will depend heavily on a variety of more enduring factors that are not directly related to the transition itself, including level of development and institutional factors. Second, as a practical matter, our analysis is constrained by the relatively recent nature of the transitions under consideration in our dataset; the Third Wave and its aftermath provides only a limited time frame in which to make judgments about the longer-run effects of transition paths.

---

[6] Schedler 2002; Levitsky and Way 2010.
[7] Bueno de Mesquita et al. 2003: 544.

Nonetheless, using the same complementary methodological approaches we have pursued in previous chapters, we do find some evidence for our expectations. We turn first to some statistical evidence, looking at the correlation between transition paths and Polity scores and Freedom House measures of political rights in the post-transition period. We do not attempt to fully disentangle the immediate and underlying causes of the transition paths through tightly specified causal identification strategies; we leave a fuller statistical exploration of these issues to further research. Nonetheless, we do find a correlation between distributive conflict transitions and subsequent political developments, even when we control for authoritarian regime type and union strength—the two factors that accounted most directly for distributive conflict transitions.

As we do throughout this book, however, we supplement our simple statistical analysis with causal process observations that permit closer attention to temporal sequences: from antecedent conditions, through the transition, to subsequent developments under democratic rule. Our design is to focus on four pairs of distributive conflict and elite-led cases. The limited number of transitions prevents us from undertaking a perfect matching of cases. But we can hold a number of factors constant, including region, level of income, and the timing of transitions. The pairs we consider are El Salvador and Honduras, Ukraine and Belarus, Zambia and Ghana, and Uruguay and Chile, with the first in each pair representing the distributive conflict path. The cross-national quantitative, within-country quantitative, and qualitative data all suggest that there are modest but consistent differences between countries undergoing these two different transition paths, extending out by as much as ten years.

COMPARING DISTRIBUTIVE CONFLICT AND ELITE-LED CASES: STATISTICAL EVIDENCE

In the preceding chapters, we treated democracy as a binary variable, identifying transitions as the movement from authoritarian to democratic rule. The CGV dataset defines democracy in dichotomous terms, and we followed the common practice of considering movement from below to above 6 as an indicator of democratization in the Polity dataset as well. In this section, however, we leverage the continuous coding of the Polity measure and the 7-point Freedom House Political Rights scale to measure differences in the institutionalization of democracy across the transition cases, a theme we take up in our discussion of reversions as well (Chapter 6). Polity scores capture the competitiveness of political participation, checks on executive discretion, and indirectly the political and civil liberties that undergird competition. Freedom House measures more directly assess political rights on a 1 to 7 scale (most to least free) and on multiple dimensions: not only whether elections are free and fair, but the extent of political pluralism (which includes freedom of parties to form, a viable opposition, lack of ethnic or religious discrimination) and whether elected governments can determine policies, are relatively free of corruption, and are accountable between elections.[8] If countries undergoing distributive conflict transitions have higher quality democracies, we should see higher Polity and Freedom House scores.

Figures 5.1 to 5.4 present descriptive data on annual average Polity and FH scores in the five years preceding and following democratic transitions in the CGV and Polity datasets respectively. In line with our findings in Chapters 2 and 3, authoritarian regimes that subsequently experience distributive conflict transitions are more authoritarian on both Polity and Freedom House measures. Largely as a result, they experience greater improvements in their democracy scores during the transition. In Figure 5.1, for example, the Polity scores of distributive conflict CGV transitions improved from –4 to 6 in the year after the regime change, whereas elite-led transitions increased from an average of –2 to a score of about 4.5, well below the Polity threshold for democratic rule. In Figure 5.2, Polity scores following Polity transitions tend to converge at the time of the transition; this is expected given the definition of a transition as moving from below to above a score of 6. Prior to the transition, however, distributive conflict cases have much lower Polity scores and thus also see larger increases. Similar findings pertain with respect to the initial level and movement of Freedom House scores, which are worse prior to the transition in both the CGV (Figure 5.3) and Polity (Figure 5.4) distributive conflict cases.[9]

What about the immediate post-transition period? We consider here the first five years of democratic rule in order to maximize the number of cases in the dataset that we can compare. Since transitions identified in the Polity dataset all had to cross a 6-point threshold, it is again not surprising that the two types of transitions showed convergent Polity scores (Figure 5.2). The Polity scores of the CGV distributive conflict cases, however, begin with Polity scores that are higher than their elite-led counterparts and the two paths only converge after five years. The Freedom House scores provide more mixed evidence. In the CGV cases distributive conflict cases end up with marginally higher (i.e., worse) political rights scores at t+5. But the distributive conflict Polity transitions show consistently lower (i.e., better) Freedom House scores than their elite-led counterparts across the entire post-transition period.

[8] Freedom House 2014b.
[9] In the FH rankings, high scores indicate greater limits on political freedom.

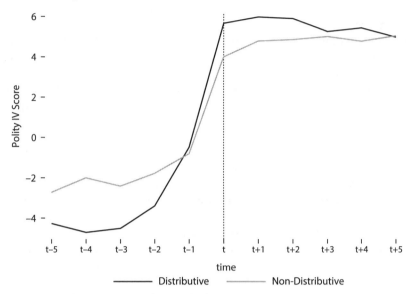

Figure 5.1 Polity IV Score Before and After CGV Transition

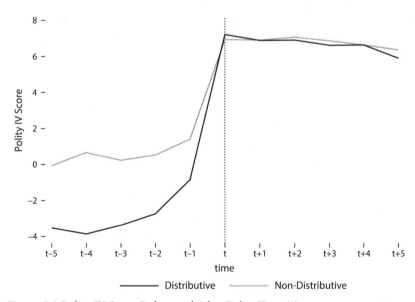

Figure 5.2 Polity IV Score Before and After Polity Transition

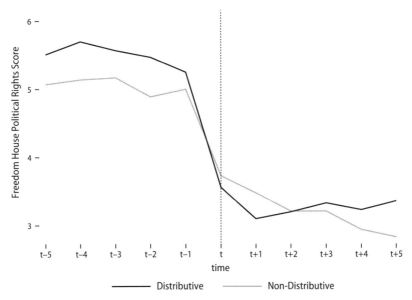

Figure 5.3 Freedom House Political Rights Score Before and After CGV Transition

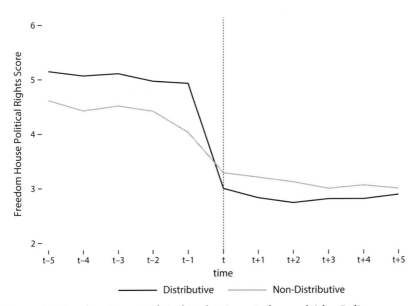

Figure 5.4 Freedom House Political Rights Score Before and After Polity Transition

To explore these relationships more systematically, we use a time-series cross-sectional (TSCS) dataset of all developing countries from 1980 to 2008 with country-year as the unit of analysis.[10] TSCS or panel data present two challenges. First, we need to account for unobserved heterogeneity at the country level, that is, country-specific factors that may not be captured by the model.[11] A fixed effects model resolves this problem by using country-varying intercepts. A fixed effects approach is particularly appropriate for our purposes here because, in contrast to the models in Chapters 2 and 6, we want to absorb cross-sectional variation to focus on the within-country effects or changes over time; country-varying intercepts have this effect.[12]

A second challenge relates to possible temporal dynamics that, if left unaddressed, may lead to biased standard errors and false inference. We use the Prais-Winsten (AR1) method to correct for autocorrelation in the dependent variable. In addition, we specify robust standard errors clustered by country.

We thus estimate the following model:

$$y_{it} = \alpha + \beta X_{it-1} + \delta_i + u_{it}$$

where y_{it} is the outcome of interest with respect to country i at time t, X_{it-1} is the vector of covariates, δ_i is a set of country dummies (fixed effects), and u_{it} is an error term. For a given country, as a variable of interest X varies by one unit, the outcome y increases or decreases by β units. Thus, the coefficients can be read as point estimates of the effect of the independent variables on the change in Polity or Freedom House scores—the dependent variable—in the given post-transition years when compared with scores in the year prior to the transition.[13]

In Tables 5.1 to 5.4, we show the effects of the different transitions paths on Polity and Freedom House scores in the first (t+1), fifth (t+5), and tenth years (t+10) following the transition. Tables 5.1 and 5.3 show the estimated *levels* of democracy scores in CGV and Polity transitions respectively, with controls held at their mean. Tables 5.2 and 5.4 present

[10] The number of countries ranges from 120 to 137 annually, subject to data availability.

[11] Beck and Katz 2001.

[12] An alternative is a random effects model. However, this model assumes zero covariance between the variables and the residuals—an assumption that is generally difficult to satisfy. Though no test exists to discern whether one should use fixed or random effects, a Hausman (1978) specification test is a typical way to assess whether significant differences exist between fixed and random effects estimates. Where such differences exist, one should use fixed effects. A Hausman test reveals that a fixed effects specification is appropriate ($\chi^2 = 158.62, p = .00$).

[13] We obtain almost identical results (not shown) when we examine the change in Polity/FH scores between the year prior to the transition and t+1 and t+3—in effect, the change over the specific period centered on the transition.

Table 5.1 CGV Transitions: Predicted Polity and Freedom House Scores. (t+1, t+5, and t+10)

	Predicted Polity Scores			Predicted FH Scores		
	t+1	*t+5*	*t+10*	*t+1*	*t+5*	*t+10*
Distributive transitions	8.46	6.74	6.40	2.27	2.40	2.74
Elite-led transitions	6.29	6.16	6.07	2.83	2.94	2.80
Difference	2.17	0.58	0.33	0.56	0.54	0.06

Note: All control variables are set to their respective means at the relevant time points.

the change models on which these estimates are based. In these models, the coefficients for Polity and Freedom House can be interpreted as point estimates for the *changes* in the democracy scores following the transition.

We include controls for other factors that are generally expected to affect the robustness of democratic rule. These include GDP per capita, a measure of inequality (capital share following Houle), and our neighborhood measure (the percentage of neighboring democracies). We also control for the authoritarian status quo ante and capacities for collective action. We include whether the authoritarian regime was military or competitive authoritarian as well as Polity or FH scores at t−3. To account for the possibility that differences in the transitions are endogenous to prior differences in underlying organizational capacity, we also include the percentage of the population in unions, which was found in Chapter 2 to have a significant impact on the likelihood of a distributive conflict transition. All of these variables are described in detail in Chapter 2.

Tables 5.1 and 5.3 show the estimated levels of Polity and FH scores for distributive conflict and elite-led transitions with all other variables held at their mean. These estimates show consistent differences across time periods. In the CGV coding (Table 5.1), a distributive conflict transition produces an initial Polity score of 8.5, as contrasted with 6.3 for elite-led transitions. By t+10, these differences have narrowed substantially, but the Polity score for transitions involving mass mobilization is still slightly higher (6.4 and 6.1, respectively), even after a decade has passed. For the Polity coding, we see a similar pattern (Table 5.2). Countries experiencing distributive conflict reach an estimated Polity score over 2.5 points higher than elite-led transitions in the initial year of transition (8.7 vs. 6.1). Again, the differences narrow after a decade, but distributive conflict transitions still score about a point higher on the Polity scale at t+10 (5.8 to 4.8).

Table 5.2 Determinants of Democratic Development: CGV Transitions.

	Change in Polity Scores			Change in Freedom House Scores		
	t+1	t+5	t+10	t+1	t+5	t+10
Distributive	8.08***	5.72***	4.15***	−2.04***	−1.67***	−1.01**
	(0.82)	(1.31)	(1.58)	(0.26)	(0.40)	(0.38)
Elite-led	5.91***	5.15***	3.82***	−1.48***	−0.76*	−1.25**
	(1.00)	(1.06)	(1.14)	(0.32)	(0.40)	(0.55)
Controls						
Union membership	0.11***	0.23***	0.44***	−0.04***	−0.07***	−0.16***
	(0.02)	(0.03)	(0.04)	(0.01)	(0.01)	(0.02)
Log GDP per capita	0.14**	0.21**	−1.00	−0.18***	−0.08***	−0.09**
	(0.07)	(0.09)	(0.12)	(0.02)	(0.03)	(0.04)
Capital share	1.45**	2.25**	0.08	−0.12	0.04	−0.15
	(0.72)	(1.06)	(1.42)	(0.26)	(0.37)	(0.46)

Growth	−0.02**	−0.05***	−0.06***	0.01	0.00	0.01
	(0.01)	(0.01)	(0.02)	(0.00)	(0.00)	(0.01)
Military/1 Party$_{t-3}$	−1.02***	−2.68***	−3.89***	0.31***	0.33***	0.16
	(0.22)	(0.31)	(0.39)	(0.08)	(0.10)	(0.13)
Polity/FH score$_{t-3}$	0.84***	0.68***	0.55***	−0.19***	−0.16***	−0.11***
	(0.01)	(0.02)	(0.03)	(0.00)	(0.01)	(0.01)
Neighboring democracies	1.64***	3.73***	3.98***	−0.56***	−1.05***	−0.83***
	(0.25)	(0.42)	(0.49)	(0.09)	(0.13)	(0.16)
N	2,399	1,872	1,318	2,397	1,874	1,329
Groups	116	117	114	117	117	115
R^2	.73	.55	.42	.61	.45	.34

Note: Baseline Prais-Winsten regressions with heteroscedastic panel-corrected standard errors in parentheses. All control variables are at t+1, t+5, and t+10, respectively, depending on the outcome.

Table 5.3 Polity Transitions: Predicted Polity and Freedom House Scores.
(t+1, t+5, and t+10)

	Predicted Polity Scores			Predicted FH Scores		
	t+10	*t+5*	*t+10*	*t+1*	*t+5*	*t+10*
Distributive-conflict transitions	8.71	6.88	5.84	2.03	2.62	2.96
Elite-led transitions	6.13	4.49	4.82	3.22	3.53	3.34
Difference	2.58	2.39	1.02	1.19	0.91	0.35

Note: All control variables are set to their respective means at the relevant time points.

This basic pattern also generally holds for Freedom House scores (Tables 5.1 and 5.3). Lower Freedom House scores indicate greater political liberties; lower estimates on the transition variables thus denote an *improvement* in the extent to which citizens acquire a full range of opportunities to organize, acquire information, and hold elected officials accountable for their actions. For CGV coding, the estimated FH scores at t+10 are 2.7 and 2.8, respectively; for Polity transitions, they are 3.0 and 3.3.

The coefficients shown in Tables 5.2 and 5.4 provide estimates of the *changes* in Polity and Freedom House scores relative to scores at t−1. The graphs, it should be recalled, indicate that, on average, distributive conflict transitions started from "further behind"; they were initiated under authoritarian regimes with histories of more severe repression. Again, however, we see that the changes in Polity and Freedom House scores are consistently larger in the distributive conflict transitions. Cases that ultimately explode in distributive conflict transitions typically begin at higher levels of repression. But popular protest appears to result in both larger *changes* and higher *levels* of Polity and FH scores than when the politics of regime change is restricted to a narrower circle of political actors.

As we noted in the Introduction, we are particularly interested in the effects of the authoritarian status quo ante and capacities for collective action on democratic quality. Exclusionary military and one-party regimes are more likely to generate distributive conflict. But their *direct* effect on democracy is predominantly negative, although in the CGV dataset that effect disappears after ten years. The effects of Polity and Freedom House scores at t−3 are also consistently significant and in the expected direction; regimes that are more repressive result in weaker democratic outcomes.

It is also important to note that the control for union membership shows a consistently positive and significant effect on the change and level of

Table 5.4 Determinants of Democratic Development: Polity Transitions.

	Changes in Polity Scores			Changes in Freedom House Scores		
	t+1	t+5	t+10	t+1	t+5	t+10
Distributive	8.33***	5.86***	3.59***	-2.26***	-1.67***	-1.01**
	(0.80)	(1.15)	(1.32)	(0.28)	(0.40)	(0.47)
Elite-led	5.75***	3.47***	2.56	-1.04***	-0.76*	-0.63
	(0.95)	(1.29)	(1.63)	(0.29)	(0.40)	(0.50)
Controls						
Union membership	0.10***	0.23***	0.44***	-0.04***	-0.07***	-0.15***
	(0.02)	(0.03)	(0.04)	(0.01)	(0.01)	(0.02)
Log GDP per capita	0.12*	0.20**	-0.09	-0.17***	-0.08***	-0.14***
	(0.07)	(1.00)	(0.12)	(0.02)	(0.03)	(0.04)
Capital share	1.70**	2.35**	0.32	-0.17	0.04	-0.15
	(0.74)	(1.08)	(1.42)	(0.26)	(0.37)	(0.46)
Growth	-0.02**	-0.05***	-0.06***	0.01*	0.00	0.01
	(0.01)	(0.01)	(0.02)	(0.00)	(0.00)	(0.01)

(*continued*)

Table 5.4 (*continued*)

	Changes in Polity Scores			Changes in Freedom House Scores		
	t+1	*t+5*	*t+10*	*t+1*	*t+5*	*t+10*
Military/1 Party$_{t-3}$	-1.04***	-2.70***	-3.92***	0.31***	0.33***	0.61***
	(0.22)	(0.31)	(0.39)	(0.08)	(0.10)	(0.12)
Polity/FH score$_{t-3}$	0.84***	0.68***	0.55***	-0.19***	-0.16***	-0.13***
	(0.01)	(0.02)	(0.03)	(0.00)	(0.01)	(0.01)
Neighboring democracies	1.68***	3.79***	4.07***	-0.58***	-1.05***	-0.78***
	(0.25)	(0.42)	(0.49)	(0.09)	(0.13)	(0.16)
N	2,399	1,872	1,318	2,397	1,874	1,328
Groups	116	117	114	117	117	115
R²	.73	.54	.42	.61	.45	.35

Note: Baseline Prais-Winsten regressions with heteroscedastic panel-corrected standard errors in parentheses. All control variables are at t+1, t+5, and t+10, respectively, depending on the outcome.

democracy as well. Union membership, it should be recalled, was a consistent predictor of distributive conflict transitions. The fact the differences between the two transition paths survive the inclusion of this control suggests that the experiences and expectations generated during mass protests against authoritarian rule have an impact that is independent of longer-term capacity for collective action.[14]

The percentages of neighboring democracies, which were shown in Chapter 2 to significantly affect elite-led transitions, continue to have positive effects on democracy scores: better neighborhoods, more robust democratic rule. Again, however, the distinction between distributive conflict and elite-led transitions holds despite the inclusion of this control. Results for distributive conflict and elite-led transitions are also robust to the inclusion of GDP per capita, capital share, and growth.

Although our regressions provide some empirical support for the proposition that transition path affects democratic quality, they rely on relatively crude and imperfect indicators of democratic quality and are largely correlational. In the next section, we turn to closer, within-case analysis of paired cases. These causal process observations provide a more nuanced picture of the evolution of democratic governance and a more dynamic analysis of the forces that affect it. In particular, they provide us more leverage on how the transitions, as distinguished from longer-run organizational and structural factors, affected subsequent outcomes.

CAUSAL PROCESS OBSERVATION: COMPARING DISTRIBUTIVE CONFLICT AND ELITE-LED CASES

To explore the differences between distributive conflict and elite-led transitions, we undertake four paired comparisons, matched to the extent possible on region, level of income, and the timing of the transition. El Salvador (1984) and Honduras (1982) are low-income Central American countries that transitioned in the context of the region's civil wars. Ukraine (1991) and Belarus (1991) are middle-income countries that became independent with the collapse of the Soviet Union. Zambia (1991) and Ghana (1993) are both low-income, aid-dependent African countries that faced similar international constraints following the end of the Cold War. Uruguay (1984) and Chile (1990) are exemplary of the middle-income Third Wave transitions from military rule in Latin America.

---

[14]We obtain virtually identical results when we substitute union membership with the size of the manufacturing sector—another "collective action" indicator found to have a significant effect on the probability of distributive transitions.

Table 5.5 Distributive Conflict and Elite-Led Transitions: Paired Comparisons.

	GDP per Capita (US$)	Polity (t-1)	Average Polity (t to t+5)
Central America, low-income			
El Salvador 1984 (CGV and Polity, distributive conflict)	2,646	–6	6
Honduras 1982 (CGV and Polity, elite-led)	1,481	–1	5.4
Former Soviet Union, middle-income			
Ukraine 1991 (Polity only, distributive conflict)	5,503	–7	6.4
Belarus 1991 (CGV and Polity, elite-led)	4,745	–7	3.5
Sub-Saharan Africa, low-income			
Zambia 1991 (Polity only, distributive conflict)	911	–9	5
Ghana 1993 (CGV only, elite-led)	753	–7	–0.8
South America, middle-income			
Uruguay 1984 (CGV and Polity, distributive conflict)	4,394	–7	9.2
Chile 1990 (CGV and Polity, elite-led)	3,349 (1987)	–6	8

Table 5.5 shows GDP per capita and pre- and post-transition Polity scores in each pair of cases, with the distributive conflict case listed first. As can be seen, the outcomes of these transitions are by no means all consolidated "high-quality" democracies; outside of South America, the record is decidedly mixed. Moreover, the post-transition averages, although conforming to expectations, are in some cases small. However, as we will see by considering both the path of Polity scores over time and more qualitative evidence, the differences are more pronounced than these indices suggest.

In the case studies, we consider how social mobilization influenced the outcomes outlined in the introduction to this chapter. We attempt to identify decisions or behaviors taken—or avoided—in the run-up to the transition and in the immediate post-transition period that appear to have had long-term consequences for the quality of democratic politics. We focus in particular on three institutional developments: the extent to which authoritarian elites and their democratic successors were able to limit the competitiveness of the electoral system; the extent of institutional prerogatives or "lock in" that gave authoritarian officeholders, their democratic successors, or the military political discretion; and the extent to which outgoing elites or their democratic successors were able to limit political rights and civil liberties. To what extent did prior features of the distributive conflict cases, or particular transitional processes, affect such limits on democratic rule?

A Civil War Context: El Salvador and Honduras

In both El Salvador and Honduras, incumbent military regimes acceded to the election of constituent assemblies and multiparty elections, won by José Napoleón Duarte (1984) and Roberto Suazo (1982), respectively. The changes in both political systems were strongly pressed by the United States, which viewed political liberalization as a necessary step in blocking the spread of insurgency in Central America. Neither of the new democratic regimes can be considered fully consolidated (Figure 5.5). However, the two cases differ in the role played by distributive conflict in the transition and, as a result, in the openness of elections, the extent of discretion on the part of nominally democratic governments, and the protection of civil and political liberties.

El Salvador constitutes a relatively rare case of a distributive conflict transition driven by insurgency:[15] a bloody civil war lasting over a decade (1980–91) between landed oligarchs and the right-wing military on the one hand, and a coalition of leftist groups (the Farabundo Martí Front for National Liberation, or FMLN) that had launched a major rural rebellion on the other. The insurgency forced the United States and incumbent elites to look for new political strategies to maintain influence and as a result produced more far-reaching political compromises than would have occurred in its absence. The 1984 transition marked the initial phase of a decline in the influence of the oligarchy and military establishment, an increase in the importance of electoral politics, and the eventual incorporation of the FMLN into a more competitive political system.

Honduras, by contrast, was spared the upheaval of civil war. The rural insurgency was smaller and more fragmented than elsewhere in Central America, and urban social forces were limited in organization and scope. As a result, neither the military regime nor the economic elite faced

---

[15] Wood 2000, 2001.

Figure 5.5 Democratization in Honduras and El Salvador

significant domestic threats from below. Rather, the shift to democratic rule was coded as "preemptive" in our dataset, motivated by military concerns about regularizing lines of succession within the coup-prone country.[16] Both the United States and the Honduran government feared contagion from other countries in Central America.[17] But in the absence of challenges from below, elite parties continued to dominate the political system, the military maintained substantial discretion, and the protection of political liberties and civil rights lagged developments in El Salvador.

The authoritarian regime in El Salvador was a particularly brutal example of a "labor-repressive" model of domination discussed in Chapter 3. Notwithstanding brief experiments with political liberalization, it was characterized by a harshly repressive alliance between the military and the agrarian oligarchy that closed off most institutional avenues of political participation. During the 1970s, the regime managed challenges from below with not only electoral fraud, but violent suppression of peaceful strikes and demonstrations. Such repression led directly to the

---

[16] Honduras had undergone thirteen coups between 1900 and 1980, and three incumbents had been overthrown in the 1970s alone (Lehoucq 2012).

[17] Booth, Wade, and Walker 2010: chap. 8.

radicalization of the rural insurgency, which in turn ultimately spurred the political transformations of the 1980s and 1990s.[18]

In October 1979, following the Nicaraguan revolution against Anastasio Somoza, a reformist coalition of junior military officers and civilian reformers overthrew Carlos Humberto Romero, the incumbent military ruler. But an escalating campaign of death squad murders and terror by hard-line military and civilian extremists undermined the junta's reform initiatives and plunged the country deeper into civil war. In response to the threat posed by the FMLN, the United States began to press the military and oligarchy to adopt a counterinsurgency strategy with a strong political component, including the election of a constituent assembly in 1982 and presidential elections, which took place in 1984. In the face of both the revolutionary threat and US pressure, the oligarchy adapted to the new political strategy. The centrist Christian Democratic Party, which had been terrorized and repressed in 1979–81, was allowed to compete for office. And the oligarchy itself transformed what had been a paramilitary organization into a right-wing party, the National Republican Alliance (ARENA), to contest the constituent assembly and presidential elections.

In the initial phases of reform, the political system seemed semidemocratic at best. Polity scores remained at the lower Polity bound (6 from 1984 to 1990), and there is a substantial debate about whether the system was democratic at all.[19] In the 1984 presidential elections, ARENA accepted the victory of a moderate Christian Democratic reformer, José Napoleón Duarte, who in the 1970s had been arrested, tortured, and sent into exile; but the oligarchy continued to control the assembly and remained intent on excluding rather than incorporating the FMLN into the political system.[20] Peace initiatives undertaken by Duarte failed, and the military continued to enjoy discretion in prosecuting the war against the FMLN.

Even though the civil war raged on, however, the political and institutional changes between 1982 and 1984 reflected an important shift in the underlying balance of power attributable to the revolutionary threat in the countryside. On the one hand, as indicated, the "counterinsurgency reforms" had widened the space for action by competing political parties, unions, NGO service providers, community organizations, and other civil society groups that had been targeted during the most repressive phases of the conflict.[21] At the same time, important changes in the oligarchy's

---

[18] Lehoucq 2012; Booth, Wade, and Walker 2010.

[19] Karl 1995; Wolf 2009.

[20] Duarte, a moderate Christian Democrat, had been blocked from the presidency by electoral fraud in 1972 and was driven into exile in 1974.

[21] Foley 1996: 74–77.

economic interests and political resources—changes induced by the insurgency itself—encouraged a greater willingness to work within the new
constitutional framework. In response to the challenges posed by the
FMLN, coffee interests had increasingly shifted investment from production to more urban-based commercial and financial activities that were
less reliant on repressive means of labor control and less threatened by
insurgent demands for agrarian reform. As a consequence, elites became
significantly more open over time to accommodation not only with the
political center, but eventually with the insurgent left itself.[22]

These accommodations were reached in the early 1990s, but only after
additional political and military struggle. In November 1989, the FMLN
launched a major offensive. The attack failed to ignite the general uprising
that the FMLN had hoped for, but also revealed the incompetence of the
military to deal with the insurgent threat, ultimately adding to the pressure for compromise. International developments were clearly crucial in
this process. Already by the late 1980s, the United States and other international actors had begun to press for a negotiated settlement with the
FMLN; and in 1990–91, as the Cold War came to a close, the most ex-
tremist combatants in the civil war faced a loss of support from their external backers. All of this clearly facilitated the effort of the United Nations to broker a peace accord.

By this time, however, domestic political circumstances were also aligned
for a breakthrough. Negotiations with the FMLN were led by Alfredo
Cristiani, a moderate ARENA politician who drew his support primarily from the commercial and urban sectors of the oligarchy. Elected to
the presidency on a "peace platform" in 1989, he played a key role over
the next several years in negotiating a peace accord, aided by the mediation of the Catholic Church and the United Nations. The formal agreements, signed in Chapultepec, Mexico, in 1992, imposed important concessions on the military establishment. They provided for a 70 percent
reduction in the size of the armed forces, the transfer of control over the
intelligence agencies to the presidency, and the dissolution of other instruments of official terror such as the National Guard and the Treasury
Police. At the same time, the agreements also provided for the integration
of the FMLN as a legitimate political party, in exchange for its commitment to demobilize its guerilla forces.

As with the initial transition in 1984, debate continues on whether
the peace agreement signaled a definitive break in El Salvador's political
history;[23] as can be seen in Figure 5.5, there are only marginal improvements in the country's Polity score. With its superior command of eco-

---

[22] Bulmer-Thomas 1987; Wood 2000, 2001.
[23] Stahler-Sholk 1994; Karl 1995; Wolf 2009.

nomic resources, the conservative ARENA party was able to compete and win in successive presidential elections in 1994, 1999, and 2004. Progress was relatively halting with respect to the human rights agenda and legal, judicial, and police reform, as well as military accountability for past human rights abuses. Consequently, Freedom House civil liberties scores for El Salvador improve in the early 1990s but remain at middling levels (3). Elections, however, were held under the auspices of international observers, and Freedom House political rights scores improve from 3 to 2 in 1997 and remain at that level through the end of our dataset. In an important marker of the institutionalization of competitive politics, an FMLN candidate, Mauricio Funes, won the 2009 presidential election and took office without incident in June of that year.

Honduras escaped the revolutionary challenges that shook El Salvador, despite even higher rates of poverty and an extreme concentration of wealth. In the absence of pressure from below, however, democratization in that country was characterized by less open contestation, continuing elite and military domination, and the erratic protection of civil and political liberties.

The weakness of the revolutionary challenge can be traced to the relative flexibility of the old regime.[24] During the 1970s, Honduras was the poorest society in Central America, and as in El Salvador, about a third of the rural families were without land.[25] During the 1960s and 1970s, however, military regimes in Honduras ruled with a lighter and less repressive touch than those in El Salvador, with counterintuitive results for the nature of democratic rule. In contrast to their counterparts in El Salvador, they undertook a modest program of colonization and land reform in response to the Alliance for Progress. Labor unions, which were based primarily in foreign-owned banana plantations, were also allowed considerable latitude to press wage claims, and the Catholic clergy was allowed to build grassroots organizations. Even in the late 1970s, when the government came under the control of more hard-line military factions, "there were no death squads, no systemized torture, and no rash of disappearances."[26] In contrast to El Salvador, the regime "negotiated differences with their opponents, and thus discouraged them from taking up arms against incumbents."[27]

In some respects, the 1982 transition in Honduras stemmed from a combination of factors that resembled those in El Salvador: external pressure from the Carter administration, military concerns about stabilizing

[24] Lehoucq 2012.
[25] Lehoucq 2012.
[26] Booth, Wade, and Walker 2010: 162.
[27] Lehoucq 2012: 60.

the succession of leadership, as well as pressure from leaders of the traditional elite parties. Roberto Suazo, a leading politician of the Liberal Party, was selected as president of a constituent assembly formed in 1980 and won the subsequent election for the presidency in 1981 against the conservative National Party candidate. The transfer of power from a military to an elected civilian government accounts for the increase in the Polity score from –1 to 6.

Also similar to El Salvador, the military and the oligarchy continued to retain influence following this transition. However, whereas military influence began to wane in El Salvador, the absence of serious pressures from below allowed for a deepening of military influence on the political process in Honduras. Under the sway of right-wing chief of the armed forces, General Gustavo Álvarez Martínez, and with encouragement from the Reagan administration, the military continued to exercise discretion outside of civilian control and launched a "small but brutal 'dirty war' of torture and assassination against suspected revolutionaries, using the army and police to infiltrate unions, student organizations, and peasant groups."[28] Álvarez was ultimately deposed in a coup in 1984, but human rights in the country showed surprisingly little improvement, and may have even deteriorated; Freedom House civil liberty scores exhibit no change as a result of the transition and stagnate (at the level of 3) through the end of our dataset.

Unlike El Salvador, moreover, the oligarchy also proved more adept at limiting the competitiveness of the electoral system. Politics was dominated by Liberal and Conservative parties, largely white elite groupings with weak accountability to a society with a large mestizo and Indian majority. Liberal Party presidents Carlos Roberto Reina (1994–98) and Carlos Flores Facussé (1998–2002) gradually reestablished formal civilian control over the military and separated the national police from the armed forces. Nevertheless, in 1994, the Freedom House political liberties measure, which had improved during the transition, actually slid backward and the country was reclassified as "partly free."[29] The effort to address spiraling gang violence through a "mano dura" policy raised new concerns about human rights violations on the part of private security forces and death squads as well as the military, police, and a weak judicial system.[30]

Limits on the openness of the political systems became especially evident when President Manuel Zelaya, elected in 2005 as a "member in good

[28]Ruhl 2011: 547.

[29]Civil liberties show no change during the transition. Political rights improve from 6 (1980) to 4 (1981) to 3 (1982–83) to 2 (1984–93), before dropping back to 3 (1994) through the end of our dataset.

[30]Manz 2008: 23–28.

standing" of the oligarchy, began to engage in populist appeals to peasants, labor unions, and the urban poor. In 2009, the same year that the FMLN gained the presidency in El Salvador, Zelaya was ousted in a coup by a coalition of military officers and conservative civilian politicians. Because conservatives in the Congress and the Supreme Court maintained legal formalities, Honduras's Polity score remained unchanged. In the view of most observers, however, the ouster represented an indicator of the weak checks on military discretion and drew widespread regional condemnation as a rupture of the democratic process, including by the OAS. Indicative of these assessments, Freedom House registered further backsliding from 3 to 4 on both political liberties and civil rights in 2010.

El Salvador and Honduras are in many respects strikingly similar, in terms of both the historical domination of the military and oligarchy and the problematic character of the post-transition democracy. Nevertheless, the preceding narratives show that within these limitations the type of transition did make a difference. In Honduras, the absence of a distributive challenge during the 1980s and 1990s contributed to a persistence of oligarchic domination of the political system, a deterioration in checks on the military, and an erosion of political rights and civil liberties. In El Salvador, the threat from below caused an economic and political reorientation of the oligarchy, impelled the military to accept the entry of centrist parties and the FMLN into the political system, and resulted in at least a marginally more robust defense of political rights and civil liberties. The origins of these differences can be found in the historical development of the insurgency in El Salvador. It was the actual mobilization from below, however—and its successes—that set in train the elite search for political alternatives and thus differentiating the two cases.

Soviet Successors: Ukraine and Belarus

Political transitions in Ukraine and Belarus occurred in the context of the breakup of the Soviet Union. In both cases former communists remained in executive office; and in both cases they joined forces or merged with emergent nationalist oppositions to declare independence after the attempt by Soviet hard-liners to reestablish control in August 1991. The governments that emerged from these transitions were limited democracies at best. At the time of their transitions, Ukraine and Belarus reached the Polity threshold scores of 6 and 7, respectively, but restrictions on political competition led Levitsky and Way to characterize them as competitive authoritarian regimes.[31]

---

[31] Levitsky and Way 2010: 201–7, 213–20.

However these regimes were initially classified, their post-transition political trajectories differed dramatically. Within a few years of its transition, a new autocratic ruler, Alexander Lukashenko, consolidated power in Belarus, while opposition forces beat back similar attempts in Ukraine. These differences are reflected in the evolution of the Polity scores as shown in Figure 5.6, as well as in the evolution of Freedom House political rights and civil liberties scores, which improve marginally over time in Ukraine and deteriorate badly in Belarus.[32]

It is important to acknowledge that these outcomes were shaped by international factors, as well as by differences in pressure from below. Belarus was closer to Russia from the outset, while Ukraine sought deeper ties with the West. But the importance of these differences should not be exaggerated. Ukraine had little chance of gaining access to the EU, unlike the Eastern European states. Like Belarus, it also had strong economic and cultural ties to Russia, including substantial energy subsidies and a large Russian-speaking population in the Crimea and the east. As is clear from the ongoing political crisis that erupted in 2013, moreover, Russian pressure placed a major constraint on democracy in Ukraine. As we elaborate below, the diverging paths of Ukraine and Belarus are attributable in large part to contrasting degrees of popular mobilization at the time of transition and following it.[33]

The movement toward independence in Ukraine was driven by an upsurge of nationalist protests, mass events, such as a human chain and large music festivals, as well as strikes and demonstrations by workers. Although prior levels of social organization were relatively low, as was also the case in Belarus, these ethnonationalist protests led decisively to the defeat of hard-line communists and the dismantling of the communist party organization. Furthermore, they proved to be enduring features of Ukrainian politics. Prior to the Russian intervention of 2014, social mobilization organized around ethnoregional cleavages served as a powerful check on the efforts of successive presidents to establish authoritarian control.[34]

In Belarus, these pressures were largely absent, both during the transition and afterward. In contrast to Ukraine, the public had become highly Russified during the Soviet era. As Way argues, "the absence of a popular alternative national idea meant that . . . the opposition had a much harder time framing anti-incumbent conflicts in ways that resonated with

---

[32] In Ukraine both political rights and civil liberties scores oscillate between 3,3 and 4,4 respectively from 1991–2003, but then improve to 3,2 after 2005. In Belarus, by contrast, Freedom House scores start marginally lower (4,4) but drop to 5,5 in 1995, 6,6 in 1996, and 7,6 in 2004.

[33] Beissinger 2002.

[34] Way 2015.

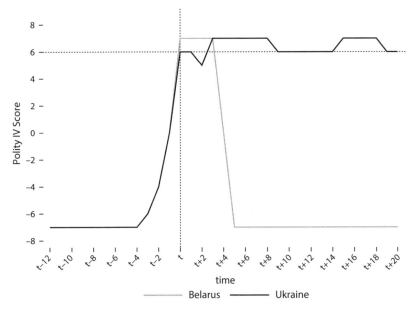

Figure 5.6 Democratization in Ukraine and Belarus

larger groups in the population."[35] The transition, consequently, was led from above, without a significant dismantling of the nomenklatura, the secret police, or economic organs of state control. In the election of 1994, the Communist officials who had led the transition were defeated by an outsider, Alexander Lukashenko. With little opposition from civil society, however, the new president proceeded to reconstitute a highly autocratic regime out of the political and economic building blocks that the transition had left intact (Figure 5.6).

We turn first to Ukraine, where nationalist protests mentioned above forced hard-liners from power in 1991, particularly in the western regions of the country. Leonid Kravchuk, the first head of government, had been a leader of the reform wing of the Communist Party, but the party organization itself crumbled in the face of the massive wave of protest, with its assets seized and its headquarters closed. As Way notes, "abandoning the Communist Party was widely seen as the only way for top level elites such as Kravchuk 'to save themselves' and remain in power."[36]

The nature of the transition had at least two long-term effects on future political developments. First, the collapse of both the party and state

[35] Way 2015: 254.
[36] Way 2014: 2.

organization meant that Kravchuk could not rely on the security forces to repress dissent during the economic and political crisis of the early 1990s.[37] At the same time, the protest that ousted the hard-liners also removed impediments to enlarging economic ties with the West. Although market reforms in Ukraine were halting and tainted with corruption, they paved the way for the emergence of independent oligarchic centers of power that further limited opportunities to consolidate political control. Kravchuk and his successors could build support by creating alliances with one or another oligarchic faction. But the need to rely on private-sector allies, in conjunction with continuing threats from below, significantly constrained the ability of incumbents to manipulate the political process.

Following the transitional presidential elections in 1991, constitutional conflicts emerged between President Kravchuk and the legislature. A key issue—as became apparent in Belarus and other former Soviet republics—was the question of how much power presidents would wield. Could they exercise discretion in ways that weakened horizontal constraints on their authority? In 1992, as the economy deteriorated, Kravchuk dismissed his first prime minister and, under pressure from the parliament, appointed Leonid Kuchma in his place. Conflicts between the branches of government escalated, however, when parliament refused to extend decree powers that it had initially granted to Kuchma to enable him to advance a major reform program. Kravchuk responded with a decree establishing a temporary Extraordinary Committee of the Cabinet of Ministers to deal with economic matters. The issuing of the decree, however, coincided with a massive strike by coal miners in the Donbas region of Eastern Ukraine that focused not only on wages and mine safety, but demanded a national referendum of confidence in the president and parliament. In response to the demands of the strikers, Kravchuk removed Kuchma and replaced him with an official sympathetic with the miners. Parliament ultimately accepted Kuchma's removal, but Kravchuk agreed to early presidential and parliamentary elections. Social as well as institutional checks proved crucial in restraining the growth of presidential power.

The more open political landscape also encouraged the emergence of a fragmented but highly competitive party system. Kuchma overcame attempts by Kravchuk to deploy state resources to stay in office and won the presidency in a runoff election in 1994. Dozens of parties stood in the legislative elections of 1994; the top vote-getter was the Communist Party, but with only 12 percent of the popular vote. A strong regional voting pattern emerged, with the left stronger in the east and south, and nationalist parties capturing support in the west. Although parties subsequently

[37]Way 2014.

coalesced less around ideology than regional oligarchs, subsequent elections were characterized by raucous political competition.

Turnover at the top did not altogether eliminate the autocratic practices that had marred the early years of independence. On the contrary, Kuchma engaged in behavior that mirrored that of his predecessor: deploying the resources of the state to build alliances with crony capitalists, intimidating the media, and manipulating the electoral process. Unlike Lukashenko in Belarus, however, Kuchma was never able to fully consolidate authoritarian control.

As Bunce and Wolchik show, civil society networks emerging in the early and mid-1990s played an indispensable role in keeping the political system competitive and providing at least some checks on the government.[38] Only a small fraction of the population belonged to civil society organizations in Ukraine,[39] as was generally the case in the post-Soviet republics; formal organizations were often short-lived. But the political elite could not close off the leadership networks that had emerged during the transition, nor close the door on the flow of US and European assistance to democratic NGOs and other civil society groups. Think tanks—particularly the Center for Economic and Political Studies of Ukraine—provided independent sources of information. From the 1994 elections, civic education and election monitoring groups began to train election observers and conduct exit polling. These groups, in turn, provided the underpinnings of the mass mobilization that escalated following revelations in 2000 that the president was implicated in the abduction of an opposition journalist. The Ukraine Without Kuchma movement, led by veterans of the student movement of the 1990s, spearheaded protests that persisted for months before ultimately being shut down by force.[40]

The organizational experience gained during these protests set the stage for the Orange Revolution, a mass movement that successfully protested not only the blatantly fraudulent presidential elections of 2004, but also the wider abuse of executive authority. The movement had its origins in the formation of a broad coalition of four opposition parties that initially included the postcommunist Socialist Party.[41] The 2004 presidential election pitted Kuchma's favored successor, Prime Minister Viktor Yanukovych, against Victor Yushchenko, an opposition figure with a career path as a banker. Following the first round of the election, mass protests occurred across the country as official tallies diverged sharply from exit polls.

[38] Bunce and Wolchik 2011: 127–38.
[39] Stepanenko 2006.
[40] Bunce and Wolchik 2011: 132.
[41] Two core pillars of the coalition, Viktor Yushchenko of Our Ukraine and Yulia Tymoshenko, subsequently established "Force of the People" as an electoral coalition and a broader social movement.

To some extent, dissident members of the oligarchy and former political insiders encouraged these challenges. Again, however, student activists and movement networks—particularly Pora! (It's Time)—were critical actors. Prior to the election, these organizations had engaged in door-to-door canvassing and information campaigns to get out the vote; following it, election monitors and student strike committees diffused the charges of fraud and organized protests.[42]

Although the Supreme Court ultimately broke the deadlock between the parties on the issue and forced a new election, there can be little doubt that the scope of the protest influenced their actions. In the aftermath of the revolution, constitutional reforms increased the power of the parliament, and electoral politics became more competitive still. These developments occurred over a decade following the transition, but it is possible to trace a lineage from the early nationalist protests to not only the Orange Revolution but also the crises of 2013–14. In this most recent episode of mass mobilization, protests on the Maidan brought down the government of Viktor Yanukovych when he reneged on a promise—under Russian pressure—to sign an association agreement with the EU. These conflicts, to be sure, left Ukraine's democracy—as well as the state itself—vulnerable to Russian incursions that exploited ethnonationalist disaffection in the eastern part of the country. But the principal challenge to democracy has been geopolitical, not domestic. Throughout most of the period considered here Ukraine was much more open than Belarus.

Indeed, political developments in Belarus took a fundamentally different path. As in Ukraine, Communist Party officials remained in control of the legislature when the Soviet republics held multiparty elections in 1990. But in contrast to Ukraine, where nationalist protests drove hardliners from power, in Belarus, where such pressures were absent, it was the old-guard faction of the party that triumphed. In the anti-Gorbachev coup of August 1991, top Belarus officials even appeared to side with the putsch, in sharp contrast to Ukraine, where the coup triggered the declaration of independence. In August 1991, parliament formally dissolved the Communist Party, but incumbents beat back an opposition petition movement for a referendum on the holding of new elections, and agreed only to a small shortening of the legislature's term.

Even after the dissolution of the party, the nomenklatura and many of the building blocks of state control remained in place. The security apparatus continued to penetrate most major state institutions, and although central planning institutions were eliminated, the government retained de jure control over most of the economy. Whereas Kuchma and his successors were highly dependent on the support of independent private-sector

[42] Bunce and Wolchik 2011: 135–37.

allies, the predominance of the state sector in Belarus offered greater opportunities for incumbents to manipulate patronage and employment for political advantage.[43] In the absence of pressure from below, these resources—inherited from the Soviet era—provided the foundations for a recentralization of power under Alexander Lukashenko.

Comparison to Ukraine can be sharpened by looking at the outcome of the second round of elections that took place in the two countries in 1994. Lukashenko came to power in the 1994 presidential elections in Belarus, held in the midst of a severe transitional economic crisis. He ran on an anticorruption platform as an outsider and a reformer, but once in office moved swiftly to consolidate power at the expense of both the legislature and the opposition. By early 1995, Lukashenko had established control over the entire state administration, the economy, and the media and imposed an "information blockade" on the activities of the opposition. He also imposed restrictions on campaign spending and coverage of the elections. The legislative elections held in May 1995 were characterized by widespread irregularities.[44]

As in Ukraine, conflicts with the opposition escalated quickly into confrontations over constitutional prerogatives. At the time of the May 1995 parliamentary elections, voters were also presented by a referendum written by Lukashenko which, in addition to other controversial issues, allowed the president to dismiss the parliament. Parliament sought to beat back the referendum in advance, and protested the outcome when it was announced as passed. In contrast to Ukraine, however—which witnessed mass mobilization over similar executive efforts—protests by parliament had no effect, despite the fact that both the Constitutional Court and external monitors, such as the OSCE, passed judgments against the administration. Lukashenko increasingly ruled by decree.

In 1996, constitutional conflicts escalated even more when Lukashenko sought to consolidate his control through yet another constitutional referendum that would further weaken the legislature, expand presidential decree powers, and extend the term of office to seven years. The parliament responded by initiating impeachment procedures against the president, and the country began to experience its first significant social protests. These proved, however, to be weaker and less costly to the leadership than those occurring in Ukraine. Lukashenko's bid to extend his control received a decisive assist from the Russian government, which pressed wavering legislators to abandon the impeachment proceedings. When the legislature gave up on this effort, protests also collapsed. The constitutional referendum went forward in 1996, with massive fraud and

---

[43] Way 2014: 8.
[44] Silitski 2005: 86.

intimidation. Lukashenko's referendum items passed overwhelmingly, while those put to the voters by parliament—on constitutional change, election of local officials, and transparency in government—were roundly defeated.

In the ensuing decade, Lukashenko consolidated his power still further, purging civil society of independent groups, eliminating the flow of Western funding for NGOs, and imprisoning or murdering opposition leaders. Mass protests did erupt over fraud in the 2006 elections, but while these echoed Ukraine's Orange Revolution of 2004, they were smaller in scale and dissipated quickly. Lack of coordination and planning among relatively weak civil society groups contributed to this outcome. As Silitski argues, "the protests ended as they began—as spontaneous, poorly organized, ill-provided, dissident-like actions." All of this, he continues, "stands in marked contrast to what happened in Ukraine, where the post-election protests were carefully planned, amply supplied with human and material resources, pursued a clear political goal, and enjoyed the full involvement of the political opposition in close coordination with civil society."[45]

As noted, the relationship with Russia constitutes an important external difference in the two cases. The Belarus nomenklatura was clearly closer and more committed to Russia from the outset and Russian support was an instrumental factor in Lukashenko's ascendency. But as the Ukrainian crisis of 2013–14 proved, the relationship with Russia was itself largely a result of domestic political differences: the presence of mass nationalist mobilization in the Ukrainian case and its absence in Belarus.

This difference had wide-ranging implications for the extent of central control over the economy and all of the three outcomes outlined in the introduction: the competitiveness of the political and electoral system, the extent of checks on the executive, and the relative power of social forces to engage in mass mobilization from below. Executives in both countries sought to exploit the benefits of office for personal as well as political gain, but the capacity to pursue this project was far more limited in Ukraine than in Belarus. Moreover, the reasons for this difference appeared to lie not in longer-standing institutional or organizational differences, but in how nationalist political forces mobilized during the transition itself.

Transitions in the Southern Cone: Uruguay and Chile

We turn next to Uruguay and Chile, two middle-income South American countries that had once been dominated by highly repressive, right-wing military regimes, but are currently considered among the more successful

---

[45] Silitski 2006: 146.

and consolidated of the Third Wave transitions. In Uruguay, distributive pressures from below disrupted efforts by the ruling elite to preserve institutional prerogatives and exclude leftist political parties. In Chile, which we code as an elite-led transition, the mobilization of de facto pressure—although extensive at an earlier point—had a less direct impact on transfer of power. Partly as a consequence, authoritarian elites retained much greater control over the transition and were able to compel the opposition to accept institutional veto power over significant aspects of the political process. As can be seen in Figure 5.7, the Polity scores of the two countries don't converge until 17 years after the transition. Differences in Freedom House scores follow a similar track; broadly converging toward full democratic norms (by 2000 in Uruguay and 2003 in Chile), but nonetheless with Uruguay showing marginally more robust protection of political rights and civil liberties in the post-transition period viewed as a whole.[46]

There were, we should note, important social and economic differences between the two cases, but it is doubtful that they influenced either the transition or post-transition in predictable ways. Uruguay had a much more equitable distribution of income than Chile, but that fact did not reduce the bitter class conflicts that erupted before the military seized power, or the labor militancy that eventually contributed to its demise. It is also unlikely that a more robust union movement, as distinguished from the transition itself, contributed to the divergence in political outcomes; indeed, according to one estimate, although unions in Uruguay were historically more centralized than in Chile, their percentage of the work force peaked at only 20 percent, as compared to 35 percent in Chile.[47]

Perhaps more significant are differences in short-run economic performance. While the Chilean economy had rebounded strongly by the time Pinochet withdrew from power, the transition in Uruguay occurred during a period of economic crisis that both discredited the military regime and spurred popular protest.[48] But popular protest itself constituted a key causal mechanism checking continuity in elite power and influence in Uruguay. In contrast, the suppression of such protest in Chile gave Pinochet much greater leverage over the transition process.

The transition in Uruguay began in the early 1980s, with a series of unsuccessful military initiatives to establish a constitutional façade that would legitimate its rule. Opposition led by traditional party leaders

---

[46] Combined civil liberties and political rights scores for Uruguay average 3.6 (on a 2–14 scale) for the first 10 post-transitions years and 2.9 from the transition in 1985 through the end of our dataset in 2008. Chile, by contrast, averaged 4.1 from the transition in 1990 through the first ten years, and 3.4 through the end of the dataset.

[47] Roberts 2014: Table 4.1.

[48] Haggard and Kaufman 1995: 48–49.

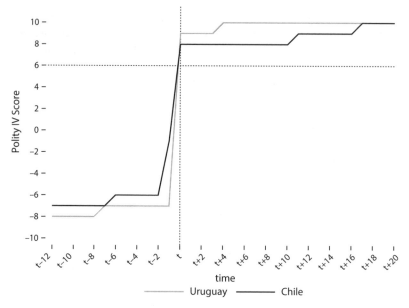

Figure 5.7 Democratization in Uruguay and Chile

played an important role in undermining these efforts, but at critical points in the process, more militant unions and leftist politicians played pivotal roles as well. The first initiative, in 1980, aimed at imposing a new constitution modeled along lines designed by the Pinochet regime in Chile. Whereas Pinochet successfully engineered a referendum approving the constitution, however, the military's initiative in Uruguay was decisively defeated. At this point, traditional parties—still nominally legal under the old regime—spearheaded the opposition. Although unions were banned in the early 1980s, and could not openly campaign against the initiative, workers also played a clandestine role in its defeat. In 1982, workers also helped to defeat a second initiative: stage-managed primary elections designed to install pro-regime politicians as heads of the traditional parties.[49] Instead, the elections resulted in victories for moderate politicians clearly committed to a political transition.[50]

Unions and popular movements began to play a more direct political role following the defeat of these initiatives, as military authorities at last began to negotiate with the traditional opposition parties over the relaxation of political controls. Military hard-liners continued to press for the

[49] Drake 1996; Silva 1998.
[50] Collier 1999: 141.

institutionalization of military veto powers through the continuation of a powerful Council of State and, even more important, for the continued exclusion of the leftist Frente Amplio from electoral participation. But the tentative political liberalization that accompanied the negotiations opened the way to the mobilization of major challenges from below, significantly raising the cost to the military of standing firm. Although unions were still officially banned, they began to mobilize large-scale protests between 1982 and 1984 that proved pivotal in making the system more open and competitive.

A huge general strike in January 1984 is widely viewed as a turning point in the negotiations. By exploiting the rivalry between the traditional Colorado and Blanco parties, the military did succeed in blocking the candidacy of Wilson Ferreira, a leading critic from the Blancos. In the aftermath of the general strike, however, the generals were impelled to abandon their demands to exclude the left from the political system altogether. Despite the fact that they had been the original targets of the military takeover, union and Frente Amplio leaders were granted a seat at the negotiating table, restrictions on their electoral participation were lifted, and the military authorities agreed to abide unconditionally by the outcome of subsequent elections.

Despite the military's abandonment of a "political project," it remained a significant political force in the Uruguayan system for several years after the transition. Julio María Sanguinetti, the winner of the transitional election in 1984, was careful to avoid "radical" policy initiatives that might have provoked a military backlash. But once the military abandoned pursuit of the institutional prerogatives it had originally sought, its influence could be retained only by overtly reentering politics, with all of the risks of a resurgence of mass mobilization that such a move would have brought.

Although politics continued to be dominated for a time by Uruguay's two traditional parties, the political space was open to the left at the outset and the Frente Amplio became an increasingly important force on the political scene. It gained 20 percent of the vote in the 1984 transitional presidential elections, and its vote share steadily increased thereafter. In 1999, the presidential bid by leftist candidate Tabaré Vázquez was forestalled only by an unprecedented coalition between the two traditional parties. In 2004, Vázquez ran again and won the presidency at the head of a broad coalition dominated by the left, and in 2009 he was succeeded by José Mujica, a former leader of the Tupamaros revolutionary movement. Chilean Socialists, as we will see, won the presidency at about the same time, but governed in coalition with a powerful and relatively conservative Christian Democratic party.

Our decision to code the Chilean transition as elite-led is subject to challenge. Unions and allies on the political left did lead massive protests against the regime during the economic crisis of 1982 and 1983, and opened space for the reconstitution of the center-left opposition after a decade of operating underground or in exile. As late as 1986, moreover, the most radical faction of the opposition—primarily from the Communist Party—continued to advocate insurrection, smuggling arms into the country and undertaking an abortive assassination attempt against Pinochet himself. These attempts, however, proved unsuccessful and even counterproductive. As early as 1984—fully five years prior to the transition—major opposition leaders, including the Socialist Ricardo Lagos, had concluded that it would be best to accept the de facto reality of the Pinochet constitution and attempt to "defeat the regime using its own rules."[51] Our coding decision rests on the view that, unlike in Uruguay, negotiations over the transfer of power occurred at a time when this view prevailed and alternative strategies of mass protest or insurrection had been decisively subdued.

The protests of the early 1980s were beaten back with some limited concessions on economic policy, but also by harsh repression. Tanks were sent into the street, a major union leader was assassinated, and on one protest day, a military patrol doused two students with gasoline and set them afire.[52] The failure of mass mobilization to unseat Pinochet intensified divisions within the opposition, with moderate voices like Lagos's (quoted above) insisting more strongly that the strategy should shift from mass mobilization to a mixture of legal challenges and negotiations to nudge the dictator from power. Radical factions continued to press for armed insurrection, but a harsh crackdown after the attempt on Pinochet's life in 1986 brought these efforts to a decisive end. The failed attempt, as Patricio Aylwin, Chile's first post-transition president, stated, was "the breaking point. Repression hardened, and we realized that clearly we had to commit ourselves to a nonviolent path in order to build broad support."[53]

With the radical opposition marginalized by the regime, the opposition coalition of Christian Democrats and Socialists turned their energies toward registering their parties under existing electoral laws and contesting a plebiscite, which the regime itself had scheduled for 1988 with the intention of legitimating Pinochet's continuation in power. Although opponents initially pressed to replace the plebiscite with a competitive election, they were compelled to accept the regime's insistence that it be restricted to an up-or-down vote on Pinochet. Nevertheless, in a surprising victory, the opposition's vigorous "campaign for the no" carried the day and placed Pinochet on the defensive.

[51] Lagos 2015: 64.
[52] Arriagada 2015: 53.
[53] Aylwin 2015: 63.

Unlike in Uruguay, however, the post-plebiscite negotiations over competitive elections and the transfer of power occurred in the absence of pressure from the street. Indeed, "Pinochet's strength continued to be great; it was mostly state and military power. He was the head of a state that functioned and also commander in chief of the armed forces, over which he had absolute power. . . . He also had the support of the upper class and business."[54] The robust performance of the economy,[55] moreover, strengthened Pinochet's hand in negotiating the terms of the transition. As a result, the opposition was forced to accede to a variety of arrangements that locked in institutional prerogatives for the military and right-wing parties, limited the authority of elected officials, and reduced the effective competitiveness of the political system. The military's direct influence on key issues of interest was ensured by permanent seats on a National Security Council, which had veto power over presidential appointments.

The transition itself can be dated to the competitive elections of 1989 that resulted in the victory of a center-left coalition headed by a moderate Christian Democratic politician, Patricio Aylwin. The design of the electoral system, however, had a particularly striking effect on the representativeness of the political system. Unlike the military's unsuccessful initiative in Uruguay, the Pinochet regime did not attempt to ban the left from electoral participation, but did successfully insist on the adoption of a "binomial electoral system" that severely restricted the left's influence. The system allotted two representatives per district and required a party to win two-thirds of the vote in order to win both seats. This arrangement allowed rightist parties to win one of the seats with slightly more than one-third of the vote. As a result, the right alliance's popular vote share of just over 34 percent translated into 40 percent of lower house seats. These electoral rules also substantially strengthened incentives for Socialists to join more conservative Christian Democrats in a center-left coalition. If that were not enough, transitional negotiations granted Pinochet the power to appoint nine "bionic senators" (out of a total of 48 seats), thus ensuring that rightist parties not only were overrepresented in the lower house but would have adequate votes to block major policy and constitutional initiatives requiring legislative supermajorities in the upper chamber.

Over time, these restrictions gradually eroded, particularly as democratically elected presidents filled the "bionic" Senate seats left vacant by the death or retirement of Pinochet appointees. In 2005, these new appointments enabled the government to muster the two-thirds congressional majority necessary to eliminate these positions entirely and to end the military's role on the National Security Council.

---

[54] Arriagada 2015: 54.
[55] Haggard and Kaufman 1995.

However, it is important to underscore that these "transitional" measures were not short-lived; Chile's Polity and Freedom House scores did not converge with Uruguay's until long after the transition (Figure 5.8). Moreover, restraints negotiated at the time of the transition placed significant limits on elected center-left governments. These governments established impressive records on both growth and poverty reduction, and in 1999 a Socialist was elected president at the head of a center-left coalition. For many years following the transition, however, the architecture of the political system guaranteed that no major social or economic policy initiative could survive without negotiation with and concessions to entrenched and overrepresented interests associated with the old regime.

Compared to the other pairs of cases discussed in this chapter, both Chile and Uruguay had the advantage of prior histories of constitutional politics, and both ultimately became "high-quality" democracies with the highest possible Polity (10) and Freedom House (1) scores. Against this shared backdrop, however, the timing and extent of mass mobilization against the regime clearly affected the bargaining power of outgoing authoritarian elites and the nature of the new democratic institutions. Concessions extracted by the outgoing authorities in Chile restricted the competitiveness of the electoral and legislative system, institutionalized provisions for elite vetoes, and at least subtly affected the level of protection for political rights and civil liberties. Indeed, in their important book on democratic consolidation, Linz and Stepan cite Chile as the "clearest case" they study of the imposition of "reserve domains," arguing that "the transition by our definition cannot be [considered] completed until these powers are removed."[56]

The Long Road to Democracy in Zambia and Ghana

The small, aid-dependent African countries faced a dramatically different landscape following the end of the Cold War, including declining Soviet and Western support. As we argued in Chapters 2 and 3, this changed external environment placed a variety of pressures on authoritarian rulers across the continent to liberalize. Both Zambia (transitioning in 1991) and Ghana (1993) faced these constraints, but differed sharply in the extent of mobilization from below, with consequences for the institutionalization of democratic rule.

In Zambia, Kenneth Kaunda's effort to consolidate his rule rested in part on a centralized labor movement linked to the ruling party. But the monopoly of membership and the control over union dues "provided the trade unions the financial and communications resources necessary to

[56] Linz and Stepan 1996: 82.

become an autonomous power."[57] Moreover, the ruling party never succeeded in eliminating the influence of churches, student groups, and civil
society organizations; these eventually coalesced into a unified opposition
under the aegis of the trade union movement. The transition occurred in
the context of strikes by copper workers, students, and postal workers,
and was accompanied by urban rioting. Kaunda's successor subsequently
engaged in practices more characteristic of competitive authoritarian rule
and underwent an outright reversion from democratic rule, a partial
anomaly for our expectations. But the country was gradually brought
back to democracy by the reemergence of mass pressures from below.

The transition in Ghana, by contrast, was initiated "from above" in response to external incentives and was stage-managed by the authoritarian incumbent Jerry Rawlings in the absence of mass mobilization from
below. Coded as a transition in the CGV dataset only, the country initially
fell far short of the standard Polity threshold. The different play of social
forces affected the transition itself, most notably in the fact that there was
a turnover in government in Zambia, while Rawlings remained in the
presidency. It is also noteworthy, however, that as in Zambia, the gradual
improvement in Ghanaian Polity scores visible in Figure 5.8 reflects the
steady emergence of more independent civil society forces after the transition. Indeed, by the end of our dataset in 2008, Ghana actually showed
more robust defense of political liberties and civil rights than in Zambia.

In 1989, the Zambia Congress of Trade Unions (ZCTU), led by Frederick Chiluba, set the Zambian transition in motion with a campaign for
multiparty politics. Chiluba's demands were rooted in part in the unions'
material interests. But he and the ZCTU carried a wider argument to the
public: that a one-party system had proven unable to deal with the prolonged economic crisis of the 1980s. Kaunda initially hoped that he could
diffuse this opposition by scheduling a referendum on "multipartism" that
would nonetheless confirm support for the dominant party he had built,
the United National Independence Party.[58] This plan was derailed, however, in the face of widespread opposition and rioting over the lifting of
maize meal subsidies in June 1990.

The regime then began planning for a snap multiparty election, hoping
to divide the opposition and allow the ruling party to retain its dominance
in a more plural setting.[59] Kaunda made ample use of state resources to
control the political opening. He refused to set a date for balloting until
eight weeks before the election—giving the opposition very little time to
prepare their campaigns—insisted on maintaining a state of emergency

---

[57] Riedl 2014: 116.
[58] Riedl 2014: 154.
[59] Riedl 2014: 154–56.

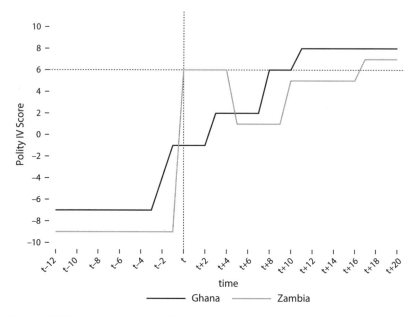

Figure 5.8 Democratization in Ghana and Zambia

throughout the negotiations, and sought to stack the deck against the opposition in disputes over districting, registration lists, and ballot-counting procedures. In short, he engaged in virtually all of the practices we associate with limited transitions.

In response, however, the opposition coalition organized itself as the National Interim Committee for Multiparty Democracy in July 1990 (later the Movement for Multiparty Democracy or MMD), spearheaded by the labor movement, but with support of business and lawyer groups. The focus—as its name implied—was on ensuring the competitiveness of the electoral system. Demands for multiparty elections were backed by large, peaceful rallies in all of the major cities. Under continuing pressure, Kaunda consented to open the electoral process to international observers, and yielded on many of the major opposition demands with respect to patronage and manipulation of the state-controlled media during the campaign. The government was forced to accept a leading role for the opposition in the organization of the transition, and to end the mandatory allegiance of the security forces to the ruling party. It is quite possible that Kaunda simply miscalculated in making these concessions because he believed his status as leader of Zambia's independence movement would carry him to victory in an open electoral contest. But the challenge from a strong, mass-based opposition, including unions, influenced the concessions he was forced to make, and in the end he suffered a crushing electoral defeat.[60]

Once in office, Chiluba was able to capitalize on the fact that his party won overwhelming control of the legislature by consolidating political power at the expense of the opposition; the case bears many of the hallmarks of the "backsliding" reversions we take up in more detail in Chapters 6 to 8. With weak checks on his authority, he subsequently used emergency decrees to rule and manipulated the constitution to limit the extent of contestation. In 1996, Chiluba engineered constitutional changes that barred Kaunda from standing in the presidential elections, permitting him to coast to reelection over a divided and weakened opposition. Chiluba's increasingly autocratic tendencies are reflected in an effective reversion to authoritarian rule; Polity scores decline from 6 to 1 in 1996, only three years after the transition (Figure 5.8), and Freedom House scores show a similar downward drift, from 2 and 3 (for political rights and civil liberties respectively) in 1991–92 to as low as 5 and 4 by the end of the Chiluba presidency.

Chiluba himself, however, ultimately faced pressure from below around the issue of term limits. As we argue in more detail in Chapter 8, term limits do not limit backsliding on their own, but serve to focus public attention on incumbents' intent and provide a focal point for mobilization. A collection of civic groups formed in 2001 under the rubric of the Oasis Forum joined together mainstream Christian churches, the Law Association of Zambia, and an umbrella organization of NGOs outside the MMD network (Nongovernmental Organizations Coordinating Committee). Increasing street protest, along with defections from within his own party, ultimately forced Chiluba to abandon efforts to amend the constitutional prohibition against a third term. In the presidential contest, Chiluba was able to engineer a very small (28 percent) plurality victory for Levy Mwanawasa, his handpicked candidate, over a highly fragmented opposition. Nonetheless, the 2001 elections brought to an end the one-party dominance that had characterized the legislature during the Kaunda and Chiluba years, increased the competitiveness of the electoral system, and restarted the transition process that would later culminate in democratic rule (Figure 5.8).

Mwanawasa, in fact, began to turn on his patron during the campaign, running as a political reformer who would clean up some of the abuses of his predecessor. In 2002, he asked parliament to lift Chiluba's immunity, leading to his arrest and prosecution. Despite the divisions this

[60] Riedl 2014: 156–61.

step caused within the ruling party, Mwanawasa won reelection over a divided opposition in 2006. When he died suddenly of a stroke in 2008, his successor won a very narrow victory over opposition candidate Michael Sata. Sata, in turn, defeated the ruling party candidate and assumed the presidency in 2011. Driven in part by mobilization from below—most notably around the "third term debate" and the elections of 2001—politics in Zambia gradually became much more competitive over the 2000s. Freedom House scores improved after 2006, and the country ultimately returned to democratic rule by Polity coding at the end of the decade.

By contrast, mass mobilization initially played a limited and indeed negligible role in the transition in Ghana. The Bar Association and student organizations had protested Rawlings's rule, and in August 1990 the Movement for Freedom and Justice was created as a forum for these and other civil society organizations to coordinate. The social base of the prodemocracy movement, however, was limited primarily to the elite and large trading and agricultural sectors, and did not effectively engage peasants, urban workers, or even students.[61] Rather, Rawlings's decision to launch a transition to constitutional rule was motivated by "official desires to conform with global and regional trends and thus preempt the application of 'political conditionalities' by international donors."[62] Like the transitions in both Honduras and Belarus, we code it as "preemptive" in nature with international constraints playing a particularly important role.

As a result of the absence of significant pressures from below, Rawlings controlled the transition process throughout and even remained in office when it was through.[63] The Consultative Assembly appointed to draft the new constitution was packed with government partisans and offered very little basis for consultations with the opposition. Throughout the period of deliberation, the government continued to ban party activities and to control the media. Appointments to the electoral commission remained exclusively in the hands of the Rawlings's Provisional National Defense Council. The new constitution, approved by referendum in April 1992, did open the way to multiparty politics and provided for a wide range of political liberties, but it was clearly a creation of the incumbent Rawlings government and vulnerable to his calculations about the extent to which it would be binding.

[61]Gyimah-Boadi 1994: 82.

[62]The incentives facing Rawlings were clearly outlined in an IMF working paper titled "Ghana: Economic Development in a Democratic Environment" (Leite et al. 2000), which traced how the multilaterals came to see broadened political support, "ownership," and participation as critical elements in the success of complex structural adjustment programs. Gyimah-Boadi 1994: 78.

[63]Riedl 2014: 136–37.

The difference between the levels of pressure from below in Zambia and Ghana was most evident in the organization and outcome of the founding elections, a useful indicator of the competitiveness of the political system. In Ghana, presidential elections were rigged in Rawlings's favor. Refusal to update the voting registration list, for example, left many opposition supporters disenfranchised, and Rawlings won an overwhelming victory (58.4 percent vs. 30.3 for his closest rival, Albert Adu Boahen) that was virtually the mirror image of Kaunda's defeat.

The changes in politics that did occur after 1992 were not altogether trivial. Opposition forces were allowed to hold rallies and won a number of important court battles over the right of assembly and access to the state-controlled media. The independent press, moreover, was allowed to flourish. However, an opposition decision to boycott the parliamentary elections of 1992 allowed Rawlings to maintain unchecked control over the legislature and further reduced the competitiveness of the political system. This changed marginally after the 1996 parliamentary elections, when the opposition won a third of the seats permitting increased scrutiny of government activities. This turnover in the legislature was the basis of the CGV coding that the system was in fact democratic, and Polity scores also turned up accordingly (Figure 5.8). Nevertheless, during his initial years in office, Rawlings had essentially unilateral control over political appointments and government finances and moved to roll back some of the constitutional limits that had been established on executive authority.

As in Zambia, the transition to more democratic politics was triggered by debates over term limits and the emergence of more sustained pressure from below. Rawlings failed in an attempt to impose his successor and accepted a transfer of office to the opposition candidate, John Kufuor, who assumed the presidency in 2001. Tense relations between the two, evenly divided political blocs marked politics in subsequent years. The Kufuor government purged Rawlings's supporters from the government bureaucracy and launched investigations into abuses of power. Supporters of the former regime responded with acts of intimidation and threats of violence. Nevertheless, electoral competition remained relatively free and open, with Kufuor winning a second term in 2004 and John Atta Mills, a Rawlings ally, regaining the presidency in 2008.

Unlike in the other pairs of cases, the transitions in Zambia and Ghana had much more ambiguous effects. Zambia experienced an outright reversion under Polity coding rules, and the CGV transition in Ghana was clearly a shallow electoral one that permitted substantial abuse of executive power. Our within-case analysis, however, confirms some theoretical expectations about these transitions, partial as they might be. First, the initial transition in Zambia, driven by union pressures and wider mobilization, was initially more robust than that in Ghana on at least two of the dimensions we outlined at the outset—the competitiveness of the electoral system, and the protection of political rights and civil liberties—even if it proved weaker in its ability to check executive abuses. In both countries, however, the mobilization of social pressures from below—particularly on the issue of term limits—contributed to the gradual transition to more competitive politics in the 2000s.

Conclusion

Neither our quantitative nor qualitative analysis supports strong claims of enduring path dependence. Only in the Ukraine-Belarus comparison do we see gross differences between the distributive conflict and elite-led cases that appear to last. In the other pairs, differences are more subtle. Moreover, the statistical analysis suggests that the effects of the transition path are subject to decay. This should not be surprising; the consolidation of democracy is clearly affected by a variety of longer-run structural factors—level of income, international linkages, and social divisions—that do not operate through the transition process itself. The cases also clearly demonstrate that the development of democracy depends on changing economic and social conditions in the post-transition period and the strategies adopted by the main political contenders.

Notwithstanding these caveats, both the statistical and qualitative evidence does show some interesting effects of transition paths on the extent of democracy in both the short and medium run. The descriptive statistics presented in Figures 5.1 to 5.4 showed particularly stark differences between distributive conflict and elite-led cases in the pre-transition period, and as a result in the extent of political change during the transitional years. Even controlling for such factors as inequality, union strength, GDP, and economic growth in the multivariate regressions, distributive conflict transitions had higher Polity and Freedom House Political Rights scores in the years immediately following the transition but extending out to as long as ten years as well. In combination, these measures capture the fact that distributive conflict transitions are followed by not only more open and competitive electoral politics but also greater limitations on the residual power of authoritarian elites, stronger horizontal checks on executives, and more robust defense of political rights and civil liberties.

Our qualitative comparisons of matched pairs of cases allow us to break out of the country-year constraints of panel designs and permit closer attention to within-country changes and mechanisms. In particular, the cases provide some leverage on how mass mobilization may matter during the transition itself. The answers can be found in both the effects of protest on the negotiations between outgoing authoritarian incumbents or democratic successors and oppositions over the rules of the game.

The qualitative comparisons suggest that the statistical differences between distributive conflict and elite-led transitions should probably be taken as a lower bound of the effects of mass mobilization. Despite the establishment of constitutional institutions and electoral competition, military and economic elites remained potent political forces in the Central American cases and the space for participation in both countries remained limited. In El Salvador, however, the existential threat posed by the FMLN motivated more wide-ranging constitutional reforms than occurred in Honduras, and the incorporation of altogether different social forces into the political arena. Opening the political system to moderate and centrist political forces in the 1980s constituted an important step toward opening it still wider in the 1990s. In Honduras, by contrast, elite parties continued to dominate the political system and the military's political role remained intrusive, with adverse effects on political rights and civil liberties.

As noted, the differences between Ukraine and Belarus were particularly marked. These could be traced to the development of nationalism in the two countries and to linguistic and regional differences. But the effects of those underlying differences became manifest and significant only through social protest. The comparison is particularly useful in showing how mass mobilization can check abuse of power. Political elites in Ukraine—including both Kravchuk and Kuchma—were much less successful in closing down the political space than were their counterparts in Belarus, where the system drifted in an increasingly authoritarian direction over time. The dynamism of civil society in the earlier period fed into the political forces that coalesced in the Ukraine Without Kuchma movement and its successors, right up through the Orange Revolution and the crisis of 2013–14.

Differences in the Uruguay-Chile pair were more subtle; both transitioned to relatively robust democratic rule in a fairly compressed time frame. But mass mobilization played an important role in differentiating the cases, particularly with respect to elite prerogatives, the design of the new political system, and the political space opened up for the left. It took over a decade for the authoritarian enclaves established at the time of the transition to be folded up in Chile, while politicians in Uruguay were free of these institutionalized restrictions from the outset, as they were in the other distributive conflicts in Bolivia and Argentina.

Finally, Zambia and Ghana appear to exhibit equifinality: both distributive and elite-led transitions were followed by the establishment of highly autocratic, personalist governments under Chiluba and Rawlings. Only over time did the two countries develop more open modes of electoral competition. This characterization is somewhat misleading, however, as the transition in Zambia led to turnover in government while the transition in Ghana did not. Moreover, the Zambia-Ghana comparison shows that the emergence of pressure from below did ultimately play a role in the gradual transition in both countries. Interestingly, these debates came to a head in both cases around the issue of term limits, and in both cases pressure from below played a role in guaranteeing that Chiluba and Rawlings stepped down. Although we have cast the argument about mass mobilization around the democratic transition itself, the Ghana-Zambia comparison suggests that the broader argument holds. The potential for contentious politics constitutes an important check on abuse of office and contributes to more accountable and competitive political systems than those in which such potential is lacking. We return to those issues again in Chapter 8 when we compare survivors and reverters. First, however, we show how the institutional limitations we use to frame these comparisons have important implications for the durability of democratic rule.

APPENDIX

Table A5.1 Descriptive Statistics.

Variable	N	Mean	SD	Min	Max
Capital share	3,927	0.67	0.09	0.29	0.93
Log GDP	4,269	22.46	2.08	16.15	28.71
Trade openness	4,085	82.62	47.88	0.18	445.91
Growth	4,279	3.45	6.90	−51.03	106.28
Capital openness	4,122	−0.20	1.46	−1.86	2.46
Multiparty legislature	4,332	0.64	0.48	0	1
FH political rights	4,531	4.19	2.08	1	7
Polity IV	3,415	−0.41	6.81	−10	10
Aid (% of GDP)	3,559	0.05	0.07	−0.01	0.89
Manufacturing	3,675	13.96	8.00	0.33	46.40
Industry	3,910	29.62	13.43	1.88	100
Union membership per capita	3,538	2.92	4.00	0	27.84

PART III

Reversions from Democratic Rule

CHAPTER 6

Inequality, Development, and the Weak Democracy Syndrome

(with Terence Teo)

THROUGHOUT THE THIRD WAVE, the spread of democracy was accompanied by an undertow of reversions to autocratic rule. Figures 6.1 and 6.2 chart the incidence of these authoritarian installations during the 1980 to 2008 period; Tables A6.1a and A6.1b provide a complete list and additional detail on the cases. The 25 reversions in the CGV dataset—better suited at capturing coups—are evenly distributed across the entire period. In the Polity dataset, by contrast, there appears to be a break in the early 1990s, with 10 reversions from 1980 to 1993 but 17 from 1994 to 2008. This difference reflects an increase in the incidence of what we call "backsliding," or a reversion to authoritarian rule carried out by democratically elected incumbents. Of the 17 reversions in the second half of the Polity dataset, 9 were the result of backsliding. As we will see in Chapter 8 by considering several out-of-sample cases, this tendency toward backsliding has continued since 2008 and generated a new wave of concern about the prospects for an expansion of democratic rule.[1]

To test distributive conflict models of regime change, we distinguish between elite-reaction reversions that conform with distributive conflict theories elaborated in Chapter 1, and "weak democracy" reversions that don't. In the former, democracies are overthrown by elites seeking to defend their material interests against redistributive policies. We identify these threats not only by the presence of governments undertaking populist or redistributive policies but by the presence of social movements pressuring governments to do so. As in our discussion of transitions, it is a separate empirical question as to whether these proximate causal processes are related to inequality, as class conflict models suggest.

Weak democracy reversions result, as the name implies, from institutional and political frailties that leave incumbent regimes vulnerable to a broader variety of threats: militaries intervene to overthrow democracy, or incumbents undermine it in the absence of redistributive challenges. The

---

[1] Freedom House divides regimes into free, partly free, and not free based on their protection of civil and political liberties. Using this metric, the number of reversions—moves from free to partly or not free—is higher still, with 75 discrete cases between 1980 and 2008.

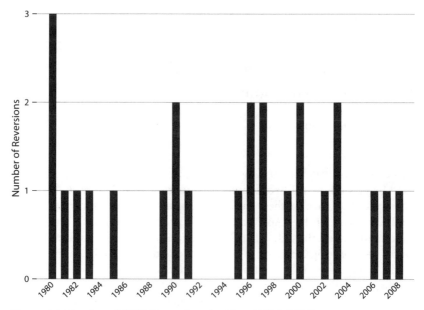

Figure 6.1 Number of CGV Reversions by Year (1980–2008)

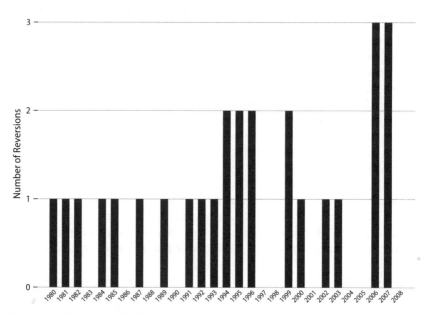

Figure 6.2 Number of Polity Reversions by Year (1980–2008)

precipitating events surrounding such cases include purely intra-elite conflicts over prerogatives and rents but also generalized public disaffection with government performance that does not have a strong distributive or class basis.

Although we focus primarily on these two reversion paths, we also identify a third type in which distributive conflict is present but operates in an altogether different fashion than anticipated by distributive conflict theories. In populist reversions, challengers to democratic rule seize power by mobilizing dissatisfaction about the *failure* of democratic regimes to respond to the distributive demands of lower-class groups. These reversions result not in right-wing coups or backsliding, as class conflict models anticipate, but in left-wing authoritarian regimes.

This classification allows us to consider both the frequency of the different types of reversion and the underlying causal factors that drive them. First, we find that even a larger share of reversions than transitions fail to conform with the proximate elite-reaction causal mechanism stipulated in distributive conflict models. This is particularly true when we take into account both the populist cases and the relatively brief and shallow nature of many elite-reaction reversions.

Second, we do not find inequality to be a causal factor in reversions, either generally or in the minority of cases coded as elite-reaction reversions. Rather we find that reversions of both sorts can be explained by what we call the "weak democracy syndrome." To some extent, the weak democracy syndrome reflects the institutional, administrative, and fiscal weaknesses associated with low per capita income. As modernization theories would predict, the very spread of democracy to lower-income countries during the latter half of the Third Wave meant greater likelihood of reversion and we do find some confirming evidence along these lines. But even when controlling for level of development, we find a cluster of political and institutional factors in our quantitative and qualitative analysis that help to account not only for "weak democracy" reversions—by far the most common type—but also elite-reaction and populist reversions as well. These include histories of military intervention and weak political institutions. We also find at least some evidence that economic crises have effects, generated in part endogenously by these very institutional disabilities.

We begin in this chapter with a more detailed outline of the elite-reaction model of reversion. We then turn to our alternative, which places greater weight on institutional and economic factors. As in the first half of the book, the empirical discussion begins with an explanation of how different reversion paths are coded and an initial consideration of the distribution of cases. We follow this with statistical tests that explore the determinants of reversions to authoritarian rule more generally as well as those that might be uniquely associated with elite-reaction and populist reversion paths. A central finding is that despite differences in proximate causal processes, we cannot rule out the possibility that reversions of both types can be traced to common causal roots in the weak democracy syndrome.

We conclude the chapter by looking again at the distribution of cases, but this time focusing not only on the proximate causes of reversion but on underlying factors that distinguish "reverters" from "survivors," including inequality, measures of political institutionalization, and economic performance.

This exercise is broadly consistent with the regression results but helps identify several classes of cases that we explore in more detail through causal process observation in Chapters 7 and 8. In Chapter 7, we focus first on the distal and proximate causes of weak democracy reversions, and then analyze how these factors are relevant to elite-reaction and populist reversions. In Chapter 8, we extend our comparisons to two classes of cases that are anomalous from the perspective of modernization theory and are, we believe, better explained by our political-institutional approach: low-income democracies that survive, and middle-income ones such as Venezuela, Russia, and Turkey that slide backward toward authoritarian rule.

THE DISTRIBUTIVE CONFLICT THEORY OF REVERSION: ELITE REACTION TO DEMOCRATIC RULE

The distributive conflict hypothesis rests on the highly intuitive assumption that democratic governments face strong incentives to redistribute. The expansion of suffrage and political freedom offers low-income majorities the opportunity to vote for parties promising redistribution through tax-and-transfer programs and regulatory measures that affect the distribution of income, from restrictions on property rights to labor market policies.

It is important to underline that the rich retain their ability to deploy their wealth and organizational resources to defend their privileges under democratic rule. Moreover, they have exit options that constrain democratic governments.[2] The responsiveness of politicians to demands "from below" will therefore depend on a variety of parameters, from electoral institutions and the nature of the party system to the organization of civil society. Ceteris paribus, however, electoral competition, and the capacity of lower-income groups to organize, should generate incentives for political actors to respond to the redistributive demands of the electorate. Moreover, the higher the level of inequality, the more substantial the redistribution that democracy would set in train and the greater the threat it would therefore pose to economic elites.

[2] Boix 2003; Freeman and Quinn 2012.

But as Christian Houle points out, the very fact that the gains from redistribution rise as inequality increases also incentivizes the wealthy to protect their income and assets, including through extraconstitutional means if necessary. For this reason, Acemoglu and Robinson, and Boix converge on the expectation that higher inequality places the stability of democracy at risk. As Acemoglu and Robinson put it succinctly, "in democracy, the elites are unhappy because of the high degree of redistribution and, in consequence, may undertake coups against the democratic regime."[3]

Slater, Smith, and Nair point out that this theory assumes that political elites, including the military, are perfect agents of economic elites.[4] But the interests of antidemocratic counterelites do not have to be perfectly aligned for the theory to hold; economic and political elites only need to act in consort. As Houle notes, "since the elites form a much smaller group than the population, those involved in coups are more likely to receive selective benefits" from regime change.[5] Although the empirical evidence remains mixed,[6] we outlined in the Introduction the long-standing observation of an elective affinity between more equal societies with robust middle classes and the stability of democratic rule. Moreover, there are at least some cross-national findings that inequality constitutes a threat to democratic rule.[7]

The idea that mass demands for redistribution can destabilize democratic rule also comports with several earlier generations of theory that—while not directly focused on inequality—link democratic failure to elite responses to "threats from below." These include the literature on bureaucratic-authoritarian installations and revisionist histories of US intervention during the Cold War. The bureaucratic-authoritarian model viewed military takeovers in middle-income countries as a consequence of economic concentration and social conflicts associated with particular stages in the process of "dependent industrialization."[8] Authoritarian rule was seen as a way of "solving" these conflicts. Brazil (1964), Argentina (1966 and 1976), and Chile and Uruguay (both 1973) were the canonical cases in this literature, but the model found extensions to other regions as well.[9]

---

[3] Acemoglu and Robinson 2006: 222.
[4] Slater, Smith, and Nair 2014.
[5] Houle 2009: 597.
[6] Teorell 2010.
[7] Przeworski, Alvarez, Cheibub, and Limongi 2000 hint at, but do not develop, a similar causal mechanism, linking it however to the level of development. In explaining why democracy typically does not fail above given income per capita threshold of about $6,000, they argue it is because wealth lowers the distributional conflicts within society "through various sociological mechanisms" (101). See also Kapstein and Converse 2008a, 2008b; Dutt and Mitra 2008; Reenock, Bernhard, and Sobek 2007; Houle 2009.
[8] O'Donnell 1973; for critiques, see Collier 1979; Linz and Stepan 1978; Valenzuela 1978.
[9] For example, Im 1987 on Korea.

Throughout the Cold War era, great-power politics compounded the risk of elite-reaction reversions.[10] Because of American concerns about the spread of communism, military leaders could count on external acquiescence or even support for intervention against left and populist governments, particularly in neighborhoods where the Soviet Union or China maintained strong relations with clients. In a highly influential article titled "Dictatorships and Double Standards," Jeane Kirkpatrick articulated the logic for tolerating authoritarian rule, arguing that Soviet-backed totalitarian regimes were both more stable than authoritarian regimes and also more likely to undermine democratic neighbors.[11] Among the cases of authoritarian reversion explored by the revisionist historians were covert US actions or direct intervention in Iran (1953), Guatemala (1954), Indonesia (1958), Cuba (1959), the Democratic Republic of the Congo (1960–65), Iraq (1960–63), the Dominican Republic (1961), Vietnam (1963–75), and the Southern Cone bureaucratic-authoritarian installations in Brazil (1964), Chile (1970–73), and Argentina (1976).[12]

THE WEAK DEMOCRACY SYNDROME

We saw in the first part of the book that modernization theories did not fare well in explaining transitions to democracy; transitions occurred in a number of low-income countries. However, a number of new democracies in our sample did face constraints associated with low levels of development, a key barrier to the consolidation of democratic rule in modernization theories.[13] The mechanisms through which low levels of development are presumed to operate include, inter alia, low levels of industrialization, education, urbanization, and income and small and weak middle classes. One particular feature of underdevelopment that is germane to our assessment of distributive conflict models is the capacity to tax and provide public goods. As Slater, Smith, and Nair have argued, a number of reverters are simply too small and poor to make the distributive conflict story plausible

[10] Boix 2011.

[11] Kirkpatrick 1979.

[12] The revisionist historical literature is vast, including numerous country and regional studies. General treatments that make the link between US intervention, anticommunism, and authoritarian rule from different perspectives include Williams 1962; Barnet 1968; Gurtov 1974; Klare and Arnson 1981; Kolko 1988; McDonald 1992; Chomsky and Herman 1979; and Westad 2005.

[13] Lerner 1958; Lipset 1959, 1960; Jackman 1973; Londregan and Poole 1990, 1996; Burkhart and Lewis-Beck 1994; Cheibub 1996; Leblang 1997; Przeworski and Limongi 1997; Przeworski, Alvarez, Cheibub and Limongi 2000; Boix and Stokes 2003; Gerring et al. 2005; Epstein et al. 2006; Svolik 2008; Kennedy 2010.

on its face; indeed, it may well be the *inability* to provide public goods and redistribute rather than excess transfers that undermines democratic rule.[14]

However modernization theory has long faced difficulties connecting the dots between level of development and the precise incentives that lead challengers to overthrow or undermine democratic rule. How, precisely, do we move from structural factors to actor incentives? Similar problems plague distributive conflict models. Inequality may create both social grievances from below and incentives to defend income and assets on the part of economic elites. But we should not assume that political elites or militaries act as agents of, or even in collusion with, economic elites. They may act instead for self-interested motives related to power, prerogatives, and rents or as agents of broader coalitions that cut across class divides. As in our discussion of transitions from democratic rule, we therefore need to understand not only the longer-run socioeconomic factors that make countries vulnerable to reversion, but also the political and institutional factors that create incentives for authoritarian reversals. These include the role of the military in politics and whether political institutions are capable of checking authoritarian tendencies on the part of incumbents or outside challengers.

It is also clear that the situational triggers that lead to reversion are by no means limited to the threats posed by redistributive governments. Rather, they include generalized government fecklessness and dysfunction and the effects of poor performance and economic crises. Even when the effects of low levels of development and redistributive pressures are in play, their causal weight must be assessed against these other institutional and economic weaknesses that might generate incumbent backsliding or coups.

In the following sections, we consider these three core components of what we call the "weak democracy syndrome": praetorianism, weak institutionalization, and poor economic performance, including crises. In each section, we define the feature of weak democracies that makes them vulnerable, demonstrate the ways these circumstances generate strategic interactions leading to reversion from democratic rule, and take up issues of measurement with respect to both our quantitative and qualitative tests.

Praetorianism

The first institutional component of the weak democracy syndrome is "praetorianism"—the failure of democratic governments to establish effective control over the military. One indicator of such failure that we use in our quantitative analysis is the historical propensity to coups. A

---

[14] Slater, Smith, and Nair 2014.

history of recurrent coups both heightens the influence of the military, even in nominally democratic contexts, and is associated with expectations and norms that facilitate future coups.[15]

In our qualitative analysis we consider a number of other indicators of praetorianism as well. Militaries in praetorian systems enjoy a presence in core decision-making bodies, such as national security councils and the cabinet (in both defense and other portfolios), control military budget and appointment processes, and directly control state assets and streams of income that are broadly outside of civilian control.[16] These institutional and political features of praetorianism are typically accompanied by an important normative dimension: doctrine that portrays the military as having a broader nation-building or developmental role, or that identifies the military as a "neutral" arbiter of the political process.[17]

The politicization of the military increases the vulnerability of democracy through at least three causal routes. First and most obviously, the military is not a neutral arbiter in such systems, but an organizational channel of upward mobility for politically and economically ambitious officers. Military intervention may be triggered not by redistribution to lower income groups, but by the efforts of democratic regimes to assert or reassert civilian dominance and control over military prerogatives and privileges.

Second, military involvement in politics also alters the structure of the broader political game. Both incumbent and opposition elites are more likely to consider appeals to militaries as potential allies in political or factional conflicts.

Finally, because militaries in praetorian systems believe in their role as arbiters of the democratic process, external events such as social mobilization, violence, or economic crises are likely to trigger military intervention at much lower thresholds. Obviously, systems characterized by widespread social violence or civil war provide ample justifications for military intervention, as we will see; civil war contexts are hardly auspicious for democracy. However we repeatedly find that militaries in countries with praetorian histories exploit—and even manufacture—crises in order to justify their entry into politics.

Institutionalization

The politicization of the military establishment is closely related as both cause and effect to a second and more fundamental causal factor: the weak institutionalization of new democratic polities. By institutionalization, we

---

[15] Londregan and Poole 1990; Collier and Hoeffler 2005; Lehoucq and Pérez-Liñán 2009; Svolik 2012; Singh 2014.
[16] Stepan 1988.
[17] Stepan 1971.

do not simply refer to specific constitutional features or what Carey calls "parchment institutions" that have been the focus of the contested literature on democratic failure.[18] These include questions such as whether presidential or parliamentary systems are more vulnerable, whether party systems influence the stability of democratic rule, and whether authoritarianism may be checked by stronger legislatures or formal checks on executive powers.[19]

Rather, institutionalization refers to a more fundamental set of expectations on the part of contending actors about the integrity of constitutional and legal constraints on the political game. Following Huntington, a well-developed literature on party systems, and an emerging literature on institutional strength, we define institutionalization as the degree to which the interactions among major political actors are coordinated around such common political expectations.[20] The core expectations in democratic regimes return us to the defining characteristics of these systems (Introduction): that the results of elections will be respected, and that governments can therefore turn over; that horizontal checks on executive authority will be respected; and that civil and political liberties will be protected, thus ensuring open political contestation.

Highly institutionalized democracies are those in which respect for these rules is not only routinized but intrinsically valued. Weakly institutionalized democracies are ones in which adherence to rules is less valued, more contingent, and therefore much more uncertain. As a result, weakly institutionalized systems are vulnerable to strategic interactions among major political actors that resemble a classic security dilemma.[21] Incumbents are unwilling or unable to make fully credible commitments to oppositions that they will adhere to the democratic rules of the game, and refrain from evading constitutional constraints when that is in their strategic personal or political interests. Expectations of such behavior similarly shape the strategies of oppositions in ways that are corrosive of democratic rule. Oppositions come to believe that losses in the constitutional game will lead

---

[18] Carey 2000. Indeed, in our quantitative analysis, we find that a dummy for presidential constitutions either has no effect on democratic stability or actually—against expectations—shows a positive effect. Our data come from the Database of Political Institutions (Beck et al. 2001). We code presidential regimes = 1, and both parliamentary regimes and those where (largely ceremonial) presidents are elected by parliaments = 0.

[19] On presidential and parliamentary systems, see Linz 1994; Mainwaring and Shugart 1997; Cheibub and Limongi 2002; Cheibub 2007; Sing 2010. On party systems, see Lai and Melkonian-Hoover 2005. On authoritarianism and legislatures, see Fish 2006. On formal checks on executive powers, see Kapstein and Converse 2008a, 2008b.

[20] Huntington 1968. For the well-developed literature on party systems, see Mainwaring and Scully 1995; Mainwaring 1999: 25; Mainwaring and Torcal 2006; and Riedl 2014: 25. For emerging literature on institutional strength, see Carey 2000; Greif and Laitin 2004; Levitsky and Murillo 2009. On institutionalization and common political expectations, see also Higley and Burton 1989, 2006.

[21] We are indebted to James Long for this point. See also Cohen 1994; Colomer 2000.

to permanent marginalization and thus create similar incentives to ignore constitutional checks and mobilize extraconstitutional resources, including violence.

There are a number of routes through which such weak institutionalization can lead to the outright undermining or overthrow of democratic rule, beginning with the arrogation of power by incumbents and its second-order effects on the ability of oppositions to serve as checks on government overreach.[22] In weakly institutionalized systems, incumbents exploit electoral victories to weaken oppositions. Weakening oppositions has the effect of simultaneously undermining the political and social foundations of institutional checks on executive discretion. Executive authority is strengthened at the expense of institutions of horizontal accountability, including legislatures, judiciaries, opposition parties, NGOs, and the media.

The weakening of checks on executive discretion also has an important political economy dimension. Corruption, fraud, and abuse of office are routine features of incumbency in weakly institutionalized systems. Unchecked control over the revenues, the budget, and particularly state-owned assets allows executives to deploy the power of incumbency to marginalize oppositions. If allowed to persist, these derogations can accumulate into the effective transition from democratic rule.

A second feature of weakly institutionalized systems is "the pursuit of politics through other means." For incumbents, political action violating constitutional boundaries includes extrajudicial harassment, repression, and detention of opponents, often defended on majoritarian grounds. All can easily cross over into abuses that effectively mark an end to the protection of civil liberties and political rights that are defining elements of democracy. These abuses extend to the mobilization of violence—whether through the armed forces or personal militias—to quell dissent. Oppositions respond accordingly, mobilizing social forces outside the political arena to offset the constraints associated with playing by the rules.[23] These dynamics create incentives for both military intervention and further arrogation of executive powers.

Finally, low institutionalization—the continuing contestation over the rules and the resort to extraconstitutional politics—all impede the capacity of government to undertake coherent and sustained policy. We find repeatedly in Chapter 7 that "wars of attrition" over policy,[24] stalemate, the incapacity and fecklessness of government, and attendant economic crises provide a motivation or pretext for military coups or executive seizure of emergency powers.

---

[22] Schedler 2009; Kapstein and Converse 2008a, 2008b; Maeda 2010.
[23] Huntington 1968; Cohen 1994; Colomer 2000.
[24] Alesina and Drazen 1991.

The Performance Dimension: Growth, Stagnation, and Crises

Vulnerabilities related to praetorianism and weak institutionalization are closely related as both cause and effect to a third condition that we associate with the weak democracy syndrome: poor economic performance.[25] It is beyond the scope of this book to consider the causes of poor performance and economic crises in detail; to be sure, small open economies are vulnerable to a variety of international and domestic shocks that are exogenous to domestic politics. Although our quantitative findings on this factor are limited, our qualitative analysis repeatedly demonstrates how poor performance and crises are effects as well as causes of weak institutional arrangements and decision-making processes and how they in turn result in the fraying of democratic institutions.

As we outlined in earlier work,[26] the mechanisms through which economic crises might lead to regime change operate both directly through the decline in output and employment and through the second-order effects of policy responses to crises, typically combining contentious macroeconomic stabilization and structural adjustment efforts.

First, crises trigger elite defections, but not because the state is engaged in excessive redistribution. Rather, policy reforms undercut elite interests by stripping away policy rents. Second, crises generate more general disaffection among the public. Finally, economic crises also have a more immediate effect on the ability of democratic governments to maintain the loyalty of civil servants and militaries through the quite obvious channel of declining fiscal capacity. Again, we see the contrast to the distributive conflict approach; the source of vulnerability arises not from the threat of redistribution by the state, but from the inability to sustain the support of key regime insiders.

We acknowledge at the outset that the three causal mechanisms that we highlight here—praetorianism, weak institutionalization, and economic crises—are highly endogenous to one another, and to the level of development as well. Disentangling them poses a virtually insuperable theoretical and empirical challenge. Nonetheless, the identification of this syndrome is useful in showing that democratic governments are vulnerable to a multiplicity of immediate political challenges other than those posed by either modernization theory or the factors that are central to distributive conflict approaches: inequality, redistributive policies, and reactionary elites. Moreover we show that the "weak democracy syndrome" can coexist with and compound the distributive conflicts that trigger elite-reaction and populist reversions as well. Indeed, we will show in both the statistical

---

[25] Haggard and Kaufman 1995; Gasiorowski 2000; Bernhard, Nordstrom, and Reenock 2001; Bernhard, Reenock, and Nordstrom 2003; Svolik 2008.

[26] Haggard and Kaufman 1995.

analysis and our causal process observations that distributive and weak democracy reversions, although occurring through different proximate causal routes, in fact share a number of underlying causal determinants.

Coding Proximate Causes: Elite, Weak Democracy, and Populist Reversions

In the remainder of this chapter, we explore these alternative models of democratic failure—distributive conflict models and the "weak democracy syndrome"—in four complementary steps: through a coding of cases, through an initial consideration of the incidence of reversions of different types, through regression analysis correlating reversion with a number of possible determinants, and through further analysis of the distribution of cases along a number of dimensions related to underlying causes postulated by competing theories.

As in the first part of this volume, we base our empirical analysis on all of the reversions from democracy in the CGV and Polity datasets between 1980 and 2008; in Chapter 8 we explore some out-of-sample cases of "backsliding" as well. As discussed in Chapter 2, these datasets capture somewhat different phenomena.[27] The dichotomous coding in the CGV dataset codes regimes as authoritarian if they do not have a competitively elected legislature and a chief executive who is either chosen by that body or is directly elected. Reversions are simply defined as any shift from democratic to authoritarian rule.[28] Because of the focus on the election of the executive and legislature, the dataset is well suited to capture coups in which militaries seize executive power and legislatures are shuttered. Of the 25 reversions in the CGV dataset, 24 take the form of military coups (see Tables A6.1a and A6.1b).

By contrast, because the Polity data are continuous, they capture both abrupt changes such as coups and incremental changes in a number of parameters that might result in backsliding. In the Polity dataset, these incremental changes include restrictions on the regulation, competitiveness, and openness of chief executive recruitment, decreasing checks on executive discretion, including through constraints on the judiciary or legislature, and measures that dilute the protection of political liberties. Of the 27 reversions in the Polity dataset, 14 are accounted for by coups (and 1 by a monarchic-military intervention), but 12 take the form of backsliding.

---

[27]Differences in the two datasets are even more marked with respect to reversions than transitions. CGV includes 15 reversions that Polity omits; Polity includes 17 that CGV omits.

[28]The four conditions are that the chief executive must be chosen by popular election or by a body that was itself popularly elected; the legislature must be popularly elected; there must be more than one party competing in the elections; an alternation in power under electoral rules identical to the ones that brought the incumbent to office must have taken place.

As in our discussion of transitions, we focus on the immediate or proximate processes through which democracy is undermined or overthrown: as an elite-reaction reversion, a weak democracy reversion, or a populist reversion. Elite-reaction reversions can occur in one of two ways. First, economic, political, and military elites can conspire to overthrow democratic governments actively committed to the redistribution of assets and income. The overthrow of the Allende government in Chile in 1973 is a canonical case. Elite-reaction reversions can also result from backsliding: actions by incumbents to prevent redistributive coalitions from winning elections and taking office or to quell mass mobilization seeking more extensive redistribution. Whether occurring through coups or backsliding, however, reversions would conform to the proximate causal processes of the distributive conflict model only under both of the following conditions:

- Clear evidence of redistributive actions on the part of the government or pressures on the government to take such actions;
- And either an overthrow of the incumbent government in response to redistributive policies or a reversal of democratic rule by incumbents in response to redistributive threats from parties or organized social forces outside the government, including from mass mobilization.

Weak democracy reversions are those in which manifest conflicts between redistributive governments and economic elites either are absent altogether or appear to play a minimal proximate role in the reversion from democratic rule. Most commonly, the military—or factions within it—stages a coup against incumbent democratic officeholders for reasons unrelated to redistribution to lower-class groups: narrow self-interest, such as loss of military budget and prerogatives, or career concerns; appeals from competing political factions; or circumstances that generate wider public support for intervention including government dysfunction and economic crises. As with elite-reaction reversions, we allow for the possibility that mass mobilization may play a role in weak democracy reversions as well. This would be the case if mass mobilization was anchored not in distributive conflicts, but rather in cross-class movements or disaffection with overall government performance that authoritarian challengers then exploit.[29]

---

[29] As in our coding of transition cases, our approach is conservative and favors the distributive conflict theory. Where mass mobilization is present prior to the reversion, we code it as elite-led conflict reversion only if the authoritarian intervention received support or "active acquiescence" on the part of significant parties and organizations representing the poor and economically excluded. In the absence of such support or in the face of active resistance on the part of lower-income groups and their representatives, we assume that the reversion is "elite-reaction" in form, and would conform with the distributive conflict model.

Populist reversions, as noted above, are cases in which democracy is overthrown or undermined not by elites seeking to limit redistribution but by populist leaders promising more extensive redistribution. The authoritarian governments that are subsequently installed need not actually pursue populist policies. But the forces that drive these democratic failures are motivated by attacks on the economic elite, appeals to lower-class groups, and promises of more extensive redistribution.

PROXIMATE CAUSES: WHAT ROLE FOR DEMOCRATIC REDISTRIBUTION IN THIRD WAVE REVERSIONS?

Tables 6.1 and 6.2 provide an initial overview of the distribution of the three types of reversion in the CGV and Polity datasets. Despite the fact that the definitions of democracy (and thus reversions from it) differ, the incidence of reversions of different types is surprisingly similar in the two datasets and raises prima facie doubts about the general validity of theories that emphasize distributive conflict as the source of democratic failure. Weak democracy reversions constitute a substantial majority—64 percent—of the CGV reversions. Although fewer Polity cases are classified as weak democracy reversions (44.4 percent), they still outnumber the elite-reaction transitions; moreover, their share increases to 50 percent of all reversions of 3 points or more.

Moreover, a closer analysis of the cases reveals two important complications that require more extended discussion, as they further reduce the incidence of elite-reaction cases. First, populist cases involve distributive conflict but do not conform to elite-reaction models. These account for 12 percent of the CGV cases and 14.8 percent of the Polity cases, leaving only 28 percent of the CGV reversions and 33.3 percent of Polity ones that do conform with them. Second, a closer examination of the elite-reaction cases suggest that many are extremely short-lived, reducing the share of reversions conforming with the class conflict model that are enduring in form.

Populist Reversions

Although our central focus in the subsequent statistical analysis is on the distinction between elite-reaction and weak democracy reversions, populist reversions constitute a distinct causal route to authoritarian rule with complex and ambiguous theoretical implications. Like elite reversions, populist reversions are characterized by evidence of distributive conflicts. Yet they arise not from the redistributive tendencies of democratic rule—a core assumption of distributive conflict theories—but rather from the perceived *incapacity* of democratic governments to respond to the interests

Table 6.1 The Distribution of CGV Reversions. (N = 25)

Elite-Reaction Reversions, n = 6	Weak Democracy Reversions, n = 16	Populist Reversions, n = 3
Bolivia 1980, Burundi 1996, Fiji 2000, Nepal 2002, *Thailand 2006*, Turkey 1980	Bangladesh 2007, CAR 2003, Comoros 1995, Congo 1997, Guatemala 1982, *Guinea-Bissau 2003*, Mauritania 2008, Niger 1996, Nigeria 1993, Pakistan 1999, Peru 1990, *Sierra Leone 1997*, Sudan 1989, *Suriname 1990*, *Thailand 1991*, Uganda 1985	Ecuador 2000, Ghana 1981, Suriname 1980
24.0% of all reversions	64.0% of all reversions	12.0% of all reversions
21.1% of reversions lasting > 2 years	63.1% of reversions lasting > 2 years	15.8% of reversions lasting > 2 years

Note: Cases in italics returned to democracy within two years.

Table 6.2 The Distribution of Polity Reversions. (N = 27)

Elite-Reaction Reversions, n = 11	Weak Democracy Reversions, n = 12	Populist Reversions, n = 4
Armenia 1995, *Dominican Republic 1994*, Fiji 1987, *Fiji 2000*, Haiti 1991, Nepal 2002, *Sri Lanka 2003*, Thailand 2006, Turkey 1980, *Ukraine 1993*, Zambia 1996	Bangladesh 2007, Belarus 1995, Fiji 2006, Gambia 1994, *Honduras 1985*, Niger 1996, Nigeria 1984, Pakistan 1999, Peru 1992, *Russia 2007*, *Sri Lanka 1982*, Sudan 1989	*Ecuador 2007*, Ghana 1981, Haiti 1999, *Venezuela 2006*
40.7% of all reversions	44.4% of all reversions	14.8% of all reversions
38.9% of all reversions of 3 points or more	50.0% of all reversions of 3 points or more	11.1% of all reversions of 3 points or more

Note: Cases in italics move from above to below 6 in the Polity coding by less than 3 points. Polity defines changes of 3 points or more as "regime transitions" (regtrans).

of newly enfranchised or excluded groups. Put differently, redistributive appeals in these settings must be understood not as a feature of democratic rule but as protests against the weakness of new democracies.

This can be seen by looking briefly at several of the five cases in the two datasets that experienced populist reversions (Suriname 1980, Ghana 1981, Haiti 1999, Venezuela 2006, and Ecuador 2000 [CGV] and 2007 [Polity]). In all of these cases, autocrats led populist takeovers of feckless democracies that showed declining ability to provide public goods of any sort. Three reversions (Ghana, Suriname, and Haiti) took place in extremely poor countries that also exhibited all of the features we associate with the "weak democracy syndrome." The military was a continuous actor in the political process, democratic experiences were brief and shallow, and all faced daunting economic problems, many as a result of government failures; we outline the Ghana and Haiti cases in more detail in Chapter 7.

Ecuador and Venezuela deviate from this pattern and appear anomalous. Both were middle-income countries with long experiences with democratic government (Ecuador since 1980 and Venezuela since 1958). However, in Chapter 8 we show that they bear close resemblance to a handful of other middle-income cases of "backsliding," including Russia, Turkey, and Hungary that also saw processes of deinstitutionalization and the adverse political effects of economic crisis. In these cases, the challenge to democracy came not from redistributive policies and demands but rather from executives exploiting popular grievances to undermine horizontal accountability and impose restrictions on political opponents.

Reversions in Context: Authoritarian Intervention and the Return of Democratic Rule

As we noted in the Introduction, an important methodological constraint associated with the country-year coding is the difficulty of capturing processes that may appear similar but have quite different structures when viewed through a longer time frame. Although any reversion from democratic rule deserves attention, some are enduring while others reflect short-term perturbations around a more prolonged transition process; they are "shallow" reversions. In the CGV dataset, we have italicized all reversions in Table 6.1 that result in a return to democratic rule in two years or less. Three of the six elite reversions witnessed a relatively rapid return to democracy as defined by the CGV dataset: Bolivia 1980 and Thailand 2006.[30]

---

[30]It is important to note that Thailand 2006 did not return to democracy in 2008 in the Polity dataset, although it was similarly coded as a reversion. It subsequently reverted again in 2014.

Only two of the Polity cases, the Dominican Republic and Fiji (2000), returned to democracy within two years, but Haiti, Turkey, Sri Lanka, and Nepal all returned to democracy within four. Moreover, reversions in the Dominican Republic, Fiji, and Sri Lanka (2003) were relatively "shallow"; they involved only incremental movements of 1 or 2 points from above to below the 6-point threshold. These are shown in italics in Table 6.2.

Closer causal process observation of the 11 discrete elite-reaction reversions in the two datasets, finally, confirms that many of these short-lived and shallow reversions should be seen as stages in a more prolonged transition process, again suggesting some of the limitations of the country-year framework required by panel econometric models.[31]

If we recalculate the share of elite reversions in the two datasets, dropping these cases and adjusting the other categories as well, the share of elite reversions in the two datasets falls, and significantly in the CGV dataset. The share of weak democracy cases rises marginally, exceeding 60 percent of all cases in both. In sum, only 5 of the 11 elite-reaction reversions exhibit the proximate causal processes associated with the distributive conflict model and result in more enduring authoritarian rule: two middle-income countries, Turkey 1980 and Thailand 2006 (on which the CGV and Polity datasets disagree), the civil war case of Nepal 2002, and Burundi 1995 and Fiji 1987, two cases in which the reversion institutionalized the political dominance of favored ethnic groups.

Modeling Reversions

The limited number of elite-reaction reversions, and the even more limited number that endure in any significant way, casts doubt on the generalizability of distributive conflict models of reversion. Nonetheless, any interruption of democratic politics deserves to be taken seriously; in none of the short-term or shallow reversions was the return to democracy a foregone conclusion. Moreover, the distribution of reversion types does not address

[31]Sri Lanka 2003 is a case of very small fluctuations in the Polity score around the democratic threshold, moving from 5 to 6 in 2001, reverting to 5 in 2003–5, and returning to democracy in 2006. The reversion was associated with the arrogation of power by sitting president Kumaratunga. When her actions were rejected by the Supreme Court in 2005, elections were called, returning the country to democratic rule. Bolivia, Fiji (2000), and Thailand are cases in which coups were followed relatively quickly by a return to democratic rule. In the Dominican Republic, similar process operated but in the context of incumbent backsliding. When it appeared that Balaguer would again lose in elections in 1994, he reverted to widespread electoral fraud. However, this move provoked a strong backlash, and he was forced to agree to limit his term to only two years. In 1996 the country staged new elections that were deemed free and fair.

the underlying causal factors at play in these reversions. Is it possible that inequality poses a challenge to democracy but operates through some other pathway than that found in class conflict models? Alternatively, could inequality explain distributive conflict reversions but not their weak democracy counterparts? Or is it possible that notwithstanding different short-run causal mechanisms, distributive and elite-led reversions might in fact be traced to common weaknesses such as those we have identified with the weak democracy syndrome?

Our empirical strategy uses both a pooled setup to examine the general determinants of reversions from democratic rule and a multinomial mixed effects model to consider the correlates of elite-reaction when compared with the other two types of reversion. The advantage of this approach is that it allows us to consider whether the elite-reaction and other reversion paths have similar or different correlates. As in Chapters 2 and 5, we run all tests separately on the reversions in the CGV and Polity datasets. To test the distributive conflict model, and whether it might help explain elite-reaction reversions in particular, we start with the effects of inequality; Houle's capital share measure, discussed in Chapter 1, is reported in the regression tables, but we discuss the effects of inequality using a Gini and the family farm measures as well.

Building on our discussion in Chapters 2 and 3, we also include two variables designed to capture collective action: union density and demonstrations. As we argued, the distributive conflict model does not explicitly incorporate mass mobilization into its theory of reversion. Nonetheless, the capacity for collective action and mass mobilization on the part of lower-income groups might nonetheless increase the likelihood of reversion, and elite-reaction reversions in particular.

Our consideration of alternative explanations begins with the modernization approach and tests for its emphasis on level of development (GDP per capita) as a determinant of reversions. However, our "weak democracy" approach focuses on institutional and shorter-run economic constraints even while controlling for longer-run structural conditions: praetorian histories, weak institutionalization, and short-run economic performance (growth in the year prior to the reversion). We measure military praetorianism through coup history, a dummy variable coded as 1 if a country had experienced a prior coup during the 1980 to 2008 period and 0 if it did not. We capture the broader institutionalization of the democratic regime by looking at Polity scores throughout the period of democratic government.[32] The index

---

[32] The period of democratic rule can be the years from the inception of the dataset (1980) to the reversion, between a prior democratic transition in the dataset and the reversion, or through the entire 1980–2008 period for the small number of countries that were continuously democratic during the period under consideration.

measures not only the extent to which elections are "free and fair," but also the extent to which incumbents are subject to institutional constraints and oppositions and civil society groups are free to operate on a relatively level playing field. We expect that countries with praetorian histories and weaker democratic institutions are more likely to revert.[33]

Controls include a measure of ethnolinguistic fractionalization and dependence on mineral wealth—both found to be adverse to democratic rule—and the proportion of neighboring democracies. We expect that "bad neighborhoods" would be associated with a higher likelihood of reverting to authoritarian rule. The description and source for these variables are found in Chapter 2.

We deploy a mixed effects or multilevel model that accounts for unit heterogeneity, but also allows the inclusion of slow-moving variables. We are therefore able to assess the effects of predictors both cross-nationally and within specific countries over time. The advantages of this model, particularly as compared with fixed effects models, are discussed in detail in Chapter 2. In the appendix to this chapter, however, we also present results for alternative specifications, including fixed effects, survival, random effects, and rare events logit models.

We deploy our time-series cross-sectional (TSCS) dataset as multilevel or hierarchical data in which level 1 units are annual observations of each variable and level 2 units are countries. The time period ranges from 1980 through 2008, with a maximum number of time points, T, of 29, and the maximum number of countries (or cross-sectional units), N, of 143. Assuming no missing data, the dataset contains 4,147 possible level 1 units nested within 143 possible level 2 units.

Table 6.3 shows results for models that pool all reversions in the CGV and Polity datasets, respectively. Tables 6.4a and 6.4b compare elite and "weak democracy" reversions within the two datasets.[34] In each table, we begin with a base model that shows only the effects of inequality, followed by models showing additional socioeconomic and political variables.

Looking first at variables reflecting the distributive conflict hypothesis, we find no evidence that democracies were destabilized by high inequality during the Third Wave. The coefficients for capital share are significant in the CGV base models of all reversions (Table 6.3) and in the elite-reaction reversions in Table 6.4a; but the significance disappears when control variables are added in subsequent models. Capital share, moreover, is not

---

[33]For the Polity measure, the mean is 1.21 and the standard deviation is 1.86, and the range is from 0 to 10. The proportion of country years with a coup history is 0.40, with a standard deviation of 0.49.

[34]The "non-elite" category excludes the small number of populist reversions, which are driven by distributive conflict. However, results do not change substantially when populist reversions are included.

Table 6.3 Likelihood of Reversion, 1980–2008: Pooled Model. (Mixed Effects Logit Regression Estimates)

	CGV				Polity			
Capital share	4.60* (2.41)	3.48 (2.18)	1.07 (2.86)	0.05 (2.99)	2.97 (2.25)	3.15 (2.31)	1.63 (3.07)	0.39 (2.88)
GDP per capita		-0.18 (0.26)	0.55 (0.52)	0.11 (0.57)		-0.16 (0.25)	-1.11** (0.49)	-0.77 (0.53)
Growth		-0.04 (0.03)	-0.08* (0.04)	-0.06 (0.04)		-0.00 (0.04)	0.00 (0.05)	0.03 (0.05)
Resource rents		0.00 (0.02)	0.02 (0.02)	0.02 (0.03)		0.00 (0.02)	-0.03 (0.04)	-0.00 (0.04)
Ethnolinguistic fractionalization		1.60* (0.91)	1.80 (1.45)	0.63 (1.40)		0.25 (0.84)	0.19 (1.29)	-0.15 (1.31)
Manufacturing				0.01 (0.07)				0.02 (0.06)
Union membership			-0.53* (0.30)				0.02 (0.08)	
Demonstrations			0.16 (0.14)	0.13 (0.16)			0.05 (0.22)	-0.01 (0.24)

Polity		-0.37***	-0.34***			-0.56***	-0.52***
		(0.08)	(0.07)			(0.18)	(0.16)
Coup history		4.61***	4.32***			3.56***	4.38***
		(1.16)	(1.17)			(0.79)	(0.82)
Proportion of democracies		-0.36	-0.20			0.70	0.64
		(1.63)	(1.54)			(1.24)	(1.20)
N	3,676	2,067	2,010	3,676	2,714	2,068	2,010
Groups	142	89	92	142	108	89	92
Log-likelihood	-126.75	-35.01	-34.84	-148.53	-116.33	-58.10	-56.98
AIC	265.50	94.01	93.67	309.05	252.67	146.20	143.97
BIC	302.76	161.62	160.94	346.31	311.73	230.72	228.05

Additional columns (N = 2,714): Log-likelihood -115.82, AIC 251.64, BIC 310.70; Groups 108.

Note: Standard errors are in parentheses. All variables are at t-1 unless otherwise specified. Cubic polynomials are not shown.
*p < .1. **p < .05. ***p < .01.

Table 6.4a Likelihood of CGV Elite Reaction and Weak Democracy Reversion, 1980–2008. (Mixed Effects Multinomial Logit Regression Estimates)

	Elite Reaction vs. No Reversion				Weak Democracy vs. No Reversion			
Capital share	11.29*	9.80	4.21	7.10	1.57	1.34	0.27	0.14
	(5.75)	(6.13)	(4.17)	(6.62)	(3.25)	(2.35)	(2.46)	(2.51)
GDP per capita		-0.10	-1.07**	-1.22**		-0.26	-1.20***	-1.09***
		(0.50)	(0.48)	(0.60)		(0.28)	(0.32)	(0.26)
Growth		-0.04	-0.05	-0.02		-0.04	-0.05	-0.06
		(0.05)	(0.04)	(0.06)		(0.03)	(0.05)	(0.04)
Resource rents		-0.04	-0.04	-0.03		0.01	0.04	0.05*
		(0.03)	(0.05)	(0.04)		(0.02)	(0.05)	(0.03)
Ethnolinguistic fractionalization		0.18	-0.84	-0.74		2.46**	2.40**	1.42
		(1.75)	(0.87)	(1.14)		(1.14)	(0.93)	(1.05)
Manufacturing				0.06				-0.02
				(0.07)				(0.05)
Union membership			-0.20				-0.35	
			(0.17)				(0.23)	
Demonstrations			-0.04	0.01			-0.09	0.09
			(0.18)	(0.27)			(0.43)	(0.13)

	(1)	(2)	(3)	(4)	(5)	(6)	(7)	(8)
Polity			-0.26*** (0.08)	-0.22** (0.09)			-0.56*** (0.15)	-0.31*** (0.10)
Coup history			10.52*** (1.67)	15.08*** (0.83)			9.02*** (2.19)	0.14 (1.02)
Proportion of democracies			-0.78 (1.36)	-2.83 (1.95)			-1.05 (1.96)	-0.32 (1.66)
N	3,676	2,714	2,104	2,069	3,676	2,714	2,104	2,039
Groups	142	108	88	92	142	108	88	92
Log-likelihood	-137.22	-124.74	-84.07	-88.77	-137.22	-124.75	-84.07	-88.77
AIC	294.44	285.48	216.14	229.54	294.44	285.48	216.14	229.54
BIC	356.54	391.79	351.78	376.05	356.54	391.79	351.78	376.05

Note: Standard errors are in parentheses. All variables are at t-1 unless otherwise specified. Cubic polynomials are not shown.

*p < .1. **p < .05. ***p < .01.

Table 6.4b Likelihood of Polity Elite Reaction and Weak Democracy Reversion, 1980–2008. (Mixed Effects Multinomial Logit Regression Estimates)

	Elite Reaction vs. No Reversion				Weak Democracy vs. No Reversion			
Capital share	2.75 (4.12)	2.82 (4.16)	0.40 (2.99)	0.95 (3.50)	3.38 (3.10)	3.69 (3.57)	5.26 (4.48)	4.56 (4.03)
GDP per capita		0.08 (0.30)	-0.78*** (0.29)	-0.78*** (0.28)		-0.48* (0.27)	-2.33*** (0.86)	-1.50*** (0.49)
Growth		0.01 (0.03)	0.02 (0.02)	0.02 (0.03)		-0.02 (0.02)	-0.08* (0.04)	-0.03 (0.08)
Resource rents		0.00 (0.03)	0.04 (0.05)	0.04** (0.02)		-0.01 (0.04)	0.01 (0.05)	-0.16 (0.13)
Ethnolinguistic fractionalization		0.36 (1.49)	2.40** (0.93)	-0.32 (0.96)		0.19 (1.05)	2.45** (0.95)	0.16 (1.41)
Manufacturing				0.04 (0.05)				-0.08* (0.05)
Union membership			-0.05 (0.06)				0.05 (0.11)	
Demonstrations			-0.87 (0.66)	-0.23 (0.33)			0.18 (0.23)	0.27*** (0.10)

	(1)	(2)	(3)	(4)	(5)	(6)	(7)	(8)
Polity			-0.31***	-0.31***			-0.93**	-0.67**
			(0.05)	(0.05)			(0.42)	(0.26)
Coup history			14.01***	14.23***			14.35***	13.77***
			(1.03)	(0.51)			(0.94)	(0.45)
Proportion of democracies			-1.60	-2.42			3.29*	2.39*
			(1.24)	(1.60)			(1.76)	(1.22)
N	3,676	2,714	2,104	2,069	3,676	2,714	2,104	2,069
Groups	142	108	88	92	142	108	88	92
Log-likelihood	-164.86	-126.86	-90.75	-89.93	-164.86	-126.86	-90.75	-89.93
AIC	349.72	289.72	229.50	231.86	349.72	289.72	229.50	231.86
BIC	411.81	396.03	365.14	378.36	411.81	396.03	365.14	378.36

Note: Standard errors are in parentheses. All variables are at t-1 unless otherwise specified. Cubic polynomials are not shown.

*p < .1. **p < .05. ***p < .01.

significant in any of the Polity models. We also find no evidence that democratic stability is threatened by either union strength or demonstrations, proxies for collective action capacity and mobilization. Indeed, in the pooled model (Table 6.3), union strength appears to *enhance* the stability of democratic regimes in the CGV dataset (a result consistent with our findings in Chapter 5), as does manufacturing in weak democracy Polity cases (Table 6.4b). In the multinomial logit regressions in Tables 6.4a and 6.4b, union strength, manufacturing, and demonstrations all have no significant effects on elite-reaction reversions.

We turn next to the impact of the political and institutional factors that we argue are components of the weak democracy syndrome. These factors fare much better in explaining reversions, both in the pooled models and across reversion types. Polity and coup history are significant in both of the pooled models in Table 6.3. Moreover, we find that they tend to operate on both types of transitions shown in Tables 6.4a and 6.4b. Polity reduces the likelihood of both elite reversions and weak democracy reversions in both datasets. Coup history uniformly increases the likelihood across both types of reversion in the Polity dataset (Table 6.4b), and falls short of significance in only one of the CGV regressions (Table 6.4a). This provides a strong indication that the short-run causal processes that we observe in the two transition paths may actually rest on deeper constraints on democratic rule that are common to both reversion types.

These results are also generally robust to alternative specifications shown in this chapter's appendix. In the pooled CGV model in the appendix (Table A6.2), both Polity and coup history are significant in all of the specifications (random effects, survival, rare events, and fixed effects). In the pooled Polity model, coup history loses significance in alternative specifications, but Polity is robust to all specifications but the fixed effects model. Although these results do not extend as neatly to the separate regressions on elite-reaction and other reversions, we find evidence there as well that praetorianism and weak institutionalization are destabilizing for democratic rule.

Figures 6.3 and 6.4 show how changes in Polity scores and the coup history variable affect the predicted probability of reversion with all other variables held at their mean. In the CGV dataset, as the average Polity score increases from 1 (for example, Suriname in 1981, prior to its reversion) to 5 (Suriname after a transition in 1991), the probability of a reversion declines from about 3 to 1 percent. In the Polity dataset, an increase from the standard 6-point cutoff (Dominican Republic 1994) to 8 (the Dominican Republic after 1998) reduces the probabilities of a reversion by about half, from about 2 to 1 percent. Coup history has an even stronger effect. A prior history of coups increases the likelihood of reversion from nearly 0 to about 4 percent in the CGV dataset and to over 7 percent in the Polity cases.

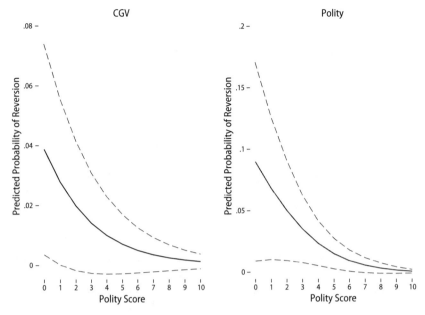

Figure 6.3 Predicted Probability of Reversion (Polity Score)

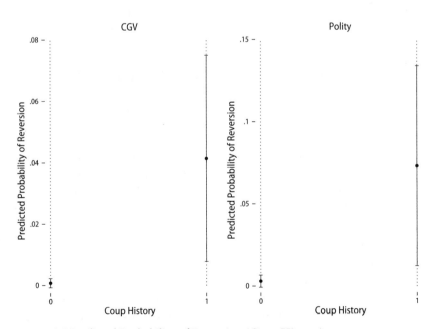

Figure 6.4 Predicted Probability of Reversion (Coup History)

Our results for growth—the third component of the weak democracy syndrome—are far weaker. Although we saw in Chapter 2 that short-term recessions generally destabilized authoritarian regimes, democratic systems appeared better equipped to survive. Economic growth in the year prior to the transition behaves as expected only in one of the pooled CGV model (Table 6.3) and in one weak democracy Polity model (Table 6.4b). But we should approach this null finding with some caution, as it exemplifies some of the limits on panel designs that we took up in the Introduction. As already noted in Chapter 2, the effects of recession may not have the same lag structure across countries for a variety of idiosyncratic reasons, making them difficult to capture in a standard panel design.

We subdivide the cases in the pooled Polity regression (which showed no significant result) into those that experienced negative or very low growth in the year prior to the reversion, those experiencing relatively modest growth rates between 1 and 4 percent, and those with growth of 4 percent or more. This breakdown suggests that the null regression results for the Polity reversions should not be taken at face value.

In ten reversions (about one-third of the total) democratic regimes did experience severe recessions or flat growth in the year preceding their reversions, often following even longer periods of economic decline. Among the seven countries experiencing relatively high growth rates, however, Russia and Sudan had experienced serious economic difficulties during earlier years. Russia, as we will elaborate in more detail in Chapter 8, was a backsliding case in which the incumbent ruler began to reap the benefits of a modest recovery and then the oil boom after a decade of economic turbulence. In Sudan, economic performance was highly volatile. The standard deviation of growth during its democratic years was 6.1, well above the overall average for reverters (4.5). The high growth rate shown in Table 6.5 was preceded by a recession in the prior year.

The plurality of the Polity cases (14 out of 31) experienced growth of only 1 to 4 percent in the year prior to their reversion, but even this mediocre performance presents a somewhat misleading picture of their economic histories in previous years. Like Russia, Venezuela and Ecuador were backsliding cases in which oil booms were just beginning to lift economies—and autocratic incumbents—after periods of secular economic crisis and decline. Honduras, like other Central American countries, had been hit hard by the debt crisis and resulting political turbulence prior to a modest upturn. As we will show in Chapter 8, Haiti's prior economic performance was even worse. Among the other moderate growth cases, Guinea-Bissau, Sri Lanka, and Fiji had also been hit by economic slumps in years relatively proximate to their reversions. We show below that growth performance in democracies that reverted was significantly lower on average than in those that survived; in Chapters 7 and 8, we show how poor performance and economic crisis were implicated in most of our reversion cases.

Table 6.5 GDP Growth Rates (%) in the Year Prior to Polity Reversions.

Negative			0–1			1–4			4 or higher		
Ghana	1981	-0.5	Niger	1996	1.0	Gambia	1994	3.5	Mali	2012	4.9
Nigeria	1984	-3.9	Zambia	1996	0.1	Guinea-Bissau	2012	3.5	Sudan	1989	7.1
Fiji	1987	-0.04	Peru	1992	0.0	Madagascar	2009	2.8	Bangladesh	2007	5.2
Armenia	1995	-10.0				Malawi	2001	2.6	Pakistan	1999	4.4
Belarus	1995	-8.1				Niger	2009	3.6	Sri Lanka	1982	5.2
Turkey	1980	-5.0				Fiji	2000	3.6	Thailand	2006	4.6
Ukraine	1993	-10.8				Fiji	2006	2.6	Russia	2007	7.2
						Nepal	2002	3.9			
						Sri Lanka	2003	2.8			
						DR	1994	3.6			
						Venezuela	2006	1.9			
						Haiti	1999	1.6			
						Honduras	1985	1.6			
						Ecuador	2007	3.7			
7			3			14			7		

Broader socioeconomic controls, finally, show mixed results. In the pooled models (Table 6.3), GDP per capita, the proxy for development, is significant in the full Polity model, but not in the CGV. It is significant in all of the full multinomial models in Tables 6.4a and 6.4b: both elite-reaction and weak democracy reversions are more likely to occur in poorer societies, even though Polity and coup history remained significant factors. Ethnolinguistic fractionalization is also significantly associated with weak democracy reversions in the full CGV model in Table 6.4a, and with both elite-reaction and weak democracy reversions in Table 6.4b. Resource rents, which were an important source of stability in authoritarian regimes (Chapter 2) and have been blamed for authoritarian resilience, had no evident effect on reversions from democracy.

IDENTIFYING CASES: INEQUALITY AND THE WEAK DEMOCRACY SYNDROME REVISITED

We have already seen in Tables 6.1 and 6.2 that the sheer incidence of reversions of different types raises prima facie doubts about the generalizability of the distributive conflict model. These doubts were supported by the regression results, which showed that there were no average treatment effects for inequality. In this section, we return to the distribution of cases, examining in more detail how specific cases fall on the core theoretical variables of interest, including both inequality and the components of the weak democracy syndrome. This exercise underlines that the determinants of different reversion paths appear similar and helps identify classes of cases and individual countries for closer causal process observation in Chapters 7 and 8.

Inequality and the Reversion Paths

In Tables 6.6 and 6.7, we consider the relationship between inequality and distributive conflict reversions in more detail, looking not at average treatment effects but actual outcomes. Although reverting through different causal mechanisms—indeed, virtually antithetical ones—both do involve elite-mass conflicts. As in Tables 1.1 and 1.2, Tables 6.6 and 6.7 array the cases of regime change by two measures of inequality, although missing data are a constraint: the capshare and Gini. We conducted a similar exercise—not shown—using the distribution of land holdings.[35]

---

[35] At each level of land concentration, there are about as many distributive and elite-led reversions in both the CGV and Polity datasets. In the CGV dataset, moreover, there are actually more elite-reaction reversions at the lowest level of land concentration (Burundi 1996, Fiji 2000, Nepal 2002, Thailand 2006, and Turkey 1980).

Table 6.6 Inequality and Distributive Conflict: CGV Cases. (N = 25)

Inequality	Capital Share of Income in Manufacturing Sector		Gini (Solt)	
	Distributive	Weak Democracy	Distributive	Weak Democracy
High	Bolivia 1980 (ER)	Guatemala 1982	Bolivia 1980 (ER)	CAR 2003
	Burundi 1996 (ER)	Nigeria 1993	Ecuador 2000 (P)	Guatemala 1982
	Ecuador 2000 (P)	Pakistan 1999	Thailand 2006 (ER)	Guinea-Bissau 2003
	Ghana 1981 (P)	Peru 1990	Turkey 1980 (ER)	Peru 1990
	Nepal 2002 (ER)	Sierra Leone 1997		Sierra Leone 1997
	Thailand 2006 (ER)	Thailand 1991		
	4 elite-reaction, 2 populist	*6 weak democracy*	*3 elite-reaction, 1 populist*	*5 weak democracy*
Medium	Turkey 1980 (ER)	Bangladesh 2007	Fiji 2000 (ER)	Niger 1996
		Comoros 1995	Ghana 1981 (P)	Nigeria 1993
		Guinea-Bissau 2003	Nepal 2002 (ER)	Sudan 1998
		Sudan 1998		Thailand 1991
				Uganda 1985
	1 elite-reaction	*4 weak democracy*	*2 elite-reaction, 1 populist*	*5 weak democracy*

(continued)

Table 6.6 (*continued*)

Inequality	Capital Share of Income in Manufacturing Sector		Gini (Solt)	
	Distributive	*Weak Democracy*	*Distributive*	*Weak Democracy*
Low	Fiji 2000 (ER)	CAR 2003	Burundi 1996 (ER)	Bangladesh 2007
	Suriname 1980 (P)	Congo 1997	Suriname 1980 (P)	Pakistan 1999
		Niger 1996		Suriname 1990
		Suriname 1990		
		Uganda 1985		
	1 elite-reaction, 2 populist	*5 weak democracy*	*1 elite-reaction, 1 populist*	*3 weak democracy*
Missing data		Mauritania 2008		Comoros 1995
				Congo 1997
				Mauritania 2008
		1 weak democracy		*3 weak democracy*

Note: ER, elite-reaction reversion; P, populist reversion.

Table 6.7 Inequality and Distributive Conflict: Polity Cases. (N = 27)

Inequality	Capital Share of Income in Manufacturing Sector		Gini (Solt)	
	Distributive	*Weak Democracy*	*Distributive*	*Weak Democracy*
High	Ecuador 2007 (P)	Gambia 1994	Armenia 1995 (ER)	Honduras 1985
	Ghana 1981 (P)	Nigeria 1994	Turkey 1980 (ER)	Nigeria 1994
	Nepal 2002 (ER)	Pakistan 1999	Thailand 2006 (ER)	Peru 1992
	Sri Lanka 2003 (ER)	Peru 1992	Zambia 1996 (ER)	
	Thailand 2006 (ER)	Sri Lanka 1982		
	Venezuela 2006 (P)			
	Zambia 1996 (ER)			
Cases	*4 elite-reaction, 3 populist*	*5 weak democracy*	*4 elite-reaction*	*3 weak democracy*
Medium	Dom. Rep. 1994 (ER)	Bangladesh 2007	Dom. Rep. 1994 (ER)	Fiji 1987
	Haiti 1991 (ER)	Russia 2007	Fiji 2000 (ER)	Gambia 1994
	Haiti 1999 (P)	Sudan 1989	Ghana 1981 (P)	Niger 1996
	Turkey 1980 (ER)		Nepal 2002 (ER)	Sri Lanka 1982
	Ukraine 1993 (ER)			Sudan 1989
	4 elite-reaction, 1 populist	*3 weak democracy*	*3 elite-reaction, 1 populist*	*5 weak democracy*

(continued)

Table 6.7 (*continued*)

Inequality	Capital Share of Income in Manufacturing Sector		Gini (Solt)	
	Distributive	*Weak Democracy*	*Distributive*	*Weak Democracy*
Low	Armenia 1995 (ER)	Belarus 1995	Sri L. 2003 (ER)	Belarus 1995
	Fiji 1987 (ER)	Honduras 1985	Ukraine 1993 (ER)	Pakistan 1999
	Fiji 2000 (ER)	Niger 1996		
	3 elite-reaction	*3 weak democracy*	*2 elite-reaction*	*2 weak democracy*
Missing data		Fiji 2006	Ecuador 2007 (P)	Bangladesh 2007
			Fiji 2006 (ER)	Russia 2007
			Haiti 1991 (ER)	
			Haiti 1999 (P)	
			Venezuela 2006 (P)	
		1 weak democracy	*2 elite-reaction, 3 populist*	*3 weak democracy*

Note: ER, elite-reaction reversion; P, populist reversion.

As we would expect, the distributions conform with the regressions in providing very little general support for the distributive conflict model. However, we do see that elite-reaction and populist reversions—if combined—appear to cluster at the middle and high levels of each dataset and that some cases might reward closer consideration. For example, if we focus on the capshare measure in the CGV dataset, Bolivia 1980, Burundi 1996, Nepal 2002, and Thailand 2006 are examples of high-inequality elite-reaction cases. Interestingly three of these—Burundi, Nepal, and Thailand—were among the five cases that experienced more enduring reversions as well. It is plausible that inequality played a causal role in the conflicts leading up to elite interventions in these cases.

However there are an ample number of anomalies that revert at low levels of inequality, and there are an equal or even larger number of cases exhibiting high or medium inequality that revert in the *absence* of the causal mechanisms stipulated in the theory. In both the CGV and Polity datasets, about half of the high-inequality reversions (both capital share and Gini) did not exhibit elite-reaction dynamics. Guatemala 1982, Nigeria 1993, Pakistan 1999, Peru 1990, Sierra Leone 1997, and Thailand 1991 are also high-inequality cases, but do not transit via the mechanisms postulated in the distributive conflict theory.

The Weak Democracy Syndrome I: Elite-Reaction, Populist, and Weak Democracy Reversions

In Tables 6.8 and 6.9, we conduct a similar exercise, focusing our attention not on inequality but on the causal factors we identify with the "weak democracy" syndrome: the presence of praetorianism; weak institutionalization; and economic performance, defined in this case as average economic growth over the entire life of the democratic regime. We also include consideration of differences in level of development, the master variable in the modernization approach.

As in the regressions, we are interested first in whether elite-reaction, populist, and elite-reaction reversions exhibit any significant differences with respect to these factors. As they constitute a small share of the total cases, we pull out the distributive conflict cases for particular scrutiny. We are also interested in whether there are differences between *all* democracies that revert ("reverters") and those that survive ("survivors"). These cases are treated at length in the next chapters, and we do not list them here. However, average results serve as benchmarks for assessing the impact of the "weak democracy" variables on the subcategories of reversion.

As in the regressions, praetorianism is captured by the existence of a coup history; the table shows the total number of countries in the

Table 6.8 Comparing Democratic Survivors and Reverters: CGV Cases.

	Cases	Per Capita GDP	Coup History (Since 1970)	Average Polity Score	Average Executive Constraints	Average Economic Growth (SD)
Survivors	44	6,193	24 (52.2%)	6.9	5.9	3.4 (5.4)
All reversions	25	2,586	24 (96.0%)	3.1	5.0	1.1 (3.9)
Elite-reaction reversions	6	3,298	5 (83.3%)	1.2	4.2	0.3 (4.5)
Bolivia (1982)		3,602	1	−7.0	1.0	−1.4 (NA)
Burundi (1993)		424	1	0	NA	−6.5 (2.0)
Fiji (1992)		3,640	1	5.1	6.0	3.0 (3.6)
Nepal (1990)		812	0	5.3	6.8	4.6 (1.9)
Thailand (2006)		5,597	1	9.0	7.0	4.6 (5.0)
Turkey (1983)		5,710	1	−5.0	1.0	−2.5 (NA)
Populist reversions	3	4,349	3 (100%)	4.6	5.9	3.0 (3.7)
Ecuador (2000)		5,431	1	8.8	6.8	2.1 (3.1)
Ghana (1983)		982	1	6.0	5.0	−1.5 (2.8)
Suriname (1991)		6,634	1	−1.0		6.1 (5.8)
Weak democracy reversions	16	1,988	16 (100%)	3.5	5.1	1.8 (3.6)

Note: Difference in means tests show a statistically significant difference between CGV survivors and reverters in per capita GDP ($t = -3.95$, $df = 67$, $p < .01$); coup history ($t = 3.93$, $df = 67$, $p < .01$); Polity scores ($t = -4.34$, $df = 66$, $p < .01$); executive constraints ($t = -2.75$, $df = 61$, $p < .10$); and growth ($t = -3.44$, $df = 67$, $p < .01$). NA = not available.

Table 6.9 Comparing Democratic Survivors and Reverters: Polity Cases

	Cases	Per Capita GDP	Coup History (Since 1970)	Average Polity Score	Average Executive Constraints	Average Economic Growth (SD)
Survivors	42	7,052	21 (50.0%)	8.1	6.4	3.5 (4.5)
All reversions	27	3,430	20 (74.1%)	6.8	5.2	1.1 (4.8)
Elite-reaction reversions	11	3,388	6 (54.5%)	6.8	4.9	−0.50 (5.7)
Armenia (1995)		1,776	0	7.0	4.6	−10.0 (19.6)
DR (1994)		3,957	0	6.0	5.0	3.6 (4.3)
Fiji (1987)		3,198	0	9.0	7.0	0 (6.4)
Fiji (2000)		3,925	1	6.0	6.0	3.6 (7.4)
Haiti (1991)		1,381	1	7.0	6.0	NA
Nepal (2002)		903	0	6.0	6.0	3.9 (2.6)
Sri Lanka (2003)		3,120	1	6.0	5.0	2.7 (3.9)
Thailand (2006)		5,738	1	9.0	7.0	4.6 (5.0)
Turkey (1980)		5,694	1	NA	NA	−2.5 (NA)
Ukraine (1993)		6,564	0	6	5.6	−10.8 (3.0)
Zambia (1996)		1,108	1	6.0	5.0	0.9 (6.0)
Populist reversions	4	4,628	4 (100.0%)	6.8	5.2	1.7 (2.6)
Ecuador (2000)		6,500	1	6.2	6.0	5.0 (2.3)
Ghana (1983)		952	1	6.0	5.0	−1.5 (2.8)
Haiti (1999)		1,113	1	7.0	6.6	1.6 (7.2)
Venezuela (2006)		9,946	1	8.0	5.7	1.9 (6.4)
Weak democracy reversions	12	2,537	14 (77.8%)	6.7	5.9	2.0 (7.5)

Note: Difference in means tests show a statistically significant difference between Polity survivors and reverters in per capita GDP ($t = -3.62$, $df = 66$, $p < .01$); coup history ($t = 2.02$, $df = 67$, $p < .05$); Polity scores ($t = -5.45$, $df = 66$, $p < .01$); executive constraints ($t = -5.55$, $df = 67$, $p < .10$); growth ($t = -2.99$, $df = 65$, $p < .05$). NA = not available.

categories with coup histories and the share with coup histories, while a 1 indicates a coup history in the country in question. We consider two measures of political institutionalization: Polity scores and the more focused Polity measure of executive constraints, a measure of checks that are lacking in what we call "weak democracies." These two measures are averaged over the countries democratic histories. Unlike in the regressions, using averages allows us to consider developments that occur up through 2013, outside of the 1980 to 2008 time span of our dataset. "Survivors" exclude three cases that subsequently reverted from 2009 to 2013: Madagascar 2009, Mali 2012, and Niger 2010. Similarly, since reversions occurring in the 1980s might have been affected by coups taking place in the previous decade, we extend our definition of coups back to 1970.

Our measures of economic conditions include level of development (GDP per capita) and economic growth. In the regressions we modeled short-run economic performance (t–1). However, here we consider the broader democratic record: average economic growth over the democratic period.[36] We also consider the standard deviation of growth over this period as a measure of volatility.

The first comparison of interest to us is whether the elite-reaction and weak democracy reversions exhibit any particular differences with respect to the causal processes stipulated in the weak democracy model. The short answer—as in the regressions—is no. In both datasets, countries experiencing elite-reaction and populist reversions are on average somewhat wealthier than elite-led reversions; but these results are driven largely by exceptionally high per capita income in Thailand and Turkey among the elite-reaction reverters and in Venezuela and Ecuador among the populists. Each category also includes some of the poorest countries in the sample (Burundi, Nepal, Ghana, Haiti, and Zambia). Clearly, distributive conflict reversions can occur in a wide variety of developmental settings.

Differences in average Polity scores in the CGV dataset mask considerable variation around the mean. The average Polity score for elite-reaction reversions, for example, was only 1.2 as compared with 3.5 for weak democracy ones and 3.1 for all reversions. Again, however, scores preceding the reversion ranged widely—from a high of 9 in Thailand to –7 in Bolivia, where the government elected in 1979 was never actually able to

---

[36] Again to be precise this includes the period from the transition to democratic rule (or the beginning of the dataset) to the end of the dataset for the survivors and the period from the onset of democratic rule (or the beginning of the dataset) to the year prior to the reversion in the cases of democracies that fail.

take power. Polity scores in the CGV populist reversion were higher on average, but the category comprised only three cases.

We see no substantial differences across reversion paths in average scores on coup history or short-run economic performance in either dataset. When we extend the time period back to 1970, most of the countries experiencing reversions of any type had already experienced at least one military coup. Growth rates among the subcategories of reversion are also broadly similar. The three populist reversions in the CGV dataset did grow at a faster rate than the other cases, but growth rates for the elite and weak democracy reversions fell between only 0.3 and 1.8 respectively. In the Polity dataset, growth rates ranged from –.50 in elite reverters to 2.0 in weak democracies. We tested for whether volatility as well as growth might have mattered. Compared to the other categories, weak democracy reversions experienced somewhat lower volatility rates in the CGV dataset and somewhat higher rates in the Polity. But none of these differences reached statistical significance.

The conclusions from these null findings are important. In contrast to the transitions described in the first part of the book—which we argued were the result of different causal processes—here we see convergence. The weak democracy and two types of distributive-conflict reversion paths appear to be rooted in common underlying causal factors. Distributive conflict may be the proximate causes of elite and populist reversions, but these proximate causes do not appear to be related to inequality in any significant way. By contrast most distributive and weak democracy reversions exhibit histories of praetorianism and weak institutionalization. The effects of economic crises are more uneven, but there is some evidence that it mattered in a number of the reversion cases, and we explore these effects in more detail in the qualitative narratives.

The Weak Democracy Syndrome II: Survivors versus Reverters

Differences between survivors and reverters are on clear display when we look at differences in growth over the long run. Average GDP per capita for survivors exceeds that of the reverters by substantively and statistically ($p < .01$) significant margins in both the CGV ($6,193 vs. $2,586) and Polity reversions ($7,052 vs. $3,430).

However, as we saw in the regressions the effects of weak democracy syndrome appeared to hold even when controlling for level of development. In the CGV dataset, the average Polity scores of survivors (6.9) are over twice those of the CGV democracies that revert (3.1). Only 11 of the CGV reversion cases transition to authoritarian rule with Polity scores higher than 6 (see Tables A6.1a and A6.1b).[37] The remaining 14 cases reverted from Polity scores below 6 and in some cases well below 6.[38] Among this group of weakly institutionalized CGV reverters are nine low-income African countries that are coded as democratic because of the staging of competitive elections, but in many cases were weakly institutionalized, as we will show in Chapter 7.[39]

Although there were no consistent differences in coup history among the distributive and weak democracy reversions, we do see a statistically significant difference in countries with coup histories if we go back to 1970. Using this longer-term measure of coup history, almost all (96 percent) of the CGV reverters have praetorian pasts; only 52.2 percent of survivors do.

Comparisons within the Polity dataset on these institutional metrics appear narrower because of the fact that a country must be above the threshold of 6 to have been a democracy in the first place. Nonetheless, as in the multivariate models, we see statistically significant differences in average Polity scores, even taking into account the regimes that reverted after the end of our dataset (8.1 to 6.8), as well as in coup histories dating back to the 1970s.[40] Three-quarters of democratic regimes suffering

[37]Turkey 1980, Thailand 2006, and Ecuador 2000 from Polity scores of 9; Niger 1996 from an 8; Sudan 1989, Peru 1990, and Pakistan 1999 from a 7; and Nepal 2002, Ghana 1981, Fiji 2000, and Bangladesh 2007 from a 6.

[38]Bolivia 1980, Burundi 1996, Central African Republic 2003, Comoros 1995, Congo 1997, Guatemala 1987, Guinea-Bissau 2003, Mauritania 2008, Nigeria 1993, Sierra Leone 1997, Suriname 1980 and 1990, Thailand 1991, and Uganda 1985.

[39]The same point about the CGV cases of electoral democracy can be made by looking at an alternative measure of regime change used in our discussion of authoritarian regime types in Chapter 3. The Hadenius-Teorell-Wahman dataset provides a more detailed coding of types of authoritarian regimes, but here we use it as a robustness check on our observations of Polity scores. Of the 25 CGV reversions, Hadenius, Teorell, and Wahman code only five as unambiguous changes from democracy to authoritarian rule (Turkey 1980, Suriname 1980, Ghana 1981, Fiji 2000, Thailand 1996). Nine cases are coded as transitions from multiparty or competitive authoritarianism to military rule (or monarchic rule in the case of Nepal). The remainder are coded as involving no fundamental change in regime at all.

[40]These differences can also be seen by comparing the share of reverters from different Polity and Hadenius-Teorell-Wahman starting points. Thirteen of the 27 Polity reversions (48 percent) occur from a Polity score of 6 and another 8 (30 percent) from a Polity score of 7; in sum, 78 percent revert from the lowest rungs of the democracy ladder. Only 6 cases revert from a Polity score of 8 (Gambia 1994, Niger 1996, Peru 1992) or 9 (Fiji 1987, Thailand 2006, and Turkey 1980) and none revert from a Polity score of 10. The Hadenius-Teorell-Wahman dataset provides confirming evidence of the relative weakness of democracy in the Polity reversion cases. Their dataset codes 10 of the Polity reversions as shifts from democracy to military or competitive authoritarian rule. But 17 of the cases are coded as multiparty authoritarian regimes to begin with, either transitioning to military rule, not transitioning at all, or in some anomalous cases actually shifting to democratic rule.

reversions had experienced prior coups, as compared with exactly half of the survivors.

Finally, survivors and reverters in both datasets differ significantly on our metrics of economic performance during their democratic periods. In the CGV cases, survivors had average growth rates of 3.4 percent, whereas reverters had average growth rates of only 1.1 percent. In the Polity dataset, survivors grew on average by 3.5 percent, whereas the growth rate among reverters was again only 1.1 percent. Differences in both datasets were significant at a .05 level. In the Polity dataset, reverters also experience much higher rates of economic volatility—as measured by the standard deviation of growth. In the CGV dataset, it appears as if the survivors are more volatile, but these differences are driven primarily by the extraordinarily deep transitional recessions of the post-Soviet cases, where volatility averaged 7.4. When they are excluded from the sample, the standard deviation for survivors is 3.0, as compared to 3.9 for reverters.

CONCLUSION

In this chapter we have replicated the methodological path we traversed in Chapters 1 and 2. We focused first on the distributive conflict model, including the distribution of cases that descriptively conformed to it and the effect of inequality on reversions in general and on the distributive conflict cases in particular. We then considered some theoretical alternatives, including modernization theory and what we call the "weak democracy syndrome." The support for distributive conflict models of reversion from democratic rule appears even weaker than for transitions. Modernization theory receives some support; poorer countries are more likely to revert. But even controlling for level of development, the econometric evidence for the weak democracy syndrome—praetorianism, weak institutionalization, and crises—is strongly suggestive of the value of taking a more political and institutional approach to reversions from democratic rule.

Nonetheless, we have also underlined the limitations on reduced form econometric models. We can strengthen causal inference about these cases by again moving from regressions and distributions to causal process observation that focuses on conformity with the distributive conflict and weak democracy models. We do this in Chapter 7 first by considering the reverters. Many of these cases appear to conform with modernization arguments, but we show that they also reflect the institutional and economic disabilities highlighted above. We then turn in Chapter 8 to two sets of anomalies: the low-income cases that "beat the odds" and survive by avoiding the weak democracy syndrome, and the middle-income cases that should enjoy structural advantages but nonetheless revert.

APPENDIX

Tables A6.1a and A6.1b provide detailed information on all reversions in the CGV and Polity datasets respectively, including whether they were the result of a military coup or backsliding, whether they were weak-democracy, elite-reaction or populist reversions, the prior regime type, changes in Polity scores pre- and post-reversion and information on the prior transition to democratic rule.

Robustness Checks

Robustness checks for the mixed effects model in Chapter 6 parallel those used in the appendix to Chapter 2. For the pooled models (Tables A6.2 and A6.3), we show random effects estimates, a survival model, and a rare events model. The hierarchical models that examine separate results for distributive and weak democracy reversions do not allow for rare events corrections, but we show results for random effects and survival models in Tables A6.4 and A6.5. Fuller discussion of these models can be found in the appendix to Chapter 2. As also noted in that appendix, we also include fixed effects models, even though these are not well suited for examining the cross-national variations we seek to capture in our theory.

In the summary tables, significant coefficients are indicated by plusses or minuses within the cells; blank cells indicate coefficients that do not meet standard thresholds of significance. Full results are provided in the online appendix at http://press.princeton.edu/titles/10879.html.

Table A6.1a Reversions from Democratic Rule: CGV Reversions. (N = 25)

	Mode of Reversion	Reversion Type	Hadenius-Teorell-Wahman Regime Type (t-1 and t)	Change in Polity Score (t-1 to t)	Legacy: Prior Transition Type
Bangladesh 2007	Military	Weak democracy	Multiparty-multiparty	6 to –6	Elite 1986
Bolivia 1980	Military	Elite-reaction	Military-military	–4 to –7	DC 1979 (not in dataset)
Burundi 1996	Military	Elite-reaction	Multiparty-military	–77 to –5	DC 1993
Central African Republic 2003	Military	Weak democracy	Multiparty-military	5 to –1	Elite 1993
Comoros 1995	Military	Weak democracy	Multiparty-multiparty	4 to –77	Elite 1990
Congo 1997	Military	Weak democracy	Military (one party)-military (rebel regime)	5 to –6	DC 1992
Ecuador 2000	Military	Populist	Democracy-democracy	9 to 6	Elite 1979 (not in dataset)
Fiji 2000	Military	Elite-reaction	Democracy-multiparty	6 to –88	DC 1992
Ghana 1981	Military	Populist	Democracy-military	6 to –7	Elite 1979 (not in dataset)
Guatemala 1982	Military	Weak democracy	Military-military	–5 to –7	Elite 1966 (not in dataset)
Guinea-Bissau 2003	Military	Weak democracy	Other-military	0 to 2	Elite 2000

(continued)

Table A6.1a (*continued*)

	Mode of Reversion	Reversion Type	Hadenius-Teorell-Wahman Regime Type (t-1 and t)	Change in Polity Score (t-1 to t)	Legacy: Prior Transition Type
Mauritania 2008	Military	Weak democracy	Multiparty-military	4 to –5	Elite 2007
Nepal 2002	Military/ monarch	Elite-reaction	Multiparty-monarchy	6 to –6	DC 1990
Niger 1996	Military	Weak democracy	Multiparty-multiparty	8 to –6	DC 1993
Nigeria 1993	Military	Weak democracy	Military (multiparty)-military	–5 to –7	Elite 1979 (not in dataset)
Pakistan 1999	Military	Weak democracy	Multiparty-military	7 to –6	Elite 1988
Peru 1990	Backsliding	Weak democracy	Democracy-democracy (multiparty in 1991)	7 to 8 (8 in 1991, –3 in 1992)	DC 1980 (not in the dataset)
Sierra Leone 1997	Military	Weak democracy	Multiparty-other (civil war)	4 to –77	Elite 1996
Sudan 1989	Military	Weak democracy	Multiparty-military	7 to –7	DC 1986

Suriname 1980	Military	Populist	Democracy-military	5 to –1	NA (prior democratic transition not in the CGV dataset)
Suriname 1990	Military	Weak democracy	Military (multiparty)-military	–1 to 2	DC 1988
Thailand 1991	Military	Weak democracy	Multiparty-military	3 to –1	Elite 1979 (not in dataset)
Thailand 2006	Military	Elite-reaction	Democracy-military	9 to –5	DC 1992
Turkey 1980	Military	Elite-reaction	Democracy-military	9 to –5	Elite 1961 (not in dataset)
Uganda 1985	Military	Weak democracy	Multiparty-military	3 to –77	Elite 1980
N = 25	24 military, 1 backsliding	6 elite-reaction, 3 populist, 16 weak democracy	Number and share that are straight democracy-authoritarian transitions: 6	Average Polity score prior to transition: 4.1	10 DC 14 elite 1 N.A.

Table A6.1b Reversions from Democratic Rule: Polity Reversions. (N = 27*)

	Mode of Reversion	Reversion Type	Hadenius-Teorell-Wahman Regime Type (at t)	Change in Polity Score (t-1 to t)	Democratic Transition Type
Armenia 1995	Backsliding	Elite-reaction	Democracy-multiparty	7 to 3	DC 1991
Bangladesh 2007	Military	Weak democracy	Multiparty-multiparty	6 to –6	DC 1991
Belarus 1995	Backsliding	Weak democracy	Multiparty-multiparty	7 to 0	Elite 1991
Dominican Republic 1994	Backsliding	Elite-reaction	Democracy-multiparty	6 to 5	DC 1978 (not in dataset)
Ecuador 2007	Backsliding	Populist	Democracy-democracy	7 to 5	Elite 2000
Fiji 1987	Military	Elite-reaction	Democracy-military	9 to –3	NA (constitutional government established at independence in 1970; enters dataset at 9)
Fiji 2000	Military	Elite-reaction	Democracy-multiparty	6 to –88	Elite 1999
Fiji 2006	Military	Weak democracy	Multiparty-military	6 to –3	2004 (omitted from the dataset)
Gambia 1994	Military	Weak democracy	Democracy-military	8 to –7	NA (constitutional government formed at independence in 1965, enters dataset at 8)
Ghana 1981	Military	Populist	Democracy-military	6 to –7	Elite 1979 (not in the dataset)
Haiti 1991	Military	Elite-reaction	Multiparty-military	7 to –7	DC 1990
Haiti 1999	Backsliding	Populist	Multiparty-multiparty	7 to –88	Elite 1994
Honduras 1985	Military	Weak democracy	Democracy-democracy	6 to 5	Elite 1982
Lesotho 1998 (omitted)					
Nepal 2002	Military/ monarch	Elite-reaction	Multiparty-monarchy	6 to –6	Elite 1999

Niger 1996	Military	Weak democracy	Multiparty-multiparty	8 to −6	DC 1992
Nigeria 1984	Military	Weak democracy	Democracy-military	7 to −7	Elite 1979 (not in the dataset)
Pakistan 1999	Military	Weak democracy	Multiparty-military	7 to −6	Elite 1988
Peru 1992	Backsliding	Weak democracy	Democracy-multiparty	8 to −3	DC 1980 (not in dataset)
Russia 2007	Backsliding	Weak democracy	Multiparty-multiparty	6 to 4	Elite 2000
Solomon Islands 2000 (omitted)					
Sri Lanka 1982	Backsliding	Weak democracy	Multiparty-multiparty (1980 is democracy)	6 to 5	NA (constitutional government established at independence in 1948, enters dataset at 7)
Sri Lanka 2003	Backsliding	Elite-reaction	Multiparty-democracy	6 to 5	Elite 2001
Sudan 1989	Military	Weak democracy	Multiparty-military	7 to −7	DC 1986
Thailand 2006	Military	Elite-reaction	Democracy-military	9 to −5	DC 1992
Turkey 1980	Military	Elite-reaction	Democracy-military	9 to −5	Elite 1973 (not in dataset)
Ukraine 1993	Backsliding	Elite-reaction	Multiparty-democracy	6 to 5	DC 1991
Venezuela 2006	Backsliding	Populist	Multiparty-multiparty	6 to 5	Elite 1958 (not in dataset)
Zambia 1996	Backsliding	Elite-reaction	Multiparty-multiparty	6 to 1	DC 1991
Two omitted; N = 27	14 military; 1 monarchy; 12 backsliding	11 elite-reaction, 4 populist, 12 weak democracy	Number and share that are straight democracy-authoritarian transitions: 10	Average Polity score prior to transition: 6.9	10 DC, 13 Elite, 4 N.A.

Note: DC, distributive conflict. Two Polity cases were omitted as a result of anomalous features of the Polity coding scheme: Lesotho and the Solomon Islands. In these cases, the transition year was initially coded as a −77, indicating "anarchy or interregnum." These cases are automatically converted to zeros for data manipulation purposes, but as we explain in more detail in the dataset, it is not clear that these codings are justified.

Table A6.2 CGV Reversions (Pooled): Summary of Robustness Checks.

Variable	Mixed Effects	Random Effects	Survival	Rare Events Logit	Fixed Effects
Capital share					
GDP per capita					
Growth	−	−	− −	−	
Resource rents					
Ethnolinguistic fractionalization					
Union membership	−	−		−	
Manufacturing					
Demonstrations				+	+
Polity	−	−	−	−	−
Coup history	+	+	+	+	+
Proportion of democracies			+	+	+

Note: In this and the following tables, marked cells indicate significant coefficients. Pluses and minuses indicate the direction of the effect. Under each model specification, the first column shows the results with union membership, the second the results with manufacturing.

Table A6.3 Polity Reversions (Pooled): Summary of Robustness Checks.

Variable	Mixed Effects	Random Effects	Survival	Rare Events Logit	Fixed Effects
Capital share					
GDP per capita					
Growth	−			−	
Resource rents		−		−	
Ethnolinguistic fractionalization					
Union membership		+		+	
Manufacturing					
Demonstrations				+	
Polity	−	−	−	−	
Coup history	+		−		
Proportion of democracies			+		

Table A6.4 Elite-Reaction and Weak Democracy Reversions (CGV): Summary of Robustness Checks.

Variable	Mixed Effects		Random Effects		Survival		Fixed Effects	
Elite-Reaction vs. No Reversion								
Capital share								
GDP per capita	–	–		+				+
Growth			–					
Resource rents			–	–				
Ethnolinguistic fractionalization			–					
Union membership							–	
Manufacturing								
Demonstrations			+	+				
Polity	–	–	–					
Coup history	+	+	+	+				
Proportion of democracies			–		+			
Weak Democracy vs. No Reversion								
Capital share								
GDP per capita	–	–						
Growth			–		–	–	–	
Resource rents				+				
Ethnolinguistic fractionalization	+		+	+				
Union membership			–					
Manufacturing								
Demonstrations								
Polity	–	–	–	–	–	–		
Coup history	+							
Proportion of democracies				+				

Table A6.5 Elite-Reaction and Weak Democracy Reversions (Polity): Summary of Robustness Checks.

Variable	Mixed Effects	Random Effects	Survival	Fixed Effects
Elite-Reaction vs. No Reversion				
Capital share				
GDP per capita	−	−		
Growth				
Resource rents		+		+
Ethnolinguistic fractionalization				
Union membership		+		
Manufacturing				
Demonstrations				
Polity	−	−	−	−
Coup history	+	+		
Proportion of democracies				
Weak Democracy vs. no Reversion				
Capital share				
GDP per capita	−	−	−	−
Growth		+		
Resource rents		−		
Ethnolinguistic fractionalization	+			
Union membership		+		
Manufacturing	−			
Demonstrations		+	+	
Polity	−	−	−	−
Coup history	+	+		
Proportion of democracies	+	+	+	+

CHAPTER 7

Pathways to Authoritarian Rule

IN THIS CHAPTER, WE SUBJECT THE COMPARATIVE EVIDENCE regarding the weak democracy syndrome to closer scrutiny by selecting individual cases for causal process observation and comparison. We have two objectives in doing so. First, do the specific causal mechanisms we have identified with the weak democracy syndrome help us account for the reversions that are *not* triggered by either elite reactions or populist protest? Do praetorianism, weak institutions, and economic crisis in these cases generate opportunities and incentives for military coups or incumbent backsliding?

Second, however, we also assess the extent to which these factors may operate in the elite-reaction and populist reversions as well. Recall that our coding is permissive, designed to be favorable to the theory under consideration. The coding does not assume that distributive conflict is the only possible cause of the transitions coded as such. Rather, the presence of such conflicts and at least some causal effect was adequate to consider cases as distributive in nature. An examination of these cases—which are limited in number despite this coding—finds that many, if not all, were *also* vulnerable to the debilities of the weak democracy syndrome. Our qualitative findings thus comport with the regression results, particularly given the null findings on the role of inequality: the alternate reversion paths—although differing in the presence of distributive conflict—might in fact be driven largely by common causal processes.

We start with the weak democracy cases themselves, the category that strongly dominates the sample of reversions. To structure our analysis, we take a regional approach that runs broadly from lower- to higher-income countries, allowing us to consider the effects of level of development that are at the center of the modernization approach. We begin with a cluster of civil war African cases, comparing them with Niger, a case we also considered as a distributive conflict transition. We then take up cases in South and Southeast Asia (Pakistan) and Latin America (Peru), closing with a discussion of European examples. With the exception of Turkey, these are represented entirely by backsliding in four former Soviet republics: Belarus, Ukraine, Russia, and Armenia, on which we focus here; we take up the Russian case in Chapter 8. As in previous chapters, this approach also allows us to hold some background conditions constant, from longer-run historical commonalities—rooted in some cases in colonial legacies—to regional "neighborhood effects," and level of development.

We then turn to a consideration of elite-reaction reversions, which comport most closely with the distributive conflict model.[1] These cases constitute over a quarter of the CGV and Polity samples (seven and nine, respectively, although with Thailand [CGV] and Fiji [Polity] accounting for two cases each). Nonetheless, the relatively small number of elite-reaction reversions makes it more difficult to find matched pairs for analysis as we did in Chapter 5. Two cases are plausible candidates for comparative analysis. First, we contrast the weak democracy reversions in a number of low-income African cases with Burundi, a very poor African country riven by deep ethnic cleavages between a dominant Tutsi minority and a large Hutu majority. We show that it shares a number of features with other post–civil war reversions on the continent.

Second, we look at the case of Thailand, a middle-income country that appears to comport closely with distributive conflict models. Rising inequality along with regional and class divisions played a role in the coup of 2006, the descent into polarization, and an out-of-sample military intervention in 2014. Yet, as with Burundi, Thailand shows evidence of the weak democracy syndrome as well, particularly with respect to its long history of military involvement in politics and weak institutionalization.

In the last section of the chapter, we focus on the much smaller subset of populist reversions, with case studies of the seizures of power in Ghana (1981) and Haiti (1999) under Jerry Rawlings and Jean-Bertrand Aristide, respectively. Despite elements of distributive conflict, these cases show strong evidence of the weak democracy syndrome as well.

WEAK DEMOCRACY REVERSIONS I: THE AFRICAN CIVIL WAR CASES

We begin with the African reversions, which account for 15 of the 52 discrete cases (28.8 percent) in the two datasets:[2] 22 percent of the Polity reversions and nearly half (48 percent) of the CGV ones, a difference that again can be traced back to the very different coding rules.[3] A cluster of seven civil war cases—six weak democracy and one elite reaction, Burundi—conform with modernization expectations. With Haiti and

---

[1] Populist reversions compose only about 15 percent, four in the CGV and five in the Polity. We touched on these cases in Chapter 6 and examine the Venezuelan case in more detail in Chapter 8.

[2] The CGV dataset codes 12 African reversions, the Polity dataset 6, with 3 overlapping cases: Sudan 1989 and Niger 1996—both elite-led—and Ghana, the sole populist case outside of Latin America.

[3] The CGV dataset defines democracy in terms of the staging of competitive elections and a relatively minimal survival rule; it thus captures reversions from democracy that would not be coded as such by Polity.

Nepal—another civil war case that closely resembles the African examples—these seven countries are among the poorest of all the reversion cases, with average GDP per capita at the time of democratic failure of only $1,006. Although poverty is a crude proxy for institutional capabilities, its depth is reflected in extreme limits on the ability of the state to extract revenue and spend on needed social infrastructure and services.[4] At the time of their reversions, total government revenue in these civil war cases—Niger, Burundi, Haiti, and Nepal—averaged only about 12 percent of GDP.[5]

Yet as the summary in Table 7.1 shows, these countries also had quite distinctive institutional disabilities: histories of praetorianism, fragile democratic settlements and weak institutionalization (measured in part by Polity scores), and histories of weak economic performance and crisis. As we detailed in Chapter 4, outside intervention, mediation of conflict, and reengagement of donors can mitigate the extremes of state failure, improve security and livelihoods, and improve accountability, including through elections. Yet it is telling that with the exception of Sierra Leone, none of these other five cases managed to consolidate sustained democratic rule through 2013 and Burundi only managed to eek out a Polity score of 6 after 2005. Democratic experiments in these cases proved unfortunately short-lived.

Praetorianism

The causal processes leading to reversion in these cases are in large part institutional and start with extreme variants of praetorianism: histories of coups, social violence and the presence of militias and armed gangs, and weak central control over territory.[6] As Table 7.1 indicates, fundamental state weakness either proved the prelude to armed challenges and the descent into civil war or strengthened the military's role in politics and paved the way for intervention. In five of the seven cases, reversion occurred via coup. This group of cases includes three countries we examined in Chapter 4 that exited civil wars with negotiated settlements

---

[4] Slater, Smith, and Nair 2014.

[5] Burundi (1996), 15.0 percent, Nepal (2002), 12.0 percent, Niger (1996), 12.8 percent, and Haiti (1991 and 1999), only 8.1 percent and 8.8 percent, respectively. Data from International Centre for Tax and Development 2014.

[6] The Nigerian Civil War of 1967–70 does not appear as a proximate cause of the reversion in that country in 1983 (CGV)–84 (Polity), and we thus omit it from this group. But the civil war was triggered in part by the complex political ramifications of the 1966 military coup, and the war served to further entrench the dominant position of the military in Nigerian politics.

brokered by outsiders that subsequently proved civil war recidivists: Uganda 1985, Sierra Leone 1997, and Guinea-Bissau 2003. In Sudan, the country's second civil war, which began in 1983, persisted through both the democratic transition in 1986 (CGV and Polity) and the subsequent reversion in 1989. As we will detail in the next section, Burundi's civil war also persisted through the democratic period and reversion.[7] We also include in this group two cases—the Congo 1997 and the Central African Republic 2003—that were preceded by coups and violence that fell short of civil war, but in which the reversion to authoritarian rule was associated with a descent into state failure.

Weak Institutionalization

As we argued in Chapter 6, institutional weakness went beyond formal arrangements that generated government immobilism and dysfunction, such as divided government, to more fundamental conflicts among competing parties. These conflicts reflected a high degree of uncertainty on the part of the main political actors about the degree of commitment of competing parties to the fundamental rules of the democratic political game. Quite apart from the veto power exercised by militaries, these weaknesses are reflected in the fragility of negotiated settlements noted in Table 7.1, captured at least in part by low Polity scores. Sudan crosses, however briefly, the Polity threshold of 6. None of the other cases do, with Polity scores for each country during the democratic period averaging from 3 to 5.

Most of these cases were only judged democracies in the CGV dataset. The staging of democratic elections was typically brokered and monitored by outside parties as a result of the lack of basic institutional infrastructure. Unwieldy or altogether dysfunctional coalitions—imposed in all cases except Sudan by externally mediated power-sharing agreements—generated ongoing conflicts over prerogatives and the spoils of office as well as policy. All were characterized by fundamental uncertainty about the willingness of incumbents to permit competitive elections and the inability of legislatures, judiciaries, or other bodies such as electoral tribunals to check the power of executives and resort to extraconstitutional means of bargaining on the part of oppositions, including through the mobilization of violence.

---

[7]As we will see, the persistence of civil war through both democratic transitions and reversions is a feature of the distributive conflict Burundi case as well.

Economic Crises

Despite the limited findings on growth in the regressions in Chapter 6, all of these reversions occurred in the immediate wake of recessions. But all experienced highly erratic growth and severe crises over the entire period of democratic rule as well; poor performance was not only a short-term phenomenon. These crises can be traced in part to external shocks and the devastating effects of the social violence itself, including the collapse of government services, degradation of basic infrastructure, and large populations of internally displaced people. However, growth collapses typically had policy roots, including macroeconomic imbalances and inability to undertake even the most modest reform measures. In all cases, these policy failures corresponded with devastating loss of access to external financial support from the multilateral financial institutions and donors on which these countries were highly dependent.

Clearly, not all of the African reversions reflect the weak democracy syndrome to the same extent as these extreme cases. Ghana, Nigeria, and Zambia provide examples of countries with higher income per capita and more differentiated political economies than the civil war cases. All three subsequently transition and survive; we discuss these survivors further in Chapter 8 and show how they differ from this cluster. The remaining African reverters, however—Gambia, Malawi, Mali, and Niger in the CGV dataset; the Comoros, Mauritania, and Niger in the Polity dataset—suggest strikingly similar headwinds. Niger provides a useful comparator to the civil war cases as it is at a comparable level of development and is coded as a reversion using both CGV and Polity coding rules.[8] Despite the absence of outright civil war, it demonstrates clearly the institutional weaknesses we seek to emphasize.

Niger: A Non–Civil War Case

As we saw in Chapter 3, Niger transitioned to democracy in 1992–93 (in the Polity and CGV datasets, respectively) following mass mobilization by unions and a coalition of opposition forces against the incumbent military government of General Ali Saibou. In 1996, the new regime was overthrown in a military coup d'état, led by Ibrahim Baré Maïnassara, in the wake of recurrent strikes by public sector workers and a stalemate between the president and the opposition in the legislature. After winning a rigged election, Maïnassara was in turn overthrown and killed in a violent coup in 1999. Although the country subsequently experienced

---

[8] Although we do not categorize Niger as a civil war or state failure case, the erosion of democracy did take place against the backdrop of an ongoing insurgency, the so-called First Tuareg Rebellion (1985–95), which raised serious concerns about military impunity.

Table 7.1 The African Civil War Cases.

Cases (GDP per Capita at Time of Reversion)	Civil War, Social Violence, and Coup History	Democrati-zation and Civil War Settlements: Average Polity Score of Democratic Period	Economic Performance and Crises	Breakdown/ Return to Democracy
Weak Democracy Reversions				
Central African Republic 2003 ($735)	1992–93. Rioting and coup attempts prior to transitional elections. 1995–96. Political crises as opposition movement coalesces, followed by three military mutinies in 1996.	1993. CGV transition with strong external involvement. 1997. Bangui Agreements facilitate second-round elections in 1999. Sustained French involvement and UN presence. Average Polity score: 5.	–0.3 percent growth 2001–2, followed by major crisis in 2003 (–7.6 percent). Terms of trade shock but also loss of access to aid as a result of failure to implement reforms.	Francois Bozize launches rebellion from Chad in October 2002 followed by descent into civil war. 2003–present. Failed peace agreements or ceasefires signed in 2007, 2008, and 2011, up-turn in fighting in 2012. No return to democracy.
Congo 1997 ($3,229)	1993. Fighting among militias loyal to compet-ing politi-cians kills thousands.	1992. CGV transition following national conference. 1994–95. Ceasefire and power-sharing agreement. Average Polity score: 5.	Severe crisis in 1994 (–5.5 percent), followed by recovery in 1995–1996 but return to negative growth (–0.6) in 1997. Oil revenues only partly offset effects of war and loss of external finance.	1997–98. Fighting be-tween military and compet-ing militias descends into civil war with Angolan intervention. 1999–2001. Peace process leads to resumption of elections. No return to democracy.

(continued)

Table 7.1 (*continued*)

Guinea-Bissau 2003 ($550)	1998. Clashes with armed Senegalese separatists. 1998–99. Attempted coup triggers short but destructive civil war. 2001–3. Repeated coup attempts.	1999. Initial peace accord fails in the wake of second coup, but ECOWAS mediates successful transitional elections, with UN involvement. Average Polity score: 4.5.	Major crisis in 2002 (–7.1 percent); crop failure but also policy failures and loss of access to external finance.	Military overthrows ineffective and corrupt Kumba Yala government following postponed elections. 2004–5 transition process reestablishes democratic rule but reverts again in 2012.
Sierra Leone 1997 ($561)	1991–2002. Continuous civil war. 1996 coup.	1996 and 1998 CGV transitions, but externally supervised power-sharing agreement under Abidjan Accords does not lead to effective control over the country. Polity score (1996): 4.	Recurrent crises (1992, –19.0 percent; 1995, –8.0 percent; and 1997, –16.7 percent). Causes include conflict but also mismanagement and collapse of government revenue and aid.	1997 coup following efforts to shrink the military. 1999. Lomé Peace Accords fail triggering British intervention, ultimate defeat of RUF, and return to democracy (CGV 2007, Polity 2009).
Sudan 1989 ($972)	1955–1972. First Sudanese Civil War. 1983–2005. Second Sudanese Civil War.	1986. Polity and CGV transition. Following coup that displaces Numeiri, a Transitional Military Council oversees transition. Polity score: 7.	Crises in 1984–85 (–5.6 percent PY) and 1988 (–0.3). Causes include war and climate shocks but also policy and loss of access to external finance after 1983.	Coup in context of virtual economic collapse, dysfunctional coalition governments, and resurgence of civil war in Darfur and the South. No return to democratic rule.

Table 7.1 (*continued*)

Uganda 1985 ($572)	1978–80. Military mutiny followed by attack by Idi Amin on Tanzania and outbreak of Tanzania-Uganda war, also involving Uganda rebel forces. 1981–86. Uganda Bush War.	1980 (CGV transition). Tanzania attempts to form unity government, but with infighting and coups among the Uganda rebel forces before Obote emerges dominant. Average Polity score: 3.	Negative growth in 1984–85 (–1.8 percent per annum). Weather shocks and war contribute but also inflation fueled by government policy.	Coup in context of brutal Uganda Bush War, militias, ethnic struggles within the military and between Obote and generals. No return to democratic rule.

Elite Reaction Reversion

Burundi 1996 ($424)	1987. Coup and Hutu uprising trigger large-scale killings of Hutus 1993. Coup sets in train civil war that persists with varying intensity until 2005.	1993. CGV transition, but first Hutu incumbent Melchior Ndadaye almost immediately assassinated as well as his successor. 1994. Externally brokered power-sharing agreement, but with effective military veto. Average Polity score: 0.	Sustained economic collapse 1993–96 (–5.3 percent per annum); loss of access to external finance is a major cause.	Military coup in wake of killing of Tutsis by Hutu rebel groups. 2003–5 peace process yields unsuccessful cease-fires but finally transitions back to democratic rule (2005 CGV and Polity).

another transition-reversion cycle,[9] we focus on the processes driving the earlier episode. This reversion is more temporally proximate to the civil war comparators and exhibits distributive conflicts that resemble those that generated the transition.

As we noted in Chapter 3, the military had been a major actor in Niger's politics since at least 1974, when it overthrew a one-party regime that had governed since independence in 1961. Despite the armed forces' retreat in 1992–93, Saibou, the displaced military head of state, continued to be an influential actor behind the scenes, and the military's "legacy party," the MNSD (Mouvement National pour la Société du Développement), remained the major opposition force.[10] The immediate triggers of democratic breakdown can be traced to fundamental conflicts between government and opposition over the country's political institutions and resulting government dysfunction.[11] The initial establishment of a French semipresidential system set the stage for severe struggles between the president and parliament. But the key risks to democracy were not simply those associated with "cohabitation"; they centered rather on the constant efforts on the part of incumbents to reduce constitutional constraints on their discretion or to ignore them altogether. In the short period of nominally democratic rule, we see attempts by the executive to undermine congressional oversight, challenges to the neutrality of the electoral administration, and widespread use of extraconstitutional resources by both the government and the opposition, including violent and disruptive street behavior.[12]

These political conflicts were intensified by ongoing economic challenges.[13] In the early 1990s, protests against the Saibou regime were spurred by civil service and student disaffection with an unpopular IMF program, and the economic protest continued after the transition. The fragile new

[9]In the CGV dataset, Niger transitions in 1993, reverts in 1996, transitions again in 2000, but experiences a coup in 2010 that is the basis for our coding of the case as a CGV reverter. In the Polity dataset, Niger transitions in 1993, reverts in 1996, and transitions in 2004; however, the coup of 2010 leaves it as a reverter in the Polity dataset as well.

[10]Villalón and Idrissa 2005: 32.

[11]Writing of the 1990s in Niger more broadly, Villalón and Idrissa note that the decade witnessed "four republics . . . ; three transitions of six, nine, and eighteen months; one National Conference and a Committee on Fundamental Texts; one Technical Constitutional Committee; a Consultative Council of Elders; three constitutional referenda and eight other national elections; four heads of state and one president of a High Council of the Republic; four National Assemblies; nine prime ministers; at least one hundred and fifty ministers; one civilian coup d'état; one electoral boycott; one strike by the president and one strike by parliamentarians; one campaign of civil disobedience; and one dissolution of the National Assembly."

[12]Villalón and Idrissa 2005: 28.

[13]World Bank 1996.

democracy was buffeted by the same forces. The massive CFA franc devaluation in 1994 triggered militant demands for unsustainable wage increases by the powerful trade union movement, the Union des Syndicats des Travailleurs du Niger. The devaluation was followed by a nominal recovery, partly as a result of compensatory financing from France and multilateral debt relief. However, the gains from the devaluation were absorbed in no small measure by the wage demands of the highly organized public sector workers.[14]

The unraveling was relatively swift in coming. Mahamane Ousmane of the opposition CDS-Rahama (Convention démocratique et sociale-Rahama) won the transitional presidential election in the second round. However, he was constrained to form a coalition with five other parties and to appoint Mahamadou Issoufou from the left-of-center PNDS-Tarayya (Parti Nigérien pour la Démocratie et le Docialisme -Tarayya) to the position of prime minister, giving rise to a situation of "cohabitation" common in semipresidential systems. From the outset of the transition, the president faced a campaign of civil disobedience on the part of the opposition MNSD, ongoing tensions with his PNSD-Tarayya prime minister, and threats of a general strike on the part of mobilized public-sector unions. Following a severe crackdown on the union movement, the PNSD withdrew from the coalition, and after a short-lived effort to construct a minority government, Ousmane was forced to call a new election in 1995. Unfortunately, the result was a virtually identical partisan lineup. The remainder of the year was characterized by complete stalemate, in which the president rejected legislation passed in the National Assembly and refused to even meet with his prime minister for long stretches of time. When the military seized power in January 1996, Maïnassara cited the constitutional crisis and the political stalemate as the reason for the coup.[15]

Weak Democracy Reversions II: Pakistan

South and Southeast Asia and Oceania account for ten reversions, but in only six countries. Four of these are coded as weak democracy cases (Sri Lanka 1982, Pakistan 1999, and Bangladesh 2007 in South Asia and Fiji in 2006 in the Pacific); six are coded as elite-reaction reversions (Nepal 2002, Sri Lanka 2003, Fiji 1987 and 2000, and Thailand 1991 and 2006). The 1982 reversion in Sri Lanka proved shallow, and the succession of reversions in Fiji reflected distinctive ethnic dynamics we noted in Chapter 3. We focus here on Pakistan, where a fragile democratic regime gave way

---

[14]Clément et al. 1996.
[15]Charlick 2007: 73.

to a prolonged period of military rule. Bangladesh, which seceded from Pakistan in 1971, showed very similar military and institutional weaknesses. The effect of short-run economic factors in these two cases is more ambiguous. Pakistan did experience a marked slowdown in growth prior to the reversion, and Ibrahim argues that Pakistan's coup history is correlated with aggregate economic performance.[16] However, these slowdowns were by no means of the magnitude of crises elsewhere; Bangladesh reverts in the context of virtually unchanged growth.[17] But other components of the weak democracy syndrome were on full display in the two countries, both of which experienced long-run oscillations between democratic and authoritarian rule.

Praetorianism

From the onset of independence in 1948, the Pakistani military establishment viewed itself as the representative of "the nation," and showed growing contempt for the weakness and corruption of civilian politicians. The military's entry into politics came early in the postindependence period, with the appointment of a career military officer-turned-civil servant (Iskander Mirza) as the last governor general (1955–56) and then president. Mirza imposed martial law in 1958 and appointed the army chief as martial law administrator. This government, in turn, was overthrown in a full-blown coup by General Ayub Khan later in the year. Military interventions followed in 1969 and 1977, and by the coup of 1999, military governments had directly ruled Pakistan for 20 of the 51 years since independence in 1948. Even during nominally democratic periods, the officer corps was an independent political force and veto player.[18]

Weak Institutionalization

As in the African cases, formal constitutional arrangements and political institutions lacked durability and posed limited constraints on political incumbents. One indicator of this weak institutionalization was a frequent change in constitutions. By the time of the 1999 coup, Pakistan had had five different constitutions as well as a period of governance under a

---

[16] Ibrahim 2009.

[17] Pakistan experienced slowed growth in 1993 (1.8 percent) and 1997–98 (1.8 percent per annum), the two years prior to the reversion. However, for the decade of the 1990s, growth averaged 4 percent. Bangladesh is even more anomalous in this regard, with consistently high growth through the 2000s, up to and including the year of the reversion in 2007 (5.7 percent).

[18] Siddiqa 2007; Jalal 2014: chap. 3.

suspended constitution (1977–85) and two periods without the benefit of a written constitution at all (1958–62, 1969–71). Cleavages within and between the major parties were cross-cut by deep institutional fissures between the president and parliament, and between political leaders and a highly politicized judiciary. These conflicts repeatedly escalated into constitutional crises as the competing institutions struggled to assert their prerogatives. It was typically such conflicts that triggered military mediation or intervention.[19]

Even in the decade prior to the coup, the cutthroat character of democratic politics was evident in the bitter conflicts between the two major clientelistic parties, both catchall coalitions headed by elite kinship groups: Benazir Bhutto's slightly left-of-center PPP and the Muslim League headed by Nawaz Sharif.[20] These conflicts not only were evident in the electoral arena, but infected core political institutions as well. The return to democracy in 1988 ushered in a period of recurrent constitutional crises, beginning with those between President Ghulam Ishaq Khan and Prime Minister Benazir Bhutto. In 1990, President Ishaq dismissed Bhutto's government for corruption under a controversial constitutional amendment (Amendment VIII or Article 58 2[b]), crafted by the authoritarian Zia ul-Haq government in 1985. The highly politicized superior courts upheld the action, setting the stage for elections won by Nawaz Sharif. But the trench warfare between branches of government continued unabated. In 1993, Sharif was first dismissed in the wake of a major banking scandal, then reinstated by allies on the Supreme Court, and then forced from power by the military.

New elections returned Bhutto to office, but did little to stabilize the political situation. Bhutto proceeded to retaliate against her political rivals, bringing charges against the Sharif family, and antagonized the Supreme Court by attempting to manipulate judicial appointments. The situation deteriorated further with the killing of her brother, Mir Ghulam Murtaza Bhutto, in an encounter with the police. Bhutto accused the president of being behind the killing; he once again had recourse to his power to dismiss the government, again quickly legitimized by a Supreme Court "still smarting from the effects of her judicial policies."[21]

The Reversion

The direct seizure of power by General Musharraf in 1999 reflected another cycle of institutional weakness inviting praetorian intervention. In

[19] Oberst et al. 2014: 186.
[20] Tudor 2013; Jalal 2014: chap. 8.
[21] Oberst et al. 2014: 226.

the election of 1997, Sharif returned to power with a very large parliamentary majority, which he used to undermine the opposition. Exploiting the advantages of incumbency, he halted the legal proceedings against his family, barred Bhutto from holding elective office, and dismissed hundreds of her political appointees. The prime minister overreached with respect to the military, however. A failed attempt by the armed forces to seize strategic heights near the Kashmiri town of Kargil resulted in a humiliating defeat and bitter political recriminations over responsibility for the fiasco. In an attempt to counter threats from the armed forces, Sharif dismissed the commanding general, Pervez Musharraf, while the general was traveling on official business. In a classic example of praetorianism, Musharraf refused to accept the decision and successfully rallied the military establishment to his side. When he returned home, he seized power after Sharif unsuccessfully attempted to prevent his plane from making an emergency landing.

Weak Democracy Reversions III: Peru

Four out of the 11 discrete reversions in Latin America were classified as weak-democracy ones: Guatemala 1982, Honduras 1985, Suriname 1990, and Peru 1992.[22] Although better off than their African and Asian counterparts, all of these were low-income countries with histories of praetorianism, military dictatorship, and severe economic crises. The first three cases, however, involved relatively limited changes in the underlying structure of power in weak democracies where the military was already the dominant actor.[23]

Although Peru ultimately returned to a democratic path, Fujimori's *autogolpe* constitutes a more significant case as it saw a more abrupt and definitive change of regime that lasted for a decade. Unlike the Central American cases and Suriname, the reversion in Peru overthrew a regime that had for over a decade been characterized by an open and highly competitive multiparty system. Prior to the *autogolpe*, there had been three successful alternations in power since the transition from military rule in 1980: from the center-right government of Fernando Belaúnde Terry (1980–85) to a left-populist government under Alan García and the APRA party (1985–90), and from García to Fujimori, who prevailed as a centrist in a campaign against the neoliberal candidacy of Mario Vargas Llosa in 1990. Despite a long history of military praetorianism prior to the democratic period,

[22]The CGV dataset codes the reversion in Peru in 1990 because of the election of a government in that year that did not survive. The Fujimori *autogolpe*, however, took place in 1992.

[23]See Chapter 5 on Honduras and Chapter 6 on short-lived returns to autocracy.

moreover, the military appeared to have made the strategic decision to refrain from entering politics directly following the manifest failures of the 1968 to 1980 dictatorship.[24] On the eve of the *autogolpe*, Peru had a Polity score of 8, as compared to –5 in Guatemala, –1 in Suriname, and 6 in Honduras, which barely crossed the democratic threshold. Closer inspection, however, reveals all the core elements of the weak democracy syndrome.

Praetorianism

First, as in a number of other weak democracies, politics in Peru took place against the backdrop of social violence that invited military entanglement. The rise of the Sendero Luminoso insurgency increased the role of the military and gradually weakened democratic institutions even prior to the *autogolpe*. Both the Belaúnde and García governments delegated emergency authority to regional commanders, and depended upon the military to carry out responsibilities normally assigned to the police. Fujimori, who campaigned on a promise to take a harder line with insurgents, extended this practice. Once in office, he issued a series of decrees that authorized military discretion to restrict the activity of journalists, confiscate property in the name of national security, and try suspected terrorists in special military courts.[25]

The military was more cautious about exerting power at the national level. Although direct coup threats were infrequent, however, they were not altogether absent. In June 1986, Alan García expressed concern about a coup after military officers massacred 270 Sendero prisoners; in April 1987, air force officers overflew the presidential palace in protest over the establishment of a centralized Ministry of Defense.[26]

All three democratic presidents made extensive use of decree authority and declared states of emergency in wide areas of the country. Persistent attacks on mayors and other elected officials left towns entirely without civilian authority, with military commanders effectively suspending constitutional protections in order to prosecute the war.[27]

Weak Institutionalization

The rise of Sendero—together with the economic crisis—also did much to erode other aspects of the institutional structure. Widespread human rights abuses were either tolerated or ignored under Belaúnde and García,

[24] McClintock 1989.
[25] Mauceri 1995: 23.
[26] McClintock 1989: 134.
[27] Mauceri 1995: 16.

as well as under Fujimori, and all three presidents delegated power to the military through emergency decrees that bypassed congress.

Although Fujimori initially governed within the framework of the 1979 constitution, moreover, he also relied heavily on claims of decree powers to counter potential legislative opposition to the austerity program that he announced unexpectedly following his election victory.[28] More broadly, Fujimori began to exploit executive powers in ways characteristic of other backsliding cases. He manipulated rivalries within the political elite, built a spy network that could bribe or blackmail political enemies, and relied extensively on decree powers both to impose his economic program and to prosecute the counterinsurgency.[29] As Roberts argues, he was able to do this in part because of the absence of effective organized social or political checks: "Competing parties had been devastated by the crisis of the 1980s, as had once-powerful labor and peasant movements, creating an atomized sociopolitical landscape that was almost entirely devoid of representative institutions."[30]

Economic Crisis

Economic factors also played a strong role in the erosion of democratic rule. The country had been battered by severe debt crises in the mid-1970s under a military government and again in the early 1980s, but it suffered an even more devastating crisis in 1988–90, the years preceding the democratic collapse. The reasons were political as much as economic. Alan García ran on a populist platform in the aftermath of the debt crisis, promising a heterodox approach. A partial default on external debt payments had the effect, however, of cutting off access to external credit and isolating the country. Expansionist monetary and fiscal policies triggered a growth collapse and high inflation, with price increases reaching over 1,220 percent on an annual basis.[31] Following a brief recovery in 1991, the country once again slid into deep recession in 1992, the year of the reversion.

The Reversion

The decision in April 1992 to close Congress and suspend the constitution was precipitated most directly by the legislature's vote earlier in the year to reject a number of Fujimori's decrees. In some respects, Fujimori's

[28] Stokes 2001.
[29] Roberts 2006: 138; Mauceri 1995: 23.
[30] Roberts 2006: 140.
[31] Lago 1991.

concerns reflected the vulnerabilities of all presidential systems to divided government and stalemate. But the roots of the authoritarian reversion went far deeper than presidentialism per se. As we just noted, Fujimori had exploited executive powers from the onset of his presidency to avoid legislative checks and had lined up military support for doing so. In response to congressional opposition, the military command announced in early 1992 that it backed his use of decree powers, sending a clear signal of support ahead of the coup.

The initial international response to the coup was unambiguously hostile. Donors, including the IMF and World Bank, suspended assistance and the OAS threatened sanctions.[32] Fearing international isolation, the reaction of the private sector was also initially negative. Under these circumstances, a full-blown military dictatorship was off the table. Fujimori turned instead to a façade of constitutional government that was more difficult to identify as openly autocratic. While hardly democratic, these moves were sufficient to restore the confidence of economic elites and secure acquiescence from the international community.

Notwithstanding opposition from the rapidly shrinking organized left, a large majority of the Peruvian poor was also attracted by a leader who promised to deal with the economic crisis and the insurgency with a strong hand. A 1992 survey showed that almost 76 percent of low-income people supported Fujimori's plan for constitutional reform,[33] a clear example of how actual political cleavages can confound distributive conflict models. Building on an initial cross-class electoral foundation, the increasingly authoritarian system subsequently combined repression and rigged institutions with policies favorable to the economic elite and clientelistic manipulation of the electorate.

Weak Democracy Reversions IV: Armenia and the Post-Soviet Cases

Peru shares a number of features with the final cluster of elite-led reversions: four former Soviet republics, including Russia itself, that managed to cross the democratic threshold in the post–Cold War period, but subsequently reverted to authoritarian rule: Ukraine very briefly in 1993, Armenia and Belarus in 1995, and Russia in 2007. Ukraine and Belarus have been examined at length in Chapter 5, and we address Russia in our consideration of middle-income reverters in Chapter 8.

---

[32] Chapter 3; Levitsky and Way 2010: 163.
[33] Rubio 1992: 7, cited in Weyland 1996: n. 16.

We focus here on the case of Armenia, another classic case of backsliding. Like only a handful of other Soviet republics, including the Baltic states and Ukraine, Armenia was democratic at independence; it sits between the more successful return to democracy in Ukraine, and the complete collapse of democratic rule in Belarus. Polity scores fell from 7 to 3 in 1995—the coded reversion—followed by two years of –6, before rebounding to sustained competitive authoritarian rule just short of the democratic threshold in 1998 (a score of 5, sustained through the end of the dataset in 2008). To what extent does Armenia conform with the weak democracy model?

Conflict, Praetorianism, and Economic Collapse

Unlike the African and Asian cases, in the post-Soviet countries the fact that communist regimes had a long history of military subordination to party control may have insulated them from coups. However there are elements of the Armenian case that conform with the failure of weak democracies to constrain the military. Armenian militias participated in the war over the Armenian enclave of Nagorno-Karabakh in neighboring Azerbaijan. The country was thus one of a number of the post-Soviet cases in which severe ethnic conflict and the emergence of militias constituted a critical backdrop for the assertion of executive powers. These include Moldova, Georgia, Russia, and two countries that fall outside of the scope of our inquiry as they remained consistently authoritarian throughout the sample period, Azerbaijan and Tajikistan. In an echo of praetorianism elsewhere, a succession of Armenian rulers used the threat of resumed violence in Nagorno-Karabakh or Azeri aggression to justify restraints on the opposition. They also effectively relied on militias as instruments of domestic repression and intimidation. As in the African civil war cases, the conflict also contributed to a particularly severe economic collapse in the early 1990s; from 1991 to 1993 the Armenian economy contracted an average of 20 percent a year.

Weak Institutionalization

The weak democracy syndrome is also strongly in evidence with respect to the solidity of political institutions. Following the overwhelming votes for independence and the Levon Ter-Petrosyan presidency in 1991, the process of moving toward a new constitution was prolonged by disagreements between Ter-Petrosyan and the opposition over executive powers. Ter-Petrosyan did not believe these issues should be resolved by negotiations. Moreover, he enjoyed the prerogative of appointing his own prime minister; his first term saw four different appointments at the position. As the process of constitutional revision became more contested, the government began a sustained attack on the opposition Armenian Revolutionary Federation for harboring loyalties to Russian interests. In the wake of mass mobilization against the regime after 1992, the government launched a campaign of assassinations of opposition figures. In January 1995, the president charged the leading opposition party (Dashnak) with being a terrorist organization and banned the party and its newspaper. Although the Constitutional Court reduced the ban to a six-month suspension, the timing of the suspension prevented the party from participating in the 1995 elections.

The strongly contested and irregular constitutional referendum of July 1995 granted the president vast powers including the capacity to declare emergencies and wide-ranging control over the judiciary. These were quickly used to tilt the political playing field. The presidential elections of 1996, narrowly won by Ter-Petrosyan, were characterized by ballot tampering, discrepancies in the tabulation of votes, and repression of opposition leaders. Efforts on the part of the opposition to appeal these irregularities were rebuffed by the Constitutional Court, which failed to serve as an effective check on the executive. Ter-Petrosyan's government ultimately fell as a result of internal divisions, but as Bunce and Wolchik document, his successors ruled in a similar way: exploiting executive powers, using private monopolies to gain access to resources, controlling the media, and responding to protest by intimidating the opposition.[34]

Regime transitions in Armenia and the other post-Soviet cases were characterized by continuity in the power of strong executives from the Soviet era, buttressed by control over economic rents, the judiciary, the police, and the media. Although not praetorian in the classic sense, civil conflicts provided the justification for the accretion of executive powers and the use of coercion against opponents. Legislatures, courts, and other institutions of horizontal accountability—historically weak under Soviet rule—proved unable to check power grabs on the part of incumbents. Economic crises also provided a justification for the expansion of executive powers and thus contributed to deinstitutionalization.

ELITE-REACTION REVERSIONS: BURUNDI AND THAILAND

In Chapter 6, we noted an important constraint on our ability to use comparative causal process observations to explore reversions: the dearth of enduring elite-reaction cases. Only 5 of the 11 elite-reaction reversions resulted in more enduring authoritarian rule that restructured politics or

[34]Bunce and Wolchik 2011, 190–98.

the underlying political economy in the way the earlier Southern Cone bureaucratic-authoritarian regimes did. Three were low-income countries: the civil war case of Nepal, which bears some resemblance to the African civil war cases; and two cases in which ethnic cleavages were implicated, Fiji 1987 and Burundi 1995. Two were two middle-income countries: Turkey 1980 and Thailand 2006 (on which the CGV and Polity datasets disagree).[35] Burundi constitutes a reasonable comparator to what we call the African civil war cases, while Thailand is one of the very few examples of a middle-income country that conforms—at least descriptively—to the distributive conflict model. Given its substantive significance as an East Asian anomaly and the reoccurrence of a coup in 2014, it provides a logical choice for consideration.

In looking at these cases, we have two purposes. As in our analysis of the elite-led transitions, we are interested in identifying how inequalities, class or ethnic conflicts, and the redistributive policies of government generated incentives for the military and its allies to overthrow democratic rule. However, as is indicated in our regression analysis, it is not the case that distributive conflicts were the only causal forces in play. We also use the cases to consider two alternative causal stories. The first is that underlying elite-mass cleavages contributed to the weak democracy syndrome and lead to reversion not only directly but indirectly through the weakening of democratic rule as well. In this story, inequality contributed to the fall of democracy through a different causal path. The second story is that the weak democracy syndrome is a codeterminant of reversion, operating alongside but independently of elite concerns about redistribution. Although we make the case for the latter claim, we must remember the broader picture: that the number of cases that revert through the distributive conflict channel is extremely limited and that substantial ambiguity exists about the causal weight of elite reactions even in countries coded as examples of class conflict dynamics.

THE AFRICAN CASES REVISITED: BURUNDI

Burundi is the only African elite-reaction case. The social foundation of distributive conflict in the country is the highly unequal distribution of political power, economic assets, and income between the dominant Tutsi minority, accounting for about 15 percent of the population, and the Hutu majority, accounting for virtually all of the non-Tutsi population. Yet as the brief summary in Table 7.1 suggests, ethnic conflict is not the only plausible cause of the reversion. Burundi shared a number of characteristics with the other civil war African cases, including a praetorian

---

[35]The CGV dataset shows a return to democracy in 2008.

history, weak institutionalization, and a particularly devastating economic crisis.

A succession of Tutsi-dominated authoritarian regimes, led by rotating factions of the Tutsi-controlled military, were particularly repressive, with a virtual genocide in 1972.[36] In 1987, Pierre Buyoya—a Tutsi—led a coup against the incumbent military regime, promising an effort to mend relations between the two dominant groups. However, a Hutu uprising against the regime precipitated savage revenge killings, with as many as 20,000 Hutu deaths.

In the wake of these killings, Buyoya appointed a commission to draft a new constitution for a democratic government, which he clearly intended to dominate through his Union for National Progress. However, in an example of the miscalculations that can occur in such "preemptive" democratizations, Hutu Melchior Ndadaye scored an overwhelming victory backed by a coalition of Hutu parties (most notably the Front pour la Démocratie au Burundi or FRODEBU).

Recognizing the delicacy of presiding over a praetorian state with entrenched Tutsi interests, including in the military, Ndadaye did everything in his power to avoid the perception that he would redistribute in favor of the Hutu. Assurances included the appointment of a Tutsi vice president and cabinet ministers. Nonetheless, a series of actions had the appearance of favoring coethnics. The administration sought to reverse contracts and concessions made by Tutsi governments that affected military, state, and private Tutsi interests, sought reforms in the military to reduce Tutsi dominance, and displaced Tutsis in the civil service and local administrations. The nominally democratic government never gained control of the Tutsi-dominated military, which weakened the government both from the inside and through its actions against Hutu rebels outside it. In October 1993, the military assassinated Ndadye, setting in train a civil war that would continue for over a decade, claim 150,000 lives, and constitute the backdrop for the continuing military role in political life.

Despite the assassination of Ndadaye, the coup did not succeed, as the installed interim president ultimately refused to support it. The FRODEBU government stumbled along first under Cyprien Ntaryamira (died in 1994), and then under Sylvestre Ntibantunganya. Yet despite the nominally democratic coding, and efforts by the UN to broker a power-sharing agreement (the 1994 Convention of Government),[37] the regime was rent by deep political fissures reflective of the weak institutionalization that plagued other civil war cases. During the democratic period, Burundi's Polity score averaged zero. As Weissman notes, "the Convention of Government virtually annihilated FRODEBU's election victory by essentially superseding the

---

[36] Lemarchand 1996.
[37] Falch 2008.

1992 constitution, guaranteeing the Tutsi-led opposition a 45 percent share in the government, and establishing a National Security Council in which the opposition could block key moves by the FRODEBU Hutu president." Weissman goes on to note that by 1995, it is difficult to argue that the country was really governed by the nominally-elected government at all; rather, "Burundi was largely controlled by an uneasy coalition of the army, various Tutsi militia, UPRONA hardliners, and small Tutsi parties."[38]

Tutsi control of the military and weak institutions created incentives for the opposition to push the edge of the political envelope by recourse to extraconstitutional means. Extremists from the Union pour le Progrès National (UPRONA) sought to undermine FRODEBU rule through provocations, which in turn sparked a cycle of Hutu retaliation and killings. Ironically, an important trigger of the actual coup that marked the 1996 reversion was an effort on the part of the president and prime minister to secure more robust international protection for the government at a summit meeting of regional heads of state. This request was vehemently rejected by UPRONA and the CNDD-FDD (Conseil National pour la Défense de la Démocratie–Forces de Défense de la Démocratie)

Severe economic problems both reflected and compounded these political and military struggles; on this dimension, too, Burundi resembles the other civil war cases. Between 1986 and the 1993 assassination of Ndadaye, the government had strong working relations with the international financial institutions. With the political turmoil and subsequent increase in ethnic violence after 1993, the economy virtually collapsed, no doubt worsened by a rupture in the multilateral and major donor pipeline. Real per capita GDP contracted by 5.8 percent in 1993, 6.7 percent in 1994, 3.7 percent in 1995, and an estimated 13 percent in the year of the reversion itself.

Gross ethnic inequities, the ascendance of a Hutu government, and redistributive measures—however modest—certainly suggest that elite-reaction dynamics were in play. But it is important to underline that features we associate with the weak democracy syndrome were also at work. The praetorian nature of the political system can no doubt be attributed to political and class inequities. The military saw itself as the bulwark—the ultimate check—against a fully democratic system in which the Hutu would dominate. But as we noted, fundamental weaknesses in government prevented it from acting in any coherent way; indeed, in important respects the government was not even in a position to undertake the redistributive policies that are seen as triggers of class conflict models. As in a number of the other civil war cases—which it resembles to a significant degree—the combination of open warfare, incentives to military involvement in politics,

---

[38]Weissman 1998: 7.

weak decision-making processes, and economic collapse conspired against maintenance of even minimalist democratic rule.

THAILAND: CLASS CONFLICT OR WEAK DEMOCRACY SYNDROME REVISITED?

Thailand appears to constitute a relatively clear elite-reaction reversion, one of the few in the sample. Yet even more than in Burundi, in Thailand the sources of the coup suggest substantial ambiguities if not outright anomalies for distributive conflict theories.

Important electoral reforms in 1997 served to consolidate what had been a highly fragmented party system and incentivize more programmatic appeals.[39] Populist tycoon Thaksin Shinawatra seized these opportunities and led his Thais Love Thais (Thai Rak Thai, TRT) to impressive electoral victories in 2001 and 2005. In the latter election, an unprecedented landslide of over 60 percent of the vote yielded control—in coalition with a smaller allied party—of more than three-quarters of the seats in the National Assembly.

Although the TRT appealed to low-income sectors, it would be wrong to classify it as a left party; it clearly had a cross-class appeal. As Kitirianglarp and Hewison note, the party "brought together business people, nationalists, communitarians, liberals and even royalists to support a capitalist political party that was seen as a 'true friend' of the poor and a promoter of nationalist-communitarian interests."[40] However, the rise of the TRT appears to comport with conditions that are conducive to reversion in distributive conflict models. First, income inequality in Thailand was already high prior to the onset of its rapid growth in the 1980s, and it increased substantially up to the eve of the financial crisis of 1997–98, when incomes fell across the board and inequality probably worsened further still.

Second, as noted, the TRT did have a social and electoral base among the poor. Its initial electoral success was supported by an upsurge of populist NGOs and social movements that had crystallized after the financial crisis of 1997–98 in opposition to the orthodox policies of the incumbent government and in favor of greater attention to social issues. Exemplary of these movements was the Assembly of the Poor, a network of NGOs capable of effective mass mobilization, including those focusing on small farmers, the landless, rural poverty, slum dwellers, and environmental

[39] Hicken 2006.
[40] Kitirianglarp and Hewison 2009: 456.

politics.[41] TRT also generated support from the Thai working class and urban poor and had a particularly strong electoral appeal in the rural northwest and northeast.

Finally, the economic program of the Shinawatra government had a strong populist component, appealing to low-income and particularly rural voters. The government undertook a wide array of social initiatives, including the effective universalization of health care, highly controversial and costly debt relief for farmers, unemployment insurance, village and community investment funds, and small and medium enterprise loans that permitted TRT to extend its patronage.[42]

In the wake of the 2005 elections, a loose coalition of forces began to form against Thaksin, including at least some of the organizations and activists that had initially supported Thaksin's rise.[43] Yet in addition to classically liberal intelligentsia and civil society defectors from the Thaksin camp, the opposition movement—the People's Alliance for Democracy (PAD)—clearly represented regional and class cleavages: Bangkok-based urban elites and the middle class, segments of the private sector that were outside of the Thaksin network, the bureaucracy, the military, the nobility, and the monarchy of King Bhumibol Adulyadej, on whose prerogatives Thaksinism seemed to impinge.

Elite-reaction reversions do not necessarily rest on a dynamic of mass mobilization. However, street demonstrations and counterdemonstrations began in September 2005 and increased dramatically following the revelation that Thaksin had sold his controlling stake in the Shin Company, a telecommunications firm that had benefitted from state concessions while enjoying an exemption from capital gains taxes. As protests continued and polarization deepened, Thaksin dissolved parliament in February 2006 in order to hold snap elections in April as a referendum on his rule, counting on strong up-country and rural support to counter urban opposition centered in Bangkok. The government pushed ahead with the elections despite an opposition boycott, further galvanizing protest and ultimately a constitutional crisis. As pressures mounted, Thaksin sought to mollify the opposition by meeting with the king, calling for constitutional reform and forming a grand coalition. But with the PAD threatening to maintain street pressure until he was removed, the king finally intervened by calling the results of the election into doubt and asking the courts to investigate electoral fraud. On September 19, 2006, the military overthrew the government.

---

[41]Missingham 2003.
[42]Haggard and Kaufman 2008.
[43]Kitirianglarp and Hewison 2009.

Although not directly relevant to an analysis of the 2006 case, it is worth noting that political-cum-social polarization did not end with the coup: rather, 2006 marked the onset of recurrent political crisis and instability that continues through the writing of this book.[44] Despite constitutional revisions, the military could not prevent the reemergence of a Thaksin proxy party in the form of the People's Power Party in 2007, a development that contributed to the reemergence of PAD mobilization and the onset of a sustained conflict between pro- and anti-Thaksin forces. The ouster of the PPP governments of Samak Sundaravej and his successor, Thaksin's brother-in-law, Somchai Wongsawat in 2008, and the subsequent dissolution of the party had features of a constitutional coup. The seating of the Democratic Party under Abhisit Vejjajiva increased the activity of "red shirt" protests by the National United Front of Democracy Against Dictatorship (UDD), a largely pro-Thaksin group that was also opposed to military and judicial overreach.

In elections in 2011 and 2014, the Pheu Thai Party—yet another reincarnation of TRT—took office under none other than Yingluck Shinawatra, Thaksin's sister. She was ultimately overthrown, however, in yet another coup in 2014, following an effort to grant amnesty to her brother. Although replaced by a nominally nonpartisan appointed legislature, Yingluck was also formally impeached in January 2015 for corruption in the management of a rice subsidy scheme that had resulted in large financial losses for the government.

In many respects, the dynamics of these reversions clearly point to the importance of distributive demands and elite reactions as destabilizing factors in the failure of the Thai democratic regime. Yet Thailand's vulnerability to coups has causal roots that extend beyond the class dynamics postulated by distributive conflict models. Unlike many of the other weak democracy cases discussed above, these vulnerabilities did not include poor economic performance; on the contrary, growth was high throughout much of this period. Other elements of the weak democracy syndrome, however, were very much in evidence.

These begin with a long history of praetorianism and a gradual process of deinstitutionalization, personalism, and abuse of power. It is virtually a cliché in Thai studies to point out its history of political instability: from 1932 to 2014, the country had 18 constitutions, 19 or 21 coups (depending on coding choices), and 36 prime ministers. A lingering challenge for all democratic governments—as the coup subsequently revealed—was the deep involvement of the military in politics, a hallmark of praetorianism. As Ockey shows, the coup was preceded by growing tensions between the

[44]Unger 2014.

administration and the military on a number of issues, including strong disagreements about how to handle a festering insurgency in the Muslim south of the country. In the months prior to the coup, the military signaled its political preferences by stating publicly that protests by the PAD should be allowed to continue and that no special measures, such as a state of emergency, were necessary.[45]

As in many coup settings, the army was also concerned about Thaksin's use of promotion powers to favor cronies over more experienced officers. The military was also implicated in complex court politics in which supporters of the monarchy—including in the military—argued that Thaksin had eroded monarchic prerogatives. In sum, the military appeared to be acting not as an agent of a particular class, but for a variety of its own interests.

Among the rationales for the coup were also a variety of purely political grievances. In fact, the weakening of democratic institutions was one of the most important focal points of critics in both the "yellow shirt" and "red shirt" camps; the social policies of the government were generally not front and center in the opposition critique. In many ways, the Thaksin governments themselves represented episodes of backsliding in which an incumbent government exploited the powers of office to weaken horizontal checks and engage in extensive corruption and patronage. A central feature of the 1997 constitution was the creation of a number of institutions designed to provide horizontal checks on government: an Election Commission, a National Human Rights Commission, a National Counter Corruption Commission, and a Constitutional Court. Yet Thaksin exploited his supermajority to pack them with allies, a feature of the backsliding cases we discuss in Chapter 8 as well. Thaksin filled positions in the armed forces and civil services with his relatives or cronies and limited the opportunities for an electoral opposition through a massive distribution of public and private patronage.

As Malesky and Samphantharak point out in addressing class polarization theories of the coup, the social composition of the opposition was in fact very heterogeneous, focused to a significant extent on competing political, rather than economic, visions: "The Yellow Shirts consist of both anti-Thaksin and pro-monarchy groups, and these two groups do not have identical goals. The Red Shirts consist of pro-Thaksin rural supporters as well as a wide swath of urban intellectuals opposed to military intervention in politics, and anti-monarchy forces."[46]

In sum, although the coding of Thailand as an elite-reaction case has some validity, there are considerable ambiguities as well. An incumbent government was committed to a populist program, in the context of very high

---

[45] Ockey 2007.
[46] Malesky and Samphantharak 2011: 7.

inequality, and a coalition of economic elites and urban middle-class forces were arrayed against the government. The military finally acted against it, and continued to attempt to check Thaksinist forces through 2014, including through yet another coup. Yet a closer examination of the case also shows that praetorianism played a role, as the military acted for a host of reasons that had little to do with redistributive concerns. Moreover, polarization did not occur solely along class lines. Purely political concerns playing a significant and cross-cutting role. We cannot, therefore, rule out that the reaction to Thaksin and his successors in fact constituted a reaction against a classic case of backsliding: a civilian attempt to exploit constitutional powers—both legally and extralegally—and thus to weaken the institutionalization of democratic rule.

The Political Logic of Populist Reversions

We turn, finally, to a brief consideration of populist reversions: those characterized by the emergence of autocratic leaders promising *more* extensive redistribution. Like elite-reaction reversions, these constitute a class of democratic failures driven by distributive conflict. But as noted in Chapter 6, these reversions reflect very different political dynamics. Elite-reaction reversions stem from the fact that democracies contain inherent incentives for redistribution that pose threats to the assets and income of the upper class. Populist reversions, by contrast, are motivated by the presumed *weakness* of democratic regimes that are perceived as unable to fulfill their popular mandates. Although distributive cleavages are important components of populist reversions, they might well reflect the weak democracy syndrome: praetorianism, low levels of institutionalization, and poor economic performance.

An empirical elaboration of this argument is again constrained by the fact that the incidence of populist reversions is quite small: we find only three (12 percent) in the CGV dataset (Ecuador 2000, Ghana 1981, and Suriname 1980) and only four (15 percent) among the Polity cases (Ecuador 2007, Ghana 1981, Haiti 1999, and Venezuela 2006). We deal with the middle-income anomaly of Venezuela in Chapter 8, focusing here on two countries that are comparable to other low-income countries discussed in this chapter: Ghana and Haiti.

Ghana

Jerry Rawlings's military coup against the elected government of Hilla Limann in December 1981 both reflected and prompted a strong upsurge of populist and radical protest among students, labor unions, and left-wing

organizations. Throughout its short term in office, the Limann government had faced strikes and confrontations over back pay and a painful
austerity program pressed by the IMF. Coup leaders themselves were
strongly influenced by radical Marxist models such as in Ethiopia, Libya,
Cuba, and Mozambique.[47] Shortly after seizing power, Rawlings actively
solicited the support of radical and populist groups by placing representatives from the left on the military's Provisional National Defense Council,
and by creating a raft of populist consultative organizations. Within just
a few years, Rawlings sharply reversed course and vigorously embraced
economic reforms closely in line with the Washington Consensus. But the
initial overthrow of the democratic regime clearly appealed to, and mobilized support from, left, populist, and lower-class groups.

Although distributive cleavages drove the initial seizure of power, the
deposed Limann government exhibited virtually all of the weaknesses of
other African democracies noted in our consideration of the other cases.
Even without taking into account the ideological and social conflicts described above, democratic institutions were clearly fragile. Limann was
the first elected head of government since 1972 and had been in office only
a little over two years before being deposed by the 1981 coup. The election itself had gone forward under the auspices of the Armed Forces Revolutionary Council (AFRC), which had seized power after a coup under the
leadership of Rawlings in June 1979. Limann had spent most of his earlier
career as a diplomat, and had little personal following inside the country.
In allowing elections to take place, Rawlings had signaled his willingness
to reenter politics if the new democratic government failed to perform.

Well before Rawlings's political ascendency, moreover, the military
had been the pivotal actor in Ghanaian politics. Military governments
held power directly between 1966 and 1969, following the overthrow of
Kwame Nkrumah, and then again from 1972 to 1979, under a succession
of palace coups and military officers. Rawlings, a flight lieutenant in the
air force, led a rebellion of junior officers in May 1979 against General
Fred Akuffo, who himself had come to power in an internal coup the year
before. Although the coup initially failed and Rawlings was imprisoned, in
June another uprising of junior officers and civilian supporters propelled
him into power. He continued to control the military throughout the Limann term, casting a strong shadow over civilian authority.

By the time of the 1981 coup, the government was confronted by the
economic results of a development strategy based on currency manipulation, rent-seeking, and transfers of wealth from cocoa producers to para-
statal enterprises, crony capitalists, civil servants, and military elites. The
corrupt military regime of Ignatius Kutu Acheampong (1972–78) had an

---

[47] Jeffries 1982; Yao 1985; Owusu 1989: 376; Oquaye 1995.

especially damaging impact. Constrained by marketing board controls and extensive smuggling, official cocoa exports fell from about 430,000 metric tons between 1969 and 1972 to 277,000 tons in 1977 and 1978.[48] Domestic inflation also became an increasingly serious problem, rising to over 100 percent by 1978. Growth was essentially flat over the 1970s, but also highly volatile: the country saw negative growth in 1975–76, 1979, and from 1980 to 1983.

Like many other regimes of the period, the Limann government was severely cross-pressured between the IMF and donors urging painful austerity and structural adjustment, and powerful urban labor and student constituencies with deep stakes in the existing policy regime. With limited political capacity or support to act and constrained by the views of radical military officers, the democratic government was unable to formulate a coherent adjustment strategy or to forestall Rawlings's decision to resume control of the government. Although the ideological polarization leading up to the coup was unusually deep, the underlying institutional and economic weaknesses were typical of those found in the "weak democracy" cases.

Haiti

In Haiti, as in Ghana, a weakly institutionalized democratic regime was undermined by highly polarized political forces. As a parish priest, Jean-Bertrand Aristide had led the opposition to the dictatorship of Jean-Claude Duvalier and to a succession of military governments. In 1990 he won the first democratic election in Haiti's history with 67 percent of the vote. But this transition marked the onset of a decade of political and social conflict between the forces arrayed around Aristide and his adversaries among Haiti's economic and military elites. Aristide was initially ousted by the military after only seven months in power (coded as an elite-reaction reversion), then regained the presidency in 1994 with broad popular support and with the military backing of the United States and the international community.

But Aristide himself also relied heavily on intimidation and harassment of opponents, including within his own political movement. After returning to office, he took steps to concentrate personal power in ways that are typical of the backsliding process. In a highly tainted election in 1995, Aristide accepted the transfer of the presidency to a handpicked successor, René Préval, but he remained the power behind the throne. When divisions emerged between moderates and radicals within his own political movement (Lavales Political Organization or OLP), Aristide left the party

[48] Jeffries 1982: 313.

to form an alternative called the Lavales Family (FL). However, the split within the movement left Préval hamstrung by legislative opposition from the OLP, which refused to confirm a series of nominees for prime minister.

In 1999, Préval dismissed the Chamber of Deputies and began to rule by decree. It was this act that we code as the genesis of the populist reversion. The ultimate objective was to pave the way for Aristide's return to the presidency with a legislative supermajority in the upcoming 2000 elections. In the run up to the election, Préval appointed an electoral council comprised of FL partisans. The elections, although won overwhelmingly by Aristide and the FL, were marked by blatant fraud and condemned by the OAS.

The severe polarization that led to the failure of democracy in Haiti distinguishes that case from the majority of weak democracy reversions in which distributive politics played only a limited role. As was the case with Ghana, however, it is also important to emphasize that these pressures unfolded within an extremely fragile institutional framework. Even during nominally democratic periods, none of the major actors unconditionally accepted the constraints imposed by the constitutional rules of the game. During his first seven-month tenure as president in 1990–91, Aristide was quickly deposed by hostile military officers unwilling to accept the constraints of civilian control. In turn, the domestic security dilemma outlined in Chapter 6 created strong incentives for Aristide and Préval to exploit the advantages of incumbency once in office to marginalize potential sources of opposition, even from within their own political movement. All sides, in other words, were motivated to pursue politics "by other means," the basic elements of praetorianism and weak institutionalization.

As was the case of most other weak democracies, finally, these conflicts occurred against the backdrop of severe economic deterioration—both a consequence and cause of the political instability. A special World Bank report provides grim details.[49] In the ten turbulent years between the fall of the Duvalier dictatorship and the rise of Aristide (1985–95), per capita income fell at an annual rate of 5.2 percent. Political instability and concomitant economic crisis continued throughout the decade of the 1990s. Politically, the decade was marked by the initial rise and military ouster of Aristide, his return to office in 1994, and his somewhat reluctant transfer of the presidency to Préval. Not surprisingly, the economy continued to deteriorate sharply. Between 1991 and 1997—the years preceding the reversion of 1999—overall annual GDP growth rates declined by an average of over 1.7 percent.

In 1996 and 1997, the Préval government attempted to address the deepening economic crisis with a program of fiscal adjustment and trade

---

[49] World Bank 1998: 1–19.

liberalization, but the initiative quickly stalled after divisions within the legislature forced the resignation of the prime minister and blocked further appointments.[50] Aristide and Préval share responsibility for the slide toward authoritarianism that followed this failure, but the more general weaknesses of the regime clearly underlay these choices. Fatton offers a virtual restatement of the main theoretical point we seek to make about the weak democracy syndrome: "Haiti's ills cannot be blamed exclusively on Aristide and/or his Fanmi Lavalas; they are also the product of the collective failure of the political class and its external allies. The emphasis on the rituals of elections has exacerbated the zero-sum game tradition of the island's politics and placed a high premium on winning at any cost. It is not surprising therefore that those who have executive power use it to maximize their opportunities, reward their clientele, and punish their adversaries."[51]

Conclusion

As we noted in Chapter 6, the debate about the role of economic development in transitions to and from democratic rule has been heated, with differences centering on whether per capita income is implicated in *transitions* to democratic rule or only in the *stability* of democratic rule once achieved.[52]

Yet a striking omission in this debate is the mechanisms through which long-run growth and level of development actually operate on the incentives facing political actors. Selecting a sample of mostly low-income countries from very different regions, we showed in this chapter how reversions arise from particular institutional arrangements compounded in many cases by the fallout from endogenous economic crises. We did not find all elements of the weak democracy syndrome in all cases in equal measure: the African civil war cases border on anarchy, while the weaknesses of democratic rule in Peru and Armenia were initially more subtle, and perhaps for that very reason more insidious. Yet we found repeatedly in these cases that democracy was constrained by continuing military involvement in politics and weakly institutionalized political systems. Despite the South Asian exceptions, economic crises also typically played a role in delegitimizing democracy, exacerbating intra-elite conflict and providing an excuse for coups or the abuse of executive authority.

[50] Fatton 2002: 125.

[51] Fatton 2002: 124.

[52] Przeworski and Limongi 1997; Przeworski, Alvarez, Cheibub and Limongi 2000; Boix and Stokes 2003; Gerring et al. 2005; Epstein et al. 2006; Svolik 2008; Kennedy 2010.

A second purpose of the chapter was to probe whether the elite reaction and populist reversions were in fact fundamentally different than their elite-led conflict counterparts. This exercise proved more difficult because of the paucity of cases that conformed—even in the proximate causal processes—with the expectations of class conflict theories. Nonetheless, even in the handful of cases that did exhibit class conflict dynamics, it was difficult to confirm that the distributive conflict model was dispositive. In Burundi, the weakness of institutions was arguably endogenous to underlying social polarization, suggesting that the distributive conflict model itself may have operated through deeper institutional and economic as well as policy routes. But in that case and particularly in Thailand, the apparent role of inequality and class cleavages was overlain with a long history of military involvement in politics and a clear process of deinstitutionalization that operated quite apart from class conflicts. Populist reversions in Ghana and Haiti, similarly, reflected long-standing patterns of praetorianism and institutional weakness as well as economic collapse. At best, these comparisons suggest the need for more complex configurative explanations in which distributive conflict is but one among a complex of institutional weaknesses explaining reversion from democratic rule.

CHAPTER 8

Learning from Anomalies

LOW-INCOME SURVIVORS, MIDDLE-INCOME REVERTERS

A CORE CLAIM IN THE MODERNIZATION LITERATURE is that as countries develop, the likelihood of authoritarian reversions decreases. We saw some evidence for this claim in Chapter 6, in both the multinomial regressions and the average differences in the per capita GDP of democratic survivors and reverters. Most of the reversions we traced in Chapter 7 occurred in relatively low-income countries. We showed, however, that independently of the structural factors that undergird modernization theories, the vulnerability of democracy seemed to hinge on institutional factors and the performance of governments as well.

In this chapter, we continue to explore the effects of political institutions and performance by examining two sets of cases that run counter to the expectations of modernization theory: low-income countries that survive and the handful of more developed middle-income countries that revert. The distribution and identity of these anomalies can be seen by listing all of the cases in our sample by level of income and whether they survive or revert (Table 8.1). We define "survivors" as cases that transition during the Third Wave and stay democratic for at least ten years without subsequently reverting. In most cases, the ten-year minimum would imply that the regime had survived at least two competitive election cycles following its initial founding election. To maximize the consideration of cases beyond the 1980 to 2008 time frame, "survivors" include cases in the CGV and Polity datasets that transition by 2003 and remain democratic through 2013.[1] In addition, we distinguish cases by GDP per capita

---

[1] Polity provides coding of all cases through 2013 and we coded all relevant cases in the CGV dataset after 2008, when the dataset ends, using CGV rules. In the CGV dataset, Madagascar and Mali survive until 2008, but subsequently revert through coups in 2009 and 2010, respectively, and are therefore counted as reverters. Mexico (2000), Niger (2000), Senegal (2000), Serbia (2000), and Peru (2001) all transition after 1998 but remain democratic through 2013 under CGV rules and are therefore counted as survivors. We exclude seven discrete cases that enter the dataset as democracies in 1980 and remain democratic throughout: Costa Rica, the Dominican Republic, India, Israel, and Jamaica in the CGV dataset and Botswana, Colombia, Costa Rica, India, Israel, and Jamaica in the Polity dataset. With the exception of Colombia, these countries were democratic from their independence, or throughout the entire postwar period in the case of Costa Rica. Although we cannot associate sheer survival with the quality of democracy, it is also worth noting that there are only five cases in the dataset that transition during the Third Wave, are democratic for ten

at the time of transition (for survivors) or reversion (for the reverters), with a cutoff of $6,000 per capita.

In one important respect, the distribution of reversions comports with theoretical expectations in the modernization literature. In both the CGV and Polity datasets, low-income reverters—the subject of our analysis in Chapter 7—outnumber middle-income reverters by a wide margin. Conversely, the vast majority of the middle-income democracies survived, dominated by postcommunist Eastern Europe and Latin American cases.

Nevertheless, we also see a large number of low-income survivors. For cases in the CGV dataset, the threshold for democracy is admittedly low. But the share of survivors among the low-income cases is roughly equal in the two datasets (51 percent in the CGV dataset and 46.5 percent in the Polity dataset). About one-third of the poor African democracies and a majority of the poor democracies of Latin America survived. The distribution of cases makes clear that status as a low-income country—even from "bad neighborhoods"—is neither a necessary nor a sufficient cause of democratic failure.

Given that low-income survivors are anomalous from the perspective of modernization approaches, is there evidence that their political institutions and economic performance differentiate them from the reverters discussed in Chapter 7? We argue there is. Survivors had some combination of more favorable civil-military relations, stronger institutional checks on incumbents, and better economic performance. However, we also note that these institutions were undergirded by the broader social checks on government we discussed in Chapter 5, including the capacity of civil society to mobilize in the face of executive derogations from democratic rule.

Examples of democratic decay in middle-income countries constitute a second cluster of anomalies. With the exception of Thailand—discussed in Chapter 7—these cases have reverted not through coups, but via backsliding. They include populist reversions in Venezuela and Ecuador and the descent into competitive authoritarianism in Russia under Putin. If we take a somewhat wider definition of "backsliding" as a deterioration in the quality of democracy that falls short of outright reversion, the list is longer. Among important out-of-sample cases are Turkey—which we consider here—and more recently Hungary, Bulgaria, and South Africa.

In contrast to the survivors, we find ample evidence of the weak democracy syndrome, typically unfolding in a particular sequence. Severe economic slumps undermined the legitimacy of incumbents and allowed

---

years, and then revert. These cases are, by date of transition, Bangladesh (1986), Pakistan (1988), Nepal (1990), and Thailand (1992) in the CGV dataset and Peru (1980), Pakistan (1988), Bangladesh (1991), and Thailand (1992) in the Polity dataset; these cases are also omitted from consideration.

Table 8.1 Survivors and Reverters, 1980–2013.

CGV Cases	Survivors 46	Reverters 25
Low income (<$6,000)	*Total: 25* *Africa* (8): Benin, Cape Verde, Ghana, Kenya, Malawi, Nigeria*, São Tomé and Principe, Senegal*, *Asia* (3): Indonesia*, Philippines, Sri Lanka* *Latin America* (10): Bolivia, El Salvador, Grenada, Guatemala, Honduras, Nicaragua, Panama, Paraguay, Peru*, Suriname *Europe and Postcommunist* (4): Albania, Armenia, Mongolia, Ukraine	*Total: 23* *Total excluding subsequent survivors: 17* *Africa* (14): Burundi, CAR, Comoros, Congo, *Ghana*, Guinea-Bissau*, Madagascar*, Mali*, Mauritania, Niger*†, *Nigeria*, Sierra Leone, Sudan, Uganda *Asia* (5): Bangladesh, Fiji, Nepal, Pakistan, Thailand *Latin America* (4): Bolivia, Ecuador, *Guatemala*, *Peru* *Europe and Postcommunist*: none
Middle income ($6,000+)	*Total: 21* *Africa*: none *Asia* (2): South Korea, Taiwan *Latin America* (6): Argentina, Brazil, Chile, Mexico*, Panama, Uruguay *Europe and Postcommunist* (13): Belarus, Bulgaria, Croatia, Czech Republic, Estonia, Hungary, Latvia, Lithuania, Macedonia, Poland, Romania, Serbia*, Turkey	*Total: 2* *Total excluding subsequent survivors: 1* *Africa*: none *Asia*: none *Latin America* (1): Suriname *Europe and Postcommunist* (1): *Turkey*
Low income (<$6,000)	*Total: 20* *Africa* (5): Benin, Cape Verde, Kenya, Lesotho, Senegal* *Asia* (3): Indonesia, Philippines, Solomon Islands*	*Total: 23* *Total excluding subsequent survivors: 18* *Africa* (10): Gambia, Ghana, Guinea-Bissau*, Madagascar*, Malawi,

Table 8.1 (*continued*)

Polity Cases	Survivors 42	Reverters 27
	Latin America (8): Bolivia, Dominican Republic, El Salvador, Guatemala, Guyana, Honduras, Nicaragua, Paraguay *Europe and Postcommunist* (4): Albania*, Moldova, Mongolia, Ukraine	Mali, Niger†, Nigeria, Sudan, Zambia *Asia* (6): Bangladesh, Fiji, Nepal, Pakistan, Sri Lanka*, Thailand *Latin America* (4): *Dominican Republic*, Haiti, *Honduras*, *Peru* *Europe and Postcommunist* (3): Armenia, Belarus, *Ukraine*
Middle income ($6,000+)	**Total: 22** *Africa* (1): South Africa *Asia* (2): South Korea, Taiwan *Latin America* (7): Argentina, Brazil, Chile, Mexico, Panama, Peru*, Uruguay *Europe and Postcommunist* (12): Bulgaria, Croatia*, Czech Republic, Estonia, Hungary, Latvia, Lithuania, Macedonia, Poland, Romania, Serbia*, Turkey	**Total: 4** **Total excluding subsequent survivors: 3** *Africa*: none *Asia*: none *Latin America* (2): Ecuador, Venezuela *Europe and Postcommunist* (2): Russia, Turkey

Notes: Cases can enter the dataset as both reverters and survivors if they revert and then subsequently transition and survive for ten years; these cases are highlighted in italics. Countries may appear in the lower-income group in one dataset and middle-income group in the other as a result of differences in income per capita over time. Asterisks indicate cases in the CGV or Polity datasets that are coded as either survivors or reverters because of developments from 2009 to 2013, i.e., they either survive for at least ten years into that period or revert during it. Daggers indicate cases that revert more than once.

political outsiders to come to office through democratic means. Subsequent economic recoveries—including oil booms in the Russian and Venezuelan cases—permitted executives to expand legislative and popular support. Supermajorities ultimately allowed them to arrogate decree and other discretionary powers—including over state financial resources—limit horizontal institutional checks, and undermine oppositions.

How Do Poor Democracies Achieve Stability?

We turn first to the factors that enable poor democracies to beat the odds. In some cases, sheer luck mattered. Some new democratic governments inherited militaries more firmly under civilian control or benefitted from self-abnegating leaders who convinced contending social and political forces—including militaries—to commit to the uncertainties of competitive politics. And finally, as we have acknowledged throughout, international actors constituted a check on coups and backsliding in a number of cases.

However, both institutions and social forces matter in generating democratic equilibriums. We likened politics in weak democracies to a security dilemma in which political competition devolved into conflicts that were ultimately destructive of democracy itself. In the survivors, by contrast, reinforcing dynamics ensued. As we will argue below, a variety of institutional mechanisms—including term limits, legislative prerogatives, and independent electoral authorities—provided incentives for incumbents to signal commitment to democratic rule. These institutions generated expectations that they would abide by constitutional limits and cede power in the face of electoral defeat. In turn, however, these institutional mechanisms were undergirded by a deeper balance of social power. As we suggested in Chapter 5, domestic checks on both militaries and incumbents ultimately stemmed at least in part from effective oppositional organization, including through parties, organized interest groups, and even the capacity for contentious politics.

Benin: A Low-Income Survivor

To motivate the more general discussion of these factors, we begin with a brief description of Benin, a poor West African survivor that provides a direct contrast to Niger, a reversion case we highlighted in Chapter 7.[2]

[2]It must be noted that Benin was somewhat better off than Niger, with GDP per capita in 1991 of $1,125 compared to Niger's $665 in 1996, the onset of democracy in the two countries, respectively. It is unlikely, however, that these differences can account for the relative success of Benin; by international standards, it was an extremely poor country.

Benin underwent a democratic transition in the early 1990s, but unlike many of its neighbors, it managed to sustain a competitive political system over the next two decades. The standard of success, to be sure, is quite low. The party system was fragmented and highly volatile, and incumbents at times sought advantages through unfair means.[3] Constitutional changes of government were often fraught. Despite its fragility, however, Benin experienced four elections and two changes of government during the 1990s and early 2000s. In 2006, the country experienced a key turning point when the longtime incumbent president, Mathieu Kérékou, decided to accept term limits and refrain from contesting for an additional term. As a result, the Polity score, which had been 6 throughout the 1990s and early 2000s, increased to 7.

The success story in Benin is attributable in part to a number of subtle but important differences from Niger and other West African neighbors. First, although Benin was wracked by a succession of military coups after winning its independence in 1960, these came to an end in the early 1970s. Major Mathieu Kérékou seized power in a coup d'état in 1972, but adopted a Marxist-Leninist ideology and ruled from 1975 to 1989 through a single-party dictatorship. He went on to defeat several additional coup attempts in 1973 and 1975, and then governed until the late 1980s without significant threats from the military.[4] By the time of the transition in 1991, Benin was far less vulnerable to the coup trap than countries with sustained histories of military dictatorship. In Niger, as we saw in Chapter 7, the military continued to play an active behind-the-scenes role throughout the transition and early democratic years. In Benin, the military generally stood aside as popular protests forced the incumbent ruler to yield power to the political opposition.[5]

A second advantage was a relatively rapid emergence from the economic crisis of the early 1990s. Reforms pressed by France and the IMF were reluctantly initiated in the final years of the Kérékou dictatorship, and protest against them contributed to its downfall. But the program continued and deepened during the interim technocratic government of Nicéphore Soglo, formerly Benin's representative at the World Bank. Although strikes and protests against the adjustment program continued throughout the early years of the first democratic government, substantial external assistance helped to soften the blow; aid, in effect, served an

[3] Riedl 2014.
[4] McGowan 2007: 12–27.
[5] Lindberg and Clark (2008: 97) note "military activity" in 1992, but emphasized that it is "ambiguous whether it was a military intervention at all. . . . It consisted of some "firing of guns around the presidential palace, which was not originally recognized as a coup attempt."

important political function.[6] In the early 1990s, the country shifted on to a moderate but more stable growth path. From the transition in 1991 to 2008, annual growth averaged about 4.5 percent, with a standard deviation of only 0.9. In Niger, the new democratic government came to office in the midst of a crisis. The country was continuously paralyzed over structural adjustment issues, and growth during the short democratic period averaged less than 1 percent, with a standard deviation of 4.3.

Finally, confidence in Benin's political institutions was strengthened by a sequence of strategic decisions by Kérékou and Soglo, his principal rival for the presidency, as each faced the prospect of relinquishing power. The most critical test of the new democracy came over the question of whether Kérékou would abide by term limit provisions as the 2006 elections approached. Earlier choices eased the way for a peaceful exit from office. Soglo, who had defeated Kérékou in the founding election of 1991, decided to accept Kérékou's bitterly disputed second round victory in 1996 after a relatively independent Constitutional Court rejected accusations of fraud. Kérékou retained power in a highly contentious electoral contest in 2001, raising questions as to whether he would respect term limits that barred him from again pursuing the presidency in 2006. As the Polity report on the country notes in explaining its increase in the country's score, the eventual "decision to abide by constitutional requirements . . . was a major step toward regular peaceful transfers of executive power in the country." As in a number of other African cases, the decision by incumbents to relinquish office set an important precedent that altered expectations and thus deepened the process of institutionalization.

Kérékou's choice to stand down is suggestive about the role of both institutions and civil society in checking incumbent backsliding. Term limits and the institutions that enforce them, such as constitutional courts, are intended to serve as a barrier to the concentration of personal power and to provide assurances to competing actors that they have a legitimate shot at winning office. At the same time, the effectiveness of such institutional constraints in new democracies is untested and opposition from both political parties and civil society organizations can play a role in encouraging compliance.

Kérékou himself never initiated an effort to remove the limits, but his advisors did float trial balloons in the years prior to the election, and he was publically urged by one close business advisor to reconsider his decision to step down.[7] Restraint was undoubtedly encouraged by a number of factors, including anticipated reaction from external donors, advancing

[6] Gazibo 2012.
[7] Idrissou-Toure 2014.

age, and a concurrent decision by Soglo to retire from the electoral arena. However, it is also clear that an effort to revise or defy term limits would have faced substantial public opposition from civil society. In October 2006, Reporters without Borders ranked Benin the top African country in terms of freedom of the press and IREX's Media Sustainability Index ranked Benin second only to South Africa among African countries in the overall rating of media independence and first in the strength of its professional and trade associations.[8] In the context of a relatively robust civil society, the cost of attempting to continue in power would have been high. As Reckya Madougou, leader of one coalition of groups (NGO ELAN), stated, "It is possible that Kerekou did not want to amend or that he wanted to but changed his mind mid-stream. . . . What's important for us is that every time the overriding interest of the nation is at stake, civil society should remain mobilized. We're proud of having fought this battle which has borne fruit."[9]

Poor Democracies: A Comparative Perspective

Benin's experience provides an example of how a country escaped the constraints of the weak democracy syndrome. Developments during the authoritarian period restrained the military, economic performance in the democratic years was relatively strong, and a crucial episode of government turnover—incentivized by term limits and civil society engagement—strengthened expectations that major political actors would abide by the rules of the political game. In this section, we explore whether similar forces are at work in other low-income survivors.

Tables 8.2 and 8.3 provide an overview of how low-income survivors and reverters compare on key dimensions of the weak democracy syndrome. In both datasets, the cases are arrayed as we would expect. Among the survivors are more cases without coup histories; indeed, among the CGV reverters virtually all had coup histories, with the sole outlier being a monarchy. In both datasets, there are more cases among the reverters with marginal Polity scores (defined as below 6 for the CGV dataset and 6 or 7 for the Polity dataset) and, conversely, more cases with higher Polity scores among the survivors. Finally, and perhaps most strikingly, we see a large share of reverters that struggled with low growth (defined as less than 2 percent on average), nearly 50 percent in each dataset.

---

[8] IREX and USAID n.d.
[9] Cited in Idrissou-Toure 2014.

Table 8.2 Comparing Low-Income CGV Survivors and Reverters.
(Cases and Shares of Survivors and Reverters)

	Survivors	Reverters
Countries without prior coup histories (since 1970)	Senegal, Indonesia, Mongolia, Sri Lanka, Armenia, Ukraine, Grenada 29.1% (7/24)	Nepal 3.9% (1/26)
Cases with Polity scores < 6	Ghana, Kenya, Malawi, Nigeria, Sri Lanka, Albania, Armenia, Croatia, Guatemala, Nicaragua 41.7% (10/24)	Burundi, CAR, Comoros, Congo, Guinea-Bissau, Mauritania, Sierra Leone, Uganda, Bangladesh, Fiji, Nepal, Bolivia, Guatemala, Suriname (1990), Thailand (1991), Turkey (1980) 61.5% (16/26)
Cases with Polity Scores of 6–10	Benin, Cape Verde, Senegal, Philippines, Macedonia, Ukraine, Bolivia, El Salvador, Honduras, Panama, Paraguay, Peru, Ghana (1993), Kenya 58.3% (14/24)	Ghana (1981), Madagascar, Mali, Niger, Nigeria, Sudan, Pakistan, Thailand (2006), Ecuador (2000), Peru (1990) 38.5% (10/26)
Countries with average economic growth during democratic years < 2%	Macedonia, Ukraine, Nicaragua 12.5% (3/24)	Burundi, CAR, Comoros, Congo, Ghana, Guinea-Bissau, Mauritania, Nigeria, Sierra Leone, Uganda, Bolivia, Guatemala, Suriname 48.1% (13/26)

Checking Praetorianism

The most effective way for democratic regimes to forestall the emergence of a politicized military, of course, is to avoid falling into the coup trap in the first place. As Tables 8.2 and 8.3 suggest, a substantial number of survivors had been free of coups since 1970. We can understand these cases in part by looking at the authoritarian status quo ante. In Chapter 2, we argued that one-party and military regimes faced greater risk of mass mobilization

Table 8.3 Comparing Low-Income Polity Survivors and Reverters.
(Cases and Shares of Survivors and Reverters)

	Survivors	Reverters
Countries without prior coup histories (since 1970)	Senegal, Indonesia, Mongolia, Moldova, Serbia, Ukraine, Dominican Republic, Guyana 42.1% (8/19)	Malawi, Nepal, Armenia, Belarus, Ukraine, DR, Zambia 30.0% (7/23)
Cases with Polity scores ≤ 7	Benin, Kenya, Lesotho, Senegal, Indonesia, Moldova, Ukraine, El Salvador, Guyana, Honduras, Nicaragua, Paraguay 60.0% (12/20)	Gambia, Ghana, Guinea-Bissau, Madagascar, Malawi, Mali, Niger, Nigeria, Sudan, Zambia, Bangladesh, Fiji, Nepal, Pakistan, Sri Lanka, Armenia, Belarus, Ukraine, Dominican Republic, Haiti, Honduras, Madagascar 95.7% (22/23)
Cases with Polity Scores of 8–10	Cape Verde, Mongolia, Philippines, Solomon I, Albania, Bolivia, DR, Guatemala, 40.0% (8/20)	Thailand 2006 4.3% (1/23)
Countries with average economic growth during democratic years < 2%	Moldova, Ukraine 10.0% (2/20)	Ghana, Niger, Nigeria, Zambia, Fiji, Armenia, Belarus, Ukraine, Haiti, Honduras 43.4% (10/23)

than competitive authoritarian regimes because of the absence of channels for representation. However, as the Benin case suggests, one-party and military regimes may have quite different implications for the subsequent stability of democratic rule. Svolik shows that civilian dictatorships are less vulnerable to coups than military regimes, and as in Benin, this pattern of military subordination may carry over to their democratic successors. Formerly one-party regimes in Africa—including Benin, but also Zambia, Senegal, and Malawi—were mostly free of coup threats following their transitions.[10]

[10] Svolik 2012.

This pattern is also clearly evident in poor postsocialist countries, such as Mongolia, Moldova, Serbia, and Ukraine. Direct military subordination to the Communist Party established a pattern of civilian control that continued during the 1990s and 2000s. In these cases, the armed forces were not independent actors during the transitions themselves, and remained in the background in subsequent years. Similar patterns are seen in nonsocialist dominant-party systems such as Mexico, where the party prevented the military establishment from posing a threat to civilian authority. In this regard, Mexico stands in sharp contrast to comparable countries in Latin America, particularly those in the Southern Cone.

Refraining from coups or other forms of intervention in politics is not the only way that militaries can affect the stability of democracy; their stance toward backsliding is also critical. When incumbents seek to shut down competition, typically by going after the opposition, or when they face potentially destabilizing protest from mobilized oppositions, the military faces critical decisions. Do they obey orders to repress and overthrow civilian authority—even if with the intention of returning to democratic rule—or simply remain quartered in their barracks? "Shirking," as Pion-Berlin et al. call the last option, is clearly a political decision with significant consequences for the stability of democratic rule.[11] The decision will depend on the cost-benefit calculus for the military. Critical in this regard is the armed forces' assessment of the opposition it would face in intervening, as we will see. By simply refusing to offer support for "backsliding" leaders, the military can act in defense of democratic rule.

What about escapes from the coup trap? How do countries with a history of military challenge to civilian rule transition to effective civilian control? This question clearly has a long pedigree, going back to Juvenal's classic question: "Who guards the guardians?" Feaver labels it "the military problemmatique": the very institution created to protect the polity is given sufficient power to become a threat to it.[12] Solutions have ranged from ensuring democratic legitimacy itself to quid pro quos over operational autonomy, institutional designs with respect to decision making and monitoring, and more fundamental efforts to train and ultimately socialize the military to a "cult of obedience," professionalism, and self-restraint.[13] The international security setting and regional institutions may play a role,[14] although the latter is contested.[15]

[11] Pion-Berlin, Esparza, and Grisham 2014.
[12] Feaver 1996.
[13] On assuring democratic legitimacy, see Kohn 2002. On quid pro quos, see Huntington 1957; Welch 1976; Bland 1999. On decision making and monitoring, see Stepan 1988; Feaver 1996 and 1999. On the "cult of obedience," see Huntington 1957; Janowitz 1960; Burk 2002.
[14] Desch 1999.
[15] Pevehouse 2005; Poast and Urpelainen 2015.

But militaries in new democracies also ultimately evaluate the costs of facing down the potential backlash from civil society and political oppositions if they choose to reenter politics. Ceteris paribus, the higher those costs, the more likely militaries will refrain from entering politics. And ceteris paribus, the more robust the checks emanating from civil society, the higher the costs of intervention will be.

In the Philippines, the first democratic government of Corazon Aquino faced no fewer than ten coup attempts.[16] The failure of these coups could be traced to divisions within the military itself. However, the coup plotters— who, had they succeeded, would have conformed in many ways with our populist model of reversion—also underestimated public resistance. These included localized efforts by civil society groups to thwart them, the role of the media, and doubts within the major opposition Nacionalista Party, factions of which might have benefited had the coups succeeded.[17] It is also important to underscore that the initial transition in the Philippines had occurred in the context of mass mobilization that had supported antiauthoritarian military factions. The perceived costs of coup efforts were clearly not estimated uniformly across the military, but memories of "people power" no doubt played a role among those factions that remained loyal to the Aquino government. These coup failures helped to inoculate subsequent administrations from such threats, although not necessarily from other institutional weaknesses.

In Indonesia, the military had been factionalized between red (nationalist) and green (Islamic) generals, in part purposefully, under Suharto.[18] The military further divided in Suharto's final days.[19] However, General Wiranto's subtle nudging of Suharto toward the exit was accompanied by purges that resulted in more cohesive control over the military and a decline in factionalism. The armed forces converged in support for Suharto's vice president, and thus de facto successor, B. J. Habibie, and ultimately accepted his role and the transition itself, although they remained a crucial behind-the-scenes player. Nonetheless, as in the Philippines, it is plausible that similar calculations deterred the Indonesian military from a more direct political role following the large-scale popular protests and rioting that triggered Suharto's resignation.

Latin America poses more of a puzzle; as can be seen from Tables 8.2 and 8.3, with a very few exceptions (the Dominican Republic and Guyana in the Polity dataset), virtually all Latin American cases have coup histories. Nonetheless, outside of countries with ongoing social violence,[20]

---

[16] Davide Fact-Finding Commission 1990.
[17] Davide Fact-Finding Commission 1990: 470–509.
[18] Crouch 1988.
[19] Honna 2013.
[20] Pion-Berlin and Trinkunas 2011.

there has been considerable progress in establishing effective civilian control in previously coup-prone countries in the region.[21] Such developments cast doubt on the idea of an enduring "coup trap."

It is still the case that in a number of countries—especially in Central America—the armed forces remain beyond full civilian control, continuing to resist efforts to hold them accountable for human rights abuses carried out under previous dictatorships. Several have intervened outright.[22] Compared to past decades, however, the constraints on overt military intervention have grown considerably; rather, irregular exit from office in Latin America is now more likely to come at the hands of legislative impeachment or mass mobilization.[23] Potential coup plotters face not only the threat of international and regional isolation in the post–Cold War era, but backlash from civil societies and mass publics as democratic rule is increasingly institutionalized.

In the most comprehensive treatment of the issue, Lehoucq and Pérez-Liñán confirm that the more recent the coup history, the more a country is at risk.[24] But they also find a process akin to what we call institutionalization: that these risks decline with cycles of democratic turnover. Both Fujimori's *autogolpe* and the 2009 coup in Honduras succeeded only under the cover of a constitutional façade and very weak domestic opposition. A highly mobilized popular opposition, conversely, contributed to the failure of the anti-Chávez coup in Venezuela in 2002. Elsewhere in the region, in both poor and middle-income countries, such as Brazil, Chile, Guatemala, and El Salvador, we see a steady chipping away of military prerogatives and legal protections: the appointment of civilian ministers of defense, increased civilian control over military budgets, and even prosecutions for crimes committed during periods of dictatorship. Although democracy has slid backward in a number of countries, it has occurred primarily through the illiberal concentration of power by elected politicians rather than through direct military intervention.

We see similar constraints, finally, in African countries that had once been plagued by military coups; as in Latin America, there are few African cases in either dataset that avoided some history of coups. Posner and Young find that of the African leaders who left power in the 1960s and

[21] For example, Stepan 1988; Hunter 1997; Pion-Berlin 2001; Barany 2012.

[22] Jean-Bertrand Aristide was deposed by the Haitian military in 2004. The military in Honduras collaborated with the elite-controlled Supreme Court and Congress as recently as 2009 to depose the incumbent president and send him into exile (Chapter 5). The armed forces also played a crucial role in backing Fujimori's *autogolpe* in Peru (Chapter 7) and, as we will see in the next section, became increasingly politicized in Venezuela in the 1990s and 2000s.

[23] Pérez-Liñán 2007; Marsteintredet and Berntzen 2008.

[24] Lehoucq and Pérez-Liñán 2013.

1970s, almost three-quarters did so through coups, violent overthrows, or assassinations.[25] Between 2000 and 2005, however, the share of leaders leaving power through irregular means declined to only 19 percent. Comparing Africa with the rest of the world, they also note a sharp convergence in patterns of leader exit. "Whereas African leaders were two to three times more likely to leave power by violent means in the 1960s, 1970s, and 1980s, they are equally likely—or to be more precise—equally *unlikely*—to leave power under violent circumstances today."[26] During the 2000s, coups have occurred largely in the civil war cases addressed in Chapter 7 and in a handful of other low-income West African states such as Niger.[27]

Again, both international and domestic forces are at work (Chapter 4). In 1999, the OAU banned heads of state installed by coups from attending its meetings. In 2000, this norm against unconstitutional changes of government was institutionalized, resulting in the temporary suspension of Mauritania's and Niger's membership in 2008 and 2010, respectively.[28] This norm is arguably self-interested, since it protects both democratic governments and civilian regimes that have overreached. Nonetheless, the change is striking.

These external pressures, however, reinforce (and are reinforced by) domestic institutional and social checks. Staffan Lindberg and John Clark analyzed 34 military interventions between 1990 and 2004 in African countries with at least some competitive electoral process.[29] As in the studies of Latin America cited above, they find that the incidence of successful military interventions dropped significantly with successive elections, with the risk becoming minimal by the time of the third election. This effect is not solely institutional, however; it is best seen as a proxy for a variety of social constraints as well, including underlying public opinion. Drawing on Afrobarometer polls from 12 countries for 2000, 2002, and 2005, Bratton queries whether African publics harbored nostalgia for military rule. Large majorities answered no. Although opposition to military government declined somewhat from 82 percent in 2000 to 73 percent in 2005, "clear majorities were still dismissing military rule and supporting democracy."[30]

In sum, in Africa and Latin America, the geographic regions historically most prone to coups, there is some cause for optimism about the role of the military. The fall in the risk of coups is not equivalent to a fall in the risk

[25] Posner and Young 2007: 128–29.

[26] Posner and Young 2007: 129.

[27] Others include Guinea-Bissau, the Central African Republic, Guinea, Mauritania, as well as Madagascar.

[28] Ndulo 2012.

[29] Lindberg and Clark 2008.

[30] Bratton 2007: 101.

of backsliding or overreach by incumbents; we take up that question in the next section. It does suggest, however, that the coup dynamic identified by Londregan and Poole may also work in reverse.[31] Just as coups breed more coups, lowering the costs of intervention, so can institutional and civil society checks produce reinforcing dynamics, raising the costs militaries face in reentering politics.

Institutionalization

As the concept of backsliding suggests, not all risks to democratic rule emanate from militaries. Even where the threat of military coups has diminished, democracies can be undermined both gradually and more decisively by the security dilemmas we associate with weakly institutionalized political systems. In these "winner-take-all" environments, elected incumbents deploy the political, economic, and coercive resources of the state to manipulate elections, eliminate constitutional checks on their authority, and undermine oppositions. Oppositions respond accordingly with resort to contentious politics and the mobilization of violence, which—even if provoked—also has destabilizing effects.

As we will see in the next section, middle-income democracies are not immune from such backsliding. But the most vulnerable are democratic regimes in low-income countries where formal institutions are lacking in durability and provide only weak constraints on incumbents. As can be seen in Tables 8.2 and 8.3, reverters count in their number many more cases with marginal Polity scores than the survivors. How did the low-income survivors beat the odds? More precisely, how did the expectations of the most significant political actors converge around a democratic equilibrium in which competition is given free rein, rights and liberties are protected, outcomes of elections are respected, and incumbents do not abuse office and exit in a timely fashion?

Deep structural factors, such as the intensity of social cleavages among groups, as well as more contingent and even highly personal factors, such as the commitments and values of individual leaders, play a role in this process.[32] In particularly fraught settings, such as in the aftermath of civil wars, third-party intervention may be required to break the security dilemma.[33] However, both institutional choices and checks emanating from civil society appear central to controlling the behavior of incumbents, just as they do in limiting military incentives to intervene.

[31] Londregan and Poole 1990.
[32] Dahl 1973: 105–89. On the role of values, see Mainwaring and Pérez-Liñán 2014.
[33] Walter 2002.

Earlier work on "consolidation" focused on how constitutional and electoral arrangements might strengthen incentives for cooperation and thus increase the prospects for democratic survival. Salient constitutional arrangements included parliamentarism versus presidentialism, electoral rules that forced coalition building, and explicit power-sharing arrangements.[34] In all of these cases, the primary concern was to design institutions that would mitigate the risks of polarization and stalemate, thus simultaneously reducing incentives for militaries to intervene to break political logjams or conflicts.

However, none of these findings appear wholly robust; indeed, all of the claims about the relationship between institutions and democratic stability noted above remain highly contested to this day. Critics have noted that the differences between proposed ideal types, such as presidentialism and parliamentarism, were often overplayed,[35] or that their effects seemed contingent on other features of the system. Semipresidential systems, including the French model, were believed to have particular disadvantages, for example,[36] but worked in Benin and failed in Niger.[37]

But these models suffered from deeper disabilities. First, they rested on the assumption that institutional arrangements were stable and actually constrained the actors in questions; the focus was on the perverse effects of operating constitutional arrangements, such as the propensity to polarization or deadlock in presidential systems that would tempt military intervention. In the settings of greatest interest to us, however, the problems are more fundamental. Constitutional arrangements are unstable and continually changing. Second, the problems confronting contemporary democracies appear to have shifted. More recently, the challenges have come not from polarization and deadlock but from incumbent executives motivated to overreach.

More recent approaches to the role of institutions have thus focused less on large-scale constitutional design and more on specific mechanisms that immediately and transparently signal to relevant political and social actors when red lines are being crossed. Kapstein and Converse focus for example on the importance of restraints on the executive for the

---

[34] On parliamentarism vs. presidentialism, see Linz 1990a, 1990b, 1994; Linz and Valenzuela 1994; Mainwaring 1993; Stepan and Skach 1993; Power and Gasiorowski 1997; Mainwaring and Shugart 1997; Cheibub and Limongi 2002. On electoral rules and coalition building, see Horowitz 1985; Reilly 2001. On explicit power-sharing arrangements, see Lijphart 1977; Sisk 1995; Hartzell and Hoddie 2003, 2007, 2015; Norris 2008.

[35] For example, Mainwaring and Shugart 1997.

[36] Skach 2005; however see also Shugart 2005 and Elgie 2004.

[37] Allen 1992.

consolidation of democratic rule.[38] In a complementary approach, Fish looks at the powers of legislatures.[39]

Such "small" institutional rules are not necessarily binding in new and relatively weak democracies. They can, however, play a signaling role that can help trigger social and political checks on incumbents and increase the costs of violations. Constitutional term limits provide a useful example. Incumbents can—and often do—find ways to circumvent these limits, but decisions to do so are highly visible acts that will register clearly with international actors, oppositions, and rivals within the ruling party.

A growing body of research has explored the implications of this "small" institution, focusing on the costs politicians face when ignoring term limits.[40] Gideon Maltz surveyed competitive authoritarian regimes over the 1992 to 2006 period and found that while incumbents retained power in 93 percent of the elections that they contested, their successors were much less likely to prevail, winning just 52 percent of the time.[41] Strikingly, these findings carry over to low-income African subsamples. Posner and Young found that, on average, governing parties in which incumbents refrained from attempts to alter term limits won by smaller majorities (17.8 percent) than those that did try (41.5 percent).[42] In one of the more comprehensive tests, covering all African elections from 1990 to 2009, Cheeseman finds that opposition parties were almost four times more likely to win non-founding elections in which the incumbent had stood down.[43] Even when incumbent parties won, moreover, their margin of victory fell by 10 percent in open-seat polls. This may have to do with the sheer charisma of early incumbents. Posner and Young note, however, that a number of political factors are also at work: new contenders from the ruling party face greater challenges in building personal networks of support, generating intra-party competition over the top spot, and facing potential conflicts with sitting incumbents.[44]

Although term limits constitute a particularly visible way of restraining incumbents, a variety of other "small" institutions have been identified that also serve to check incumbent power. Constitutional courts provide horizontal checks.[45] The Constitutional Court in Benin played an important role in persuading Soglo to accept defeat in the 1996 Benin elec-

---

[38] Kapstein and Converse 2008a, 2008b.
[39] Fish 2006.
[40] Baturo 2014.
[41] Maltz 2007.
[42] Posner and Young 2007.
[43] Cheeseman 2014.
[44] Posner and Young 2007.
[45] Epstein, Knight, and Shvetsova 2001; Ginsburg 2003.

tion. Electoral commissions have also received substantial attention as an institution crucial for the integrity of democratic processes.[46] An independent electoral commission was established in Ghana following opposition protests against alleged electoral fraud in the early 1990s. The commission added credibility to elections going forward and was credited in part with the decision by the ruling party to accept defeat in a closely contested election in 2009.[47]

In sum, where the military has been tamed and does not constitute a threat, particular institutional innovations may be effective in checking potential backsliding on the part of incumbents. But in weak institutional environments, the stabilization of expectations ultimately depends not on "parchment institutions"[48] but on the capacity of oppositions, political parties, organized interest groups, and mass publics to mobilize against the efforts of executives to arrogate powers. In this regard, it is worth underlining that the stabilization of expectations rests on two, somewhat contradictory mechanisms. On the one hand, for both incumbents and their opponents, restraint of the contending actors depends on credible assurances of restraint by their rivals. Both incumbents and oppositions are more likely to play by the formal rules of the game if the risk of conceding defeat does not bring with it permanent defeat, marginalization, or worse. Cheeseman notes, for example, that rulers such as Kérékou "found it relatively easy to walk away from power because they had not committed crimes that were likely to make them targets for domestic and international prosecution and because they trusted future governments not to persecute them."[49]

But calculations of this sort did not depend entirely on the strategic self-restraint of competing political leaders. As several of our case studies also indicate, and as we argued at greater length in Chapter 5, executives were also less likely to abuse their power if doing so risked a backlash from opposition political parties and active civil societies. The importance of pressure from below is most visible, of course, in cases where adherence to the constitutional rules of the game is openly at risk. For example, we showed how a groundswell of opposition from civil society groups, opposition party members, and even a significant majority of his own party helped to prevent an attempt by Frederick Chiluba to secure a third presidential term in Zambia in 2001 (Chapter 5). Popular mobilization was instrumental in defeating other abuses of power as well. It forced a return to constitutional norms in Ukraine in 1993 (Chapter 5) and helped to defeat

[46] For example, Eisenstadt 2004.
[47] Cheeseman 2014: 154–55.
[48] Carey 2000.
[49] Cheeseman 2014: 16.

attempts by Balaguer to continue in power through rigged elections in the Dominican Republic (Chapter 6). Conversely, as we saw in our discussion of Peru in Chapter 7, Fujimori's *autogolpe* in Peru succeeded at least in part because the unions and the political left had been devastated by years of economic crisis and were unable to launch significant resistance.

It is important to acknowledge that the effect of civil society mobilization on democratic continuity is not entirely straightforward, and we return to the risks in more detail in the Conclusion. In the absence of mechanisms of accommodation and mutual assurance among competing elites, mobilization can also increase the likelihood of political polarization or stalemate noted in earlier studies of consolidation. Strong opposition from unions and other sectors of civil society can also impede economic adjustments that—though painful and unpopular—are necessary for the sustained growth that facilitates democratic rule. Nonetheless, strong civil societies and popularly based collective action do raise the cost of backsliding. A civil society that is weak and quiescent presents a far greater threat to the institutionalization of democratic politics than the occasional disruption it may bring.

Economic Performance: Avoiding—and Overcoming— Economic Crises

How economic performance affects the survival of democracies remains at issue. Our regressions in Chapter 6 provided only limited support for the claim that weak performance destabilizes democracy. But as we argued as well in Chapter 6, this null finding also reflects the rigid lag structure required by panel designs. In Tables 6.8 and 6.9 we showed that economic performance of those democratic countries that ultimately reverted was distinctly inferior over their entire democratic life spans to the performance of those that survived (1.3 vs. 3.4 in the CGV dataset; 2.02 vs. 3.48 in the Polity dataset). The distribution of low-income cases identified in Tables 8.2 and 8.3 is also consistent with these findings. In both datasets, over 40 percent of the reverters had endured low growth during their democratic years (less than 2 percent, the average rate of all reverters in the Polity dataset), whereas only a handful of survivors had such weak growth records, most of them postsocialist cases (Macedonia, Ukraine, and Nicaragua in the CGV dataset; Moldova and Ukraine in the Polity dataset). More important, our consideration of the low-income cases found clear evidence of poor performance and economic crises playing a catalytic role in the collapse of democratic rule; indeed, crises were nearly ubiquitous features of the reversion cases.

Nevertheless, it seems clear that while some democratic regimes can be brought down by the political fallout from short-term shocks to the economy, others survive or avoid crisis, as happened throughout the 1980s and 1990s in the middle-income countries of Latin America and Eastern Europe. Why are some regimes able to survive or avoid crises and sustain relatively high rates of growth? The reasons for these differences have been the subject of a very long debate in which we have ourselves participated,[50] and a systematic discussion of this issue is beyond the scope of this book. However, a scrutiny of the cases in our sample suggests a number of hypotheses.

To begin with, we cannot rule out the role of sheer luck. For example, poor democracies in natural-resource-rich countries that transitioned just before or during the commodity boom of the 2000s had a decent run of good economic performance in their early democratic years. They were subsequently insulated from the global economic crisis, in part because of the role that China played as a demandeur of commodities. In the Polity dataset, these cases included Kenya (2002), Senegal (2000), and Peru (2001), all of which experienced growth rates over 4 percent in the years following their transitions. In Nigeria (1999), included in the CGV dataset, growth rates averaged 5.6 percent through the 2000s.[51] It should be noted, however, that high growth helped to stabilize at least some autocratic regimes as well. As we will see below, commodity-fueled booms also contributed significantly to the entrenchment of backsliding regimes in Venezuela and Russia after long periods of economic stagnation and crisis under democratic governments.

The likelihood that democracies can overcome—as well as avoid—crises may also depend on timing and political circumstances in which they hit. The fate of democracy may depend on whether the old authoritarian regime or the new democratic government is held responsible for the economic difficulties associated with crisis and adjustment. The new democratic regime in Benin benefited from the fact that the outgoing Kérékou dictatorship took much of the blame for initiating IMF-sponsored reforms, allowing the new democratic administration to deepen the program and reap the benefits. In Ghana, which transitioned in 1993, early adjustments under the Rawlings dictatorship contributed to subsequent growth rates of over 5 percent during the 1990s and 2000s.[52]

Focusing blame on authoritarian incumbents was also an important factor in enabling democracies in other regions to survive or work their

[50] Haggard and Kaufman 1995.

[51] Although our ten-year rule precluded us from including low-income democracies that transitioned after 2003 as survivors, these regimes were typically stabilized by high, commodity-fueled growth rates as well.

[52] These reform efforts and political stability in these and other African "success stories" were reinforced and enhanced by substantial external assistance. We return to this issue in the Conclusion.

way through economic crisis. The "crony-capitalism" of the Marcos regime was a central target of the democratic opposition in the Philippines, and this provided leverage for the Aquino and Ramos governments to initiate reforms. Democratic regimes in Eastern Europe and Latin America, similarly, gained an advantage from the evident failures of their communist and military predecessors. However, where reforms faltered or failed to deliver results, as was the case, for example, in Bolivia and Ecuador, blame eventually shifted from incumbent officials to the democratic regime itself, sometimes with highly destabilizing political consequences.

Recovery from earlier crises, finally, increases the chances that democracies could survive and make corrections in subsequent struggles. The "second round" crises that hit the middle-income countries of both Eastern Europe and Latin America in the late 1990s and early 2000s followed still more devastating collapses in the 1980s and early 1990s. However, those crises had been accompanied by quite fundamental reforms—for example, with respect to exchange rates, fiscal policy, and foreign borrowing—that reduced vulnerability the second time around.[53] When these new crises hit, democratic regimes were also more firmly entrenched. Both economic and political circumstances allowed more effective responses to the Great Recession of 2007–8. Governments could let exchange rates depreciate and pursue modest countercyclical monetary and fiscal policies that permitted a more rapid rebound than had occurred during the 1980s.

In presenting these hypotheses, it is important to acknowledge the obvious issue of endogeneity between political and institutional conditions and poor economic performance. Resource endowments and external shocks clearly affect growth, but so too do political and institutional features of new democracies. It is far beyond the scope of this book to untangle the reciprocal causal relations that operate here. But it is worth stating the obvious point that the superior economic performance of the survivors could well be related to their more robust institutionalization; this is clearly an important direction for future research.

WHY DO MIDDLE-INCOME DEMOCRACIES FAIL?

We turn in this final section to an issue that has become an increasing subject of concern during the 21st century: the incremental erosion of democracy in middle-income countries. Our Polity and CGV datasets identify only three examples of outright middle-income reversion via backsliding: Venezuela (2006), Ecuador (2007), and Russia (2007); Thailand, discussed in Chapter 7, reverted in 2006 through a military coup d'état.

---

[53] Haggard 2013.

But if we cast our conceptual net more broadly to consider incremental political shifts that fall short of outright regime change, we see disturbing trends in a much broader range of middle-income cases. The Freedom House Index of Political Rights and Civil Liberties captures one component of this backsliding.[54] From the end of our dataset in 2008 to 2013, there were at least slight declines in nine middle-income survivors in the CGV dataset, while only eight improved.[55] The record of the Polity survivors shows deterioration in 15 middle-income survivors and improvements in only 7. In most of these cases, changes were only at the margins, often merely a point. Turkey, however—a case we explore in detail below—saw a decline of 6 points in this rights and liberty index, and several other middle-income countries—Bulgaria, Latvia, and South Africa—display scores that declined by 5 points. In Hungary, a relatively developed member of the EU, the majoritarian dominance of the conservative ruling party has also caused considerable consternation; its score declined by 4 points. While these trends stopped short of outright reversion as measured in the two principal datasets we use in this study, they clearly constitute worrisome steps backward.

We begin our analysis of this phenomenon with case studies of two iconic and unmistakable cases of reversion: Venezuela under Hugo Chávez and Russia under Vladimir Putin. The former had previously enjoyed a long-standing democratic system, and provides an especially striking case of poor economic performance and political deinstitutionalization over a prolonged period. In contrast, although Russia received a Polity coding of 6 in 2000, "democracy" in that society was clearly much more fragile, and there is significant debate over whether it was ever actually democratic at all.[56] During the 2000s, however, each of these moved decisively toward competitive authoritarian rule, and each has provided models, and at times material support, for other countries in Latin America and postcommunist Europe.

Not coincidentally, both of these countries (as well as Ecuador) are oil states. The decline of democratic politics and the emergence of autocratic

---

[54] Between 2006 and 2013, more countries have declined on their index than have improved; in 2013, the last year of their survey, 40 countries improved a point or more, while 54 declined. (Freedom House 2014a).

[55] Polity backsliders were South Africa, South Korea, Taiwan, Bulgaria, Croatia, Czech Republic Hungary, Latvia, Lithuania, Turkey, Chile, the Dominican Republic, Mexico, Panama, and Peru. Those that increased were Albania, Estonia, Macedonia, Romania, Serbia, Brazil, and Uruguay. CGV backsliders were Bulgaria, Czech Republic, Hungary, Latvia, Lithuania, Turkey, Mexico, Chile, and Peru. The increases came in Croatia, Estonia, Macedonia, Romania, Serbia, Uruguay, Brazil, and Grenada.

[56] Fish 2005.

leaders arguably had to do with opportunities provided by dramatic increases in the price of oil and corresponding rents that could be used to political ends.[57] We argue, however, that the dynamics of reversion also reflected more general institutional and economic weaknesses that can affect non-oil producers as well. To make this point, we extend our analysis to include recent, out-of-sample developments in a non-oil case: Turkey under Recep Erdoğan (prime minister, 2003–14; president, 2014–present). Although it might be somewhat premature to suggest that democracy has failed in Turkey, the decline in Turkey's Freedom House score between 2008 and 2013 was the largest of any middle-income survivor in our sample. After significant progress in democratization during the early 2000s, the end of the decade was marked by substantial restrictions on civil liberties and a significant decrease in horizontal checks on the executive.

Why did these middle-income democracies move backward? Part of the explanation lies in the international arena: rather than the positive neighborhood effects discussed in the first part of this chapter, we see evidence of the limited leverage available to otherwise powerful democratic neighbors. In Venezuela, the collapse of petroleum prices in the 1990s paved the way for the rise of Chávez. However, the subsequent boom substantially increased his capacity to resist external pressure. Western pressure on Putin was also limited by the surge in oil prices of the mid-2000s. In the case of Turkey, the pull of the EU initially provided a powerful incentive for democratic reforms. But the positive effects of both linkage and leverage diminished substantially after the failure of Turkey's accession bid in the mid-2000s and the subsequent onset of economic crisis in Europe.

Although the weakness of external constraints enlarged the space for backsliding, in each of these cases we also see institutional and economic weaknesses that expanded opportunities for the concentration of political power. In this regard, the cases provide evidence of the weak democracy syndrome visible in the low-income reverters.

A background of poor economic performance was the vulnerability most commonly shared by the three countries. In all three cases, autocratic rulers were eventually buoyed by economic booms; but the inability of previous governments to respond to severe economic difficulties had already significantly weakened support for democratic rule. Ironically, this is a mirror image of our discussion in the preceding section. In the survivors, bad economic conditions helped undermine incumbent authoritarian regimes and delegitimize autocratic rule more generally. Democracies

---

[57] Ross 2013.

that could weather crises inherited from their authoritarian predecessors saw subsequent recoveries that stabilized democratic rule. In the backsliding cases, by contrast, poor economic performance delegitimated democratic regimes rather than authoritarian rulers and opened the way for challengers—typically political outsiders—who then exploited recoveries to concentrate executive powers.

Institutions also mattered. Although the level of democratic institutionalization differed significantly across the three cases, the route to the consolidation of autocratic executive power was paved by the fact that courts, legislatures, and parties had fallen into disrepute if not total dysfunction. Incumbents who subsequently undermined democratic rule were able to exploit these institutional weaknesses, as well as the widespread dissatisfaction over economic performance. Supermajorities allowed them to concentrate executive power, marginalize opposition groups, and curtail political rights and civil liberties. The consolidation of power typically extended to control over state financial resources, including those generated by state-owned enterprises. Access to these resources—including through outright corruption—enabled alliances with crony capitalists, and clientelist and patronage networks that strengthened the power of the incumbents while weakening oppositions.

Finally, although the military did not directly seize power, and in fact opposed Chávez and Erdoğan at certain points, it was ultimately a pivotal political actor in the accumulation of executive power. Rulers in the three countries relied heavily on military acquiescence, if not active collaboration, in deploying the security apparatus and police against critics.

Venezuela

Explanations of the rise of Hugo Chávez must begin by confronting the puzzle that for many decades Venezuela was not a "weak democracy," but a highly institutionalized constitutional system. From the overthrow of a military dictatorship in 1958 until at least the early 1990s, the country was often portrayed as one of the few democratic success stories in Latin America, characterized by stable electoral competition between two deeply rooted centrist parties, and by a military establishment that remained largely outside the political realm. Serious strains began to emerge, however, with the onset of the debt crisis in the early 1980s and the collapse of oil prices after 1985. In the 1990s, the key institutional and political pillars of the regime began to crumble. As the economy continued to deteriorate, the route to a populist reversion was paved by collapse of a once highly institutionalized party system, the decline of cooperative norms among contending political elites, and the erosion of barriers that separated the military from political life.

ECONOMIC DECLINE

The prolonged crisis of the oil-based economy directly affected living standards and reduced revenues governments of both parties had used to provide public goods as well as clientelistic benefits. As in other systems where democracy was well entrenched, voters initially reacted to hard times by voting out incumbents rather than by turning against the system itself. But as a succession of democratic governments failed to deal with the country's economic challenges, the legitimacy of the entire political system eroded.

The most decisive effort to halt the economic deterioration came under Carlos Andrés Pérez, elected in 1988. But the tough adjustment program he attempted to put in place quickly encountered political resistance. In 1989, attempts to reduce subsidies for public transportation triggered massive protests and a bloody response by the police. In 1992, military dissatisfaction with Pérez's neoliberal program prompted Hugo Chávez and a coterie of nationalist military officers to attempt the first coup d'état since the 1960s, and one that nearly succeeded in dislodging the president. Politically, Pérez's economic adjustment initiative also left him isolated from political and union leaders affiliated with his own party, as well as those from the opposition. He was ultimately driven from office in 1993, before the official end of his term, by accusations of corruption and a vote of impeachment. Pérez's failure did much to accelerate the erosion of support for the established political parties and the regime itself.

PRAETORIANISM

Although Chávez's 1992 coup attempt failed, it catapulted him into prominence as a populist critic of a corrupt and ineffective democratic regime and provided him a base of factional support among junior military officers. More generally, the coup recast the military establishment as a critical swing player in the ensuing battles following Chávez's election in 1998. In 2002, opposing military factions temporarily ousted Chávez, only to be beaten back by loyalist factions and widespread popular protests. Following this second failed coup attempt, political purges and material rewards transformed the officer corps into a central pillar of the Chávez presidency.

DEINSTITUTIONALIZATION

Even more important than the politicization of the military was the collapse of the established party system, which had historically provided the institutional foundation of Venezuelan democracy. By the late 1980s, the practice of relying on elite agreements between two dominant parties that monopolized the political space had come under increasing criticism.[58] But the system fragmented entirely in the years following Pérez's defeat. The vote share of the two major parties fell from almost 93 percent in the 1988 presidential election to only 45 percent in 1993. The winner, with only 31 percent of the vote, was Rafael Caldera, who was once a top leader of the major opposition party, but was now running as an anti-establishment independent. In office, Caldera's policies shifted erratically between populism and austerity, and the political and economic crisis deepened further. Caldera's term ended in 1999, with the old political system in profound disarray. The way was open for Chávez, the former coup conspirator, to contest for the presidency with a populist campaign against the elitism and corruption of the entire political system.

BACKSLIDING

Chávez's first order of business following his election was to convene a constituent assembly, exploiting widespread disaffection with the existing constitutional system. In the meantime, the Supreme Court was pressed by the highly popular new president to suspend the Congress while the assembly was under way. The assembly itself was dominated primarily by Chávez's supporters and acted to increase executive control over the legislature by abolishing the Senate, extending the presidential term, and providing for extensive decree powers. Once the legislature was weakened, "it became easier for the president to pack the court and tighten control over the attorney general, the comptroller general, and the [National Election Council] . . . the electoral monitoring body."[59] By 2001, Chávez had used a large majority in the new legislature to increase the control of the central government over education, and new decree powers over hydrocarbons and agriculture. Corrales and Penfold argue that although the onset of the oil boom of 2003–8 enabled Chávez to consolidate and expand these initiatives, some of the most important were achieved prior to that time, as a consequence of the discrediting of the old system and Chávez's initial political honeymoon: "The availability of economic resources alone would not have sufficed as a condition enabling the rise of a hybrid regime. In the presence of stronger political parties and institutions of accountability, the political impact of an economic windfall would have been different."[60] Unlike many of the reversions discussed in Chapter 7, however, by about 2001 Chávez's authoritarian initiatives did encounter fierce political and civil society opposition. Between 2001 and 2004—in addition to the 2002 coup noted above—Chávez weathered large-scale demonstrations,

[58] Coppedge 1997.
[59] Corrales and Penfold 2015: 19.
[60] Corrales and Penfold 2015: 15.

a business lockout, and a prolonged stoppage by managers and technical workers in the critical petroleum sector.

Attempts to unseat Chávez failed for many reasons, including both the prior institutional changes and the fortuitous upsurge in oil prices in 2003. But the effectiveness of the opposition was also undermined significantly by its association with the old order and the ambiguity of its own democratic commitments. The 2002 coup was tainted by a hasty expression of support from the US government, and it fell apart entirely after the coup leaders announced that they intended to dissolve the National Assembly and dismiss elected state governors.[61] On returning to power, Chávez resumed his appeal to broad sectors of the population with fiery attacks on the United States and the elites of the old order. In 2003, he drew on his political capital to fend off a potentially fatal work stoppage in the petroleum sector and to replace striking employees and managers with political loyalists. Even more important, the formerly semiautonomous management of the state oil company was brought under direct presidential control, providing Chávez with unimpeded access to the flow of petroleum revenues.[62]

The decisive turning point in this struggle came in 2003–4, and the resurgence of oil prices now played a crucial political role. Having failed at extraconstitutional efforts to depose Chávez, the opposition seized on a provision in the new constitution to petition for a referendum on his continuation in office. Rising oil prices, however, allowed Chávez to counter with a massive social spending program—food subsidies, health facilities, and clientelistic benefits—that built a large electoral following among low-income groups. Chávez won the referendum with over 60 percent of the vote.

This reversal of fortune further stunned and demoralized the opposition. The regime's opponents offered only a weak challenge in 2004 local elections, leaving Chavistas in control of 21 of the 23 state governments and more than 90 percent of the country's municipalities. Opposition leaders then boycotted the 2005 legislative elections, which left Chávez entirely in control of that branch of government as well. Buoyed by both oil resources and a weak opposition, Chávez won a relatively clean 2006 presidential election and another five-year term with 63 percent of the vote.

Following this electoral victory, the same combination of presidential powers and oil resources combined to further expand presidential powers and weaken the opposition. Immediately following the election, the National Assembly voted the president the power to rule for decree for

[61] Corrales and Penfold 2007: 102.
[62] Corrales and Penfold 2015.

the following 18 months. Among the important "reforms" of this period were measures that limited the autonomy of the central bank and put the president in charge of managing international reserves. Following his success in seizing control of the state-owned oil firm, the government went on to seize control of other sectors of the economy, including telecommunications, energy, and banking. The regime also moved to further tighten controls on the media, a key battleground in the effort to tame the opposition. The most significant augmentation of the presidential power came in the 2009 referendum, which wrote these and other institutional changes into the constitution and abolished term limits.

With the onset of the 2010s, the Chávez regime faced increasingly severe challenges from the resurgence of the opposition under a younger and more dynamic leadership, the collapse of oil prices, and the death of the highly personalist and charismatic leader himself in 2013. Over the next two years, with the regime now under the leadership of Nicolas Maduro, Venezuela entered a period of severe, potentially fatal, economic and political crisis. As inflation rates reached triple digits and consumer goods disappeared from the shelves, popular support for the government fell dramatically and the regime faced opposition both in the streets and in the electoral arena. In congressional elections held in December 2015, a coalition of opposition forces won a stunning victory, winning two-thirds of the legislative seats and increasing the chances for a crippling political and economic stalemate. As of this writing, the fate of the regime remains uncertain; but it is clear that, to remain in power, it will need to both overcome strains within its own ranks and rely increasingly on coercion against its opponents.

Whatever the fate of the regime going forward, however, the rise of Chávez shows how even a relatively robust constitutional system can become vulnerable to institutional decay, which opens the way to a competitive authoritarian reversion. The recovery of oil prices in the early 2000s played a vital role in Chávez's ability to capitalize on this opening, but the building blocks of personalist authoritarian rule rested on the discrediting and decay of the prior political system and the opportunity provided for the construction of an illiberal supermajority. For almost two decades, the political opposition proved unable to challenge growing state control over democratic institutions, the coercive apparatus, and wide swaths of the economy.

Russia

In contrast to the decades of relatively stable democratic politics preceding the onset of the Chávez regime, the years prior to Putin's rise to power were characterized by profound political and economic challenges; from the collapse of the Soviet Union onward, Russian "democracy" was precarious at best. Constitutional changes in the early 1990s were not only frequent but swung between those granting the Duma wide powers and those formally granting Yeltsin extraordinary discretion. Actual politics unfolded as a free-for-all among contending centers of power: the president; the legislature; the bureaucracy, self-interested and only partly under executive control; and regional centers of power. Public policy was characterized by shadowy relations between government officials, economic oligarchs, and uncertain property rights. The economic nadir came with a crushing financial crisis in 1998, triggered by a default on government debt. These developments opened the way to the emergence of a strongman such as Putin. Thus, the reversion to authoritarian rule (2007 in the Polity dataset)[63] is arguably less counterintuitive; indeed, a number of analysts have concluded that the system was never really democratic at all.[64]

But Boris Yeltsin, who had been elected to the presidency during the Soviet period in 1991, was reelected in 1996 in a relatively free election. Vladimir Putin's victory in the next election, in 2000, was marked by a number of irregularities but was nonetheless considered by at least some outside observers as "free and fair." Moreover, Putin's election in 2000 offered some hope that Russia had turned a corner. Despite the economic chaos, market reforms under Yeltsin had thoroughly transformed the economy, and by 1999 Russia had begun to bounce back from the financial crash of the preceding year. The election itself, as Polity put it, marked "the first peaceful and democratic transfer of power in the nation's history."[65] By the middle of the 2000s, however, it was increasingly clear that Putin was pursuing a trajectory quite similar to that of Chávez. What explains the authoritarian turn?

ECONOMIC DECLINE AND RECOVERY

The springboard for this consolidation of power was, as in Venezuela, the timing of both the economic collapse and the subsequent recovery. On the one hand, the economic collapse at the end of the Yeltsin years was accompanied by widespread public cynicism about the promises of both democracy and market-oriented reform; poll results in 1999 showed that more than 90 percent disapproved of President Yeltsin's performance.[66] On the other hand, although Putin initially became prime minister and acting president in 1999–2000, the final years of Yeltsin's term, he came

[63] The case is not coded as an authoritarian reversion in the CGV dataset because of the staging of elections and apparent turnover to Medvedev in 2008.

[64] Fish 2005. See also McFaul 2002.

[65] Polity IV 2010b: 1.

[66] Treisman 2011.

in as an outsider and reaped credit for the turnaround from the financial crisis. In 2000, just as the positive results of the crisis-induced devaluation were beginning to appear, Putin's approval rating soared to about 85 percent.

The Russian economy, like Venezuela's, was highly dependent on oil, and this ultimately played a significant role in Putin's consolidation of power. However, just as Chávez was able to exploit a political honeymoon prior to the oil boom, Putin's initial popularity surged while oil prices were still low.[67] The effects of the oil boom in Russia began to be felt by about 2005.[68] But until that time, much of Putin's popularity stemmed from a recovery from the 1998 financial crisis, which saw improved exports, new capital inflows, and a degree of domestic protection provided by the drop in the value of the ruble.[69] Put differently, the key to Putin's rise was not oil wealth per se—important though that eventually was—but the resumption of growth. As the economy improved, so did Putin's popularity and his political power. The share of legislative seats controlled by progovernment parties increased from 18 percent in 1999 to 58 percent in 2003. In 2007, with the oil boom in full gear, Putin gained control of 78 percent of legislative seats through party switching and the bandwagoning of opposition politicians.[70]

BACKSLIDING

In principle, the construction of a supermajority did not imply an inevitable reversion to competitive authoritarian rule. It did, however, mean that there were no significant institutional or political checks on Putin's ambitions. With respect to formal institutions, one of the early moves of Putin's first administration was a flurry of judicial reforms in 2001–3 that dramatically increased the executive control over the courts and thereby weakened horizontal checks on the executive.

Another important target of government action during the first administration was the independent media. Justified in part on national security grounds as a result of the conflicts in Chechnya, the Kremlin acted to defang opposition media prior to the 2000 elections, but these efforts intensified in subsequent years. The withdrawal of government subsidies in 2004

[67]The Urals oil price per barrel averaged about $27 between 2000 and 2004. In 2005, it nearly doubled to $50 and increased to $61 and $69 in the next two years. OECD 2006; Rutland 2008.

[68]Rutland 2008; Treisman 2011.

[69]Even as the commodity boom accelerated in the 2000s, Russia was slightly less dependent than Venezuela. In Venezuela, oil counted for 64 percent of government revenues and 92 percent of its exports by 2008. In Russia, oil and gas constituted about 40–50 percent of state revenues and only 68 percent of exports during the 2000s.

[70]Treisman 2011.

made the media vulnerable to economic pressures from private groups with close ties to the Kremlin. As a result, it became virtually impossible for the opposition to get balanced coverage, or coverage at all.

As in Venezuela, another crucial component of presidential control centered on the continuing role of state-owned enterprises in the economy, the emergence of new crony firms, and the leverage the president could wield as a result of the weakness of property rights protections.[71] Privatization had created the so-called oligarchs in the first half of the 1990s, and played a central role in Yeltsin's reelection in 1996. Yet as Dawisha has documented in extraordinary detail, Putin proved masterful at using these economic levers to generate both public and private resources under his direct control. A turning point in this regard was the dismantling of the energy giant Yukos after 2003 and the transfer of many of its assets to state-owned and crony companies—a move that not only increased Putin's economic power but also attacked the political independence of the oligarchs and their ability to advocate for a more liberal political course.

Unlike in Venezuela, the military stood down from a political role after its intervention in support of Yeltsin in 1993. The KGB, however, provided an important base for Putin's rise to power, and he aggressively exploited security issues to political ends. By the end of the 2000s, there were nearly two dozen of these *silovye ministerstva*—literally "ministries of force." But personnel from security backgrounds also occupied a wider range of state positions and were turned increasingly turned to the task of actively undermining any independent centers of political, civil, or economic power. As more active opposition resurfaced at the end of the 2000s, it was increasingly exposed not only to legal restraints but also to outright intimidation by both public security forces and a shadowy mafia of their supporters.

Following the 2003–4 elections, centralizing moves continued, including a completion of the effort begun during Putin's first term to reassert control vis-à-vis regional leaders. Putin relieved governors of the right to sit in the Federation Council, which removed their immunity from criminal prosecution and exposed them to executive threat. New legislation weakened regional bases of opposition by empowering the president to dismiss governors and regional legislators under a variety of pretenses. These political moves culminated in 2007 in the stacking of the electoral commission, election rigging, and the effective circumvention of term limits by Putin's handpicking of his presidential successor, the actions responsible for Polity's downgrade. With an eviscerated opposition, Medvedev secured over 70 percent of the vote in what was effectively a

[71]Dawisha 2014.

referendum on Putinism. Putin maintained the position of prime minister, continuing his political dominance and exploiting the malleability of formal institutions in an increasingly personalized system.

Russia faced the exact same shocks as the Chávez regime in the form of the global financial crisis, a sharp decline in oil prices, a slowdown in capital inflows, and a weak recovery in the early 2010s. These economic events naturally had an effect on Putin's popularity. Undeterred, Putin ran an aggressive electoral campaign for the presidency in 2012 that rested on strong nationalist appeals and secured 63.5 percent of the popular vote. Following the pattern of earlier elections, Putin was able to put together legislative coalitions around a host of restrictive legislation, moving the country further into hard authoritarian territory: limits on public assemblies, the recriminalization of libel, an expanded legal definition of treason that included involvement in human rights issues, and expansive control on Internet content and foreign ownership of media.

The foreign policy gambits of 2014–15—the involvement in Ukraine, the annexation of Crimea, and the engagement in Syria—appeared to boost Putin's popularity, but it is not clear that they will pay out in the long run. The nationalist strategy proved highly costly in economic terms. Growth had already begun to slow as Putin was assuming office for his third term, but ground to a virtual standstill in 2014 before turning sharply negative in 2015. Even with a controlled press and the initial burst of public support, Russians may increasingly come to doubt the benefits of sustaining a presence in former Soviet territories and the increasing involvement in the complex wars of the Middle East.

On the other hand, the Putin regime enjoys advantages not available to its Venezuelan counterpart. Unlike in Venezuela, the opposition remains badly crippled and demoralized, and the regime does not hesitate to use increasingly repressive measures to keep it cowed. Unlike Maduro in Venezuela, moreover, Putin does not face a military or police establishment of uncertain loyalty, or strong political rivals within the incumbent elite. On the contrary, horizontal checks are limited: public prosecutors and the "security police" have served as loyal agents of the regime and have been instrumental in controlling critics in the political sphere, and the press and legislators have tended to bandwagon to the power presidency.

Finally, despite sanctions, Russia clearly has a greater capability to shape its external environment than does the Maduro regime in Venezuela. Notwithstanding the diplomatic support that Venezuela has received from allied populist regimes, it operates in a neighborhood that is unfavorable to the open use of force. Indeed, when faced with mass protests in 2014, the regime encountered significant international pressure to engage in compromise with moderate sectors of the opposition. Putin faces far fewer constraints from his immediate neighbors, former Soviet republics that are either themselves "competitive authoritarian" regimes or, like the Baltics, small democracies that cannot seriously challenge Russia's domestic political practices. Thus, although the future of Russia's competitive authoritarian regime—like Venezuela's—remains uncertain, it is in a better position to survive the challenges to the authoritarian equilibrium.

Turkey: A Non-Oil Case

Economic dependence on petroleum in Venezuela and Russia was, as we have argued, not the only factor explaining the rise of Chávez and Putin. But it does raise the question of whether political developments in those societies are endogenous to well-known disabilities of rentier states, and therefore not relevant to the political fate of other middle-income countries. A consideration of Turkey—an out-of-sample case—shows how substantial backsliding can occur in non-oil cases as well, and in a country of geopolitical significance to the United States, NATO, and the EU. We emphasize that the slide has been incremental, and unlike the cases of Venezuela or Russia, has not so far crossed the CGV or Polity thresholds for reversion to authoritarian rule. Nevertheless, following continuing moves in the direction of more democracy after the Justice and Development Party (AKP in Turkish) came to power in 2003, the period from the end of the decade saw the prime minister and then president, Recep Erdoğan, moving in the opposite direction. To understand this reversal, we again need to consider key features of the weak democracy syndrome, including the crisis-and-rebound cycle in the economy, military threats, and political institutions that could only weakly balance executive overreach.

ECONOMIC DETERIORATION AND RECOVERY: THE BUILDING OF A SUPERMAJORITY

The initial election of Erdoğan and the Islamist AKP party in a coalition government in 2003 occurred against a fraught historical backdrop characterized by fundamental uncertainties about the limits of Turkish democracy. Would the AKP challenge the secularist military and political elite that had dominated Turkey since its formation as a national state under Ataturk? Six years earlier, in fact, the military had forced the resignation of Islamist Prime Minister Necmettin Erbakan, and it yielded only reluctantly to EU pressure to accept Erdoğan's coalition victory.

However, Erdoğan's ability to face down his opponents and rise to political dominance rested on economic foundations that bore a close resemblance to the developments that carried Chávez and Putin to power. A decade of political and economic instability during the 1990s, and a severe financial crisis in 2000 and 2001 provided the political opening. The crisis, and an unpopular IMF austerity program that followed, led to a crushing defeat of the incumbent government and a victory for an AKP-led coalition in 2002. The economy then turned around quickly, and the AKP was able to claim credit. In 2001, GDP contracted by almost 6 percent, but annual growth under the AKP government averaged almost 6.8 percent between 2002 and 2008. The euro crisis hit Turkey hard in 2008 and 2009, but the economy again bounced back rapidly, growing 9.2 and 8.5 percent in 2010 and 2011.

As in Venezuela and Russia, economic recovery had a strong impact at the polls; riding the boom, the AKP was able to shed its coalition partners and form a government on its own. Its vote share increased from 34.3 in 2002 to 46.6 in the 2007 parliamentary elections, and to close to 50 percent in 2011. With representational biases toward the largest party, these pluralities translated into outsized majorities of 60 percent of the parliamentary seats. Electoral support drew on religious conservative sentiment that had suffered discrimination under secularist rule, but it also ranged across the class spectrum: from Anatolian business groups to the rural and urban poor, who were the targets of traditional vote-buying practices and increasingly generous social programs.[72] The mirror image of this process was the marginalization of the principal opposition party, the CHP, which drew support from secular liberals and Kemalist groups.

PRAETORIAN POLITICS AND WEAK INSTITUTIONALIZATION

Prior to Erdoğan's rise, Turkish politics—although democratic—was still characterized by several deep institutional uncertainties. The Turkish military had long positioned itself as a defender of Kemalist secular values, and even after the withdrawal of the military dictatorship in 1983, it sought to maintain a veto power over political competition. In the aftermath of Erdoğan's election in 2003, continuing struggles between the civilian government and the "deep state" of military and bureaucratic elites exposed fundamental elements of the constitutional framework to bitter contestation.

These constitutional conflicts came to a head in 2007 and 2008 around the efforts of the AKP to both strengthen and control the indirectly elected presidency. With the AKP's supermajority in parliament, Erdoğan appeared to believe that his choice for the position was a foregone conclusion. But—ironically—the weakening of military checks on the government actually increased concern among secularists that the AKP was accreting too much power at the center that would be used to advance Islamist policies. In response to a parliamentary stalemate over the selection of Erdoğan ally Abdullah Gül, for the presidency, the prime

[72] Öniş 2013: 116.

minister called new parliamentary elections and placed a constitutional referendum on the ballot providing for direct election of the president. Despite mass mobilization by secular groups in April and May 2007, both votes resulted in sweeping victories for the AKP.

In the meantime, rumored coup plots and ongoing conflicts with the Kurdish insurgency offered Erdoğan the opportunity to organize a wave of arrests and trials that swept up unrelated journalists, bureaucrats, and other military officers. Throughout these conflicts and later ones over constitutional reform, Erdoğan repeatedly made majoritarian arguments to justify his actions, including open criticism of the Constitutional Court.

As in the other cases, the press was the target of executive pressure brought to bear both through new legislation—such as the 2006 antiterrorism law—and through the exercise of executive discretion. As in Russia, the largest media group in the country was investigated for tax irregularities and hit with unusual fines. Lest there be any doubt about the intent, other media outlets were also warned about the risks of editorials critical of the government. As in Venezuela, the purges of the military allowed Erdoğan to appoint their successors, as well as political allies to the National Security Council. The victory over the military, however, came at the price of increasing politicization of the judiciary and greater polarization between the AKP and secularists over constitutional issues.

Ultimately, these conflicts cleared the way for increasing concentration of power in the hands of Erdoğan and the AKP leadership. Following the controversy over the presidency, the prime minister embarked on a revision of the constitution—including measures that would weaken the Constitutional Court and Supreme Board of Judges and Prosecutors, crucial horizontal checks—and pushed them through in a referendum that also would establish direct presidential elections in 2010. Again making strongly majoritarian appeals, Erdoğan and the AKP won with over 70 percent of the vote. In 2014, Erdoğan himself won the first presidential election, permitting a significant increase in his personal power, mirroring the way in which Putin retained dominant personal influence while changing institutional roles. As of this writing, Erdoğan has not gone as far as Chávez or Putin in consolidating personal power. Nonetheless, the case exhibits a number of parallels. During the preceding decade, the ruling party's unilateral control of the government enabled Erdoğan to increase pressure on the judiciary, the press, and opposition in response to charges of abuse of power and corruption. In 2013, he responded to antigovernment protests over crony capitalism with police repression. Five protesters were killed, over 8,000 injured, and nearly 5,000 detained. Intra-elite conflicts were also on full display.

In 2014, Erdoğan assumed the presidency in a context of a severely weakened opposition and continuing disputes over constitutional limits on executive power. His bid to expand the power of his presidential office suffered a temporary setback with the loss of the AKP's legislative majority in the 2015 parliamentary elections. But throughout the post-constitutional period, Erdoğan was able to maintain support against a fragmented field of opponents, even in the face of a leveling of economic performance. The failure of the opposition to coalesce into a governing alternative inadvertently shifted the balance of decision-making power to the president and in elections later in 2015 the AKP exploited popular fears of terrorism and its control over the media to increase its share of the popular vote by 9 percent, once again permitting it to rule without coalition partners.

As is the case with the oil states, neither Europe nor the United States was in a good position to constrain Erdoğan's backsliding. The evident failure of Turkey's candidacy for EU membership in the mid-2000s removed a strong incentive for democratic reform, and the EU's prolonged recession increased skepticism about the economic value of links to Europe. Such considerations encourage a "pivot" from ties to Europe to a focus on the Middle East. By 2015, Turkey was still at the threshold between democracy and competitive authoritarianism, but international constraints appeared less and less likely to be able to tip the balance.

CONCLUSION

In this chapter, we have extended our effort to assess our "weak democracy" theory of reversion alongside the expectations of modernization approaches. In Chapter 7, we sought to show that although the failure of democracy in low-income countries comports broadly with the structural claims of modernization theories, the reversions can ultimately be traced to identifiable political, institutional, and economic pathways: praetorian histories, weak institutionalization, and, at least in most cases we considered, economic stagnation or crisis.[73] We did not seek to untangle the underlying endogeneity between level of development and these proximate political parameters. But any complete theory needs to provide an account of the mechanisms that lead to military intervention and backsliding; level of development is simply too blunt an instrument to provide these causal links.

In the current chapter, we have focused on low-income democracies that survived, and middle-income countries that—despite the advantages of higher levels of per capita income—slid back to authoritarian rule. In both instances, we find that differences in praetorianism, institutional strength,

---

[73]The South Asian cases of Pakistan and Bangladesh are the most striking exceptions to this generalization.

and economic performance—the main components of the weak democracy syndrome—made an important difference.

We showed in the first part of the chapter that the low-income survivors tended to differ from reverters on all three of the political characteristics we identified as salient. In general, low-income survivors enjoyed better luck at avoiding crises, or made difficult choices that had positive effects over the long run. Their less successful counterparts were more likely to struggle economically, which undermined support for their democratic systems.

Perhaps even more important, political actors in surviving democracies were relatively more successful at overcoming the security dilemmas described in Chapter 6. In the reversion cases, militaries and incumbents could not or would not commit to limits on the bounds of political competition, and oppositions responded accordingly, also resorting to extra-constitutional tactics. The survivors, by contrast, were characterized by increasing restraint on the part of both militaries and incumbents, the ultimate source of coups and backsliding reversions. Over time, regimes in the survivor cases tended to become more institutionalized: expectations increasingly converged around the perception that democracy was "the only game in town" and contending parties increasingly signaled that they were willing to accept the risks of political defeat and exit from office.

Such decisions do not take place in a political vacuum; they depend both on prior institutional choices and ultimately on organized social forces that can act as checks. It may seem circular to say that coups breed coups and democracy breeds democracy. But the apparent tautology dissipates if we think of political systems resting on expectations and understand the consolidation of democratic rule as a process of more gradual but tectonic institutional change.[74]

Elections and turnover of government are the absolute minimum conditions for defining a democracy. For that reason, we used the example of term limits as one potentially powerful institutional lever. Term limits, however, do not restrain on their own. They have wider effects by creating new centers of institutional power and through their signaling effects vis-à-vis organized political and social forces. A variety of other "small" institutional changes, from electoral commissions to central banks, audit bodies, and corruption commissions, can have similar effects. These institutions are likely to be effective, however, only if they are accompanied by strong social checks on political power: through opposition parties, interest groups, NGOs, and the threat of contentious politics and mass mobilization.

Reversions in the middle-income countries that we discussed in the second part of this chapter reflected economic, institutional, and political

[74]Mahoney and Thelen 2010.

trends that moved in the opposite direction. First, like democratic failures in the low-income countries, support for the political regime was undermined in each case by deep recessions and/or prolonged periods of economic stagnation. Political and economic crisis conditions, in turn, provided opportunities for challengers to enter the political system riding broad waves of disaffection and to argue for expanded powers.

Second, although only Turkey had a history of military praetorianism, the military in Venezuela also became increasingly politicized as tensions among the major political actors grew increasingly severe.

Finally, the reversions underscore the dangers that majoritarian governments can pose to democratic rule by both weakening of institutions and social checks on incumbents. Competitive pressures and political fragmentation, to be sure, can impede effective and coherent governance. The principal source of the middle-income failures, however, was the absence of checks on overweening executives and the slide toward rubber-stamp legislatures, subservient judiciaries, and security forces deployed ultimately for political ends.

It should be emphasized that the vast majority of middle-income countries have remained democratic. It is also important to emphasize that neither the Chávez model nor the Putin model is fully consolidated, and the outcome of Erdoğan's bid for power is far from clear. Indeed, given their personalist features, it may be difficult for such models to become fully institutionalized at all. Erdoğan was shaken in Turkey by defeats in the legislative elections of 2015. And the rapid decline in the price of oil in 2014–15 has impeded the ability of Putin's and Chávez's successors to sustain bases of domestic support.

Whatever the eventual fate of these regimes, however, there is little doubt that they have had adverse effects beyond their own borders. In Latin America, Chávez's brand of authoritarian populism materially and ideologically encouraged similar developments in a number of other low-income Latin American countries, including Ecuador, Bolivia, and Nicaragua. Putin's grab for power has also attracted admirers in the postsocialist democracies, and not only in the post-Soviet space, but in cases such as Hungary, Bulgaria, and Greece as well.[75] We take up this problem of authoritarian diffusion in more detail in the Conclusion.

---

[75]Hungary, in recent years, has also indicated cause for concern. As a recent Freedom House report states, "Hungary's multiyear decline . . . remains the most poignant reminder that democratization in post-communist Europe is neither complete nor irreversible . . . any further deterioration in governance, electoral process, media freedom, civil society, judicial independence or corruption . . . will expel Hungary from the category of 'consolidated democratic regimes'" (Habdank-Kołaczkowska 2014).

Conclusion

WHITHER DEMOCRACY?

WE HAVE ENGAGED PREVALENT STRUCTURAL APPROACHES to democratization—including modernization and distributive conflict theories—by testing them against the rich experience of the Third Wave. The transitions to democracy that constituted this "wave" marked a fundamental expansion of opportunities for people around the world to exercise political rights and hold their leaders accountable. But the political changes of those decades also included a number of reversions and increasing evidence of the resilience of authoritarian rule, including its competitive authoritarian variant. In this conclusion, we reiterate our findings and focus on their relevance for the period since 2008, the year our dataset ends, and looking forward.

It was around 2008 that the Third Wave crested. Transitions slowed, the number of democracies flattened, and backsliding and outright reversions increased. The events of the Arab Spring hit like a cold shower, an unpleasant reminder that not all pushes for democracy—including those driven by mass protest—end in success. The slowdown in the pace of democratic change demonstrated not only the durability of "hard" authoritarian regimes but the apparent stability of competitive authoritarian rule as well: authoritarian regimes with democratic façades. Far from a transitional form, the number of these intermediate regimes proved surprisingly stable from 1990 through the mid-2010s. Was a study of the Third Wave looking in a rearview mirror?

We focus our analysis of democratic progress and stagnation around four more specific questions posed in this book. The first was the extent to which transitions to and from democracy could be explained by structural factors, including level of development and inequality. Our findings on this issue were generally negative, particularly on the effects of inequality on regime change. Level of development did not affect the incidence of transitions in our sample. And although level of development did have a statistically significant effect on the likelihood of reversions, anomalies abounded and the political factors we associated with the weak democracy syndrome also appeared in play. The findings on inequality were less ambiguous, with inequality not appearing to play a role in either transitions or reversions. Our conclusions by no means rule out concerns about the possible effects of inequality on the quality of democratic rule. We can imagine a variety of adverse effects that fall short of outright regime collapse, including polarization, corruption, and popular alienation and anomie. But inequality does not appear to be a driving force behind changes in political regime.

Although inequality was not implicated in regime change, however, we did find that distributive conflicts frequently played a role in transitions. A second set of questions was therefore raised as to why some democracies emerged "from below" as a response to mass pressure while others emerged more exclusively "from above" as a result of elite initiatives and bargains. We found that transitions from below—what we called "distributive conflict transitions"—depended on political factors: institutional and political practices of the old regime and the capacity for collective action. At the same time, a high incidence of transitions "from above" forced us to consider altogether different causal pathways, including the reciprocal impact of international factors and elite calculations.

The third question was whether the different paths to democracy had substantive effects. We found some modest evidence that distributive conflict transitions weakened defenders of the old order and increased the accountability of new democratic leaders. Yet these findings deserve closer scrutiny in the face of the Arab Spring and other failed assaults on authoritarian rule. Not only can mass mobilization fail, generating elite backlashes, it can also polarize society and threaten the integrity of institutionalized political processes. In cases as diverse as Ecuador, the Philippines, and Ukraine, mass mobilizations have driven democratically elected governments from office, with mixed effects on the stability of democratic rule.

Finally, and most important given the ambiguous status of the Third Wave, what makes democracy durable or fragile? How do we account for reversions from democratic rule? Our explanation again differs from those of both modernization and distributive conflict approaches. We again emphasize political and institutional challenges: curbing the military, institutionalizing the rules of the political game, and managing at least adequate economic performance. Our brief accounts of Venezuela, Russia, and Turkey show that these weaknesses are not restricted entirely to poor countries and suggest the risks for backsliding in a broader range of democratic regimes.

Transitions to What? Defining Outcomes

Before addressing these issues, we need first to revisit our definitions of democracy and democratization spelled out in the introduction to this book. These definitions raise both conceptual and methodological questions. Conceptually, we follow the norm in political science by emphasizing the procedural aspects of democracy. Elections are a defining feature, but they are only one dimension of democratic rule, and even the electoral component requires nuance. Electoral democracies require a relatively level playing field and incumbents must surrender office if they lose.[1] But broader definitions of "liberal" democracy also take into account the importance of horizontal checks on executive power, the guarantee of civil and political liberties, and even citizen commitments to democracy as an intrinsic value.[2]

Since the degree to which a given regime satisfies each of these criteria will inevitably vary, the extent to which any case rises above a minimum democratic threshold is a function of coding rules that are subject to both conceptual and empirical contestation. The challenge of identifying "transitions to democracy" is particularly acute in analyzing the Third Wave, in which a large number of new regimes occupy a "gray zone"[3] in which the line can be extremely thin between a democracy "with imperfections" and a regime that is still fundamentally authoritarian but tolerates a limited competition.

Such problems might conceivably be solved in part by seeing democracy as a continuous variable and looking at changes in the *level* of democracy—something akin to liberalization—as the principal dimension of interest.[4] We, however, left this route to others because of our concern that such an approach would not adequately capture the fundamental institutional changes that we sought to explain. In any case, moreover, it is not clear that this approach is actually able to sidestep the problem of thresholds. An increase of 3 points in a Polity score obviously need not comport with a transition to democratic rule. Nor did we believe similar changes in the level of democracy would necessarily have common explanations. Did we really believe, for example, that a shift in the Polity score from -10 to -7 was likely to result from the same causal factors that moved it from 7 to 10? Despite the advantages of continuous variables, we think and speak in terms of thresholds: regimes meet some minimum standard that distinguishes them as democracies or they don't. We believe these qualitative differences, however imperfect they are, should be reflected in empirical research.

To ensure complementarity with existing quantitative research and internal consistency, we defined democracy through reference to two datasets that have figured prominently in empirical work on democratization, CGV and Polity. Each reflects subtle and not-so-subtle differences in the very definition of the concept. The CGV dataset is based strictly on a largely electoral and turnover-oriented conception of democracy, and is

---

[1] Levitsky and Way 2010.

[2] On horizontal checks on executive power, see Schedler 1999. On citizen commitments to democracy, see Diamond 2009.

[3] Carothers 2002.

[4] For example, Teorell 2010; Acemoglu et al. 2013.

purposefully categorical; although it captures important political changes, it often includes democracies in the "gray zone" that would fall well short of the criteria for liberal democracy. Polity provides a linear measure that incorporates a wider array of institutional features we associate with democratic rule, including checks on executive discretion, the extent of political competition, and, more indirectly, protection of political liberties.

Notwithstanding these differences, the two datasets—particularly if viewed in tandem—provided a useful basis for our assessment of the determinants of regime change. As just noted, the minimalist CGV index was more likely than the Polity to overestimate the extent of democratic change. But in its emphasis on the shift to relatively competitive elections and government turnover, it also captured limited but normatively meaningful changes that would not register in analyses that established more demanding thresholds. Moreover, the CGV and Polity measures yielded similar results on many—although not all—of the questions of interest to us. Yet the exercise of establishing a baseline for measurement, including the manifest differences between the datasets, is a reminder that any such endeavor depends strongly on what is being explained. More or less demanding conceptions of regime change—including those posed by advocates of a more stringent "liberal" conception of democracy[5]—might well yield different findings.

What Is the Role of Inequality and Distributive Conflict in the Emergence of Democratic Rule?

One important finding of this study, as noted, is a negative one. Contrary to views closely linked to the contemporary modernization literature, we find no systematic relation between levels of inequality, distributive conflict, and democratic transitions (or reversions, to which we return below). Our conclusion is based not only on the absence of a statistical correlation, but also on a methodological innovation: the use of focused causal process observation to assess the incidence and impact of distributive conflict across all of the regime transitions identified in the statistical analysis. Although we did find that a substantial number of transitions were driven, at least in part, by distributive conflict, there was little evidence that these protests were systematically driven by differences in the concentration of assets and income.

We cannot, however, definitively dismiss the claim that inequality affects democratization. Several lines of research might modify or even re-

[5] For example, Diamond 2009.

verse our findings, including more work on the income distribution data itself. Standard measures of the income and asset distribution—Gini coefficients and land concentration indices—have well-known problems of comparability and reliability and do not necessarily correspond with politically salient cleavages. Measures constructed from the distribution of manufacturing income, which we also used in our statistical analysis, are vulnerable to similar critiques, depending on how politics and society are structured in specific societies. A gross measure like a Gini does not capture inequalities that are well recognized and politically salient—for example, between landlords and peasants or urban capitalists and workers—or might reflect class cleavages in which such conflicts are much less clear. For example, significant components of the social structure in developing countries—such as the informal sector—are both undertheorized and understudied with respect to their political preferences and behavior.[6]

We have also only begun to tap the spatial or ethnic dimensions of inequality, which are emerging as promising frontiers in the study of civil conflict.[7] Could regional inequalities—particularly those that overlap with horizontal inequalities between ethnic groups—also play a role in transitions to and from democratic rule?[8] For example, regional inequalities played a significant role in the political polarization in Thailand that contributed to the breakdown of democratic rule. Regional cleavages are an ongoing political issue in countries as diverse as Ukraine, Kenya, and Sri Lanka, where they overlapped with interethnic inequalities.

The effects of inequality should also be examined in a more dynamic context. Given the limits on the data, we generally focused on levels of inequality rather than changes in it.[9] It is possible that further refinements might permit more credible tests of the effects of improvements or deteriorations in the distribution of income or cognate factors, such as social mobility. A long intellectual tradition suggests that movements in relative incomes may be more destabilizing than inequalities that are enduring but constant.[10]

Finally, the absence of a connection between objective measures of inequality and democratic transitions does not rule out the importance of a complex universe of perceptual and cognitive factors that have now received sustained study in both political science and behavioral economics,

[6] Haggard, Kaufman, and Long 2013.
[7] Stewart 2000; Ostby 2007; Cederman, Gleditsch, and Buhaug 2013.
[8] Horowitz 1985.
[9] Although fixed effects specifications effectively captured changes in inequality, we are skeptical that the quality of the data merits placing too much emphasis on these findings one way or the other.
[10] Hirschman and Rothschild 1973.

ding through surveys and both field and laboratory experiments.
_ _ is significant evidence that citizens are largely unaware of the
level of inequality or even their position in the distribution of income,[11]
and there is an ample literature that generally finds a surprisingly weak
connection between class position and preferences for redistribution.[12]
But survey evidence also shows that *perceptions* of inequality do affect
distributive preferences,[13] and experimental research indicates that people will reject offers they deem unfair.[14] We cannot reject the possibility
that perceptions of inequality and unfairness are indeed a powerful motivating force behind the rejection of institutions that sustain the distributional status quo and could be a driving force in changes in political
regimes. Indeed, we suggested as much in our finding that highly repressive authoritarian regimes are more likely to fall as a result of distributive
conflict.

Short of a revolution in the data, we suspect that the most likely path
forward is to delve more deeply into the conditions under which inequality and perceptions of inequality might matter, which is where current
research is now moving.[15] We generally steered away from such conditional approaches in favor of simplicity and a focus on the determinants
of different transition paths, but we can imagine a host of candidates that
might trigger an "inequality effect." These include the presence of economic crises, strong left parties, or insurgencies. Inequality is clearly an
important feature of social life, but its effect on complex institutional developments such as changes in political regime is likely to be conditional
at best.

SO WHAT DOES EXPLAIN TRANSITIONS TO DEMOCRATIC RULE?

It is one thing to reject someone else's theory; it is quite another to pose
a compelling alternative. We found quickly, however, that an overarching
theory of transitions may be a chimera because of the fact that transition
processes varied in significant ways. The identification of distributive conflict and elite-led transitions forced us to take seriously the "many path-

[11] Gimpelson and Treisman 2015.
[12] Svallfors 1997; Benabou and Ok 2001; Finseraas 2008; Alesina and Giuliano 2009;
De La O and Rodden 2008; Cramer and Kaufman 2010; Haggard, Kaufman, and Long
2013.
[13] Gimpelson and Treisman 2015.
[14] Kahneman, Knetsch, and Thaler 1986; Rabin 1993; Fehr and Schmidt 1999; Henrich
et al. 2004.
[15] Freeman and Quinn 2012; Houle 2015.

ways, many endpoints" injunction that characterized earlier generations of scholarship on the Third Wave.[16] Of course, complex typologies can proliferate to the point of yielding only idiographic accounts. But our research leads to the conclusion that the greatest analytical gains are most likely to come through modeling different transition pathways. Transitions driven by distributive demands are not likely to be driven by the same factors as those in which elite-mass conflicts were absent.

Distributive Conflict Transitions: Authoritarian Institutions and Collective Action

Our accounts of both types of transition focus less on longer-term structural factors—levels of development or concentration of wealth—than on the high drama of politics that these transitions appear to reflect. In cases where protest from below was a proximate cause, we argued that both the nature of the authoritarian regime and the organizational resources of civil society groups played an important role in incentivizing and enabling mass groups to turn out in the streets, forcing authoritarian exit. Exclusionary and repressive regimes were found more likely to generate mass protest, suggesting another source of grievance from those emphasized in distributive conflict models. We also found that unions or other ethnic and civil-society organizations were pivotal in overcoming barriers to collective action, raising questions about the role such organizations may play in the future of authoritarian rule.

In our datasets, the trend toward distributive conflict transitions was not altogether straightforward, appearing to increase over time in the Polity dataset, but not among the CGV cases. However, new research by Kendall-Taylor and Frantz on how autocrats exit office suggests a much more definitive trend. Their definition of "mass led exits" includes both revolts and civil wars and is more permissive than ours as it is not tied to distributive conflict models.[17] Nonetheless, in the 1950s, only about 5 percent of autocratic exits were from revolts or civil wars. In the 2000s it had doubled to 10 percent and by the 2010s had leapt to over 35 percent. Most commentary on the Arab Spring has focused on the limited successes of democratic challengers: except for the brief democratic moment in Egypt, the only real successful case was Tunisia. But if there is a relationship between long-run growth, globalization, and the deepening of civil society, we are likely to see more, not fewer, challenges to autocrats coming from below.

[16] O'Donnell, Schmitter, and Whitehead 1986c; Collier 1999.
[17] Kendall-Taylor and Frantz 2014. See also Pion-Berlin, Esparza, and Grisham 2014.

In considering the role of social organization, we also engaged a literature of long-standing on "prairie fire"—or more technically, information-cascade—models of protest.[18] These models emphasize the significance of small—even random—triggers, and the centrality of individual choice over elite leadership of mass mobilization. We expressed skepticism. Protest can appear spontaneous, triggered by apparently small events that snowball. Our causal process observation of cases found repeatedly, however, that organizations mattered: by turning out their members, coordinating otherwise decentralized loci of mobilization, and articulating demands for regime change. Moreover, there are strong theoretical reasons to believe that prairie fire protests and mobilizations may prove fickle. If incumbent authoritarians believe that protests are ephemeral, why not gamble on co-ercion or transitory concessions to wait them out?

Looking forward, however, it is important to acknowledge that our sample includes numerous cases that predated altogether the dramatic growth in cell phone penetration and the explosion of social media in developing countries. In the wake of the failed Green Revolution in Iran in 2009 and the Arab Spring of 2010–11, an exciting new literature has emerged on the extent to which these protests were elite or mass led and to what extent social media played a catalyzing role. Advocates of the importance of social media claim that these platforms shaped substantive debates over politics, led—rather than followed—mass mobilization, and also contributed to the international diffusion of protest across borders.[19] Moreover social media allow for incredibly detailed micro-level work on the location, content, and timing of online communications, from viral videos to cell phone traffic, from Facebook posts to Tweets.[20]

It is important to underscore that this literature is appropriately cautious, noting that new means of communication are only a partial substitute for enduring organization and are best seen as a complement to it: a means for organizations to overcome communication problems posed by dictatorships. Moreover, the success of such communication will depend on state capacity to dampen it—as the Chinese case shows clearly—and the willingness of authoritarian incumbents to resort to physical coercion to overcome the technological advantages these media generate for op-positions. It bears repeating that of the many Middle Eastern cases where the effects of media have been explored, only Tunisia saw an enduring transition to democratic rule. Nonetheless, technological change might

---

[18]Kuran 1989; Lohmann 1994.

[19]For example, Howard 2011; Howard et al. 2011; Aday et al. 2012; Tufekci and Free-lon 2013; Gunning and Baron 2014.

[20]For example, Pierskalla and Hollenbach 2013 on cell phones; Tufekci and Wilson 2012 on social media in the Arab Spring; Earl et al. 2013 on Twitter.

well alter the balance of power between elites and masses to the benefit of the former precisely through its effect on organizational capabilities, and this topic is likely to remain an enduring research program for years to come.

Elite-Driven Transitions: The International Dimension, and Elite Calculations and Processes

Even if there are debates about whether protest is generated through organizations or is spontaneous, it is clear that transitions to democratic rule can come from above as well as below. Indeed, roughly half of our sample of transitions during the 1980 to 2008 period occurred in the absence of pressures from below. We therefore need to understand the incentives— the games—that operate in the absence of an elite-mass dynamic.

International factors are clearly more likely to play a role in these cases. We review a dense literature on international influences in Chapter 4, but began with the big picture: that fundamental changes in the international system during the Third Wave proved highly consequential for the survival of dictatorship. These included the collapse of multinational empires in the Soviet Union and Yugoslavia, the profound effects these events had on alliances with authoritarian regimes elsewhere, and the propensity to provide assistance to clients previously supported largely for geostrategic reasons. We also noted the role that international institutions, democracy promotion, and direct intervention played in this process—albeit still debated[21]—and the effects of "neighborhoods." As regions became more densely populated with democracies, institutions and norms evolved and pressures on "holdouts" increased.

The emphasis on international influences, however, is subject to two caveats. The first is related to what might be called "the end of the end of history." The triumphalism of the early post–Cold War period did not last long, and we are clearly entering a period in which the diplomatic reach of the advanced industrial democracies—and the United States in particular—is increasingly circumscribed. Virtually all of the arguments made above on international institutions, aid, democracy promotion, and neighborhoods can be reversed where powerful authoritarian states exercise influence. Five significant authoritarian regimes—China, Russia, Iran, Saudi Arabia, and Venezuela—pose direct challenges to the development of democracy in their regions and beyond. Institutions, aid, diplomacy, and neighborhood effects from these countries are anything but benign for the future of democracy, and indeed constitute one of our major sources of

---

[21] See, for example, Poast and Urpelainen 2015.

concern. How authoritarianism—as well as democracy—diffuses is likely to be a much more important topic in the future than we had hoped.[22]

Our second caveat is more theoretical than empirical: international factors ultimately operate through the incentives facing domestic political actors and in any case must be tested against such domestic dynamics. In the smallest, most aid-dependent countries, democratization might arise largely as a result of international constraints on authoritarian incumbents. But even in such cases, we have doubts and believe that two-level games are likely in play.

We found at least three ways in which elite politics might lead to democratic outcomes: when intra-elite competition dislodges incumbents in favor of democratization; when rulers calculate (and sometimes miscalculate) that they can compete effectively in a multiparty context; and when incremental changes nudge semicompetitive regimes in a more open direction. All of these routes again raise a question that we have posed repeatedly in this project: Adam Przeworski's puzzlement about why rulers would willingly share—or even cede—power with others.

Several answers suggested themselves apart from pressure from below, and each raises questions about the future of authoritarian rule. Intra-elite conflicts often involved factional disputes within the military about the utility of continued involvement in politics. An important empirical and policy point follows: that the socialization of the military to a more professional role—even in authoritarian or semiauthoritarian countries—might well serve the cause of democratization.

In other cases, we found that authoritarian elites did sometimes lead countries out of authoritarian rule because they thought they themselves could compete effectively in more open settings. In an important contribution, Slater and Wong have noted that single-party or party-dominant systems are more likely to be persuaded of the benefits of democratic rule because of their organizational capacity to compete and even prevail; Taiwan and Mexico provide nonsocialist examples.[23] The big fish in this regard is clearly China, but the dilemma is clear: the advantages that such single or dominant parties may have in a more open political setting also give them advantages in maintaining authoritarian rule. Why take risks? Among those that did, we found that incumbents frequently miscalculated their ability to survive in power, not only in the longer run (both Taiwan and Mexico) but in the short run as well (for example, Kaunda in Zambia).

What we called institutional transitions revealed a similar point, but may hold forth more promise than "big bang" democratizations from

---

[22] Whitehead 2015.
[23] Slater and Wong 2013.

above. In these transitions, authoritarian elites could, through incremental changes, abide by commitments they themselves had made, which moved systems in a more open direction. These cases hold some important and less pessimistic lessons. The literature on competitive authoritarianism has rightly focused on the fact that these regimes may prove more stable than we think: that they can constitute a political equilibrium of their own, and not just a way station on the route to democracy.[24] However, our findings suggest that competitive authoritarian regimes exhibit evidence of a number of related endogenous political processes that might lead to their demise, including intra-elite conflicts, gambles on more democratic futures, and the uncertainty—and surprises—of even stage-managed elections. As we will see, these gambles relate directly to the question of how transition paths might matter.

THE QUALITY OF DEMOCRACY: DO TRANSITION PATHS MATTER?

From the moment we first made the observation about the substantial number of elite-led transitions,[25] colleagues have challenged us with the proverbial "so what?" question.[26] An earlier generation of research had tried to track down the differences between pacted and non-pacted transitions and other "transitions with adjectives"[27] and made surprisingly little headway; the research program was not picked up, and to the extent it was, doubts surfaced quickly about the value of such distinctions.[28]

We pursued this question in Chapter 5 and argued that transitions from below appear to have, at least at the margins, a favorable impact on political rights and democratic procedures, both in terms of the immediate quality of the transition and over the longer term. We hypothesized that mass mobilization might weaken rulers' control over coercive resources, preclude institutional "lock-ins" of reserve domains of autocratic power, and—more generally—remind incumbents that they are vulnerable to a resurgence of protest. We can get to the same results by considering the prospects for democracy in the elite-led transitions explored in Chapter 4. Displacement, preemptive democratization, and institutional transitions are all more likely to leave incumbents and their elite allies with influence, and in some cases even allow them to remain in power. Such

---

[24] Levitsky and Way 2010.

[25] Haggard and Kaufman 2012.

[26] We made a similar kind of argument in *The Political Economy of Democratic Transitions* (Haggard and Kaufman 1995): that "crisis" transitions had different effects from "non-crisis" ones.

[27] Collier and Levitsky 1997.

[28] Carothers 2002; Diamond et al. 2014.

systems may thus exhibit greater continuity with the authoritarian status quo ante than their distributive conflict counterparts.

Although these findings are suggestive, we acknowledge that more than any other findings in the book, more research is needed to tease out—and hopefully resolve—possible endogeneity problems. As we showed in Chapter 3, mass challenges to authoritarian rule depend in part on the longer-standing ability of social forces to overcome problems of collective action. It may not be the short-run dynamics of the transition that matter, but the longer-run nature and depth of civil society and its capacity to organize. Our analysis in Chapter 5 distinguished between these stories through quantitative controls, but primarily through paired qualitative comparisons. We stop short, however, of offering a definitive answer with respect to causal effects.

Whatever role transition paths may play in the quality and durability of democracy, civil society provides important extrainstitutional checks against executive overreach. If Kendall-Taylor and Frantz are correct and more and more authoritarian regimes exit through a distributive conflict path, then it behooves us to think more clearly about the implications, particularly where such movements falter and reverse as they did in the Arab Spring.[29] Mobilization may lead to a clean pro- and antiregime divide, but there is clearly a downside risk of polarization and backlash. The implications can be especially disappointing if authoritarian elites maintain adequate political control of coercive resources to simply suppress mass challenges.

We are also aware of the fine line between the checks that mass mobilization might yield and the risks that democracy is degraded by repeated resort to extraconstitutional as opposed to electoral or legislative means of managing political failures. The Philippines, Ecuador, and Ukraine all provide examples. Ferdinand Marcos was ousted by a mass "people power" movement reflecting a wide social coalition. Less than 15 years later, "People Power II" ousted a democratically elected president, "Erap" Estrada. The case could be argued on its merits, given the manifest corruption and incompetence on display. But "People Power II" was not the end, and Estrada's successor also had to face down social movements that sought to displace her. In Ecuador, massive protests in the late 1990s and early 2000s forced three successive presidents to resign from office. Although constitutional formalities generally guided the choice of successors, the democratic regime was clearly troubled; in fact, a faction of the military did briefly take control of the presidential palace for about 24 hours in January 2000. The protests that drove Ukraine's president Yanukovych from office in 2014 preserved a democratic regime in the west-

[29]Kendall-Taylor and Frantz 2014.

ern region of the country but also triggered a Russian-backed insurgency, outright intervention, and a loss of control over the Crimea and large swathes of the eastern region.

A second set of questions returns us more immediately to the theoretical tradition we sought to engage. If democracy is motivated by distributional pressures, then an important and obvious test would be to consider whether transitions driven by distributive conflict generate more redistribution; a positive finding might help salvage class conflict approaches. We are skeptical, however, as the evidence with respect to the propensity of new democracies to redistribute remains contested, the assumptions of Meltzer and Richard notwithstanding.[30] As with other claims in this vein, the answers are likely to be conditional on how left parties and civil society evolve in the aftermath of the democratic transition. Moreover, these developments may be slow-moving and thus more distal from transition paths. In Chapter 2 we noted how the interests of politicians and publics can diverge in the aftermath of distributive conflict transitions. Huber and Stephens find that it can take as long as 20 years for the progressive features of democratic rule to yield significant changes in patterns of redistribution.[31] We suspect that while distributive conflict is likely to have positive effects with respect to political accountability, the links to distributive politics are subject to a range of mediations.

WHAT SUSTAINS DEMOCRATIC RULE?

We close with what are, in many ways, the most important and pressing of questions: What determines the stability of democratic rule? Are we entering a phase in which democracy has either reached limits or is proving more fragile?[32] And if so, why?

To address this issue, it is important to revisit the overall trends that have occurred since the onset of the Third Wave, but also some particular developments from 2008 through 2015. As we noted above, the number of democracies in the world increased at a steady pace over the 1980s, accelerated dramatically between 1988 and 1992, and continued to rise at a somewhat slower pace through about 2008. But developments since 2008 have changed our picture of the Third Wave in important ways:

---

[30]Haggard and Kaufman 2008; Rudra 2008; Albertus and Menaldo 2014; Huber and Stephens 2012; Slater, Smith, and Nair 2014.

[31]Huber and Stephens 2012.

[32]Zakaria 2003; Diamond 2008; Economist Intelligence Unit 2010, 2013; Freedom House 2013, 2014a; Plattner 2014; Kurlantzick 2014.

- The number of democracies has clearly plateaued, and conversely, the number of autocracies has also bottomed out and is no longer falling.
- Related to this, the number of "competitive authoritarian" regimes, or anocracies in Polity usage, has held roughly constant over the entire 1990 to 2014 period, even if their share of all regimes has fallen somewhat. Competitive authoritarianism is clearly an enduring form.[33]
- There has been somewhat more churning in the post-2000 period, with a rising net number of democracies masking an increase in the number of reversions in both the Polity and Freedom House datasets. As we noted in Chapter 6, some reversions in our sample proved in hindsight to be way stations in longer transitional processes; the aggregates can hide this more hopeful possibility. Nonetheless, we have an ample number of cases that reverted and did not return to democratic rule.
- And finally, as we outlined in Chapter 8, Freedom House measures have shown a deterioration in political rights and civil liberties, even in countries that have not undergone outright reversions to authoritarian rule. The fate of democracy is a question of its vulnerability not only to outright reversal but to more subtle erosion as well.

How are we to understand this more reserved portrait of the Third Wave? Several explanations present themselves, starting with the "law of asymptotes." As the number of democracies increases, the number of remaining cases that are even theoretically available for democratization shrinks. We have only indirectly addressed the question of what to make of the significant number of countries that remained authoritarian over the entire period.[34] Naturally, the cases left in this group of potential democratizers are—virtually by definition—those in which authoritarian rule is strongly entrenched and the structural conditions conducive to democracy are lacking. The Middle East and former Soviet Union remain among the most impervious to democratic trends, although because of the large number of countries on the African continent it is strongly represented among the difficult cases as well. Particularly in the Middle East, most movements for democratic rule collapsed in the face of ruthless autocratic responses. Others descended into civil war and complete state

[33] Levitsky and Way 2010.
[34] The following countries were consistently nondemocratic using the Polity metric: in Latin America, Cuba; among the postsocialist states, Bosnia, Georgia, Azerbaijan, Turkmenistan, Tajikistan, Uzbekistan, and Kazakhstan; in Africa, Equatorial Guinea, Gambia, Guinea, Burkina Faso, Togo, Cameroon, Gabon, Chad, Democratic Republic of the Congo, Tanzania, Rwanda, Somalia, Djibouti, Eritrea, Angola, Mozambique, Zambia, Zimbabwe, Swaziland; in North Africa and the Middle East, Morocco, Algeria, Tunisia, Libya, Iran, Iraq, Egypt, Syria, Lebanon, Jordan, Saudi Arabia, Yemen, Kuwait, Bahrain, Qatar, United Arab Emirates, Oman, Afghanistan; in Asia, China, North Korea, Bhutan, Myanmar, Cambodia, Laos, Vietnam, Singapore, Papua New Guinea.

failure. Inverting an important observation by Svolik on democracies, it may be worthwhile to study authoritarian regimes only by first distinguishing between those that are consolidated—in the sense of being relatively invulnerable to democratization—and those that are potentially at risk of democratization.[35]

As with transitions, international factors may play a role in reversions to authoritarian rule as well. In an important contribution, Boix notes that the Third Wave overlapped with a period of Western, and particularly American, triumphalism.[36] But during the late 2000s, the distribution of power shifted.[37] China continued to rise, Russia drew increasingly inward, while both the United States and Europe fell into economic crisis. The international system not only became more multipolar, but a number of new authoritarian powers asserted themselves in regional settings where they may have produced "contagion in reverse." These included the Cuba-Chavista-populist authoritarian model in Latin America (Ecuador, Bolivia, Nicaragua); Iran in the Middle East, playing a destabilizing role with respect to democracy or its prospects in Lebanon, Iraq, Syria, and Yemen; Saudi Arabia's support for Salafist political as well as religious models across the globe; Russia, with its effort to extend its influence not only in the former Soviet Union, but in Eastern Europe as well; and the ongoing question of whether China's global economic reach might have adverse effects on politics through direct connections such as aid or through the presentation of a developmental authoritarian state model.[38]

Whatever the influence of these external factors, the spirit of our inquiry is to always link them back to the domestic political factors that ultimately anchor robust democratic rule. Again, it is important to reiterate several significant negative results of our research. Although level of development did prove a significant headwind to democratic consolidation in some of our econometric models, we found numerous anomalies in the form of low-income survivors. We do not find that inequality rendered new democracies more vulnerable to reversion.

Equally important for our purposes was the fact that only a small percentage of reversions occurred—at any level of inequality—as a result of elite fears of progressive democratic forces. Indeed, all but a few reversions occurred under new and poorly institutionalized democratic systems with little realistic capacity for redistribution.[39] In a large majority of cases, as we have seen, democracies in both poor and middle-income countries fail less because of class divisions than because of an inability

[35] Svolik 2012.
[36] Boix 2011.
[37] Zakaria 2008; Acharya 2014.
[38] For example, Ramo 2004; Halper 2010.
[39] Slater, Smith, and Nair 2014.

to withstand destructive rivalries among civilian and military elites, and because they are unable to deliver material benefits to their populations.

This is not to say that inequality has no effect on democratic rule. Money can pervert the functioning of democratic regimes in myriad ways. In most of the countries we have examined, vote buying and clientelism are facilitated by small middle classes and large pools of poor voters.[40] The concentration of income also increases opportunities for elites to influence electoral outcomes, government institutions, and even mass culture through campaign contributions, direct access to political office, control of cultural and communications institutions, and bribery.[41] The pernicious effects of high inequality are thus an ongoing issue of concern, even though those effects may not extend to outright reversion per se.

As an alternative to distributive conflict explanations of reversion, we focus on a wider array of vulnerabilities that we have labeled a "weak democracy" syndrome. At most, this syndrome was only partially related to underlying patterns of development. Reversions were, to be sure, more likely to occur in poor countries; but a surprising number of low-income democracies survived, and middle-income countries (Thailand, Venezuela, Russia, Turkey, and possibly even Hungary) were not altogether invulnerable to reversion or backsliding that fell just short of it. Instead of focusing on underlying structural factors to explain the instability of democracies, we emphasized more immediate and interrelated political and economic challenges: the threat of military praetorianism, the challenge of strengthening weak political institutions, and the effects of the government's management of the economy.

Military praetorianism has traditionally been a core component of the "weak democracy" syndrome; we found significant quantitative and qualitative evidence of self-reinforcing cycles of military political involvement. Some countries, to be sure, managed to escape this "coup trap," and others—particularly those emerging from one-party communist systems—managed to avoid it entirely. Even so, in countries with prior histories of coups, military officers were less inhibited about challenging civilian authority and had a greater capacity to sustain the cohesion necessary to launch a successful coup.

The good news is that—despite this pattern—the overall incidence of coups has declined in recent decades. This decline can be attributed both to the end of Cold War sponsorship of military regimes, and to anticipated reactions to military reentry into politics, particularly where military regimes manifestly failed to deliver in the past. For the military, these circumstances increase the cost of direct seizures of power relative to the

---

[40] Stokes et al. 2013; Weitz-Shapiro 2012.
[41] Rueschmeyer 2004; Solt, Habel, and Grant 2011.

advantages of professionalization, or at least more circumscribed rent-seeking. But more subtle issues of civilian control and military accountability remain. Beyond the question of transitional justice, which has received considerable attention, there is a host of underresearched ways in which militaries may impede democratic development via means that fall below the radar: the assumption of policing functions in high crime areas, tacit support for civilian militias and death squads, or other means of effectively subverting political rights and civil liberties.

Even in the absence of direct coup threats, democracies remain vulnerable to backsliding as long as adherence to norms of democratic competition is tentative and contingent. "Institutionalization" implies a process in which expectations and behaviors begin to converge around constitutional norms. In weakly institutionalized democracies, actors face a security dilemma. Uncertainty about whether competitors will conform to constitutional norms creates strong incentives for them to hedge their own bets through recourse to extraconstitutional behaviors. With respect to officeholders, these behaviors include exploiting the advantages of incumbency, corruption, and intimidation of the opposition. Significantly, a large number of democratic failures during the Third Wave period arose from the efforts by incumbents to exploit state resources to remain in power: by stacking the electoral deck, reducing horizontal checks, partaking in corruption, and attacking and undermining loyal oppositions. Yet oppositions may not be altogether blameless. The security dilemma we describe can generate opposition activities that are corrosive of democracy as well, including continual resort to contentious politics and even the mobilization of violence.

We also found that government performance matters for the consolidation of democratic rule. Low growth and particularly crises increase the odds of democratic reversals. In many instances, these stem from exogenous shocks—for example, the debt crises of the 1980s and 1990s—which also brought down incumbent authoritarian regimes. Clearly, however, the capacity to deal with these shocks is diminished by the political vulnerabilities discussed above. In weakly institutionalized democracies, perceptions of fecklessness or corruption can quickly shift the target of opposition from incumbent officeholders to the regime itself. Even more established democracies, such as Venezuela, can become "deinstitutionalized" and eventually be undermined by the repeated economic failures of democratic governments and the election of outsiders with autocratic ambitions.

How can these cycles of weak institutionalization and poor performance be broken? We acknowledge that the reasons for democratic stability rest in large measure on historical or structural factors, which—like the initial level of economic development or a history of military subordination to civilian authority—provide clear advantages. But not all democracies are born with these advantages, and some do survive anyway.

In weakly institutionalized regimes, mutual assurance strategies between civilian and military elites are clearly an important component of political stability, and have received a deservedly prominent place in the literature. Attention to the role of pact making goes back at least as far as the seminal work of Rustow, and O'Donnell and Schmitter.[42] There has been considerable debate over the form and efficacy of such pacts. Nonetheless, elite strategies aimed at conciliating opponents and lowering the stakes of losing are clearly an important step toward reducing the domestic security dilemma, even if such assurances alone may not suffice to secure authoritarian acquiescence to democratic rule.[43]

But to emphasize—as O'Donnell and Schmitter do[44]—the role of *fortuna* and *virtu* is to beg the question of the incentives that might shape the propensity to exercise *virtu* in the first place. In Chapter 8, we highlighted two points that appeared to be consistent with evidence from experiences in the Third Wave and invite continued research and debate.

The first is the potential importance of relatively narrow, functionally specific institutional arrangements in encouraging compliance with democratic procedures. As the risk of coups recedes, the arrogation of power by elected executives is emerging as the primary threat to democracy. In this respect, "small" institutions that establish clear rules and procedures aimed at checking executive power can make important contributions to democratic stability. These include term limits, independent electoral commissions, anticorruption agencies, auditors, and enhanced powers of legislative oversight. Such constraints, to be sure, carry a risk of stalemate and immobilism, which can be extraordinarily crippling in periods of economic crisis. In recent decades, however, the major problems arise from executives who are overly strong, rather than ones who are too weak and ineffectual.

We distinguish these types of institutional mechanisms from the broader design of constitutional or electoral systems. In transitional situations, where institutional commitments are still uncertain, the complex web of formal rules codified in these broad designs have consequences that cannot be foreseen ex ante by powerful participants; consequently, they are frequently changed or simply ignored. On the other hand, more discrete and specific institutional rules such as term limits or electoral commissions provide more straightforward benchmarks through which contending groups can signal

[42] Rustow 1970; O'Donnell and Schmitter 1986.

[43] With respect to Egypt, for example, debate persists on whether Morsi failed to provide adequate assurances or whether the military was simply intent on retaining power regardless of what the Muslim Brotherhood did. Springborg 2016.

[44] O'Donnell and Schmitter 1986: 5.

their intentions to each other. In situations where elite buy-in to democratic procedures is contingent and uncertain, adherence offers a clear indication of an intent to abide by the rules of the game; attempts to undermine them raise red flags, in effect focal points for the mobilization of oppositions.

Our second major point follows from the first: the effectiveness of the institutional rules will depend not only on their signaling function, but on the underlying balance of power in civil and political society. In this study, the preponderance of evidence points to the importance of a mobilized civil society as a constraint on decisions made by both political and military elites. We showed in Chapter 5 that regimes emerging via distributive conflict transitions might have an edge in this regard. But strong civil society checks on executive power can also emerge in democracies established "from above" in the wake of the transition. For example, we found that unions—one proxy for civil society organization more generally—directly contributed to a more robust defense of political liberties, regardless of the transition path.

Strong political oppositions typically mobilize support through links to civil society organizations, but they are themselves a crucial component of the underlying balance of power. This is especially important in majoritarian situations in which legislative supermajorities have the effect of undermining democracy itself. Effective party opposition is important not only because it offers a choice to voters; it is the first line of defense against executive attempts to use constitutional procedures to rewrite the rules of the game.

It is important to acknowledge that the effect of the political constraints imposed by civil society and political party opposition is not entirely straightforward. Professionalized NGOs, which usually receive preferred treatment from international funders, may make contributions to public policy, but often lack roots in the societies they purport to represent. More socially rooted civic organizations may have only a limited interest in engaging in democratic politics and may be at times even complicit in abuses of state power.[45] Strong civil society opposition to executive initiatives can also impede economic adjustments that—though painful and unpopular—can be necessary for recovery and growth.

On balance, however, a weak and passive civil society and political opposition poses a far greater threat to the institutionalization of democratic politics than the occasional disruption it brings. Strong civil societies and vigorous political challenges to incumbents reduce the likelihood that the rules of the game will be restricted to "parchment documents." They raise the cost to the military of seeking to control the government,

[45] Carothers and Ottaway 2000.

and increase incentives for them to pursue professional careers outside the political arena. A well-organized, robust, and dynamic civil society is also more likely to hold elected incumbents accountable and to reduce the chances for elite pacts made at the expense of the public. Viewed over the long run, the key to more stable democratic regimes may depend less on institutional design than on the social organizations in which they are nested.

References

Acemoglu, Daron, Suresh Naidu, Pascual Restrepo, and James Robinson. 2013. "Democracy, Public Policy, and Inequality." *Comparative Democratization* 11 (3): 2–20.

Acemoglu, Daron, and James A. Robinson. 2000. "Democratization or Repression?" *European Economics Review* 44 (4–6): 683–93.

———. 2001. "A Theory of Political Transitions." *American Economic Review* 91 (4): 938–63.

———. 2006. *Economic Origins of Dictatorship and Democracy.* New York: Cambridge University Press.

Acharya, Amitav. 2014. *The End of American World Order.* Cambridge: Polity.

Ackerman, Paul, and Jack DuVall. 2000. *A Force More Powerful.* New York: Palgrave Macmillan.

Ackerman, Paul, and Christopher Kruegler. 1994. *Strategic Nonviolent Conflict.* Westport, CT: Praeger.

Aday, Sean, Henry Farrell, Marc Lynch, John Sides, and Deen Freelon. 2012. "Blogs and Bullets: New Media and Conflict After the Arab Spring." Washington, DC: United States Institute of Peace.

Adebajo, Adekeye. 2002. *Building Peace in West Africa: Liberia, Sierra Leone, and Guinea Bissau.* Boulder, CO: Lynne Rienner.

Adler, Glenn, and Eddie Webster. 1995. "Challenging Transition Theory: The Labor Movement, Radical Reform, and Transition to Democracy in South Africa." *Politics and Society* 23 (1): 75–106.

———. 2000. *Trade Unions and Democratization in South Africa, 1985–97.* New York: St. Martin's.

Albertus, Michael, and Victor Menaldo. 2014. "Gaming Democracy: Elite Dominance during Transition and the Prospects for Redistribution." *British Journal of Political Science* 44 (3): 575–603.

Alesina, Alberto, Arnaud Develeeschauwer, William Easterly, Sergio Kurlat, and Romain Wacziarg. 2003. "Fractionalization." *Journal of Economic Growth* 8:155–94.

Alesina, Alberto, and Allan Drazen. 1991. "Why Are Stabilizations Delayed?" *American Economic Review* 81 (5): 1170–88.

Alesina, Alberto F., and Paola Giuliano. 2009. "Preferences for Redistribution." Working Paper 14825, National Bureau of Economic Research.

Alexiev, Alexander R. 1983. "Dissent and Nationalism in the Soviet Baltic." Santa Monica, CA: RAND.

Allen, Chris. 1992. "Restructuring an Authoritarian State: 'Democratic Renewal' in Benin." *Review of African Political Economy* 19 (54): 42–58.

Andersen, Sigrid Bjerre. 2010. "In All Sovereignty? An Inquiry into the 'Essential Elements' of the Cotonou Agreement." Working Paper OA3 (2010), Roskilde University.

Ansell, Ben, and David Samuels. 2010. "Inequality and Democratization: A Contractarian Approach." *Comparative Political Studies* 43 (12): 1543–74.

———. 2013a. "Rethinking Inequality and Democratization: How Inequality Divides Elites and Underpins Regime Change." *Comparative Democratization* 11 (3): 1, 8–11.

———. 2013b. "Rethinking Democracy and Inequality." *Comparative Democratization Newsletter* 11 (3): 1–11.

———. 2014. *Inequality and Democratization: An Elite-Competition Approach.* New York: Cambridge University Press.

Arriagada, Genaro. 2015. "Chile's Successful Transition: From Intense Polarization to Stable Democracy." In Bitar and Lowenthal, *Democratic Transitions*, 50–59.

Ash, Timothy Garton. 2002. *The Polish Revolution: Solidarity.* New Haven, CT: Yale University Press.

Aydin-Düzgit, Senem, and E. Fuat Keyman. 2004. "European Integration and the Transformation of Turkish Democracy." EU-Turkey Working Papers No. 2, Center for European Policy Studies, Brussels.

———. 2013. "EU-Turkey Relations and the Stagnation of Turkish Democracy." In *Global Turkey in Europe: Political, Economic, and Foreign Policy Dimensions of Turkey's Evolving Relationship with the EU*, edited by Senem Aydin-Düzgit, Anne Duncker, Daniela Huber, E. Fuat Keyman, and Nathalie Tocci. Rome: Edizioni Nuova Cultura.

Aylwin, Patricio. 2015. "Interview with Patricio Aylwin." In Bitar and Lowenthal, *Democratic Transitions*, 60–72.

Baker, Chris, and Pasuk Phongpaichit. 2002. *Thailand: Economy and Politics.* 2nd ed. Oxford: Oxford University Press.

Banks, Arthur S. 2013. "Cross-National Time-Series Data Archive." www.cnts data.com

Barany, Zoltan. 2012. *The Soldier and the Changing State: Building Democratic Armies in Africa, Asia, Europe, and the Americas.* Princeton, NJ: Princeton University Press.

Barkan, Joel D. 2008. "Legislatures on the Rise?" *Journal of Democracy* 19 (2): 124–37.

Barnet, Richard. 1968. *Intervention and Revolution: The United States and the Third World.* New York: Dutton.

Bartels, Larry. 2008. *Unequal Democracy: The Political Economy of the New Gilded Age.* Princeton, NJ: Princeton University Press.

Bates, Robert H., Avner Greif, Margaret Levi, Jean-Laurent Rosenthal, and Barry R. Weingast. 1998. *Analytic Narratives.* Princeton, NJ: Princeton University Press.

Baturo, Alexander. 2014. *Democracy, Dictatorship and Term Limits.* Ann Arbor: University of Michigan Press.

Beach, Derek, and Rasmus Brun Pedersen. 2013. *Process-Tracing Methods: Foundations and Guidelines.* Ann Arbor: University of Michigan Press.

Beck, Nathaniel. 2001. "Time-Series-Cross-Section Data: What Have We Learned in the Past Few Years?" *Annual Review of Political Science* 4 (1): 271–93.

———. 2006. "Is Causal-Process Observation an Oxymoron?" *Political Analysis* 14 (3): 347–52.

———. 2010. "Causal Process 'Observation': Oxymoron or (Fine) Old Wine." *Political Analysis* 18 (4): 499–505.

Beck, Nathaniel, and Jonathan N. Katz. 2001. "Throwing Out the Baby with the Bath Water: A Comment on Green, Kim, and Yoon." *International Organization* 55 (2): 487–95.

Beck, Thorsten, George Clarke, Alberto Groff, Philip Keefer, and Patrick Walsh. 2001. "New Tools in Comparative Political Economy: The Database of Political Institutions." *World Bank Economic Review* 15 (1): 165–76.

Beissinger, Mark R. 2002. *Nationalist Mobilization and the Collapse of the Soviet State*. New York: Cambridge University Press.

Bellin, Eva. 2012. "Reconsidering the Robustness of Authoritarianism in the Middle East: Lessons from the Arab Spring." *Comparative Politics* 44 (2): 127–49.

Benabou, Roland, and Efe A. Ok. 2011. "Social Mobility and the Demand for Redistribution: The Poum Hypothesis." *Quarterly Journal of Economics* 116 (2): 447–87.

Bennett, Andrew, and Jeffrey T. Checkel, eds. 2015. *Process Tracing: From Metaphor to Analytical Tool*. Cambridge: Cambridge University Press.

Berlin, Isaiah. 1953. *The Hedgehog and the Fox: An Essay on Tolstoy's View of History*. London: Weidenfeld & Nicolson.

Bermeo, Nancy. 2003. *Ordinary People in Extraordinary Times: The Citizenry and the Breakdown of Democracy*. Princeton, NJ: Princeton University Press.

———. forthcoming. *War and Democracy*. Oxford: Oxford University Press.

Bernhard, Michael, Timothy Nordstrom, and Christopher Reenock. 2001. "Economic Performance, Institutional Intermediation, and Democratic Survival." *Journal of Politics* 63 (3): 775–803.

Bernhard, Michael, Christopher Reenock, and Timothy Nordstrom. 2003. "Economic Performance and Survival in New Democracies: Is There a Honeymoon Effect?" *Comparative Political Studies* 36 (4): 404–31.

Biberaj, Elez. 1999. *Albania in Transition: The Rocky Road to Democracy*. Boulder, CO: Westview Press.

Birikorang, Emma. 2005. "Democracy for Guinea-Bissau? An Analysis of the 2005 Presidential Elections." Kofi Annan International Peacekeeping Training Center, KAIPTC Paper No. 8 (August).

Bitar, Sergio, and Abraham F. Lowenthal, eds. 2015. *Democratic Transitions: Conversations with World Leaders*. Baltimore: Johns Hopkins University Press.

Bland, Douglas L. 1999. "A unified theory of civil-military relations." *Armed Forces & Society*, 26, 1: 7–25.

Blaydes, Lisa. 2010. *Elections and Distributive Politics in Mubarak's Egypt*. New York: Cambridge University Press.

Boix, Carles. 2003. *Democracy and Redistribution*. New York: Cambridge University Press.

———. 2008. "Economic Roots of Civil Wars and Revolutions in the Contemporary World." *World Politics* 60 (3): 390–437.

———. 2011. "Democracy, Development, and the International System." *American Political Science Review* 105 (4): 809–28.

———. 2013. "RMDs." *Comparative Democratization* 11 (3): 2, 12–15.

Boix, Carles, and Susan Stokes. 2003. "Endogenous Democratization." *World Politics* 55:517–49.

Boix, Carles, and Milan Svolik. 2013. "The Foundations of Limited Authoritarian Government: Institutions, Commitment, and Power-Sharing in Dictatorships." *Journal of Politics* 75 2 (2): 300–316.

Booth, John A., Christine J. Wade, and Thomas W. Walker. 2010. *Understanding Central America: Global Forces, Rebellion and Change.* Boulder, CO: Westview Press.

Bradley, Andrew. 2005. "An ACP Perspective and Overview of Article 96 Cases." Discussion Paper No. 46D, European Centre for Development Policy Management.

Brady, Henry E., and David Collier, eds. 2004. *Rethinking Social Inquiry, Diverse Tools, Shared Standards.* Lanham, MD: Rowman & Littlefield.

Bratton, Michael. 2007. "Formal versus Informal Institutions in Africa." *Journal of Democracy* 18 (3): 96–110.

Bratton, Michael, and Nicolas van de Walle. 1997. *Democratic Experiments in Africa: Regime Transitions in Comparative Perspective.* New York: Cambridge University Press.

Brinks, Daniel, and Michael Coppedge. 2006. "Diffusion Is No Illusion: Neighbor Emulation in the Third Wave of Democracy." *Comparative Political Studies* 39 (4): 463–89.

Brownlee, Jason. 2007. *Authoritarianism in an Age of Democratization.* New York: Cambridge University Press.

Bueno de Mesquita, Bruce, Alastair Smith, Randolph M. Siverson, and James D. Morrow. 2003. *The Logic of Political Survival.* Cambridge, MA: MIT Press.

Bulmer-Thomas, Victor. 1987. *The Political Economy of Central America since 1920.* Cambridge: Cambridge University Press.

Bunce, Valerie J., and Sharon L. Wolchik. 2011. *Defeating Authoritarian Leaders in Postcommunist Countries.* New York: Cambridge University Press.

Burk, James. 2002. "Theories of Democratic Civil-Military Relations." *Armed Forces & Society* 29 (1): 7–29.

Burkhart, Ross E. 1997. "Comparative Democracy and Income Distribution: Shape and Direction of the Causal Arrow." *Journal of Politics* 59 (1): 148–64.

Burkhart, Ross E., and Michael S. Lewis-Beck. 1994. "Comparative Democracy: The Economic Development Thesis." *American Political Science Review* 88 (4): 903–10.

Bush, Sarah. 2015. *The Taming of Democracy Assistance: Why Democracy Promotion Does Not Confront Dictators.* New York: Cambridge University Press.

Carey, John M. 2000. "Parchment, Equilibria, and Institutions." *Comparative Political Studies* 33 (6–7): 735–61.

Carothers, Thomas. 1999. *Aiding Democracy: The Learning Curve.* Washington, DC: Carnegie Endowment for International Peace.

———. 2002. "The End of the Transition Paradigm." *Journal of Democracy* 13 (1): 5–21.

———. 2004. *Critical Mission: Essays on Democracy Promotion.* Washington, DC: Carnegie Endowment for International Peace.

Carothers, Thomas, and Marina Ottaway, eds. 2000. *Funding Virtue: Civil Society Aid and Democracy Promotion.* Washington, DC: Carnegie Endowment for International Peace.

Carter, David B., and Curtis S. Signorino. 2010. "Back to the Future: Modeling Time Dependence in Binary Data." *Political Analysis* 18 (3): 271–92.

Cavarozzi, Marcelo. 1986a. "Peronism and Radicalism: Argentina's Transition in Perspective." In *Elections and Democratization in Latin America, 1980–85*, edited by Paul Drake and Eduardo Silva, 143–74. La Jolla, CA: Center for Iberian and Latin American Studies.

———. 1986b. "Political Cycles in Argentina since 1955." In O'Donnell, Schmitter, and Whitehead, *Transitions from Authoritarian Rule: Latin America*, 49–72.

Cederman, Lars-Erik, Kristian Skrede Gleditsch, and Halvard Buhaug. 2013. *Inequality, Grievances, and Civil War*. New York: Cambridge University Press.

Charlick, Robert. 2007. "Labor Unions and Democratic Forces in Niger." In *Trade Unions and the Coming of Democracy in Africa*, edited by Jon Kraus, 61–83. New York: Palgrave Macmillan.

Cheeseman, Nic. 2014. *Democracy in Africa: Why It Has Failed and How to Make It Work*. New York: Cambridge University Press.

Cheibub, José Antonio. 1996. "What Makes Democracies Endure?" *Journal of Democracy* 7 (9): 39–55.

———. 2007. *Presidentialism, Parliamentarism, and Democracy*. New York: Cambridge University Press.

Cheibub, José Antonio, and Jennifer Gandhi. 2004. "Classifying Political Regimes: A Six-Fold Measure of Democracies and Dictatorships." Paper presented at the annual meeting of the American Political Science Association, Chicago.

Cheibub, José Antonio, Jennifer Gandhi, and James R. Vreeland. 2010. "Democracy and Dictatorship Revisited." *Public Choice* 143:67–101.

Cheibub, José Antonio, and Fernando Limongi. 2002. "Democratic Institutions and Regime Survival: Parliamentary and Presidential Democracies Reconsidered." *Annual Review of Political Science* 5:151–79.

Cheng, Tun-jen and Stephan Haggard, eds. 1992. *Political Change in Taiwan*. Boulder, CO: Lynne Rienner.

Chenoweth, Erica, and Maria J. Stephan. 2011. *Why Civil Resistance Works: The Strategic Logic of Nonviolent Conflict*. New York: Columbia University Press.

Christensen, Maya M., and Mas Utas. 2008. "Mercenaries of Democracy: The 'Politricks' of Remobilized Combatants in the 2007 General Elections, Sierra Leone." *African Affairs* ā107 (429): 515–39.

Chomsky, Noam, and Edward Herman. 1979. *The Washington Connection and Third World Fascism*. Toronto: University of Toronto Press.

Clark, John F. 1994a. "Elections, Leadership and Democracy in Congo." *Africa Today* 41 (3): 41–60.

———. 1994b. "The National Conference as an Instrument of Democratization in Francophone Africa." *Journal of Third World Studies* 11 (1): 304–35.

Clément, Jean A. P., Stéphane Cossé, Johannes Mueller, and Jean Le Dem. 1996. "Aftermath of the CFA Franc Devaluation." IMF Occasional Paper 138.

Cohen, Youssef. 1994. *Radicals, Reformers, and Reactionaries: The Prisoner's Dilemma and the Collapse of Democracy in Latin America*. Chicago: Chicago University Press.

Collier, David, ed. 1979. *The New Authoritarianism in Latin America*. Princeton, NJ: Princeton University Press.

Collier, David, Henry E. Brady, and Jason Seawright. 2010. "Sources of Leverage in Causal Inference: Toward an Alternative View of Methodology." In Brady and Collier, *Rethinking Social Inquiry*, 161–200.

Collier, David, and Steven Levitsky. 1997. "Democracy with Adjectives: Conceptual Innovation in Comparative Research." *World Politics* 49 (3): 430–51.

Collier, Paul, and Anke Hoeffler. 2005. "Resource Rents, Governance, and Conflict." *Journal of Conflict Resolution* 49 (4): 625–33.

Collier, Ruth. 1999. *Paths Toward Democracy: The Working Class and Elites in Western Europe and South America*. New York: Cambridge University Press.

Colomer, Josep M. 2000. *Strategic Transition: Game Theory and Democratization*. Baltimore: Johns Hopkins University Press.

Cooper, Andrew Fenton, and Thomas Legler. 2001. "A Model for the Future?" *Journal of Democracy* 12 (4): 123–36.

———. 2005. "A Tale of Two Mesas: The OAS Defense Democracy in Peru and Venezuela." *Global Governance* 11 (4): 425–44.

Coppedge, Michael. 1997. *Strong Parties and Lame Ducks: Presidential Partyarchy and Factionalism in Venezuela*. Palo Alto, CA: Stanford University Press.

Corrales, Javier, and Michael Penfold. 2007. "Venezuela: Crowding Out the Opposition." *Journal of Democracy* 18 (2): 99–113.

———. 2015. *Dragon in the Tropics: The Legacy of Hugo Chavez*. 2nd ed. Washington, DC: Brookings Institution Press.

Cramer, Brian D., and Robert R. Kaufman. 2010. "Views of Economic Inequality in Latin America." *Comparative Political Studies* 44 (9): 1206–37.

Crasnow, Sharon, and Stephan Haggard. 2015. "Bridging Cultures: A Multimethod Approach to the Study of Rare Events." Paper presented at the annual meeting of the American Political Science Association, San Francisco.

Creevey, Lucy, Paul Ngomo, and Richard Vengroff. 2005. "Party Politics and Different Paths to Democratic Transitions: A Comparison of Benin and Senegal." *Party Politics* 11 (4): 471–93.

Crouch, Harold. 1988. "Indonesia: The Rise or Fall of Suharto's Generals." *Third World Quarterly* 10 (1): 160–75.

Crowther, William. 2003. "The European Union and Romania: The Politics of Constrained Transition." In *The European Union and Democratization*, edited by Paul Kubicek, 87–110. London: Routledge.

Dahl, Robert A. 1973. *Polyarchy: Participation and Opposition*. New Haven, CT: Yale University Press.

Davide Fact-Finding Commission. 1990. *The Final Report of the Fact-Finding Commission (Pursuant to R.A. No. 6832)*. Makati City: Bookmark.

Davis, John Uniack, and Aboubacar B. Kossomi. 2001. "Niger Gets Back on Track." *Journal of Democracy* 12 (3): 80–87.

Dawisha, Karen. 2014. *Putin's Kleptocracy: Who Owns Russia?* New York: Simon & Schuster.

De La O, Anna L., and Jonathan A. Rodden. 2008. "Does Religion Distract the Poor? Income and Issue Voting around the World." *Comparative Political Studies* 41 (4–5): 437–76.

Desch, Michael. 1999. *Civilian Control of the Military: The Changing Security Environment*. Baltimore: Johns Hopkins University Press.

de Tocqueville, Alexis. 1835. *Democracy in America*. Vol. 2. New York: Schocken Books.

Deyo, Frederick. 1993. *Beneath the Miracle: Labor Subordination in the New Asian Industrialism*. Berkeley: University of California Press.

Diamond, Larry. 2008. "The Democratic Rollback." *Foreign Affairs* 87 (2): 36–48.

———. 2009. *The Spirit of Democracy: The Struggle to Build Free Societies throughout the World*. New York: St. Martin's Griffin.

Diamond, Larry, Francis Fukuyama, Donald L. Horowitz, and Marc F. Plattner. 2014. "Reconsidering the Transition Paradigm." *Journal of Democracy* 25 (1): 86–100.

Di Palma, Giuseppe. 1990. *To Craft Democracies*. Berkeley: University of California Press.

Drake, Paul. 1996. *Labor Movements and Dictatorships: The Southern Cone in Comparative Perspective*. Baltimore: Johns Hopkins University Press.

Dunkerly, James. 1994. *Rebellion in the Veins: Political Struggle in Bolivia, 1952–1982*. London: Verso.

Dutt, Pushan, and Devashish Mitra. 2008. "Inequality and the Instability of Polity and Policy." *Economic Journal* 118 (531): 1285–1314.

Duverger, Maurice. 1972. "Factors in a Two-Party and Multiparty System." In *Party Politics and Pressure Groups*, 23–32. New York: Thomas Y. Crowell.

Earl, Jennifer, Heather McKee Hurwitz, Analicia Mejia Mesinas, Margaret Tolan, and Ashley Arlotti. 2013. "This Protest Will Be Tweeted: Twitter and Protest Policing during the Pittsburgh G20." *Information, Communication & Society* 16 (4): 459–78.

Economist Intelligence Unit. 2010. "Democracy Index 2010: Democracy in Retreat." *Economist*. https://graphics.eiu.com/PDF/Democracy_Index_2010_web.pdf.

———. 2013. "Democracy Index 2013: Democracy in Limbo." *Economist*. http://www.eiu.com/Handlers/WhitepaperHandler.ashx?fi=Democracy_Index_2013_WE B-2.pdf&mode=wp&campaignid=Democracy0814.

Eisenstadt, Todd. 2004. *Courting Democracy in Mexico: Party Strategies and Electoral Institutions*. New York: Cambridge University Press.

Ekiert, Grzegorz. 1996. *The State Against Society: Political Crises and Their Aftermath in East Central Europe*. Princeton, NJ: Princeton University Press.

Elgie, Robert. 2004. "From Linz to Tsebelis: Three Waves of Presidential/Parliamentary Studies?" Working Papers in International Studies 6/2004, Center for International Studies, Dublin City University.

Elkink, Johan A. 2011. "The International Diffusion of Democracy." *Comparative Political Studies* 44 (12): 1651–74.

Ellis, Christopher J., and John Fender. 2011. "Information Cascades and Revolutionary Regime Transitions." *Economic Journal* 121 (553): 763–92.

Enterline, Andrew J., and J. Michael Greig. 2008. "The History of Imposed Democracy and the Future of Iraq and Afghanistan." *Foreign Policy Analysis* 4 (4): 321–47.

Epstein, David L., Robert Bates, Jack Goldstone, Ida Kristensen, and Sharyn O'Halloran. 2006. "Democratic Transitions." *American Journal of Political Science* 50:551–69.

Epstein, Lee, Jack Knight, and Olga Shvetsova. 2001. "The Role of Constitutional Courts in the Establishment and Maintenance of Democratic Systems of Government." *Law and Society Review* 35 (1): 117–64.

Escribà Folch, Abel, and Joseph Wright. 2010. "Dealing with Tyranny: International Sanctions and the Survival of Authoritarian Rulers." *International Studies Quarterly* 54 (2): 335–59.

Falch, Ashild. 2008. "Power-Sharing to Build Peace? The Burundi Experience with Power Sharing Agreements." Centre for the Study of Civil War Policy Brief 2/2008.

Falleti, Tulia G. 2010. *Decentralization and Subnational Politics in Latin America.* New York: Cambridge University Press.

Falleti, Tulia G., and Julia F. Lynch. 2010. "Context and Causal Mechanisms in Political Analysis." *Comparative Political Studies* 42 (9): 1143–66.

Fatton, Robert, Jr. 2002. *Haiti's Predatory Republic: The Unending Transition to Democracy.* Boulder, CO: Lynne Rienner.

Fearon, James D., and David D. Laitin. 2008. "Integrating Quantitative and Qualitative Methods." In *Oxford Handbook of Political Methodology*, edited by Janet M. Box-Steffensmeier, Henry E. Brady, and David Collier, 756–78. Oxford: Oxford University Press.

———. 2011. "Sons of the Soil, Migrants, and Civil War." *World Development* 39 (2): 199–211.

Feaver, Peter D. 1996. *Armed Servants: Agency, Oversight, and Civil-Military Relations.* Cambridge, MA: Harvard University Press.

———. 1999. "Civil-Military Relations." *Annual Review of Political Science* 2: 211–41.

Fehr, Ernst, and Klaus M. Schmidt. 1999. "A Theory of Fairness, Competition, and Cooperation." *Quarterly Journal of Economics* 114 (3): 817–68.

Finseraas, Henning. 2008. "Income Inequality and Demand for Redistribution: A Multilevel Analysis of European Public Opinion." *Scandinavian Political Studies* 32 (1): 94–119.

Fish, Michael Steven. 2005. *Democracy Derailed in Russia: The Failure of Open Politics.* New York: Cambridge University Press.

———. 2006. "Stronger Legislatures, Stronger Democracies." *Journal of Democracy* 17 (1): 5–20.

Fithen, Caspar, and Paul Richards. 2005. *Making War, Crafting Peace: Militia Solidarities and Demobilization in Sierra Leone.* Suffolk: James Currey.

Foley, Michael W. 1996. "Laying the Groundwork: The Struggle for Civil Society in El Salvador." *Journal of Interamerican Studies and World Affairs* 38 (1): 67–104.

Fomunyoh, Christopher. 2001. "Democratization in Fits and Starts." *Journal of Democracy* 12 (3): 37–50.

Fortin, Jessica. 2010. "A Tool to Evaluate State Capacity in Post-Communist Countries, 1989–2006." *European Journal of Political Research* 49 (5): 654–86.

Freedom House. 2013. "Freedom in the World 2013." https://freedomhouse.org/report/freedom-world/freedom-world-2013#.VUo8JVPF9RB.

———. 2014a. "Freedom in the World 2014." https://freedomhouse.org/report/freedom-world/freedom-world-2014#.VUo8a1PF9RA.

————. 2014b. "Freedom in the World: Aggregate and Subcategory Scores." http://www.freedomhouse.org/report/freedom-world-aggregate-and-subcategory-scores.

Freeman, John R., and Dennis P. Quinn. 2012. "The Economic Origins of Democracy Reconsidered." *American Political Science Review* 106 (1): 58–80.

Fukuyama, Francis. 2011. *The Origins of Political Order: From Prehuman Times to the French Revolution*. New York: Farrar, Straus and Giroux.

Galvan, Dennis. 2001. "Political Turnover and Social Change in Senegal." *Journal of Democracy* 12 (3): 51–62.

Gamson, William A. 1992. *Talking Politics*. New York: Cambridge University Press.

Gandhi, Jennifer. 2008. *Political Institutions under Dictatorship*. New York: Cambridge University Press.

Gandhi, Jennifer, and Ellen Lust-Okar. 2009. "Elections under Authoritarianism." *Annual Review of Political Science* 12:403–22.

Gandhi, Jennifer, and Adam Przeworski. 2006. "Cooperation, Cooptation, and Rebellion under Dictatorships." *Economics & Politics* 18 (1): 1–26.

————. 2007. "Authoritarian Institutions and the Survival of Autocrats." *Comparative Political Studies* 40 (11): 1279–1301.

Gasiorowski, Mark J. 1995. "Economic Crisis and Political Regime Change: An Event History Analysis." *American Political Science Review* 89 (4): 882–97.

————. 2000. "Democracy and Macroeconomic Performance in Underdeveloped Countries: An Empirical Analysis." *Comparative Political Studies* 33 (3): 319–49.

Gazibo, Mamoudou. 2012. *Beyond Electoral Democracy: Foreign Aid and the Challenge of Deepening Democracy in Benin*. WIDER Working Paper No. 2012/33.

Geddes, Barbara. 1995. "A Comparative Perspective on the Leninist Legacy in Eastern Europe." *Comparative Political Studies* 28 (2): 239–74.

————. 1999. "What Do We Know about Democracy after Twenty Years?" *Annual Review of Political Science* 2:115–44.

Geddes, Barbara, Joseph Wright, and Erica Frantz. 2014. "New Data on Autocratic Regimes." Unpublished manuscript, University of California, Los Angeles.

George, Alexander L., and Andrew Bennett. 2005. *Case Studies and Theory Development in the Social Sciences*. Cambridge, MA: MIT Press.

George, Alexander L., and Timothy J. McKeown. 1985. "Case Studies and Theories of Organizational Decision Making." *Advances in Information Processing in Organizations* 2:21–58.

Gerring, John. 2006. "Single-Outcome Studies: A Methodological Primer." *International Sociology* 21 (5): 707–34.

————. 2007a. *Case Study Research: Principles and Practices*. New York: Cambridge University Press.

————. 2007b. "The Mechanismic Worldview: Thinking Inside the Box." *British Journal of Political Science* 38 (1): 161–79.

————. 2010. "Causal Mechanisms: Yes, But. . . ." *Comparative Political Studies* 42 (3): 327–59.

Gerring, John, Philip Bond, William T. Barndt, and Caroloa Moreno. 2005. "Democracy and Economic Growth: A Historical Perspective." *World Politics* 57: 323–64.

Gervais, Myriam. 1997. "Niger: Regime Change, Economic Crisis and the Perpetuation of Privilege." In *Political Reform in Francophone Africa*, edited by John F. Clark and David Gardinier, 86–108. Boulder, CO: Westview Press.

Giliomee, Hermann. 1995. "Democratization in South Africa." *Political Science Quarterly* 110:83–104.

Gimpelson, Vladimir, and Daniel Treisman. 2015. *Misperceiving Inequality*. Unpublished manuscript, University of California, Los Angeles.

Ginsburg, Tom. 2003. *Judicial Review in New Democracies: Constitutional Courts in Asian Cases*. New York: Cambridge University Press.

Gjomema, Eranda. 2007. "The EU and Consolidating Democracy in Post-Communist States: The Democratization Process in Albania." PSI Papers in Culture, Ideas, and Policy, WP 2, University of East Anglia School of Political, Social and International Studies and Centre for Research in European Studies.

Gleditsch, Kristian Skrede. 2002. *All International Politics Is Local: The Diffusion of Conflict, Integration, and Democratization*. Ann Arbor: University of Michigan Press.

Gleditsch, Kristen Skrede, and Michael D. Ward. 2006. "Diffusion and the International Context of Democratization." *International Organization* 60 (4): 911–33.

Gleditsch, Nils Petter, Lene Siljeholm Christiansen, and Havard Hegre. 2007. "Democratic Jihad? Military Intervention and Democracy." World Bank Policy Research Working Paper 4242.

Goertz, Gary, and James Mahoney. 2012. *A Tale of Two Cultures: Qualitative and Quantitative Research in the Social Sciences*. Princeton, NJ: Princeton University Press.

Goffman, Irving. 1974. *Frame Analysis: An Essay on the Organization of Experience*. London: Harper & Row.

Goldsmith, Benjamin. 2007. "A Liberal Peace in Asia?" *Journal of Peace Research* 44 (1): 5–27.

Goldstein, Judith L. 2008. *The Evolution of the Trade Regime: Politics, Law, and Economics of the GATT and the WTO*. Princeton, NJ: Princeton University Press.

Goldstone, Jack, and Charles Tilly. 2001. "Threat (and Opportunity): Popular Action and State Response in the Dynamics of Contentious Action." In *Silence and Voice in the Study of Contentious Politics*, edited by Ronald Aminzade, 179–94. New York: Cambridge University Press.

Goodwin, Jeff. 2001. *No Other Way Out: States and Revolutionary Movements, 1945–1991*. New York: Cambridge University Press.

Gourevitch, Peter, David Lake, and Janice Stein. 2012. *The Credibility of Transnational NGOs: When Virtue Is Not Enough*. New York: Cambridge University Press.

Grabbe, Heather. 2001. "How Does Europeanisation Affect CEE Governance? Conditionality, Diffusion and Diversity." *Journal of European Public Policy* 8 (6): 1013–31.

Graham, Yao. 1985. "The Politics of Crisis in Ghana: Class Struggle and Organization, 1981–1984." *Review of African Political Economy* 12 (34): 54–68.

Green, Donald P., and Ian Shapiro. 1994. *Pathologies of Rational Choice Theory*. New Haven, CT: Yale University Press.

Greif, Avner, and David D. Laitin. 2004. "A Theory of Endogenous Institutional Change." *American Political Science Review* 98 (4): 633–52.

Gunning, Jeroen, and Ilan Zvi Baron. 2014. *Why Occupy a Square? People, Protests and Movements in the Egyptian Revolution*. Oxford: Oxford University Press.

Gupta, Dipak K., Harinder Singh, and Tom Sprague. 1993. "Government Coercion of Dissidents: Deterrence or Provocation?" *Journal of Conflict Resolution* 37 (2): 301–39.

Gurtov, Melvin. 1974. *The United States Against the Third World: Antinationalism and Intervention*. Westport, CT: Praeger.

Gyimah-Boadi, Emmanuel. 1994. "Ghana's Uncertain Political Opening." *Journal of Democracy* 5 (2): 75–86.

Habdank-Kołaczkowska, Sylvana. 2014. "Nations in Transit 2014: Eurasia's Rupture with Democracy." Freedom House. https://freedomhouse.org/report /nations-transit-2014/nations-transit-2014-eurasias-rupture-democracy#.VUJN jlPF9RB.

Hadenius, Alex, and Jan Teorell. 2007. "Pathways from Authoritarianism." *Journal of Democracy* 18 (1): 143–57.

Hadenius, Axel, Jan Teorell, and Michael Wahman. 2012. "Authoritarian Regimes Data Set, Version 5.0: Codebook. September 2012." http://www2.srv .svet.lu.se/uploads/specialsidor/svet-mwaARD_dataset_3.pdf.

Hafner-Burton, Emilie M. 2013. *Forced to Be Good: Why Trade Agreements Boost Human Rights*. Ithaca, NY: Cornell University Press.

Hafner-Burton, Emilie, and James Ron. 2009. "Seeing Double: Human Rights Impact through Qualitative and Quantitative Eyes?" *World Politics* 61 (2): 360–401.

Haggard, Stephan. 1990. *Pathways from the Periphery*. Ithaca, NY: Cornell University Press.

———. 2013. "Politics in Hard Times Revisited: The 2008–9 Financial Crisis in Emerging Markets." In *Politics in the New Hard Times: The Great Recession in Comparative Perspective*, edited by Miles Kahler and David Lake, 52–74. Ithaca, NY: Cornell University Press.

Haggard, Stephan, and Robert Kaufman. 1995. *The Political Economy of Democratic Transitions*. Princeton, NJ: Princeton University Press.

———. 2008. *Development, Democracy and Welfare States: Latin America, East Asia and Eastern Europe*. Princeton, NJ: Princeton University Press.

———. 2012. "Inequality and Regime Change: Democratic Transitions and the Stability of Democratic Rule." *American Political Science Review* 106 (3): 495–516.

———. 2016. "Democratization during the Third Wave." *Annual Review of Political Science* 19.

Haggard, Stephan, Robert Kaufman, and James Long. 2013. "Income, Occupation, and Preferences for Redistribution in the Developing World." *Studies in Comparative International Development* 48 (2): 113–40.

Haggard, Stephan, Robert Kaufman, and Terence Teo. 2016. "Distributive Conflict and Regime Change Dataset, Online Appendix." http://press.princeton.edu/titles/10879.html.

Haggard, Stephan, and Lydia Tiede. 2011. "The Rule of Law and Economic Growth: Where Are We?" *World Development* 39 (5): 673–85.

Halper, Stefan. 2010. *The Beijing Consensus: How China's Authoritarian Model Will Dominate the Twenty-First Century*. New York: Basic Books.

Harris, David. 2012. *Civil War and Democracy in West Africa: Conflict Resolution, Elections, and Justice in Sierra Leone and Liberia*. London: I.B. Tauris.

Hartzell, Caroline A., and Matthew Hoddie. 2003. "Institutionalizing Peace: Power Sharing and Post–Civil War Conflict Management." *American Journal of Political Science* 47 (2): 318–32.

———. 2007. *Crafting Peace: Power-Sharing Institutions and the Negotiated Settlement of Civil Wars*. University Park: Pennsylvania State University Press.

———. 2015. "The Art of the Possible: Power Sharing and Post–Civil War Democracy." *World Politics* 67 (1): 37–71.

Hausman, Jerry A. 1978. "Specification Tests in Econometrics." *Econometrica* 46 (6): 1251–71.

Hazelzet, Hadewych. 2005. "Suspension of Development Cooperation: An Instrument to Promote Human Rights and Democracy?" Discussion Paper No. 46B, European Centre for Development Policy Management.

Hedstrom, Peter, and Petri Ylikoski. 2010. "Causal Mechanisms in the Social Sciences." *Annual Review of Sociology* 36:49–67.

Helvey, Robert L. 2004. "On Strategic Nonviolent Conflict: Thinking About the Fundamentals." Boston: Albert Einstein Institution.

Henrich, Joseph, Robert Boyd, Samuel Bowles, Colin Camerer, Ernst Fehr, and Herbert Gintis. 2004. *Foundations of Human Sociality: Economic Experiments and Ethnographic Evidence from Fifteen Small-Scale Societies*. Oxford: Oxford University Press.

Hicken, Allen. 2006. "Party Fabrication: Constitutional Reform and the Rise of the Thai Rak Thai." *Journal of East Asian Studies* 6:381–407.

Higley, John, and Michael G. Burton. 1989. "The Elite Variable in Democratic Transitions and Breakdowns." *American Sociological Review* 54: 17–32.

———. 2006. *Elite Foundations of Liberal Democracy*. Lanham, MD: Rowman & Littlefield.

Hirschman, Albert O., and Michael Rothschild. 1973. "The Changing Tolerance for Income Inequality in the Course of Economic Development." *Quarterly Journal of Economics* 87 (4): 544–66.

Honna, Jun. 2013. *Military Politics and Democratization in Indonesia*. London: Routledge.

Horowitz, Donald. 1985. *Ethnic Groups in Conflict*. Berkeley: University of California Press.

Houle, Christian. 2009. "Inequality and Democracy: Why Inequality Harms Consolidation but Does Not Affect Democratization." *World Politics* 61:589–622.

———. 2013. "Inequality, Democratization and Democratic Consolidation." *Comparative Democratization* 11 (3): 2, 21–24.

———. 2015. "Ethnic Inequality and the Dismantling of Democracy: A Global Analysis." *World Politics* 67:469–505.

Howard, Philip N. 2011. *The Digital Origins of Dictatorship and Democracy: Information Technology and Political Islam.* Oxford: Oxford University Press.

Howard, Philip N., Aiden Duffy, Deen Freelon, Muzammil Hussain, Will Mari, and Marwa Mazaid. 2011. "Opening Closed Regimes: What Was the Role of Social Media during the Arab Spring." Working Paper 2011.1, Project on Information Technology & Political Islam.

Huber, Evelyne, and John D. Stephens. 2012. *Democracy and the Left: Social Policy and Inequality in Latin America.* Chicago: University of Chicago Press.

Hunter, Wendy. 1997. "Continuity or Change? Civil-Military Relations in Democratic Argentina, Chile, and Peru." *Political Science Quarterly* 112 (3): 435–75.

Huntington, Samuel P. 1957. *The Soldier and the State: The Theory and Politics of Civil-Military Relations.* Cambridge, MA: Belknap.

———. 1968. *Political Order in Changing Societies.* New Haven, CT: Yale University Press.

———. 1991. *The Third Wave: Democratization in the Late Twentieth Century.* Norman: University of Oklahoma Press.

Hutchful, Eboe. 1997. "Military Policy and Reform in Ghana." *Journal of Modern African Studies* 35 (2): 251–78.

Ibrahim, Amina. 2009. "Guarding the State or Protecting the Economy: The Economic Factors of Pakistan's Military Coups." Working Paper No. 09-02, Development Studies Institute, London School of Economics and Political Science.

Idrissou-Toure, Ali. 2014. "Politics: Africa's Big Men Cling to Power." Inter Press Service. http://www.ipsnews.net/2005/07/politics-africas-big-men-cling-to-power/.

Im, Hyung Baeg. 1987. "The Rise of Bureaucratic Authoritarianism in South Korea." *World Politics* 39 (2): 231–57.

International Centre for Tax and Development. 2014. "ICTD Revenue Dataset." http://www.ictd.ac/en/about-ictd-government-revenue-dataset.

Jackman, Robert. 1973. "On the Relation of Economic Development to Democratic Performance." *American Journal of Political Science* 17:611–21.

Jacobs, Lawrence R., et al. 2004. "American Democracy in an Age of Rising Inequality." *Perspectives on Politics* 2 (4): 651–66.

Jalal, Ayesha. 2014. *The Struggle for Pakistan: A Muslim Homeland and Global Politics.* Cambridge, MA: Harvard University Press.

James, Daniel. 1994. *Resistance and Integration: Peronism and the Argentine Working Class, 1946–1976.* Cambridge: Cambridge University Press.

Janowitz, Morris. 1960. *The Professional Soldier: A Social and Political Portrait.* Glencoe, IL: Free Press.

Jeffries, Richard. 1982. "Rawlings and the Political Economy of Underdevelopment in Ghana." *African Affairs* 81:307–17.

Kahneman, Daniel, Jack L. Knetsch, and Richard Thaler. 1986. "Fairness as a Constraint on Profit Seeking: Entitlements in the Market." *American Economic Review* 76:728–41.

Kandeh, Jimmy D. 2003. "Sierra Leone's Post-Conflict Elections of 2002." *Journal of Modern African Studies* 41:189–216.

Kapstein, Ethan, and Nathan Converse. 2008a. *The Fate of Young Democracies.* New York: Cambridge University Press.

———. 2008b. "Why Democracies Fail." *Journal of Democracy* 19 (4): 57–68.

Karl, Terry Lynn. 1990. "Dilemmas of Democratization in Latin America." *Comparative Politics* 32 (1): 1–21.

———. 1995. "The Hybrid Regimes of Central America." *Journal of Democracy* 6 (3): 72–86.

Kaufman, Robert R. 1979. "Industrial Change and Authoritarianism: A Concrete Review of the Bureaucratic-Authoritarian Model." In Collier, *New Authoritarianism in Latin America,* 165–255.

———. 2009a. "Inequality and Redistribution: Some Continuing Puzzles." *PS: Political Science & Politics* 42:657–60.

———. 2009b. "The Political Effects of Inequality in Latin America: Some Inconvenient Facts." *Comparative Politics* 41 (3): 359–79.

Kegley, Charles W., and Margaret G. Hermann. 1997. "Putting Military Intervention into the Democratic Peace: A Research Note." *Comparative Political Studies* 30 (1): 78–107.

Kelley, Judith. 2006. "New Wine in Old Wineskins: Promoting Political Reforms through the New European Neighborhood Policy." *Journal of Common Market Studies* 44 (1): 29–55.

Kendall-Taylor, Andrea, and Erica Frantz. 2014. "How Autocracies Fall." *Washington Quarterly* 37 (1): 35–47.

Kennedy, Ryan. 2010. "The Contradiction of Modernization: A Conditional Model of Endogenous Democratization." *Journal of Politics* 72 (3): 785–98.

Kieh, George Klay. 2011. "Warlords, Politicians and the Post–First Civil War Election in Liberia." *African and Asian Studies* 10 (2–3): 83–99.

King, Gary, Robert O. Keohane, and Sidney Verba. 1994. *Designing Social Inquiry: Scientific Inference in Qualitative Research.* Princeton, NJ: Princeton University Press.

King, Gary, and Langche Zeng. 2001. "Logistic Regression in Rare Events Data." *Political Analysis* 9 (2): 137–63.

Kirkpatrick, Jeane J. 1979. "Dictatorships and Double Standards: A Critique of US Policy." Washington, DC: Georgetown University, Ethics and Public Policy Center.

Kitirianglarp, Kengkij, and Kevin Hewison. 2009. "Social Movements and Political Opposition in Contemporary Thailand." *Pacific Review* 22 (4): 451–77.

Kitschelt, Herbert, and Steven I. Wilkinson. 2006. *Patrons, Clients and Policies: Patterns of Democratic Accountability and Political Competition.* New York: Cambridge University Press.

Klare, Michael T., and Cynthia Arnson. 1981. *Supplying Repression: US Support for Authoritarian Regimes Abroad.* Washington, DC: Institute for Policy Studies.

Klein, Herbert S. 1992. *Bolivia: The Evolution of a Multi-ethnic Society.* 2nd ed. New York: Oxford University Press.

Kohn, R. H. 2002. "The Erosion of Civilian Control of the Military in the United States Today." *Naval War College Review* 55 (3): 9–59.

Kolko, Gabriel. 1988. *Confronting the Third World: United States Foreign Policy, 1945–1980.* New York: Pantheon.

Kraus, Jon. 2007. *Trade Unions and the Coming of Democracy in Africa*. New York: Macmillan.

Kricheli, Ruth, and Yair Livne. 2011. "Mass Revolutions vs. Elite Coups." Paper presented at the annual meeting of the American Political Science Association, Toronto. http://ssrn.com/abstract=1449852.

Kubik, Jan. 1994. *The Power of Symbols against the Symbols of Power: The Rise of Solidarity and the Fall of State Socialism in Poland*. University Park: Pennsylvania State University Press.

Kuehn, David. 2012. "Combining Game Theory Models and Process Tracing: Potential and Limits." *European Political Science* 12:52–63.

Kuran, Timur. 1989. "Sparks and Prairie Fires: A Theory of Unanticipated Political Revolution." *Public Choice* 61:41–74.

———. 1991. "Now Out of Never: The Element of Surprise in the East European Revolution of 1989." *World Politics* 44:7–48.

Kurlantzick, Josh. 2014. *Democracy in Retreat: The Revolt of the Middle Class and the Worldwide Decline of Representative Government*. New Haven, CT: Yale University Press.

Lago, Ricardo. 1991. "The Illusion of Pursuing Redistribution through Macropolicy: Peru's Heterodox Experience, 1985–1990." In *The Macroeconomics of Populism in Latin America*, edited by Sebastian Edwards and Rudiger Dornbusch, 263–331. Chicago: University of Chicago Press.

Lagos, Ricardo. 2015. "Interview with Ricardo Lagos, President of Chile 2000–2006." In Bitar and Lowenthal, *Democratic Transitions*, 73–96.

Lai, Brian, and Ruth Melkonian-Hoover. 2005. "Democratic Progress and Regress: The Effect of Parties on the Transitions of States to and away from Democracy." *Political Research Quarterly* 58 (4): 551–64.

Lambert, Peter. 2000. "A Decade of Electoral Democracy: Continuity, Change and Crisis in Paraguay." *Bulletin of Latin American Research* 19 (3): 379–96.

Laporte, Geert. 2007. "The Cotonou Partnership Agreement: What Role in a Changing World? Reflections on the Future of ACP-EU Relations." Policy Management Report 13, European Centre for Development Policy Management.

Leblang, David. 1997. "Political Democracy and Economic Growth: Pooled Cross-Sectional and Time-Series Evidence." *British Journal of Political Science* 27:453–72.

Leeson, Peter T., and Andrea M. Dean. 2009. "The Democratic Domino Theory: An Empirical Investigation." *American Journal of Political Science* 53 (3): 533–51.

Lehoucq, Fabrice. 2012. *The Politics of Modern Central America: Civil War, Democratization, and Underdevelopment*. New York: Cambridge University Press.

Lehoucq, Fabrice, and Aníbal Pérez-Liñán. 2009. "Regimes, Competition, and Military Coups in Latin America." Paper presented at the annual meeting of the American Political Science Association, Toronto.

———. 2013. "Breaking Out of the Coup Trap: Political Competition and Military Coups in Latin America." *Comparative Political Studies* 47 (8): 1105–29.

Leite, Sérgio Pereira, Anthony Pellechio, Luisa Zanforlin, Girma Begashaw, Stefania Fabrizio, and Joachim Harnack. 2000. "Ghana: Economic Development in a Democratic Environment." IMF working paper. http://www.imf.org/external/pubs/nft/op/199/.

Lemarchand, René. 1996. *Burundi: Ethnic Conflict and Genocide*. Washington, DC: Wilson Center Press and Cambridge University Press.

Lerner, Daniel. 1958. *The Passing of Traditional Society: Modernizing the Middle East*. New York: Macmillan.

Levitsky, Steven. 2003. *Transforming Labor-Based Parties in Latin America: Argentine Peronism in Comparative Perspective*. New York: Cambridge University Press.

Levitsky, Steven, and Scott Mainwaring. 2006. "Organized Labor and Democracy in Latin America." *Comparative Politics* 39 (1): 21–42.

Levitsky, Steven, and María Victoria Murillo. 2009. "Variation in Institutional Strength." *Annual Review of Political Science* 12 (2009): 115–33.

Levitsky, Steven, and Lucan Way. 2002. "The Rise of Competitive Authoritarianism." *Journal of Democracy* 13.2 (2002) 51–65.

———. 2005. "International Linkage and Democratization." *Journal of Democracy* 16 (3): 20–34.

———. 2006. "Linkage versus Leverage: Rethinking the International Dimension of Regime Change." *Comparative Politics* 38 (4): 379–400.

———. 2010. *Competitive Authoritarianism: Hybrid Regimes after the Cold War*. New York: Cambridge University Press.

Levitt, Barry Steven. 2006. "A Desultory Defense of Democracy: OAS Resolution 1080 and the Inter-American Democratic Charter." *Latin American Politics & Society* 48 (3): 93–123.

Lichbach, Mark. 1987. "Deterrence or Escalation? The Puzzle of Aggregate Studies of Repression and Dissent." *Journal of Conflict Resolution* 31 (2): 266–97.

Lieberman, Evan. 2005. "Nested Analysis as a Mixed-Method Strategy in Comparative Politics." *American Political Science Review* 99 (3): 435–52.

———. 2015. "Nested Analysis: Towards the Integration of Comparative-Historical Analysis with Other Social Science Methods." In *Advances in Comparative-Historical Analysis*, edited by James Mahoney and Kathleen Thelen, 240–63. Cambridge: Cambridge University Press.

Lijphart, Arend. 1977. *Democracy in Plural Societies: A Comparative Exploration*. New Haven, CT: Yale University Press.

Lindberg, Staffan. 2006. "The Surprising Significance of African Elections." *Journal of Democracy* 17 (1): 139–51.

———. 2009. "The Power of Elections Revisited." In *Democratization by Elections: A New Mode of Transition*, edited by Staffan Lindberg, 25–46. Baltimore: Johns Hopkins University Press.

Lindberg, Staffan I., and John F. Clark. 2008. "Does Democratization Reduce the Risk of Military Interventions in Politics in Africa?" *Democratisation* 15 (1): 86–105.

Lindert, Peter. 2004. *Growing Public: Social Spending and Economic Growth since the Eighteenth Century*. New York: Cambridge University Press.

Linz, Juan J. 1978. "The Breakdown of Democratic Regimes: Crisis, Breakdown & Reequilibration." In *The Breakdown of Democratic Regimes*, edited by Juan J. Linz and Alfred Stepan, 3–124. Baltimore: Johns Hopkins University Press.

———. 1990a. "The Perils of Presidentialism." *Journal of Democracy* 1 (1): 51–69.

———. 1990b. "The Virtues of Parliamentarism." *Journal of Democracy* 1 (4): 84–91.

———. 1994. "Presidential or Parliamentary Democracy: Does It Make a Difference?" In *The Failure of Presidential Democracy: Comparative Perspectives*, edited by Juan J. Linz and Arturo Valenzuela, 3–87. Baltimore: Johns Hopkins University Press.

Linz, Juan J., and Alfred Stepan. 1978. *The Breakdown of Democratic of Regimes*. Baltimore: Johns Hopkins University Press.

———. 1996. *Problems of Democratic Transition and Consolidation: Southern Europe, South America, and Post-communist Europe*. Baltimore: Johns Hopkins University Press.

Linz, Juan J., and Arturo Valenzuela, eds. 1994. *The Failure of Presidential Democracy: Comparative Perspectives*. Baltimore: Johns Hopkins University Press.

Lipset, Seymour M. 1959. "Some Social Requisites of Democracy: Economic Development and Political Legitimacy." *American Political Science Review* 53: 69–105.

———. 1960. *Political Man: The Social Bases of Politics*. New York: Doubleday.

Lizzeri, Alessandro, and Nicola Persico. 2004. "Why Did the Elites Extend the Suffrage? Democracy and the Scope of Government, with an Application to Britain's Age of Reform." *Quarterly Journal of Economics* 119 (2004): 707–65.

Lohmann, Suzanne. 1994. "The Dynamics of Informational Cascades: The Monday Demonstrations in Leipzig, East Germany, 1989–91." *World Politics* 47 (1): 42–101.

Londregan, John B., and Keith T. Poole. 1990. "Poverty, the Coup Trap, and the Seizure of Executive Power." *World Politics* 42:151–83.

———. 1996. "Does High Income Promote Democracy?" *World Politics* 49:1–30.

Lust-Okar, Ellen. 2006. "Elections under Authoritarianism: Preliminary Lessons from Jordan." *Democratization* 13 (3): 456–71.

Mackie, James, and Julia Zinke. 2005. "When Agreement Breaks Down, What Next? The Cotonou Agreement's Article 96 Consultation Procedure." Discussion Paper No. 64A, European Centre for Development Policy Management.

Maeda, Ko. 2010. "Two Modes of Democratic Breakdown: A Competing Risks Analysis of Democratic Durability." *Journal of Politics* 72 (4): 1129–43.

Magaloni, Beatriz. 2006. *Voting for Autocracy: Hegemonic Party Survival and Its Demise in Mexico*. New York: Cambridge University Press.

Magaloni, Beatriz, and Ruth Kricheli. 2010. "Political Order and One-Party Rule." *Annual Review of Political Science* 13:123–43.

Mahler, Vincent A. 2002. "Exploring the Subnational Dimension of Income Inequality: An Analysis of the Relationship between Inequality and Electoral Turnout in the Developed Countries." *International Studies Quarterly* 46 (1): 117–42.

Mahoney, James. 2008. "Toward a Unified Theory of Causality." *Comparative Political Studies* 41 (4–5): 412–36.

Mahoney, James, and Kathleen Thelen. 2010. "A Theory of Gradual Institutional Change." In *Explaining Institutional Change: Ambiguity, Agency, and Power*, edited by James Mahoney and Kathleen Thelen, 1–37. Cambridge: Cambridge University Press.

Mainwaring, Scott. 1993. "Presidentialism, Multipartism, and Democracy." *Comparative Political Studies* 26 (2): 198–228.

———. 1999. *Rethinking Party Systems in the Third Wave of Democratization: The Case of Brazil.* Palo Alto, CA: Stanford University Press.

Mainwaring, Scott, Daniel Brinks, and Aníbal Pérez-Liñán. 2001. "Classifying Political Regimes in Latin America, 1945–1999." *Studies in Comparative International Development* 36 (1): 37–65.

Mainwaring, Scott, and Aníbal Pérez-Liñán. 2014. *Democracies and Dictatorships in Latin America: Emergence, Survival, and Fall.* Pittsburgh: University of Pittsburgh Press.

Mainwaring, Scott, and Timothy Scully, eds. 1995. *Building Democratic Institutions: Party Systems in Latin America.* Stanford, CA: Stanford University Press.

Mainwaring, Scott, and Mathew Shugart. 1997. "Conclusion: Presidentialism and the Party System." In *Presidentialism and Democracy in Latin America*, edited by Scott Mainwaring and Mathew Shugart, 394–439. New York: Cambridge University Press.

Mainwaring, Scott, and Mariano Torcal. 2006. "Party System Institutionalization and Party System Theory after the Third Wave of Democratization." In *Handbook of Party Politics*, edited by Richard S. Katz and William Crotty, 204–27. Thousand Oaks, CA: Sage.

Malesky, Edmund, and Krislert Samphantharak. 2011. *Understanding Thailand's Ongoing Political Crisis: Wider Implications for Southeast Asia and the West.* Washington: German Marshall Fund.

Malesky, Edmund, and Paul Schuler. 2010. "Nodding or Needling: Analyzing Delegate Responsiveness in an Authoritarian Parliament." *American Political Science Review* 104 (3): 482–502.

Maltz, Gideon. 2007. "The Case for Presidential Term Limits." *Journal of Democracy* 18 (1): 128–42.

Mansfield, Edward D., and Jon C. Pevehouse. 2006. "Democratization and International Organizations." *International Organization* 60 (1): 137–67.

Manz, Beatriz. 2008. *Central America (Guatemala, El Salvador, Honduras, Nicaragua): Patterns of Human Rights Violations.* Writenet Report, commissioned by the UN High Commissioner for Refugees, Status Determination and Protection Information Services. http://www.refworld.org/docid/48ad1eb72.html.

Marinov, Nikolay. 2005. "Do Economic Sanctions Destabilize Country Leaders?" *American Journal of Political Science* 49 (3): 564–76.

Marshall, David, ed. 2014. *The International Rule of Law Movement: A Crisis of Legitimacy and the Way Forward.* Cambridge, MA: Harvard University Press.

Marshall, Monty G., Ted Robert Gurr, and Keith Jaggers. 2013. "Polity IV Project: Political Regime Characteristics and Transitions, 1800–2012." Vienna, Virginia: Center for Systemic Peace.

Marshall, Monty G., and Keith Jaggers. 2002. "Polity IV Project: Political Regime Characteristics and Transitions, 1800–2002." Vienna, VA: Center for Systemic Peace.

Marshall, Monty G., and Donna Ramsey Marshall. 2010. "Coup d'état Events, 1946–2009: Codebook." Vienna, VA: Center for Systemic Peace.

Marshall, T. H. 1950. *Citizenship and Social Class*. New York: Cambridge University Press.

Marsteintredet, Leiv, and Einar Berntzen. 2008. "Reducing the Perils of Presidentialism in Latin America through Presidential Interruptions." *Comparative Politics* 41 (1): 83–101.

Martin, Terry. 2001. *The Affirmative Action Empire: Nations and Nationalism in the Soviet Union 1923–1939*. Ithaca, NY: Cornell University Press.

Mauceri, Philip. 1995. "State Reform, Coalitions, and the Neoliberal Autogolpe in Peru." *Latin American Research Review* 30 (1): 7–37.

McAdam, Doug. 1999. *Political Process and the Development of Black Insurgency, 1930–1970*. 2nd ed. Chicago: University of Chicago Press.

McAdam, Doug, Sidney Tarrow, and Charles Tilly. 2003. *Dynamics of Contention*. New York: Cambridge University Press.

McCarty, Nolan, Keith T. Poole, and Howard Rosenthal. 2006. *Polarized America*. Cambridge, MA: MIT Press.

McClintock, Cynthia. 1989. "The Prospects for Democratic Consolidation in a 'Least Likely' Case: Peru." *Comparative Politics* 21 (2): 127–48.

McCoy, Jennifer L. 2006. "International Response to Democratic Crisis in the Americas, 1990–2005." *Democratization* 13 (5): 756–75.

McDonald, Douglas. 1992. *Adventures in Chaos: American Intervention for Reform in the Third World*. Cambridge, MA: Harvard University Press.

McFaul, Michael. 2002. *Russia's Unfinished Revolution: Political Change from Gorbachev to Putin*. Ithaca, NY: Cornell University Press.

McGowan, Patrick K. 2007. "African Military Intervention Events, January 1, 1955 to December 31, 2006." Unpublished manuscript, Temple, AZ.

McGuire, James W. 1995a. "Interim Government and Democratic Consolidation: Argentina in Comparative Perspective." In *Between States: Interim Governments and Democratic Transitions*, edited by Yossi Shain and Juan J. Linz, 179–210. New York: Cambridge University Press.

———. 1995b. "Political parties and democracy in Argentina." In Mainwaring and Scully, *Building Democratic Institutions*, 200–246.

———. 1997. *Peronism without Perón: Unions, Parties, and Democracy in Argentina*. Stanford, CA: Stanford University Press.

Meachem, Carl. 2014. "Crisis in Venezuela: Where's the OAS?" Washington, DC: Center for Strategic and International Studies. http://csis.org/publication/crisis-venezuela-wheres-oas.

Meltzer, Allan, and Scott Richard. 1981. "A Rational Theory of the Size of Government." *Journal of Political Economy* 89:914–27.

Middlebrook, Kevin J. 1995. *The Paradox of Revolution: Labor, the State, and Authoritarianism in Mexico*. Baltimore: Johns Hopkins University Press.

Missingham, Bruce. 2003. *The Assembly of the Poor in Thailand: From Local Struggles to National Protest Movement*. Seattle: University of Washington Press.

Moore, Barrington, Jr. 1966. *Social Origins of Dictatorship and Democracy: Lord and Peasant in the Making of the Modern World*. Boston: Beacon.

Moore, William H. 1998. "Repression and Dissent: Substitution, Context and Timing." *American Journal of Political Science* 42 (3): 851–73.

Mora, Frank O. 1998. "From Dictatorship to Democracy: The US and Regime Change in Paraguay, 1954–1994." *Bulletin of Latin American Research* 17 (1): 59–79.

Motyl, Alexander J. 1992. *Soviet Nationalities: History and Comparison in the Study of the USSR.* New York: Oxford University Press.

Muller, Edward N. 1985. "Income Inequality, Regime Repressiveness, and Political Violence." *American Sociological Review* 50 (1): 47–61.

Munck, Gerardo Luis. 1998. *Authoritarianism and Democratization: Soldiers and Workers in Argentina, 1976–1983.* University Park: Pennsylvania State University Press.

National Democratic Institute. 2007. "National Democratic Institute Final Report on Sierra Leone's 2007 Elections." Washington, DC: National Democratic Institute.

Ndulo, Muna. 2012. "The Prohibition of Unconstitutional Change of Government." In *The African Union: Legal and Institutional Framework: A Manual on the Pan-African Organization,* edited by Abdulqawi A. Yusuf and Fatsah Ouguergouz, 251–74. Leiden, Netherlands: Martinus Nijhoff.

Norris, Pippa. 2008. *Driving Democracy: Do Power-Sharing Institutions Work?* New York: Cambridge University Press.

Oberst, Robert C., Yogendra K. Malik, Charles H. Kennedy, Ashok Kapur, Mahendra Lawoti, Syedur Rahman, and Ahrar Ahmad. 2014. *Government and Politics in South Asia.* Boulder, CO: Westview Press.

Ockey, James. 2007. "Thailand in 2006: Retreat to Military Rule." *Asian Survey* 47 (1): 133–40.

O'Donnell, Guillermo. 1973. *Modernization and Bureaucratic-Authoritarianism: Studies in South American Politics.* Berkeley: University of California, Institute of International Studies.

———. 2004. "Democracy, Human Rights, Human Development." In *The Quality of Democracy: Theory and Applications,* edited by Guillermo O'Donnell, Osvaldo Iazzetta, and Jorge Vargas Cullell, 7–120. Notre Dame: University of Notre Dame Press.

O'Donnell, Guillermo, and Philippe C. Schmitter. 1986. *Transitions from Authoritarian Rule: Tentative Conclusions about Uncertain Democracies.* Baltimore: Johns Hopkins University Press.

O'Donnell, Guillermo, Philippe C. Schmitter, and Laurence Whitehead, eds. 1986a. *Transitions from Authoritarian Rule: Comparative Perspectives.* Baltimore: Johns Hopkins University Press.

———, eds. 1986b. *Transitions from Authoritarian Rule: Latin America.* Baltimore: Johns Hopkins University Press.

———, eds. 1986c. *Transitions from Authoritarian Rule: Prospects for Democracy.* Baltimore: Johns Hopkins University Press.

Olson, Mancur. 1965. *The Logic of Collective Action: Public Goods and the Theory of Groups.* Cambridge, MA: Harvard University Press.

Öniş, Ziya. 2013. "Sharing Power: Turkey's Democratization Challenge in the Age of the AKP Hegemony." *Insight Turkey* 15 (2): 103–22.

Ooi, Can-Seng. 2009. "Soft Authoritarianism, Political Pragmatism and Cultural Policies." Government Encounters May 2009 Working Paper, Copenhagen Business School.

Opp, Karl-Dieter, and Wolfgang Roehl. 1990. "Repression, Micromobilization, and Political Protest." *Social Forces* 69 (2): 521–47.

Oquaye, Mike. 1995. "Human Rights and the Transition to Democracy under the PNDC in Ghana." *Human Rights Quarterly* 17 (3): 556–73.

Organisation for Economic Co-operation and Development. 2006. "Economic Survey of the Russian Federation." *Economic Outlook* 82.

Osa, Maryjane. 2003. "Networks in Opposition: Linking Organizations through Activists in the Polish People's Republic." In *Social Movements and Networks: Relational Approaches to Collective Action*, edited by Mario Dani and Doug McAdam, 77–104. Oxford: Oxford University Press.

Ost, David. 2006. *The Defeat of Solidarity: Anger and Politics in Postcommunist Europe*. Ithaca, NY: Cornell University Press.

Ostby, Gudrun. 2007. "Horizontal Inequalities, Political Environment and Civil Conflict: Evidence from 55 Developing Countries, 1986–2003." World Bank Policy Research Paper 4193, Post-Conflict Transition Working Paper No. 7.

Ottaway, Marina. 2003. "Promoting Democracy after Conflict: The Difficult Choices." *International Studies Perspectives* 4 (3): 314–22.

Owusu, Maxwell. 1989. "A Rebellion, Revolution, and Tradition: Reinterpreting Coups in Ghana." *Comparative Studies in Society and History* 31 (2): 372–97.

Pape, Robert A. 1997. "Why Economic Sanctions Do Not Work." *International Security* 22 (2): 90–136.

Peksen, Dursun. 2011. "Economic Sanctions and Human Security: The Public Health Effect of Economic Sanctions." *Foreign Policy Analysis* 7 (3): 237–51.

Pérez-Liñán, Anibal. 2007. *Presidential Impeachment and the New Political Instability in Latin America*. Cambridge: Cambridge University Press.

Persson, Torsten, and Guido Tabellini. 1994. "Is Inequality Harmful for Economic Growth?" *American Economic Review* 84:600–621.

Pevehouse, Jon C. 2002. "Democracy from the Outside-In? International Organizations and Democratization." *International Organization* 56:515–49.

———. 2005. *Democracies from Above: Regional Organization and Democracy*. New York: Cambridge University Press.

Phillips, Kevin. 2003. *Wealth and Democracy*. New York: Broadway Books.

Pierskalla, Jan H., and Florian M. Hollenbach. 2013. "Technology and Collective Action: The Effect of Cell Phone Coverage on Political Violence in Africa." *American Political Science Review* 107 (2): 207–24.

Pierson, Paul. 2004. *Politics in Time: History, Institutions and Social Analysis*. Princeton, NJ: Princeton University Press.

Piketty, Thomas. 2013. *Capital in the Twenty-First Century*. Cambridge, MA: Harvard University Press.

Pion-Berlin, David. 2001. *Civil-Military Relations in Latin America: New Analytical Perspectives*. Chapel Hill: University of North Carolina Press.

Pion-Berlin, David, Diego Esparza, and Kevin Grisham. 2014. "Staying Quartered: Civilian Uprisings and Military Disobedience in the Twenty-First Century." *Comparative Political Studies* 47 (2): 230–59.

Pion-Berlin, David, and Harold Trinkunas. 2011. "Latin America's Growing Security Gap." *Journal of Democracy* 22 (1): 39–53.

Plattner, Marc F. 2014. "The End of the Transitions Era." *Journal of Democracy* 25 (3): 5–16.

Poast, Paul, and Johannes Urpelainen. 2015. "How International Organizations Support Democratization: Preventing Authoritarian Reversals or Promoting Consolidation?" *World Politics* 67 (1): 72–113.

Polity IV. 2010a. "Polity IV Country Report 2010: Benin." Center for Systematic Peace. http://www.systemicpeace.org/polity/Benin2010.pdf.

———. 2010b. "Polity IV Country Report 2010: Russia." Center for Systematic Peace. http://www.systemicpeace.org/polity/Russia2010.pdf.

Posner, Daniel N., and Daniel J. Young. 2007. "The Institutionalization of Political Power in Africa." *Journal of Democracy* 18 (3): 126–40.

Power, Timothy J., and Mark J. Gasiorowski. 1997. "Institutional Design and Democratic Consolidation in the Third World." *Comparative Political Studies* 30 (2): 123–55.

Price, Robert. 1991. *The Apartheid State in Crisis: Political Transformation in South Africa 1975–1990*. New York: Oxford University Press.

Przeworski, Adam. 1985. *Capitalism and Social Democracy*. New York: Cambridge University Press.

———. 1991. *Democracy and the Market: Political and Economic Reforms in Eastern Europe and Latin America*. New York: Cambridge University Press.

———. 2005. "Democracy as an Equilibrium." *Public Choice* 123:253–73.

———. 2008. "The Poor and the Viability of Democracy." In *Poverty, Participation and Democracy: A Global Perspective*, edited by Anirudh Krishna, 125–47. Cambridge: Cambridge University Press.

———. 2009. "Conquered or Granted? A History of Suffrage Extensions." *British Journal of Political Science* 39 (2): 291–321.

Przeworski, Adam, Michael Alvarez, José Antonio Cheibub, and Fernando Limongi. 1996. "What Makes Democracies Endure?" *Journal of Democracy* 7: 39–55.

Przeworski, Adam, Michael Alvarez, José Cheibub, and Fernando Limongi. 2000. *Democracy and Development*. New York: Cambridge University Press.

Przeworski, Adam, and Fernando Limongi. 1997. "Modernization: Theories and Facts." *World Politics* 49 (2): 155–83.

Putnam, Robert. 1988. "Diplomacy and Domestic Politics: The Logic of Two-Level Games." *International Organization* 42:427–60.

Rabin, Matthew. 1993. "Incorporating Fairness into Game Theory and Economics." *American Economic Review* 83:1281–1302.

Ramo, Joshua Cooper. 2004. *The Beijing Consensus*. London: Foreign Policy Center.

Rasler, Karen. 1996. "Concessions, Repression and Political Protest in the Iranian Revolution." *American Sociological Review* 61:132–52.

Reenock, Christopher, Michael Bernhard, and David Sobek. 2007. "Regressive Socioeconomic Distribution and Democratic Survival." *International Studies Quarterly* 51 (3): 677–99.

Reilly, Benjamin. 2001. *Democracy in Divided Societies: Electoral Engineering for Conflict Management*. New York: Cambridge University Press.

Reuter, Ora John, and Graeme B. Robertson. 2015. "Legislatures, Cooptation, and Social Protest in Contemporary Authoritarian Regimes." *Journal of Politics* 77 (1): 235–48.

Riedl, Rachel Beatty. 2014. *Authoritarian Origins of Democratic Party System in Africa*. New York: Cambridge University Press.

Rigger, Shelley. 1999. *Politics in Taiwan: Voting for Democracy*. New York: Psychology Press.

Roberts, Adam, and Timothy Garton Ash, eds. 2009. *Civil Resistance and Power Politics: The Experience of Non-violent Action from Gandhi to the Present*. New York: Oxford University Press.

Roberts, Kenneth M. 2006. "Populism, Political Conflict, and Grass-Roots Organization in Latin America." *Comparative Politics* 38 (2): 127–48.

———. 2014. *Changing Course in Latin America: Party Systems in the Neoliberal Era*. New York: Cambridge University Press.

Roberts, Kevin W. S. 1977. "Voting over Income Tax Schedules." *Journal of Public Economics* 8 (3): 329–40.

Robinson, Pearl T. 1994. "The National Conference Phenomenon in Francophone Africa." *Comparative Studies in Society and History* 36 (3): 575–610.

Robinson, William I. 1996. *Promoting Polyarchy: Globalization, U.S. Intervention and Hegemony*. New York: Cambridge University Press.

Romer, Thomas. 1975. "Individual Welfare, Majority Voting, and the Properties of a Linear Income Tax." *Journal of Public Economics* 4 (2): 163–85.

Ross, Michael. 2001. "Does Oil Hinder Democracy?" *World Politics* 53:325–61.

———. 2013. *The Oil Curse: How Petroleum Wealth Shapes the Development of Nations*. Princeton, NJ: Princeton University Press.

Rudra, Nita. 2008. *Globalization and the Race to the Bottom in Developing Countries: Who Really Gets Hurt?* New York: Cambridge University Press.

Rueschemeyer, Deitrich. 2004. "Addressing Inequality." *Journal of Democracy* 15:4.

Rueschemeyer, Dietrich, Evelyne Huber Stephens, and John Stephens. 1992. *Capitalist Development and Democracy*. Chicago: University of Chicago Press.

Ruhl, J. Mark. 2011. "Honduras: Democracy in Distress." In *Latin American Politics and Development*, edited by Howard J. Wiarda and Harvey F. Kline, 543–58. Boulder, CO: Westview Press.

Rustow, Dankwart A. 1970. "Transitions to Democracy: Toward a Dynamic Model." *Comparative Politics* 2 (3): 337–63.

Rutland, Peter. 2008. "Putin's Economic Record: Is the Oil Boom Sustainable?" *Europe-Asia Studies* 60:1051–72.

Schedler, Andreas, ed. 1999. *The Self-Restraining State: Power and Accountability in New Democracies*. Boulder, CO: Lynne Rienner.

———. 2002. "The Menu of Manipulation." *Journal of Democracy* 13 (2): 36–50.

———, ed. 2006. *Electoral Authoritarianism: The Dynamics of Unfree Competition*. Boulder, CO: Lynne Rienner.

———. 2009. "Electoral Authoritarianism." In *The Sage Handbook of Comparative Politics*, edited by Todd Landman and Neil Robinson, 381–94. Thousand Oaks, CA: Sage.

Schillinger, Hubert René. 2005. "Trade Unions in Africa: Weak but Feared." Occasional Papers, International Development Cooperation, Friedrich Ebert Stiftung.

Schimmelfennig, Frank, and Ulrich Sedelmeier. 2004. "Governance by Conditionality: EU Rule Transfer to the Candidate Countries of Central and Eastern Europe." *Journal of European Public Policy* 11 (4): 669–87.

Schmitter, Philippe C. 1974. "Still the Century of Corporatism?" *Review of Politics* 36 (1): 85–131.

Schock, Kurt. 2005. *Unarmed Insurrections: People Power Movements in Nondemocracies.* Minneapolis: University of Minnesota Press

Seawright, Jason, and John Gerring. 2008. "Case Selection Techniques in Case Study Research: A Menu of Qualitative and Quantitative Options." *Political Research Quarterly* 61 (2): 294–308.

Shanin, Teodor. 1989. "Ethnicity in the Soviet Union: Analytic Perceptions and Political Strategies." *Comparative Studies in Society and History* 31 (3): 409–24.

Share, Donald. 1987. "Transitions to Democracy and Transition through Transaction." *Comparative Political Studies* 19 (4): 525–48.

Sharp, Gene. 1973. *The Politics of Non-violent Action: Power and Struggle.* Boston: Porter Sargent.

Shugart, Matthew S. 2005. "Semi-presidential Systems: Dual Executive and Mixed Authority Patterns." *French Politics* 3 (3): 323–51.

Siani-Davies, Peter, ed. 2003. *International Intervention in the Balkans since 1995.* London: Routledge.

Siddiqa, Ayesha. 2007. *Military Inc.: Inside Pakistan's Military Economy.* London: Pluto Press.

Silitski, Vitali. 2005. "Preempting Democracy: The Case of Belarus." *Journal of Democracy* 16 (4): 83–97.

———. 2006. "Belarus: Learning from Defeat." *Journal of Democracy* 17 (4): 138–52.

Silva, Eduardo. 1998. *The State and Capital in Chile: Business Elites, Technocrats, and Market Economics.* Boulder, CO: Westview Press.

Simmons, Beth A., Frank Dobbin, and Geoffrey Garrett. 2006. "Introduction: The International Diffusion of Liberalism." *International Organization* 60 (4): 781–810.

Sing, Ming. 2010. "Explaining Democratic Survival Globally (1946–2002)." *Journal of Politics* 72 (2): 438–55.

Singh, Naunihal. 2014. *Seizing Power: The Strategic Logic of Military Coups.* Baltimore: Johns Hopkins University Press.

Sisk, Timothy D. 1995. *Democratization in South Africa: The Elusive Social Contract.* Princeton, NJ: Princeton University Press.

Skach, Cindy. 2005. "Constitutional Origins of Dictatorship and Democracy." *Constitutional Political Economy* 16 (4): 347–68.

Slater, Dan. 2010. *Ordering Power: Contentious Politics and Authoritarian Leviathans in Southeast Asia.* New York: Cambridge University Press.

Slater, Dan, Benjamin Smith, and Gautam Nair. 2014. "Economic Origins of Democratic Breakdown? The Redistributive Model and the Postcolonial State." *Perspectives on Politics* 12 (2): 353–74.

Slater, Dan, and Joseph Wong. 2013. "The Strength to Concede: Ruling Parties and Democratization in Developmental Asia." *Perspectives on Politics* 11 (3): 717–33.

Smith, Benjamin. 2005. "Life of the Party: The Origins of Regime Breakdown and Persistence under Single-Party Rule." *World Politics* 57 (3): 421–51.

Smith, Karen. 2000. "The Conditional Offer of EU Membership as an Instrument of EU Foreign Policy: Reshaping Europe in the EU's Image." *Marmara Journal of European Studies* 8 (2): 33–46.

Smolar, Aleksander. 2009. "Toward 'Self-Limiting Revolution': Poland 1970–89." In Roberts and Ash, *Civil Resistance and Power Politics*, 127–43.

Solt, Frederick. 2008. "Economic Inequality and Democratic Political Engagement." *American Journal of Political Science* 52 (1): 48–60.

———. 2014. "The Standardized World Income Inequality Database." SWIID Version 5.0. Working paper.

Solt, Frederick, Philip Habel, and J. Tobin Grant. 2011. "Economic Inequality, Relative Power, and Religiosity." *Social Science Quarterly* 92 (2): 447–65.

Sparks, Allister. 1996. *Tomorrow Is Another Country: The Inside Story of South Africa's Road to Change.* Chicago: University of Chicago Press.

Springborg, Robert. 2016. "Democracy vs. Rule of Law: The Case of the Egyptian Military." In *Building Rule of Law in the Arab World*, edited by Eva Bellin and Heidi Lane, 89–108. Boulder, CO: Lynne Rienner.

Stahler-Sholk, Richard. 1994. "El Salvador's Negotiated Transition: From Low Intensity Conflict to Low Intensity Democracy." *Journal of Interamerican Studies and World Affairs* 36 (4): 1–59.

Staniszkis, Jadwiga. 1981. "The Evolution of Forms of Working-Class Protest in Poland: Sociological Reflections on the Gdańskszczecin Case." *Europe-Asia Studies* 33 (2): 204–31.

Stepan, Alfred. 1971. *The Military in Politics: Changing Patterns in Brazil.* Princeton, NJ: Princeton University Press.

———. 1988. *Rethinking Military Politics: Brazil and the Southern Cone.* Princeton, NJ: Princeton University Press.

———. 2001. *Arguing Comparative Politics.* Oxford: Oxford University Press.

Stepan, Alfred, and Cindy Skach. 1993. "Constitutional Frameworks and Democratic Consolidation: Parliamentarianism versus Presidentialism." *World Politics* 46 (1): 1–22.

Stepanenko, Victor. 2006. "Civil Society in Post-Soviet Ukraine: Civic Ethos in the Framework of Corrupted Sociality?" *East European Politics and Societies* 4:571–97.

Stewart, Frances. 2000. "Crisis Prevention: Tackling Horizontal Inequalities." *Oxford Development Studies* 28 (3): 245–62.

Stokes, Susan. 2001. *Mandates and Democracy: Neoliberalism by Surprise in Latin America.* New York: Cambridge University Press.

Stokes, Susan, Thad Dunning, Marcelo Nazareno, and Valeria Brusco. 2013. *Brokers, Voters, and Clientelism: The Puzzle of Distributive Politics.* New York: Cambridge University Press.

Svallfors, Stefan. 1997. "Worlds of Welfare and Attitudes to Redistribution: A Comparison of Eight Western Nations." *European Sociological Review* 13:283–304.

Svolik, Milan. 2008. "Authoritarian Reversals and Democratic Consolidation." *American Political Science Review* 102:153–68.

———. 2009. "Power-Sharing and Leadership Dynamics in Authoritarian Regimes." *American Journal of Political Science* 53 (2): 477–94.

————. 2012. *The Politics of Authoritarian Rule*. New York: Cambridge University Press.

Swidler, Ann. 1986. "Culture in Action: Symbols and Strategies." *American Sociological Review* 51 (2): 273–86.

Tarrow, Sidney G. 1994. *Power in Movement: Social Movements and Contentious Politics*. New York: Cambridge University Press.

————. 1998. *Power in Movement: Social Movements and Contentious Politics*. 2nd ed. New York: Cambridge University Press.

Taylor, Verta. 1989. "Social Movement Continuity: The Women's Movement in Abeyance." *American Sociological Review* 54 (5): 761–75.

Taylor, Verta, and Alison Dahl Crossley. 2013. "Abeyance." In *Blackwell Encyclopedia of Social and Political Movements*, edited by David Snow. Malden, MA: Blackwell.

Teitelbaum, Emmanuel. n.d. "High Profile Strikes Dataset." Data provided by the author.

Teorell, Jan. 2010. *Determinants of Democratization: Explaining Regime Change in the World, 1972–2006*. Cambridge: Cambridge University Press.

Tien, Hung-mao, and Tun-jen Cheng. 1997. "Crafting Democratic Institutions in Taiwan." *China Journal* 37:1–27.

Tilly, Charles. 1978. *From Mobilization to Revolution*. New York: McGraw-Hill.

————. 1986. *The Contentious French*. Cambridge, MA: Harvard University Press.

Titlebaum, Emmanuel. n.d. "High Profile Strikes Data Set." In *Measuring Political Protest and Class Conflict: A New Data Set on High Profile Strikes*. Unpublished manuscript, George Washington University.

Treisman, Daniel. 2011. "Presidential Popularity in a Hybrid Regime: Russia under Yeltsin and Putin." *American Journal of Political Science* 55 (3): 590–609.

Tucker, Joshua Aaron, Peter Lange, Robert H. Bates, Ellen Comisso, Peter Hall, Joel Migdal, and Helen Milner. 2006. *Regional Economic Voting: Russia, Poland, Hungary, Slovakia, and the Czech Republic, 1990–1999*. Cambridge: Cambridge University Press.

Tudor, Maya. 2013. *The Promise of Power: The Origins of Democracy in India and Autocracy in Pakistan*. New York: Cambridge University Press.

Tufekci, Zeynep, and Deen Freelon. 2013. "Introduction to the Special Issue on New Media and Social Unrest." *American Behavioral Scientist* 57:843–47.

Tufekci, Zeynep, and Christopher Wilson. 2012. "Social Media and the Decision to Participate in Political Protest: Observations from Tahrir Square." *Journal of Communication* 62 (2): 363–79.

Udo, Augustine. 1985. "Class, Party Politics and the 1983 Coup in Nigeria." *Africa Spectrum* 20 (3): 327–38.

Ulfelder, Jay. 2004. "Baltic Protest in the Gorbachev Era: Movement Content and Dynamics." *Global Review of Ethnopolitics* 3 (4): 23–43.

Unger, Daniel. 2014. "The Politics of Polarization and Democratic Breakdown in Thailand." Unpublished manuscript, Northern Illinois University.

United Nations Development Program. 2013. *Humanity Divided: Confronting Inequality in Developing Countries*. New York: UNDP.

University of Texas Inequality Project. 2008. "Estimated Household Income Inequality (EHII) Dataset." http://utip.gov.utexas.edu/data.html.

Valenzuela, Arturo. 1978. *The Breakdown of Democratic Regimes: Chile*. Baltimore: Johns Hopkins University Press.

Valenzuela, Arturo, Larry Diamond, Juan J. Linz, and Seymour M. Lipset. 1989. *Democracy in Developing Countries: Latin America*. Boulder, CO: Lynne Rienner.

Vanhanen, Tatu. 2003. "Democratization and Power Resources, 1850–2000." Tampere: Finnish Social Science Data Archive.

Vardas, V. Stanley. 1966. "How the Baltic Republics Fare in the Soviet Union." *Foreign Affairs* 44 (3): 512–17.

Villalón, Leonardo A., and Abdourahmane Idrissa. 2005. "Repetitive Breakdown and a Decade of Experimentation: Institutional Choices and Unstable Democracy in Niger." In *The Fate of African Democratic Experiments: Elites and Institutions*, edited by Leonardo A. Villalón and Peter VonDoepp, 27–49. Bloomington: Indiana University Press.

Wahman, Michael, Jan Teorell, and Axel Hadenius. 2012. "Authoritarian Regime Types Revisited." *Contemporary Politics* 19 (1): 19–34.

Walter, Barbara F. 2002. *Committing to Peace: The Successful Settlement of Civil Wars*. Princeton, NJ: Princeton University Press.

Way, Lucan. 2005a. "Authoritarian State Building and the Sources of Regime Competitiveness in the Fourth Wave: The Cases of Belarus, Moldova, Russia, and Ukraine." *World Politics* 51:231–61.

———. 2005b. "Kuchma's Failed Authoritarianism." *Journal of Democracy* 16 (2): 131–45.

———. 2014. "Civil Society and Democratization." *Journal of Democracy* 25 (3): 35–43.

———. 2015. *Pluralism by Default: Weak Autocrats and the Rise of Competitive Politics*. Baltimore: Johns Hopkins University Press.

Weissman, Stephen R. 1998. *Preventing Genocide in Burundi: Lessons from International Diplomacy*. Washington, DC: United States Institute of Peace.

Weitz-Shapiro, Rebecca. 2012. "Curbing Clientelism: Politics, Poverty, and Social Policy in Argentina." Unpublished manuscript, Brown University.

Wejner, Barbara. 2005. "Diffusion, Development, and Democracy, 1800–1999." *American Sociological Review* 70:53–81.

Welch, Claude E., ed. 1976. *Civilian Control of the Military: Theory and Cases from Developing Countries*. Albany: State University of New York Press.

Westad, Odd Arne. 2005. *The Global Cold War: Third World Interventions and the Making of Our Times*. New York: Cambridge University Press.

Weyland, Kurt. 1996. "Neoliberalism and Neopopulism in Latin America: Unexpected Affinities." *Studies in Comparative International Development* 31 (3): 3–31.

Whitehead, Laurence. 1986. "Bolivia's Failed Democratization 1977–1980." In O'Donnell, Schmitter, and Whitehead, *Transitions from Authoritarian Rule: Latin America*, 49–72.

———, ed. 1996. *The International Dimensions of Democratization: Europe and the Americas*. Oxford: Oxford University Press.

———. 2015. "Anti-Democracy Promotion: Four Strategies in Search of a Framework." *Taiwan Journal of Democracy* 10 (2): 1–24.

Williams, William A. 1962. *The Tragedy of American Diplomacy*. New York: Dell.

Wintrobe, Ronald. 1998. *The Political Economy of Dictatorship*. New York: Cambridge University Press.

Wolf, Sonja. 2009. "Subverting Democracy: Elite Rule and the Limits to Political Participation in Post-war El Salvador." *Journal of Latin American Studies* 41 (3): 429–65.

Wood, Elisabeth Jean. 2000. *Forging Democracy from Below: Insurgent Transitions in South Africa and El Salvador*. New York: Cambridge University Press.

———. 2001. "An Insurgent Path to Democracy: Popular Mobilization, Economic Interests, and Regime Transition in South Africa and El Salvador." *Comparative Political Studies* 34 (8): 862–88.

World Bank. 1996. "Implementation Completion Report, Republic of Niger Economic Recovery Credit (Credit 2581-NIR)." Report no. 15772. http://documents.worldbank.org/curated/en/1996/06/733462/niger-economic-recovery-credit-project.

———. 1998. "Haiti: The Challenges of Poverty Reduction." Report no. 17242-HA, Poverty Reduction and Economic Management Unit, Latin America and the Caribbean Region. http://www- ds.worldbank.org/external/default/WDSContentServer/WDSP/IB/1999/06/03/000009265_3981005111938/Rendered/PDF/multi_page.pdf.

———. 2010. *World Development Indicators 2010*. Washington, DC: World Bank.

———. 2013. *World Development Indicators 2013*. Washington, DC: World Bank.

Wright, Joseph. 2008. "Do Authoritarian Institutions Constrain? How Legislatures Affect Economic Growth and Investment." *American Journal of Political Science* 52 (2): 322–43.

Wright, Joseph, and Abel Escribà Folch. 2012. "Authoritarian Institutions and Regime Survival: Transitions to Democracy and Subsequent Autocracy." *British Journal of Political Science* 42 (2): 283–309.

Yao, Graham. 1985. "The Politics of Crisis in Ghana: Class Struggle and Organization, 1981– 1984." *Review of African Political Economy* 34:54–68.

Zack-Williams, Alfred B. 1999. "Sierra Leone: The Political Economy of Civil War." *Third World Quarterly* 20 (1): 143–62.

Zakaria, Fareed. 1997. "The Rise of Illiberal Democracy." *Foreign Affairs* 76 (6): 22–43.

———. 2003. *The Future of Freedom: Illiberal Democracy at Home and Abroad*. Rev. ed. New York: Norton.

———. 2008. *The Post-American World*. New York: Norton.

Zunes, Stephen. 1994. "Unarmed Insurrections Against Authoritarian Governments in the Third World: A New Kind of Revolution." *Third World Quarterly* 15 (3): 403–26.

Zunes, Stephen, Lester Kurtz, and Sarah Beth Asher, eds. 1999. *Nonviolent Social Movements: A Geographical Perspective*. Hoboken, NJ: Wiley-Blackwell.

Index

Page numbers in *italics* refer to tables.